Arrogance and Accords

Arrogance and Accords

The Inside Story of the Honda Scandal

Steve Lynch

Pecos Press
Dallas

Library of Congress Catalog Card Number: 97-091854

ISBN: 0-9657766-1-1

Portions of "John Paul Jones and the Temple of Deals" and "A Bribe Too Small to Keep" first appeared in *Automotive News.*

Printed in the United States of America.

Pecos Press
P.O. Box 630496
Irving, Texas 75063

Contents

Prelude ix

1 HONDA: Hold On, No Discount Anytime 1

2 John Paul Jones and the Temple of Deals 11

3 Mr. Honda 25

4 Lean and Mean 45

5 Jack and Jim 60

6 Good Ol' Boys 80

7 Top Speed 97

8 Flushing the Cards 115

9 The Acura Disaster 129

10 Christiaan and the Lions 144

11 A Bribe Too Small to Keep 159

12 Confessions 177

13 Den of Denial 180

14 Parallel Lies 202

15 The Race to the Courthouse 221

16 The Trial 250

17 Ethics/Epilogue 291

Acknowledgments 307

Notes 309

Anyone who says he works for a company out of loyalty is a liar. Everyone works for himself.

— Soichiro Honda, founder of Honda Motor Company

Prelude

Two anal retentives were talking. One of the men wore a white dress shirt so heavily starched that he had to wriggle into it like a tight pair of jeans. The other kept a meticulous record of the bribes he received, making notations in a black leather notebook kept stashed in his den just for that purpose. The Federal Bureau of Investigation was hounding the pair, and they wondered about their future. They sat in an office at a Costa Mesa, California, automobile dealership, hard by the Pacific Ocean. It was 11:30 on the morning of November 2, 1993.

"Is there any way to protect our assets?" asked Ed Temple, running a finger around his cardboard-hard collar.

"It's not a quick fix," replied Jim Cardiges. "It takes months to do it. You have an off-shore or international company that has title to your house. It's very typical for them to deal with international law to go after that piece of property, though."

Both men had been among the top executives of the American arm of one of the most successful Japanese automobile companies. They had also masterminded the largest commercial corruption scheme in U.S. history, topped off in its final days by flat-out embezzlement. Both men were millionaires, though each had reached that level via different routes. The balding Temple had been the up-and-coming worker bee, the consummate politician who used his maze of connections to put deals together. It was easier for the Hollywood-handsome Cardiges — his position as national sales manager guaranteed him a wealth of kickbacks from greedy owners of car dealerships.

During the previous year and a half, their idyllic lives had suddenly, horribly unraveled because of two small-town deals gone wrong, one in Concord and one in Conway.

"Honda knows everything," said Cardiges, "but doesn't want this to go any farther. They just want to know if there's anybody else left in this company that they can weed out."

Both men had watched their former peers fall over the last 18 months. All officials fired by their former employer, American Honda Motor Company, and subsequently pursued by the Department of Justice, were Americans.

"They're trying to protect the Japanese, that's why Honda's doing it," said Cardiges. "The Japanese are trying to divorce themselves from us and from anything we did. Now the next step is Amemiya is going to be pulled out. Whether you regard it as a promotion or demotion for his problems, it doesn't make any difference. I'm surprised they didn't know things about Amemiya." Like the Mercedes-Benz convertible parked in the garage of American Honda's Japanese president, a gift from a Honda dealership owner who had also paid off Cardiges.

The FBI was suddenly paying unannounced visits to the pair's old mates, five months after Cardiges had lied to the feds and nearly convinced them they had no case. The men wondered which ex–Honda officials might roll over when grilled by the authorities. "Josleyn's going off the deep end," Temple said nervously. "Cooper's getting worked up. Novelly is hearing shit from Finley. Mazzitelli's ass has gone berserk. He called me at three-thirty this morning his time and woke me up. He's worried about every damn thing that's happened from day one. I'm telling you, this son of a bitch is gonna go down to the police station and knock on the door and tell them."

"He's the weakest link," agreed Cardiges. "And they always go after the weakest link."

Temple and Cardiges believed that only one man could be counted on, the patriarch who had started it all. "Jack will not talk," said Cardiges, about his former boss, Jack Billmyer. "He will not know anything. He's got too much to lose."

"They've tried to talk to me," said Temple.

"Just keep on avoiding them until you can't avoid them anymore," advised Cardiges. "But you don't go to them volunteering."

"Do you think that they're tapping calls?"

"Definitely. The FBI asked me about Pedersen and they said: well, we have recorded conversations."

"You think they did that at Honda?"

"If they did, we're all screwed," Cardiges responded.

Both agreed that the uncertainty of their predicament was the killer. "The toughest part is the morning 'cause you don't know what the day will bring," said Cardiges. "And you'll have a lot of anxiety in the morning and as the day goes through and nothing seems to be happening that's bad, you start getting a little more confident. Then you can do what normal people do and I feel great. The next morning comes around and I feel down again."

Cardiges revealed that he had visited his priest. "I went in April and that's the time you go for confession," said Cardiges. "It was just like you and I talking. I told him, listen, I did this, I did this, I did this. I did not think I was hurting anybody. Believe me, to this day, did I ever hurt anybody?"

"None of us did." The normally unflappable Temple was shaking.

They talked about notorious white-collar criminals and the prison sentences they had received, of Liddy, Milken, and Boesky. And of John De Lorean, the former General Motors executive caught buying cocaine to finance his own car company, the automobile business's biggest scandal until the Honda boys came along.

"You and I as individuals have to fight it as much as possible all the way down the line," said Cardiges.

"Just hold to your story?"

"That's exactly right. You'd get eighteen months, two years or whatever, but you just got to hold."

Temple was visibly upset, not wanting to hear the J-word.

"Just calm down, just calm down," assured Cardiges. "You're going to jail, you see. You and I are going to jail. You gotta put it in your mind that you'll go to jail for a while. Do you understand?"

"No, I don't."

"Well, you should. You run a damn high risk of going to jail."

CHAPTER 1

HONDA: Hold On, No Discount Anytime

> Almost everywhere you looked, district employees were allocating cars to their (dealer) friends in return for gifts or financial favors.
>
> —Lee Iacocca, on Ford Motor Company in the late 1940s

ONE OF their attorneys called them the most unlikely bunch of criminals he had ever known. None had ever been arrested. Most were college-educated, churchgoing family men, volunteers in their communities — one a former Eagle scout, another a former Detroit police officer. One hailed from a family of small-town Iowa mayors. One had taught elementary school. Their ringleader was voted the most admired automobile industry official in America.

Eighteen of my peers, all former top executives of American Honda Motor Company, the U.S. subsidiary of automobile manufacturer Honda Motor Company of Japan, along with four other conspirators, were convicted between 1994 and 1997 on federal charges of racketeering, mail and wire fraud, conspiracy, and obstruction of justice. The officials included the highest-ranking Americans at Honda: senior vice president and national sales manager Stanley James "Jim" Cardiges and his predecessor John W. "Jack" Billmyer. The pair ruled over the automobile sales division, Honda's most powerful and profitable department, from 1980 through 1992. Ten of the next twelve highest-ranking Honda sales officials were also found guilty for their participation in the multitude of scams. Another 16 managers were fired by Honda but not indicted by the Department of Justice.

It was the most improbable of scandals, in a company with a squeaky-clean reputation for building superior automobiles and listening to its customers. Leveraging the enormous profits generated by Honda dealers on sales of the popular cars, the executives received millions of dollars in kickbacks from dealers in exchange for additional franchises and larger shipments of autos. The nationwide pattern of corruption ran unchecked from the late 1970s through the early 1990s, peaking during the so-called Decade of Greed in America, the 1980s. Honda dealers became overnight millionaires, thanks to the superior Honda product, and were more than willing to shower the officials with bribes. The ill-gotten booty among the thousands of transactions included briefcases stuffed with up to $750,000 in cash, palatial homes, luxury German automobiles, secret ownerships in dealerships and other businesses, and Hong Kong shopping sprees.

"These guys were so cocky, they'd come in here and put their feet up on my desk and tell me what I had to give them," says the owner of an Ohio dealership, a willing participant in the gift giving. About one-third of Honda's 1,000 dealers participated to varying degrees in the chicanery, while the rest refused. Years later, a morass of civil lawsuits would name the two camps "dirty" and "clean" dealers.

"The dealers treated us like kings," remembers Cardiges, the charismatic leader of the band of thieves from 1988 through 1992. "They were willing to pay money, swimming pools, gift certificates, houses, cars, you name it. It was a good time for everybody." Honda managers with five-figure salaries parlayed their payola into multimillion-dollar fortunes.

The crooked conspirators were as quick to spot a trend in their shady dealings as Honda was when developing a new automobile. When customers stopped standing in line to buy Hondas in the early 1990s, the officials sensed the end to their easy extortion and concocted schemes to embezzle money directly from Honda. They diverted millions of dollars in Honda advertising funds into numerous front companies they established, which provided little or no services in return to the Honda dealer groups forced to participate in the campaigns. The executives coerced retailers into attending dubious sales training seminars, funneling the profits through Honda and back into their own pockets. They sold used Honda company cars and granted lucrative Honda contracts, both in exchange for kickbacks. Every time money was handed from party to party in a legitimate business deal, a third hand would appear.

The greedy Honda executives formed a clandestine "boys' club," with its own unwritten rules of conduct. The club credo came from Jack Billmyer, who preached, "At American Honda, they don't pay you a million dollars, but you can live like a millionaire." The elders tutored underlings on the importance of being discreet and how to establish "consulting" companies to shelter their cash. They joked about the size of their "G & C (graft and corruption) Accounts." Promotions went to those who joined the kickback camp.

The corruption adversely affected all areas of American Honda's sales efforts, from how it marketed automobiles and granted franchises to the establishment of the Acura luxury car division. The activities were common knowledge in the auto industry world, but the profits generated by both Honda and its dealers kept everyone's mouths shut for a long time. When Honda dealers' profitability began to sink in the 1990s due to a stagnant market and increased competition, some began to complain about what was going on. By then, the executives figured they were untouchable and became sloppy in their dealings, ignoring the advice from their superiors about never leaving a paper trail.

The 15-year-long scam came to a halt when Honda belatedly began an internal investigation in 1992 and quickly fired a dozen managers. One year later, a court battle bungled by Honda attorneys led to the FBI probe, which culminated in guilty pleas by 19 of the conspirators and a raucous trial of two former Honda executives in Concord, New Hampshire, in 1995. Assistant U.S. Attorney Michael Connolly, the man in charge of the investigation and prosecution, deemed it the largest commercial bribery case in American history, citing more than $15 million in cash and prizes changing hands. Connolly acknowledges that figure represents only a fraction of all the thousands of transactions. The lack of a paper trail on the majority of the graft makes it difficult to ascertain an accurate total, which I estimate to be easily over $50 million.

There was a remarkable lack of quid pro quo in most of the arrangements between dealer and Honda executive — no yen for yang. One of the club's unspoken regulations was that you could ask a dealer for something but could not promise anything in return beyond the unspoken agreement of a little back-scratching. Dealers who participated opened a pipeline to additional Honda stores and more truckloads of Honda automobiles.

Many of the retailers initiated the transactions, some motivated by fear of losing their gold mine and others by simple greed. New Jersey dealer William Vince, who paid off Honda execs to the tune of over $200,000, said, "If you wanted to get anywhere with Honda, you'd better make sure you kept on the good side of the right people." Gifts were often sent unsolicited: an airfreight letter filled with $100 bills, a bulging envelope slid into a coat pocket in a rest room, or an unannounced delivery of furniture. To the tainted officials, every retailer was Santa Claus and every gift a heart-pounding rush. An innocent dealer gratuity of a holiday fruit basket would turn a Honda exec into a crazed border inspector, flinging fruit as he ripped the gift apart to find a prize that was not there.

Some of the officials went both ways, both giving and receiving gifts. When several resigned from American Honda to become Honda dealers, they dutifully paid their former peers the under-the-table money necessary to keep their showrooms filled with Hondas.

Like alcoholics, the Honda executives found they needed progressively larger doses of graft to achieve the same level of euphoria found in earlier bribes. They rejected the notion that what they were doing was wrong. "I was in denial the whole time that it was anything other than gifts from friends," explains Cardiges. "My sense of right and wrong went right out the window in the first year of my career in the automobile business." The officials figured that the only downside to their activities was they might be fired for violating Honda's Conflict of Interest and Business Ethics Policy, which prohibited employees from accepting gifts from dealers or from holding a financial interest in a dealership. The executives never imagined they were breaking federal laws.

No automaker enjoyed demand higher than supply for a longer time than Honda, which saw 15 years of dealers and consumers crying for cars. Owning a Honda automobile dealership was a permit to print money. The more cars and franchises a dealer could purloin from the factory, the more money he would make. Hondas were the most praised cars of the era — from *Consumer Reports* to *Car & Driver,* the accolades accumulated on the high-value, tightly crafted Accords, Civics, and Preludes. The soaring demand for the cars and the Voluntary Restraint Agreement, the 1980s import quota limiting the number of automobiles Japanese automakers could export to America, combined to drive prices and dealer profits skyward. Dealers routinely charged thousands of dollars over sticker price for Hondas, boldly calling the added assessments "Additional Dealer Profit" or "Quota Tax," but customers were not deterred. One Honda dealership sported a sign on its usually empty showroom during the zenith: "We Are Not Out of Business . . . Just Out of Cars."

Honda was at the top of dealer surveys as the most desirable franchise throughout the 1980s. Owners of Honda dealerships raked in the cash, and American Honda executives wanted part of the action.

There have been other cases of employee bribery and fraud against automakers in America, though all pale in comparison to the Honda scandal. The incidents occur when manufacturers have consumers clamoring for more cars than they can build and when dealers and suppliers are eager to do business with them. Most Detroit automakers in the immediate post–World War II era — and sporadically throughout the 1960s and 1970s — and some Japanese imports and German luxury brands during the 1970s and 1980s experienced incidents of their employees being greased by car dealers and suppliers.

In 1960 the newly appointed president of the Chrysler Corporation, William Newberg, was found to have hidden ownership in two Chrysler suppliers, a violation of the company's ethics policies. Newberg had plenty of notice to stop his activities. Nine months earlier, his predecessor had summoned him and 35 other officials suspected of being on the take and given them an ultimatum: if any had financial ties with Chrysler vendors or dealers, they had 24 hours to severe them or face termination. Everyone complied except Newberg. He was subsequently fired and agreed to make restitution to Chrysler for the $450,000 he profited on his side deals.

At General Motors the opportunities for thievery revolved around dealers' service departments because of the vast amount of cash flowing to repair GM's poor-quality vehicles. In 1974 its Chevrolet division was involved in a bizarre case dubbed "Motorgate." The scheme unraveled when a Chevrolet field service manager visited a Lowell, Massachusetts, dealership and went out drinking with the dealer's service department manager. The factory man's bullet-riddled body was found floating in the Merrimac River the next day, and the dealership manager was arrested for the crime. The two were part of a partnership gone sour — the dealership had received reimbursement from Chevrolet for more than $600,000 in bogus warranty repair claims, the pair splitting the proceeds. Chevrolet's subsequent investigation uncovered other service division executives involved in the scheme, as well as its field sales managers receiving payments from dealers in exchange for extra vehicles. Dealers told of factory reps calling on them in December driving Caprice station wagons to pick up the Christmas presents they demanded. Chevrolet terminated 25 employees in a pair of East Coast offices. The dealership's service manager was later acquitted of murder but was sentenced to five years in prison for fraud.

In 1976 three executives of Toyota's American sales arm were indicted on charges of receiving gifts totaling $528,000 from a variety of vendors. Between 1969 and 1972, they solicited payoffs from a Toyota distributor, a real estate agency, and car dealers wanting Toyota franchises. Two of three officials were Americans and pleaded guilty, one receiving a six-month sentence and the other probation. The third conspirator was Japanese executive vice president Shoji Hattori, who fled to Japan after being terminated and was never extradited to face charges.

Chrysler, General Motors, and Toyota all took swift action to end the fraud — unlike Honda, whose higher-ups sat on their hands for more than a decade after first hearing the rumors of rampant corruption within their ranks.

Cynics wonder whether there are cases of reverse corruption—where an automobile manufacturer executive pays off dealership personnel to buy his company's coldest cars. Makers of off-brand cars like Yugo or Peugeot may have had such a problem. One such case in 1985 involved the owner of a Chicago Dodge dealership confessing to personally receiving $1,200 for each vehicle he purchased from a builder of customized vans. In the mid-1970s, Detroit automakers began offering above-the-table bribes called incentives: cash payoffs to dealers and their salespeople to move their slowest-selling products, eliminating the need for any backward bribery.

The Honda scandal was born from the peculiar relationship between factory and dealer in the cyclical and capital-intensive world of the retail automobile business. Car dealers are often characterized as being hustlers sporting white shoes and loud sport coats, men who would peddle their grandmothers for a buck. The fact is they are no more or less honest than owners of other businesses and most are ethical, hardworking entrepreneurs. However, they are no strangers to the temptations of fast cash in a business where such opportunities abound, indeed where the philosophy is geared around how much money can be made today.

The male-dominated retail car business is one in which even high school dropouts can become wealthy. Careers typically began on the ballooned and bannered car lots of America, under the old Chevrolet "OK Used Car" sign. They started as salesmen and their needs were simple, summed up by the "3 Ds" of these drifters: a desk, a day off, and a demo (company car). The so-called "lot lizards" were taught to chase the home run, the mullet customer who would pay full sticker price for a car and also arrange the loan through the dealer—at a 19 percent interest rate for even more profit for the retailer—not caring that they would never see that customer again. As each pigeon drove off in his or her new car, the salesman would stand in the showroom and gleefully swing an imaginary baseball bat toward the upper deck, pleased with his large commission.

Salesmen soon discovered another unethical shortcut to cash—"curbing" a car, or arranging for a customer to sell his or her trade-in to the salesman rather than to the dealer. The salesman then resells the vehicle on the side and pockets enough cash to equal the commissions from selling five new units. When promoted to sales department managers, the men learned the time-honored tradition of pocketing a $100 bill every time they peddled a car to a "wholesaler"—the gypsies who broker used vehicles among dealerships. They discovered the best way to motivate salesmen was through cash bonuses, preferably off the books. Behind every bundle of money given to a Honda exec was a dealer principal (dealership owner) who believed in the power of fast money as a shortcut to wealth.

While a Honda district sales manager, the person responsible for day-to-day contact with the dealers, I witnessed a dealer principal hand a mysterious envelope to a local government official to obtain a lower property tax assessment. The owner previously had assured me that, if I purchased a home in his community, my property taxes would be "taken care of."

To this day, a Southern California Honda dealer principal, who enjoys a net worth of over $20 million, walks into his service department each Friday and meets with a supplier who installs window tinting on new vehicles. "Got anything for me?" asks Mr. Dealer. The vendor hands over a $10 bill for each job he finished that week, a tradition he has honored for years. He is buying the right to continue to be the supplier to the dealer, but for the dealer principal, now isolated from the front lines of the automobile business by the demands of his empire, it is a reminder of why he got into the racket in the first place: the fast buck. The dealer principal may negotiate million-dollar deals, but the thrill of someone handing you cold cash is still more fun.

The retail automobile business is filled with men who feel they have little control over their destinies, that they are the poor working stiffs fighting faceless bureaucracies. They feel cheated by state regulatory agencies that dictate how automobile dealers can advertise, while other retail businesses have few such restrictions. Cheated by the federal government, which requires that new automobiles display a Manufacturer's Suggested Retail Price (MSRP) window sticker, a statute unique to the car business. Cheated by consumer magazines that publish the dealers' confidential costs on purchasing cars from the factory and tell people how to demand a vehicle for $50 over invoice, less markup than the same customer would pay on a piece of jewelry or furniture.

And most of all, the dealer principals feel cheated by the automakers they represent. The cars are junk and they're overpriced, say dealers. Customers won't buy them. The factory won't stand behind them. There are always too many or too few vehicles available. The factory reps from Detroit are college-educated idiots who don't know a closing booth from a phone booth.

When Honda came along and caught fire during the late 1970s, the dealers found their Holy Grail. It was during a time when their Pontiac or Oldsmobile franchises were in a steep nosedive as Detroit struggled against new government regulations, an oil crisis, and a new consumer they did not understand. With Honda, the dealers felt a glimpse of control. They dictated the prices of the Hondas and who would buy them. It was like the tales their fathers had told them about the glory days of the car business, the 1940s and 1950s, when demand always exceeded supply.

American Honda's relationship with its dealers went against the grain of the automobile business, and it contributed to the corporation's success as well as to the corruption. Automakers like to crow about their association with dealers as being a partnership. In reality, the alliance extends little beyond the common goal of selling cars and is often mired in mistrust, despite the fact that neither can survive without the other. The independent businessmen who hold the franchises consider themselves a different breed from automakers' executives, whom they view as being elitist and isolated from the true sales arena — the showroom floor. Because they have never been "belly-to-belly" with a customer, the dealers ask, how can the factory people dare to tell us how to sell a car? The manufacturers rush to condemn our high-pressure sales systems, say the retailers, but do not understand the reality of the showroom where "buyers are liars," coached by consumer publications on how to mislead dealers about their trade-in vehicles. It is our life savings on the line, say the dealer principals, and we have to do what is necessary to survive today.

Dealers believe they have little input on the factory's product, programs, or pricing and feel abandoned when carmakers will not back up their automobiles. It is the retailers who have to mollify irate consumers on their service drives, customers who see dealer and manufacturer as one entity. Dealers differ from consumers in that they have no choice in the cars they buy — if the automaker they represent builds an unpopular product, the dealers still have to buy it and try to resell it to the public.

The automaker, shackled by franchise laws that make it difficult to intervene in a dealer's business, criticizes the retailers' inherent short-term strategy that often leads to poor treatment of customers, all to make a dollar today. The factory believes in long-term success through the nurturing of the consumer, ultimately leading to customer retention and increased market share. Automakers press dealers to improve their customer satisfaction index (CSI), the industry measure of consumer handling, even to the point of offering cash incentives to dealers to treat customers right.

However, when business is slow, dealers who are able to "move the iron" will be lauded by the factory, regardless of their tactics.

Manufacturers may not approve of how a dealer represents them in a market, but automobile dealers have succeeded in persuading states to enact legislation—unique to the car business—limiting how and where automakers may grant new dealerships. This movement began in the 1970s, when dealers feared the factories had become large enough to begin establishing company-owned dealerships. These regulations, some appropriately titled "Dealer Day in Court," are slanted against the car companies and governed by state motor vehicle commissions often made up of automobile dealers. An automaker may have a dealer with poor sales and disgraceful customer satisfaction but be prohibited from establishing another dealership in the same market. Ironically, these same laws force dealers to be faithful to the manufacturers they represent—even if a dealer cannot be profitable with a certain make, he often cannot simply cancel the franchise and move in another brand.

Honda's uniqueness in working with its dealers began with its hiring practices. Some automakers have policies that discourage employing anyone with dealership experience for a position calling on retailers. This paradox is justified by the fear that their sales rep will become "too dealer oriented"—forgetting who writes his paycheck and siding with the dealer in disputes. Honda preferred a retail automobile background for any candidate applying for a position involving meeting with dealers: "I can teach the wholesale (factory) business to our field reps," said Jack Billmyer. "But I don't want anyone who never sold a car out there telling our dealers how to do it." Many Honda executives had been automobile dealers or managers before their tenure with Honda. Those with retail experience achieved instant credibility with the retailers, often earning the highest compliment from a dealer principal—recognizing his Honda rep as a "car man" like himself.

Honda genuinely listened to its dealer body and had the reputation for fast response to their concerns. Dealers could ring up the top managers at Honda, while Detroit carmakers' executives were too isolated and unskilled in the ways of dealing with their retailers and thus avoided any meaningful contact. Dealer surveys rated Honda the top franchise based on factory personnel understanding and reacting to their problems.

The dealerships were lucrative, and the Honda sales division executives understood the business. It was a car dealer's dream.

Bribers and bribees usually only meet under clandestine conditions—not so in the Honda world. The dealer principals would do anything to curry favor with the Honda executives: They invited them into their opulent homes; they golfed, traveled, and partied together. The factory men heard "you are the reason for my success, for my lifestyle" too many times from the dealers, not understanding that "you" really meant the Honda automobiles, not the officials themselves. They began to carry themselves, in the words of one dealer, "like Honda Gods," kingmakers to be kowtowed to. Lack of power corrupts just as surely as does too much power, and many dealers perceived they were powerless, that the Honda executives decided which lucky owners would become millionaires.

The majority of Honda's dealers grew rapidly during the rocking 1980s without bribing any Honda officials, as sales roared from 375,388 cars in 1980 to 716,495 in 1990, due in part to Honda establishing three North American assembly plants. Every Honda dealer had the capability to expand and earn more cars under Honda's distribution system, based solely on the strength of his operation and market, but many retailers doubted this system and looked for shortcuts by paying off Honda officials. Most of the operators who participated in the venality were those who could not sell a $15,000 car with a $20,000 rebate, the graduates of the bribe-your-way-through business school, the ones also blowing customers and employees out the door. But some of Honda's best and brightest dealer principals also played the game.

Honda's tight relationship with its dealers is just one piece in the puzzle of why the corruption blossomed. A lean corporate structure that granted unchecked power to too few individuals, Honda's legal counsel that coached executives to perjure themselves in court, a clueless corporate personnel department, and the Japanese executives at Honda who were accused of quietly condoning the payola by ignoring rumors, whistleblowers, and hard evidence, all contributed to the antics rolling out of control for so long.

The Honda scandal was homage to the bygone days of the automobile business — one final caper for the quick cash. The gluttonous Honda executives raised corruption to a higher level than any other group of businessmen. The smartest of the bunch was Ed Temple.

CHAPTER 2

John Paul Jones and the Temple of Deals

> Temple was the Master. Nobody had his hands in more deals than him
>
> — Anonymous American Honda executive

ED TEMPLE did not need a house to fall on him. A Honda dealership would be okay, though.

As California zone sales manager for American Honda, Temple was responsible for the distribution and sale of 120,000 new Hondas annually, nearly one-sixth of the company's U.S. sales. He was becoming concerned about issues other than selling cars: He sensed the impending downturn of the Honda heyday and the resultant end to the dealer gravy train. Time was limited to squeeze a few million dollars more out of car dealers willing to lease their souls to obtain Honda franchises. Temple wanted to retire by the time he was 40 years old. It was late 1988, and he was 39.

I had just transferred from Dallas to Los Angeles to work as a district sales manager under Temple. All I knew of Temple was when he called on the Honda dealership where I worked before I joined the factory. He and my dealer principal always seemed to be huddling and whispering. I had heard the rumors of high-stakes corruption by fellow Honda executives, but I was now about to witness it firsthand. And from a man who had honed his graft better than anyone.

Temple was a decorated Vietnam War veteran who had gone bust as a Ford dealer in his hometown of Sylvester, Georgia. He joined Honda as Arkansas district sales manager in 1983. An affable, prematurely bald man with a commanding bass voice, the meticulously organized Temple loved stiffly starched dress shirts and would often don a fresh one after lunch. He was forever working the phones, staying in contact with car dealers nationwide, looking for opportunities to convert into cash. Temple was the most politically astute of the Honda executives. He bragged about how

American Honda president Koichi Amemiya sought out his advice. Amemiya would occasionally physically embrace Temple, an unusual act by the normally reserved Japanese.

"If Ed had been Catholic, he would be Pope by now," says one Honda dealer. "If he had stayed in the military, he would be a general." Respected by the retailers, adored by Honda sales chief Jim Cardiges, and feared by officials one step above him, Temple was on a march toward the top of Honda's powerful sales division. He rose to become California zone sales manager only four years after joining Honda, a climb that would take a decade at other carmakers. Temple was the most productive of Cardiges's soldiers, a member of the inner sanctum of officials granted the freedom to steal all they could — as long as they split the loot with Cardiges.

The unchecked establishment of new Honda dealerships was the main course in a crooked Honda executive's menu of corruption. While any of Honda's ten zone sales managers could bleed a dealer for cash in exchange for extra shipments of cars, selling a new franchise was the Big Score, one that took risk and effort.

The establishment of a new dealer by an auto manufacturer is a tedious endeavor. It involves adhering to endless state franchise laws, performing market studies, screening dealer applicants, and enforcing strict guidelines for proposed facilities, all in an effort to represent the automaker well in the marketplace. At American Honda, executives didn't play by those rules during the rollicking 1980s when dealers were begging for more Honda stores. Cardiges and his predecessor, Jack Billmyer, had Honda's market representation department, the division responsible for granting new dealerships, under their thumbs, so they had the freedom to establish Honda stores at will — and without any bothersome guidelines or committee meetings.

Although no automobile company charges a franchise fee for a new dealership, when the crooked Honda officials identified new markets, or "open points" as they are called, they would peddle the rights to them to drooling dealers. With existing Honda dealerships selling for upwards of $2 million "blue sky," or profit, for the seller, buying a new open point from a Honda executive for substantially less was a bargain. Sometimes the execs would just sell the letter of intent, Honda's document granting the franchise and assigning the territory to the new dealer, a transaction prohibited by other automakers. However, opening a new dealership — as cheaply and quickly as possible — and then immediately selling it aroused less suspicion. The profit from the sale was split between the zone sales managers and Cardiges.

The deals were in direct violation of Honda's employee conflict of interest policy and standard automobile industry practice. Years later, the government would determine that it was also against the law.

Most of the ill-gotten franchises went to operators with successful records as both automobile dealers and gift givers. But by the late 1980s the executives threw business sense out the window as they foresaw the end to Honda's meteoric rise in America. They settled for any deal that would pad their pockets, regardless of the talents of the chosen dealer principal or the viability of his location. Water cooler talk in Honda offices revolved around which new dealerships were the most absurd, the ones established in backwater towns or those in broken-down buildings. Or both.

There is no question in my mind which new store was the national champion of bizarre: Santa Paula Honda in Southern California. The Santa Paula saga symbolized all that was wrong at Honda.

Ed Temple desperately wanted to establish a new Honda point in Southern California. A prospect would pay handsomely for a Honda store in the nation's largest import car market. Consumers were still lining up to buy Hondas in Los Angeles in 1988, as they had been doing for a remarkable 12 years. The collapse of the California economy was still two years away, and the average Honda dealer in the state was profiting over $800,000 annually. The very best were netting over $5 million a year. Becoming a Honda dealer in Los Angeles was better than winning the lottery.

Temple got out a map of California and began plotting. California Motor Vehicle laws make it difficult for an automaker to establish a same-make dealership within ten miles of an existing one. If they plan to, other dealers within that loop may, and usually do, file a protest with the Motor Vehicle Commission. Even in legitimate market representation action, American Honda — headed by their lawsuit-loathing Japanese officials — avoided any such sort of litigation. They certainly would not go to court for a rogue zone sales manager initiating a questionable new deal. Temple knew that any new point would have to be farther than ten miles from an existing Honda store.

Temple drew ten-mile rings around each of the 60 Honda dealers in Southern California. The Los Angeles metro was ruled out: a half-dozen Honda stores would fall within ten miles of any location. He turned his attention to the outlying areas, but even there another Honda dealer usually fell within the forbidden radius. Where no other Honda store existed, usually neither did a city. A potential buyer would probably not warm up to Honda of Death Valley.

Normally, Temple never involved his underlings in his dealings. The executives above him were already part of the game; those below him were as yet untested. He knew that the more of his employees involved, the greater the risk. But time was running out—he was leaving Honda in three months, come what may. He dispatched his district sales managers to all corners of California to survey potential sites. In my case, it was to the San Joaquin Valley town of Bakersfield, a working-class burg known for fertile farm fields and oil wells and as the destination of the migrating "Okies" of the 1930s. Unless Honda started building tractor-trailer rigs, the one existing Honda store in Bakersfield would be more than adequate to serve the market.

Temple surmised that a spot northeast of the town would be farther than ten miles from the local dealer, Barber Honda. And be sellable for about $500,000. It was irrelevant that Barber represented Honda well, with good market penetration and fine customer handling. Nor did it matter that dealer principal John Barber was the wealthiest man in Bakersfield and could raise a cloud of Tulare dust in protest. There was no sound business reason for a second Bakersfield Honda dealership, but Temple needed a point fast and was already lining up buyers.

My marching orders were to stealth into Bakersfield, collect market demographic information he could use to justify the deal, and inspect potential sites for a new dealership. Temple did not tell me why, but I was beginning to catch on. "I have only one piece of advice," cautioned Temple. "Do not be seen by Barber. If you do, you are on your own."

This was a dicey situation. I was most concerned about Barber Honda, because I would have to placate a raging John Barber if we put a second dealership in his community. I did not want to jeopardize my relationship with Barber, but since Temple signed my paycheck, I headed out for Bakersfield.

I snuck into the city down a back road to dodge Barber Honda, which sat on the main highway from Los Angeles. Every person on the street and every face in passing cars looked to me like a Barber employee. An hour later, I walked out of the Greater Bakersfield Visitors and Convention Bureau with literature extolling the virtues of life in Bakersfield ("Not Just Oil Rigs and Agriculture"). I surveyed the locations farther than ten miles from Barber Honda. I was not the most inconspicuous sleuth. Wearing my corporate-blue suit and wing tips, I walked around a dozen windy fields of oil derricks and pistachio nuts far from civilization, drawing only about a hundred stares from passing rednecks. This is not in my job description, I thought. Temple must have assumed that Bakersfield had suburbs of some kind, but in reality the city limits were the city limits. It was clear that a Bakersfield point would be semirural. Temple was not happy with my report that Bakersfield was out.

I left Bakersfield and crossed the desolate high plains of central California, headed for more open point fun. The Pacific Coast village of Pismo Beach was my next destination. Not much happens in tiny Pismo — its claim to fame is that renowned TV sportscaster John Madden met his wife in a bar there. A sign in the town announces that fact proudly. Jim Cardiges was awarding a letter of intent for Pismo Beach to a man named Dick Kennedy, who wanted to retire on the coast. Kennedy was a journeyman dealership manager and a friend of Cardiges's. I was to do the Pismo paper — and dirty — work, my first big assignment from the sales chief.

Like Bakersfield, there was no rational business reason for Honda to open a dealership in Pismo Beach. Honda outsold its two primary competitors (Toyota and Nissan) combined in Pismo, thanks to the efforts of Sunset Honda, the excellent San Luis Obispo dealer located 10.2 miles to the north. A Honda store would succeed in Pismo — they were profitable everywhere in the 1980s — but at the expense of Sunset Honda. I inspected Kennedy's proposed site south of town, a small field next to a gas station off the Pacific Coast Highway, invisible from the main road. It was a terrible location, but I was not about to tell Cardiges that. A carefully cropped photograph of the property would be enough to fool Honda's market representation department into thinking that Pismo was a real deal.

Next I had to give Sunset Honda's dealer principal, the improbably named Had Burger, the bad news. It was my first meeting with the dealer. The gist of my conversation with Burger was: "Hi. I'm your new Honda rep. We're going to stick a dealership up your tailpipe, causing your store to lose sales and profits, and jeopardizing the millions you have invested. We've done no market studies. We can give you no good reason. Hey, deal with it. Wanna go to lunch?"

I was nicer than that, but what could I say? We both knew it could not be stopped — it was outside of ten miles. Burger did not relish the deal but knew he had no choice. If he had balked, we were prepared for Plan B — to offer him a letter of intent to open a second Honda dealership in a market to be determined. This strategy was consistent with Honda's philosophy of working with its dealers during the go-go 1980s. If a dealer is miffed about something, send him an extra load of cars. If he is really steamed or threatens to sue or expose corruption, give him another dealership. It's hard to talk with a mouthful of money.

Meanwhile, Temple was having to deal with distractions about a legitimate (read: nonprofit) open point. Robertson Honda of North Hollywood was the second-largest-volume Honda dealership in the nation. Despite being located in a run-down neighborhood, Robertson was moving over 5,000 new Hondas per year, a volume three to four times higher than adjacent Honda dealers. Owner Jack Robertson succeeded through tenacity and long hours — I could call the store at 6:00 A.M. and find him already at work. His dealership was considered the best of Honda's 900 stores nationwide.

Jack Robertson wanted a second Honda store. His disdain for Honda zone sales managers and their hijinks was legendary. Robertson made his request directly to the top Japanese Honda officials and they gave him the green light to pursue any location he desired. The respect the Japanese had for Robertson was evident in their commitment to go to court to fight any protests from dealers within the ten-mile radius of any sight he chose, an unusual move by the litigation-shy managers.

Robertson first received permission to establish a store in Calabasas, just west of the San Fernando Valley. An annoyed Temple had to give a within-ten-miles dealer a letter of intent for a Honda store in Bountiful, Utah, to convince him not to protest the Calabasas point. Robertson ran into obstacles from the regulation-happy city of Calabasas and canceled the proposed dealership. Honda's Japanese officials then gave him a point in Palmdale, north of Los Angeles, yanking the rug out from underneath Temple, who had just targeted Palmdale and was trying to peddle it to another dealer.

Bakersfield, Pismo Beach, Calabasas, Bountiful, and Palmdale had put a collective zip into Ed Temple's pocket. He was doing better in Northern California, establishing dealerships in the burgs of Tracy and Vacaville and profiting handsomely, but it was a Southern California point he wanted.

Back at the circle-drawing table, he discovered a market he had overlooked in his search for a location more than ten miles from an existing Honda dealer: Santa Paula.

I was about to get a lesson from the Master.

Ed Temple looked at Santa Paula and saw Las Vegas.

A dusty farming community of 20,000 residents, the city of Santa Paula siestas in the shadow of the Sierra Madre Mountains, 45 miles northwest of downtown Los Angeles. In the late 1980s, Santa Paula had avoided any of the exploding growth of its Ventura County neighbors, Ventura and Oxnard. But Temple knew that Santa Paula was going to become his Santa Claus. The city was about to get a Honda dealership.

Honda targets the 25- to 54-year-old college-educated-plus consumer, the baby boomers called yuppies during the Decade of Greed. All of the people fitting this description who lived in Santa Paula could have piled into the backseat of a Honda Civic. Santa Paula was not exactly a town receptive to foreign cars — no other import automobile company had even considered it as a potential market. Temple surmised that no prospective dealer would buy a letter of intent to build a Honda store in Santa Paula. No, this would have to be a going concern — he would have to actually open the franchise and then sell it. The credibility of Honda establishing a new dealership would make it salable.

Building a new showroom was out of the question. Temple had to find an existing facility, the cheaper the better. Unlike other automobile manufacturers, Honda had no standard building guidelines for dealers. The only templates were some vague minimum square-footage numbers based on sales volumes from the 1970s. Temple could put a Honda dealership in a Dairy Queen if he wanted.

Temple cruised the streets of Santa Paula. The lack of energy in the town was striking. The only activity came from the area's migrant orange-grove farm workers gathered on street corners. You expected to see Jed Clampett pull up at any moment.

Temple wanted a facility on at least one of the two main drags. A closed auto repair shop or a retail establishment with a showroom big enough to display one Honda, anything cheap and fast, was all Temple desired. It took all of ten minutes for him to eliminate the main thoroughfares.

He turned down Mill Street, a two-lane avenue of closed businesses and rundown houses. It was a street so narrow you had to move over for oncoming traffic. There stood an abandoned stucco structure with a one-car showroom and a single garage door. Its narrow parking lot would be large enough to display a handful of Hondas. Temple contacted the owner of the building and found it had been a Chrysler-Plymouth dealership during the 1950s. Since then, the facility had been through dozens of lessees, including one tenant who had boarded horses there.

The dilapidated building at 118 North Mill Street was perfect for Temple's new Honda store. All he needed was someone to play dealer principal for a few weeks. He called his old friend John Paul "Bud" Jones, a man who had drifted through several Honda dealerships in Texas and Oklahoma. Jones was the consummate "car man," right down to his cowboy boots and the yellow used-car guidebook sticking out of his back pocket. Jones negotiated a $5,000 per month lease and he and Temple began the paperwork to open Santa Paula Honda.

Temple knew he had one potential problem: Honda of Oxnard. The neighboring dealer was not your typical family-owned car dealership. It was owned by the Dah Chong Hong (DCH) Trading Company, a gigantic Hong Kong import/export company. The firm operated Honda stores in New York City and Los Angeles, its flagship dealership being Gardena Honda, the number-one-volume Honda dealership in the United States, located five minutes from American Honda's Torrance, California, headquarters. Scuttlebutt had it that DCH executives enjoyed an underground relationship with top Honda brass that guaranteed Gardena Honda the highest allotments of cars of any Honda store in America — and the dealer who received the most, sold the most. When perennial bridesmaid Jack Robertson complained about his dealership never getting enough cars to beat Gardena, he was told "out behind the body shop" by Honda officials that his store would always be number two.

Dah Chong Hong would not be happy about Santa Paula Honda.

At that time, Honda of Oxnard was located 10.5 miles from 118 North Mill Street, skirting the state's ten-mile limit. However, Dah Chong Hong was currently building a new $3 million dealership located just 9.6 miles from the Santa Paula location. The relocation of Honda of Oxnard to this new facility was imminent. Temple had to open Santa Paula Honda before Honda of Oxnard moved or all bets were off.

Temple pushed the paperwork through, and John Paul Jones Enterprises (doing business as Santa Paula Honda) opened on January 15, 1989. On a back street in a tiny town. With a one-car showroom, three service bays, and the five employees hired by Jones. It was a day many people will not forget.

Honda district service manager Udo Gietl was responsible for working with the service departments of the 17 Honda dealers in my territory. On the morning of January 15, Gietl was on Honda of Oxnard's service drive speaking to a Honda owner whose car had a mechanical problem. The customer pointed out to Gietl and to Oxnard's service manager that, if he could not get satisfaction, he could visit the new dealer in Santa Paula. The customer had seen a newspaper ad that morning announcing Santa Paula Honda's grand opening.

"There is no Honda dealer in Santa Paula," replied Gietl. Honda of Oxnard's service manager backed him up. The customer was adamant, so Gietl called his boss, who also confirmed that no such dealership existed. The customer walked away, shaking his head.

Gietl decided to drive to Santa Paula to see for himself. "And there I find this whitewashed chicken coop that has a sign on it, Santa Paula Honda," said Gietl. "The building was a joke."

Ed Temple knew that Honda's service division executives would throw a rod when they saw the facility. They might have slowed him down. He also realized that they would have required the purchase of some outlandish equipment for the service department—like tools to fix cars. So he simply did not inform Honda service division officials about the new dealership.

When it sunk in that Santa Paula Honda was indeed franchised and living in his territory, Gietl mused, "Why didn't Steve Lynch tell me?"

I was having my own problems that day.

Temple had informed me on January 14 that Santa Paula Honda was opening in my territory the next day. That situation was strange enough, since I usually handled the paperwork for a new point. But the big embarrassment was that I did not know where Santa Paula was.

On the morning of January 15, I headed for Santa Paula. A call came in on my car phone from a frantic Larry Lee, general manager of Honda of Oxnard. "Mr. Lynch, Mr. Sheng wants to see you this morning," he said. "We need to talk about Santa Paula." I realized DCH did not know until that day, either.

I drove to Honda of Oxnard. The Chinese officials of DCH were the most businesslike people I had ever dealt with. Not this morning. Led by West Coast manager Alfredo Soon Nam Sheng, the executives vented their anger. Why, they asked, were we not informed of this ahead of time? We know it is outside the ten-mile limit, but we still should have been notified. We are spending millions on our new facility, raged Sheng, and Santa Paula may draw customers from Oxnard. My honest reply, that I did not know about Santa Paula Honda until the day before, was met with derision.

What really steamed Al Sheng was that he and other DCH executives had given Honda sales boss Cardiges and other officials over $300,000 in cash and gifts to obtain additional franchises and shipments of cars. The unspoken fringe benefit of the arrangement was the safeguarding of their Honda stores, protection that included Honda not opening new dealerships near any DCH Honda dealers. What Sheng did not understand was that each layer of Honda management cut its own deals with the retailers. DCH officials may have paid off Cardiges and Jack Billmyer, but since they chose to ignore Temple they were fair game.

I left the encounter and headed to Santa Paula to meet my new dealer. I drove right past the dealership the first time without noticing it. I laughed out loud when I first saw Santa Paula Honda. So this is how it works, I thought. I had heard the wild rumors about how Temple operated, but now it was clear they were true.

Jones and Temple began an immediate search for a buyer for Santa

Paula Honda. It did not take them long. Three weeks later, Temple ordered me to begin the paperwork for a buy/sell agreement between Jones and a Ford dealer named Steve Shuken.

It was said that Shuken had the Midas touch in the car business. The owner of Vista Ford and Vista Lexus in the San Fernando Valley, Shuken had built a dealership empire the right way. His stores were the rare combination of high volume and high customer satisfaction. Vista Ford had the best customer satisfaction index of any high-volume Ford dealership in California. Shuken respected and empowered his employees, and they reciprocated with fierce loyalty. He hosted his top salespeople and their spouses to an annual all-expenses-paid holiday in Hawaii, a rarity in a business where owners generally treat salespeople like dirt. Shuken would be good for Honda.

I met Shuken at his Ford store. A 6′4″ former college basketball standout, Shuken looked ten years younger than his age of 49. He introduced me to Alan Busby, the general manager of his operations. Shuken was going to give Busby his shot at owning a dealership, selling him 20 percent interest in the new Santa Paula Honda.

Both men were somewhere between giddy and shocked at their good fortune. Shuken could not contain his enthusiasm for the opportunity to become a Honda dealer: "It is every dealer's dream to have the Honda franchise." He presented a thorough outline of his dealerships' operations and philosophies. Even though it was clear that he would be approved as the new dealer, he treated our meeting as if he had to sell American Honda on his plans.

Shuken expressed some concern about the facility and location of Santa Paula Honda. "There is no way I would ever buy this store if it was to stay in Santa Paula," he said. "I know it will be tough at first, but since Temple said we would be allowed to move to Ventura after a few months, I know we'll be successful." This was news to me.

Ventura, California, was indeed a more logical location than Santa Paula for a new store. An affluent coastal community just north of Oxnard, Ventura was home to dealerships representing all major automobile franchises except Honda. Honda was the best-selling import car in California at the time, but Toyota and Nissan were both killing Honda in Ventura and Oxnard; adding a Honda store to the market would make good business sense. However, any location in Ventura would be well within a ten-mile radius of Honda of Oxnard. There was no way Honda or DCH would allow Santa Paula Honda to relocate there.

The promise to let him move the Santa Paula dealership to Ventura had been Temple's closing tool on Shuken. Temple knew he would be gone from Honda in a couple of months and would not have to face Shuken again.

I did not relay my doubts to Shuken. Temple emphasized the importance of completing the buy/sell agreement as soon as possible. I pressed on with the paperwork, happy to have Shuken on the Honda team.

Shuken paid for the assets plus approximately $400,000 "blue sky" to Bud Jones for Santa Paula Honda. The day the deal closed, Jones and Temple met with Cardiges at the vice president's beyond-luxurious Laguna Hills home to discuss the split of the booty.

Shuken took over Santa Paula Honda on March 15, 1989.

Jones saddled up a brand-new white Ford pickup truck and rode back to Oklahoma. He said that he sold the dealership because he "just didn't like California."

Temple resigned from American Honda, saying his wife had inherited a large sum of money. He gave away his collection of blue suits and moved to Hilton Head Island, South Carolina. Appropriately, he had just arranged for a new Honda dealership to be established there. This one would be his own.

For Steve Shuken, the nightmare was only beginning.

"You could lay down in the middle of Mill Street and not worry about being hit by a car. The only traffic was to the crack house across the way," remembered Alan Busby, co-owner and general manager of the Steve Shuken–owned Santa Paula Honda.

The store struggled from the start, rarely achieving a sales volume over 20 cars a month. Aggressive advertising in neighboring newspapers attracted a few consumers who were dissatisfied with other Honda dealers. The vast majority of Santa Paula Honda's business came from Oxnard and Ventura.

Service and parts business was dismal, since there were few Honda automobiles in Santa Paula. Customers from surrounding communities who purchased cars at Santa Paula were not willing to return for service. Those who did endured a cramped building with no customer waiting lounge. The dealership could not bolster its profitability with used car sales, either. There was no room on the lot to display any — the eight or ten cars visible from the street had to be new units or people would not realize it was a Honda dealership.

In May American Honda's sales were not enjoying the traditional spring surge of previous years. More unsold Hondas sat on dealers' lots than at any time in history. So Honda did the unthinkable: It offered its first incentives ever, $500 per sold car in dealer cash. "Our timing was awful," said Shuken. "I become a Honda dealer and the market turns soft." Santa Paula Honda was losing money fast, but the promise from Temple kept Shuken motivated. He did not realize that Temple was not speaking on behalf of Honda.

Shuken formulated his plans to move the dealership to Ventura. As luck would have it, Ventura Toyota was about to relocate. Its old building was not the best, but it looked like the Taj Mahal next to Santa Paula Honda. Shuken jumped at the opportunity. He prepared a detailed report for Honda, outlining the Ventura market and the proposed facility. He enclosed a "Welcome Honda" letter from the president of the Ventura Chamber of Commerce, who stated he had always wondered why there was no Honda dealership in his city.

The shadow of DCH and Honda of Oxnard would make a relocation tough. DCH had just been burned once, despite its relationship with Honda executives. If Shuken was a politician, someone with the right connections, it might be different. Shuken was not a "player"—but his chance to get into the Honda game was imminent.

Enter Ed Temple's replacement, new California zone sales manager Dennis Josleyn, a man who considered every Honda dealer an ATM machine. He only had to learn which buttons to push to access the money.

Josleyn invited Shuken to dinner to discuss the dealership's move to Ventura. Shuken brought along his outline on his organization and on the Ventura market. This meeting was Shuken's first with Josleyn and he was pumped. Because Josleyn had called the meeting and already given him positive feedback on his proposal, Shuken assumed Honda was going to rubber-stamp the relocation.

Josleyn and two other Honda officials met Shuken at an Italian restaurant in tony Newport Beach. "The course of the conversation was very strange," recalls Shuken. "They asked, what will you do for us if we let you move? My reply was to point out my record of CSI (Customer Satisfaction Index), the stats on the Ventura market and so on. Nothing seemed to impress them. Dennis asked the question again, what will you do for us? I rattled on about my plans. They would not commit. Looking back, I was very naive."

Josleyn was trying to get Shuken to pay him for the chance to relocate. He dropped the hints, but Shuken did not bite. Josleyn was not concerned about Cardiges's relationship with DCH. For the right amount of money, he would have done anything.

Soon thereafter, Josleyn sent me to tell Shuken the bad news: that Honda would not support Santa Paula Honda relocating to Ventura. Josleyn indicated that Cardiges had made the decision after having dinner with DCH officials. The supposed rationale was that Honda of Oxnard had just opened its new facility and should be given the opportunity to improve Honda's market penetration before any other moves were made in the area. The real agenda was twofold: Cardiges had already stabbed DCH in the back once by approving the Santa Paula deal; he could not afford to do it again. And Shuken was not someone who would pay to play—DCH was.

Shuken insists that even if he had known about Josleyn's expectations he would not have participated in the kickback game. He felt that Honda had breached its promise to him. "I was screwed," he said. He was stuck for an answer. He was the new dealer on the block and could not go over Cardiges's head to complain. He had also heard rumors that suing Honda meant decreased allocations of hot-selling Hondas. Litigation was not Shuken's style, anyway. Nor was it in his nature to close Santa Paula Honda and put his employees on the street. He decided to press on.

Still riding above the undercurrents, Shuken moved ahead with his simple objective of doing a good job selling Hondas. He looked for a spot to build a new facility within the city of Santa Paula. The only piece of land that made sense was located on Highway 126, visible to all who passed by Santa Paula on their way to somewhere else. It was also the most expensive piece of property in town.

Shuken bought the land and built a $1.3 million dealership for Honda. The resulting building would make any manufacturer proud. The modern architecture, backed up by the green mountains of Santa Paula, was a sight to behold. Opened in late 1990, Shuken renamed it Vista Honda 126 East, a shrewd move designed to achieve synergy with his other stores and to remind consumers of his location.

Dennis Josleyn never visited the dealership.

Shuken's good intentions, effort, and expertise were not enough to succeed in Santa Paula. The sudden downturn in the California economy and the limitations of operating in a small town conspired against Shuken. Vista Honda 126 East lost over $500,000 during its first two years of operation. Shuken had never given up and closed a dealership in all his years, and he would not consider that option. He needed a solution.

He found it in the 1994 arrests of the Honda officials. It became public news that DCH officials had paid Cardiges and others to protect its stores, including Honda of Oxnard, to the tune of over $300,000. Ed Temple and Dennis Josleyn were exposed as fast-buck artists.

"The light bulb finally went on in my head," said a bitter Shuken. "Temple had lied to me, DCH had paid off Cardiges to block the move, and Josleyn tried to shake me down. I was caught in a crooked card game. I had never dealt with dishonest factory people before."

What happened next may never be explained. Shuken had contacted a Honda vice president and told him the Santa Paula story. A pair of Honda corporate attorneys were dispatched to visit Shuken and discuss the matter. "They were very impressed with my new store, and best of all, they were obviously shocked when they saw 118 North Mill Street," said Shuken. "They started mumbling to themselves."

They returned to Shuken's office and were casually discussing the situation. "I mentioned that I should sue DCH because of the potential restraint of trade violations," Shuken said. "(Attorney Mark) Brooks stood up, went to my office door and closed it. He said: 'Look, you have to very careful what you say. You don't know who you are dealing with when you speak about these people. We switched cars on the way here today because we were concerned about our safety.' 'Do you mean DCH?' I asked. They wouldn't confirm that. They just said, don't ever say that again. I thought, what have I gotten myself into here? Honda's own lawyers are even afraid of DCH!"

Shuken took away from the meeting the idea that DCH was a bunch not to mess with. The never-ending series of strange incidents with Honda officials was beginning to wear on Shuken. His lawyers pressed him to sue Honda. They said the Santa Paula yarn had all the ingredients to be the blockbuster Honda case that would draw national media coverage. The thought of a multimillion-dollar settlement did not sway Shuken — he preferred the simple opportunity to do a good job selling Hondas in Ventura.

Steve Shuken resolved his differences with Honda in 1995. It is likely he will finally be allowed to move Vista Honda 126 East from Santa Paula to Ventura. In effect, Honda will be paying him to relocate, instead of him having to bribe Honda officials for that right.

The house would eventually fall on Ed Temple, but not before it was revealed that he had another reason for his haste in leaving American Honda.

As for Dah Chong Hong, its relationship with Honda officials began with Soichiro Honda himself.

CHAPTER 3

Mr. Honda

> We do not make something because the demand, the market, is there. With our technology, we can create the demand, we can create the market.
>
> — Soichiro Honda

SOICHIRO HONDA would have been unemployable by any car company but his own. A rebel in a society that emphasizes conformity, Honda Motor Company's founder was a free-spirited mechanical genius whose corporation reflected his personality. He would never learn that his company's philosophies ultimately contributed to the Honda scandal in America.

Born in 1906, Honda was the son of a poor blacksmith. His fascination with machinery began as a child. He recalled seeing the first automobile in town and covering his hands with the black engine oil dripping underneath. "I was literally intoxicated with the smell of that oil," he reminisced. "I think it was from that moment I knew I would one day build a car myself."

Honda dropped out of school at age 16 to work for an automobile repair shop. Six years later he opened his own garage in the city of Hamamatsu. The shop grew quickly and had the reputation of being able to fix vehicles that other garages deemed irreparable. Honda's knack for developing new ideas began here, with his invention of metal wheel spokes to replace the rickety wooden ones used on the cars of the time.

The business became profitable, and young Honda became the Wild Man of Hamamatsu, partying with *geisha* girls and racing through town in one of his favorite foreign cars — usually a Ford. Honda was a man of the common people. "I learned about the feelings of people who travel the back ways of life," said Honda. "I was able to acquire knowledge of human nature through exposure to life in the raw."

During his recuperation from a 1936 auto racing accident, Honda realized the limitations of the car repair business, saying, "No matter how good a repair job is done by a garage, requests for repair work wouldn't come from Tokyo or America." Honda wanted to fulfill a dream: to start a manufacturing operation to supply goods to the world.

Post–World War II Japan was in desperate need of transportation because food shortages had forced people to travel to rural areas to buy staples. Honda purchased some war-surplus gasoline engines and attached them to bicycles. The bikes were a sales success, but the supply of motors soon evaporated and Honda set out to build his own. The first was produced in 1947, a noisy 50cc two-stroke engine dubbed "The Chimney" for the black smoke it spewed. In 1948 Honda renamed the company Honda Motor Company, Ltd., and began development on a true motorcycle.

Honda was a man obsessed with engine design and had little time for the customs of the business world. He irritated bankers by wearing brightly colored suits or grimy shop coveralls to meetings. Honda began seeking a partner to manage the nontechnical end of the business. In 1949 he met Takeo Fujisawa, the owner of a tool and die company. Fujisawa, like Honda, came from a poor family and had only a middle-school education. His dream was to build a corporation different from other Japanese giants, one with the entrepreneurial spirit of a small enterprise. Fujisawa became the director of finance and marketing for Honda Motor Company. His knack for salesmanship and management was the perfect complement to grease-monkey Honda. The partnership the pair forged was a juxtaposition of personalities: the gregarious Honda was the tinkerer, the introspective Fujisawa the salesman.

In 1949 Honda Motor built its first motorcycle, the 98cc Dream, to be produced in Honda's first factory planned for Tokyo. Honda immediately had its first run-in with the Ministry of International Trade and Industry (MITI), the powerful government agency that controls Japanese industry. MITI's mission is to develop industrial policy, though its regulations are often suffocating and anticompetitive. MITI decides how many companies are allowed to build a certain product, how much production is allowed, how a company borrows money, and who may import and export. MITI decreed that Honda's proposal to build a factory to produce 300 motorcycles a month was too ambitious and threatened to deny its application. Honda and Fujisawa spent hours convincing MITI officials of the merits of their plans and were eventually granted the permit. "I probably would have even been more successful had we not had MITI," Honda said years later.

By 1951 Fujisawa had expanded Honda's dealer network from 200 to

5,000 outlets. As sales grew, Honda instituted policies unheard of in the motorcycle business. It gave consumers a one-year warranty on its products and tutored dealers on the importance of customer service.

The combination of Honda's technological advances, such as the development of an overhead camshaft engine small enough for motorcycle use, and Fujisawa's marketing prowess vaulted Honda's sales skyward. Honda bikes were recognized for their high quality and fusion of economy and performance. That success was due in part to Honda reinvesting a higher percentage of profits back into research and development than other manufacturers. By 1954 Honda was Japan's top motorcycle producer.

Honda Motor cultivated an environment different from the consensus style of management practiced in Japanese businesses. Honda wanted his workers to have independence, feeling that the conformity required in other firms stifled creativity. "First, each individual should work for himself," Honda directed. "People will not sacrifice themselves for the company. They come to work at the company to enjoy themselves. That feeling would lead to innovation." The rebel Honda attracted independent thinkers like himself, engineers who did not want to suffer the oppressive environments of the larger Japanese firms.

Honda stressed youthfulness in his hiring practices. New hires were given immediate responsibility and found themselves working alongside the firm's founder. The corporation's development of new products involved people from all departments, who would participate in brainstorming sessions called *waigayas,* a Japanese term meaning noisy.

The youthful vitality of Honda Motor Company was further advanced by the founders' commitment to promoting employees without regard to seniority or age. Fujisawa believed that corporation presidents should be in their 40s — 20 years younger than the typical Japanese CEO.

Honda and Fujisawa put their philosophies into writing in 1956, when they created Honda Motor Company's mission statement:

> COMPANY PRINCIPLE
> Maintaining an international viewpoint, we are dedicated to supplying products of the highest efficiency yet at reasonable price for worldwide customer satisfaction.
>
> MANAGEMENT POLICY
> 1. Always proceed with ambition and youthfulness.
> 2. Respect sound theory, develop fresh ideas, and make the most effective use of time.
> 3. Enjoy your work and always brighten your work atmosphere.

4. Strive constantly for harmonious work flow.
5. Be ever mindful of the value of research and endeavor.

The company principal was a bold statement for the young motorcycle maker, even omitting Honda's philosophy of remaining independent from other companies. Honda had rejected overtures to join several *keiretsu* corporations, large conglomerates of firms merged together at the encouragement of MITI. Soichiro Honda lectured his troops on the importance of developing their own technology and not copying others' ideas. "I don't want to walk on the path that is already created by other people," said Honda.

Though free spending for the development of technology, Honda Motor was a fiscally conservative company. Despite its rapid growth, Fujisawa resisted establishing a bureaucratic organizational structure. The lean staffing helped the company weather several financial crises in the 1950s, as did Fujisawa's expertise in money management and his ability to dissuade banking institutions bent on loan foreclosures.

In 1958 Honda introduced what would become the most significant motorcycle in history: the Super Cub. Considered to be Soichiro Honda's crowning achievement, the Super Cub project was initiated by the foresight of Fujisawa. While Mr. Honda concentrated on developing large, high-performance motorcycles, the intuitive Fujisawa foresaw a market for a small, inexpensive, easy-to-ride bike practical enough for people other than motorcycle enthusiasts. The resultant Super Cub did not resemble any bike that had come before: It sported a light, almost feminine look. The frame did not have a horizontal frame member between the seat and handlebars, causing it to be dubbed a "step-through" motorcycle and making it easier for women to ride. The 50cc motor featured an automatic gearbox, adding to its appeal to first-time riders.

The Super Cub was an overnight sensation. Honda began construction of a production plant in the city of Suzuka with an output of more than 360,000 units per year—an incredibly confident plan that would triple Honda's volume. The Suzuka plant would be the world's largest motorcycle factory when it opened in 1960. A year later, 60 percent of the Hondas sold worldwide were Super Cubs. The Super Cub became the best-selling motorcycle in world history and propelled Honda to the number-one spot in the world motorcycle industry.

Honda quickly expanded internationally, building factories in Taiwan and Belgium and establishing subsidiaries in 20 other nations. Honda applied to MITI for permission to set up shop in the United States, a proposal the agency rejected, saying Honda had not "earned the right" to export to America. MITI eventually relented, and American Honda Motor Company was established in 1959, initially setting up a three-man office in Los Angeles.

The first few years were difficult for American Honda. It had signed up only 15 dealers during its first six months. In early 1960, a rash of mechanical problems plagued the first batch of motorcycles in consumers' hands. The large-displacement bikes were being ridden harder and longer than they had been in Japan. Honda bought the motorcycles back and worked night and day to fix the maladies.

Slowly, a dealer body took shape, and Honda flew dealers to Japan to tour its factories and learn its philosophies about customer service. Dealers were impressed with Honda's commitment to airfreight parts to them until a distribution system could be set up.

Fujisawa's marketing plan for selling motorcycles in America emphasized promoting Honda's larger machines. But Honda employees soon caused a stir with Californians as they ran errands on their Super Cubs. Spurred by the interest, Honda studied the U.S. consumer and recognized a niche that American motorcycle makers had missed. Said Honda, "We knew that more and more Americans in those days were using motorcycles for different reasons, to enjoy their leisure, not (just) as a practical means of transportation." Honda decided to feature the Super Cub in their first serious marketing effort.

The 1963 campaign was recognized as one of the most effective in advertising history. Honda's agency, Grey Advertising, developed the "You Meet the Nicest People on a Honda" campaign from a strategy of positioning the motorcycle as socially acceptable. The ads featured lighthearted drawings of people using Super Cubs for work, school, or play. Honda directed the advertisements at women as well as men, a first for the industry. The campaign single-handedly changed Americans' image of the motorcycle rider from a leather jacket–clad delinquent to one of the girls or boys next door.

Honda had established over 600 dealers by 1963, and the retailers could not keep the bikes in stock. The Honda brand image — that of a fun company that built unique motorcycles and stood behind them — was forming. The rock group the Beach Boys, under the name the Hondells, hit the charts with a song entitled "Little Honda." Honda sold almost 100,000 motorcycles in 1963 and became the number-one-selling brand in America, capturing nearly 50 percent of the market.

Back in Japan, Soichiro Honda turned his attention to achieving his childhood dream of building an automobile. Creating a new car company is a bold undertaking; no major automaker had been established anywhere in the world since before World War II. The capital needed for research and development, as well as for factories and a distribution system, is staggering.

Again, Honda's first obstacle was MITI. The agency felt too much competition within Japan's car industry would be detrimental to future growth. In 1961 MITI proposed that Japan's ten automakers merge into three groups, with giants Toyota and Nissan keeping their independence and the remaining eight combining to form one company that would concentrate on building mini-cars. The new law would also bar other companies from becoming automakers, legislation aimed squarely at Honda. Soichiro Honda was livid about the government interference, telling MITI officials, "If you want to control us, you will have to be a shareholder. Only our shareholders have the right to dictate to the management of this organization. Only then will we listen to you!"

Honda sped up development of its first car so that it would be recognized by the government as an auto manufacturer before the legislation passed. Honda needed to raise capital to fund engineering and build a factory, especially since it had just finished construction of the giant Suzuka motorcycle plant and was strapped for cash. Obviously, MITI would not be any help in arranging for banks to loan money to the company. Honda was hesitant about approaching its primary financial institution, Mitsubishi Bank, since the bank's parent company was a major car manufacturer itself.

Enter the gang from Dah Chong Hong (DCH), the huge Hong Kong trading company that 20 years later would own Gardena Honda in Los Angeles, America's highest-volume Honda dealership. The privately owned DCH conglomerate — that in 1989 would cause American Honda lawyers to cower and Steve Shuken to lose his shot at moving Santa Paula Honda — came to Honda's rescue.

In 1961 DCH was the leading automobile distributor for Hong Kong, selling vehicles from General Motors, Nissan, Isuzu, Renault, and British Leyland. Dah Chong Hong and Honda Motor reached an agreement for DCH to provide the cash for Honda to continue its automobile project in exchange for DCH becoming Honda's car distributor for Hong Kong. MITI was furious about the arrangement, the rebel Honda having used funding from another country without the ministry's approval.

This deal was a key moment in Honda's history, DCH arguably being its savior. Without DCH's help, Honda would have delayed introduction of its first automobile and its fate would have changed — particularly in America, where Honda's success would be determined as much by timing as by the cars themselves. The word at American Honda during the rollicking 1980s that DCH would get whatever it wanted in terms of product and dealerships stemmed from this 1961 arrangement — and from DCH's showering American Honda officials with gifts.

In 1962 Honda introduced a prototype of its first automobile, the S360 convertible. The two-seat roadster had a motorcycle drivetrain, right down to its chain-driven rear wheels. Its smooth, rounded styling was reminiscent of British sports cars of the day. Honda marketed the car in 1963 as the S500, powered by a 531cc, twin-cam, four-cylinder motor producing an astounding 44 horsepower — more than most 1,000cc engines of the time. The Honda roadsters were the "Little Ferraris" of Japan: high-performance, hand-built, limited-production sports cars.

The legislation that would have prevented Honda from building automobiles was defeated in 1963. Honda developed a small four-seater car for mass consumption and began building an auto factory in Sayama. Going against the grain of most automakers, the tiny Honda N360 sedan featured a front-wheel-drive drivetrain. It was a first by a Japanese automaker, and every subsequent Honda automobile would be powered by this layout. Said Honda, "A front-wheel drive car does not require a long drive shaft to transmit power from the engine to the rear wheels, an advantage for a small car, as a lot of (interior) space can be saved. Furthermore, a car of this type, being pulled from the front rather than pushed from behind, has greater running stability." Another advantage of this configuration was better bad-weather traction, a benefit also enjoyed by the rear-engine, rear-wheel-drive Volkswagen Beetle from Germany, the best-selling small car in the world in the early 1960s.

The Honda N360 was introduced just as the Japanese auto market was undergoing huge growth, most of it in the mini-car segment. Honda's timing was perfect. The N360 became the best-selling mini-car in Japan. Ironically, Honda would rarely see such success again in its home market.

Honda's increasing revenues and status enabled it to afford another of old racer Honda's dreams: to enter a car in the international Formula One automobile racing series. Honda had dominated the worldwide motorcycle racing circuits for five years and planned to use auto racing as a test bed for new technology and to enhance the corporation's worldwide image as an innovator. Unlike most Grand Prix competitors, who produced their own engines but used chassis built by specialized racing firms, Honda's car was built entirely in-house. The machines suffered from mechanical woes for two years before Honda won the season-ending Mexico Grand Prix in 1965. After an accident in the 1968 French Grand Prix claimed the life of a Honda driver, the company withdrew from automobile racing.

During the early 1970s Honda was embroiled in a series of legal battles unheard of in litigation-shy Japan. A consumer group called the Japan Automobile Users' Union was formed in 1970 and immediately began demanding settlements from automakers on behalf of people injured in automobile accidents, claiming that defective cars caused the wrecks. The organization was particularly tough on the Honda N360. Without admitting guilt, Honda grudgingly agreed to settle several of the cases.

The Japan Automobile Users' Union and the union's legal counsel, Haruo Abu, were not through with Honda. Abu and the director of the union attempted to blackmail Honda Motor for 1.6 billion yen (around $5 million), in exchange for the union backing off on litigation surrounding Honda automobiles. The two men were tried and convicted of extortion. It was revealed in court that the union was funded by a group of non-Honda automobile dealers.

Another Honda corporate philosophy was born: Lawyers are extortionists and litigation is to be avoided at all costs.

Honda Motor never moved beyond being a small player in the Japanese auto market. With all other Japanese automakers established prior to 1936, Honda was hard-pressed to establish a competitive dealer body in Japan. Japanese car dealers are loyal to their chosen brand, so Hondas could not be sold by existing retailers. The high cost of land prevented Honda from establishing the number of locations or dealers with the physical size of a Toyota or Nissan outlet. Honda's reputation with consumers in Japan was one of a top motorcycle and racing company, but it lacked both a wide selection of cars and the dealers to service them. Honda's global philosophy was going to be necessary for it to succeed in the automobile business. Wide-open America presented the best opportunity — it was the world's largest automobile market and had car dealers willing to add additional brands to their showrooms.

In 1969 American Honda recruited 50 U.S. dealers, mostly those who sold Honda motorcycles, to try the car franchise. Honda dropped a 600cc engine in the N360, renamed it the Honda N600, and shipped it to America.

The car was introduced in March 1970 at a price of $1,275. It was a hilariously small vehicle by American standards, the White Castle hamburger of cars. The ten-foot-long, roller-skate-shaped auto was perceived as an extension of a Honda motorcycle — dealers reported that customers peered into the N600 expecting to see handlebars. The car took 24 seconds to agonize from 0 to 60 miles per hour.

Automobile magazines praised the car's surprising roominess but wondered who would buy it. Wrote *Road & Track* magazine, "What happens mostly to people riding around in Honda 600 Coupes is, they get laughed at." Few customers noticed the car's advanced features, such as the front-wheel-drive layout, overhead camshaft engine, and power front disk brakes. The N600's impressive fuel economy of 42 miles per gallon was not a selling point in those days of 39-cents-per-gallon gasoline.

Honda's reputation as the company that revolutionized the American motorcycle market meant little to automobile buyers. Worse, American Honda's advertising agency, different from the one handling its motorcycle business, bungled the N600's marketing. One ad made light of the car's lack of automatic transmission and air-conditioning, while another showed a woman sitting on the fender of the car, inadvertently emphasizing the N600's Lilliputian size. Hampered by public resistance and a limited number of dealers, Honda sold only 3,772 copies of the N600 during 1970. The automobile that was a hit in Japan was a mere curiosity in the United States.

Honda was a latecomer to both building automobiles and exporting them to the United States. Toyota and Datsun (Nissan's American name till 1982) had been selling automobiles in the United States since 1958. Toyota was already moving over 200,000 cars annually by 1970, and Datsun 100,000 — and both offered a selection of models and body styles. Mazda, Mitsubishi, and Subaru also preceded Honda across the Pacific. The importer enjoying the greatest success was Volkswagen, with a cult-like following of customers buying its Beetles at the staggering rate of over 350,000 per year. The small car boom was about to begin in America, but the Honda N600 was too tiny, a micro-car by industry and consumer measurements. At one point, Honda officials huddled to consider whether to abandon selling cars in the America. They decided to press on.

Domestic manufacturers had built compact automobiles since the early 1960s — such vehicles as the Ford Falcon and Plymouth Valiant — all little more than chopped-down full-size cars. Detroit automakers' executives were skeptical about producing smaller cars because they thought those vehicles would take sales away from their larger automobiles. Ultimately, it was the bigger profits from their huge, chrome-laden behemoths that held Detroit back from developing true small cars.

Detroit thought that since customers bought every car they built, the makers were in touch with the market. Domestic executives' view of the consumer was limited to what they could see in isolated Detroit, where few people owned imported cars. American automakers thought small cars were a fad, and they refused to believe foreign companies could be a force in the United States. The four domestic manufacturers — General Motors, Ford, Chrysler, and American Motors — assumed they competed only with each other.

The compact car market had grown steadily since the mid-1960s, as consumer interest in environmental issues grew and as baby boomers graduated from college. By 1970 the segment had grown to 29 percent of the total industry, with over 1.8 million sales, a trend too big for Detroit to ignore. Half of those cars were imports, 45 percent of which were from Japan. Detroit's entries were three-quarter-scale versions of their full-sized cars, while the foreigners offered smaller, fuel-efficient machines. Japanese autos were lauded for their quality. Customers buying imports were young and college-educated, many of them first-time car buyers, and would turn out to be fiercely loyal to the brand. They wanted fun-to-drive cars with innovation and good gas mileage.

The growth of small car sales marked the beginning of the greatest sea change in the American automobile market and the first challenge to Detroit's stranglehold on the consumer. Watching import sales rise every year, the domestic automakers had no choice but to respond and develop genuine small vehicles. They hastily cobbled together their first counterattack cars.

The 1970 debut of the first domestic small autos included three of the biggest lemons ever foisted off on the American public. The Ford Pinto had an annoying habit of exploding when struck from behind. American Motors' Gremlin *looked* like it had been struck from behind: the company had taken its midsized Hornet, chopped 12 inches off its rear, and added a hatchback. The Gremlin inexplicably featured a gas-guzzling six-cylinder motor, instead of the four-cylinder engines of its competitors. The overweight and overpriced Chevrolet Vega suffered meltdowns of its aluminum motor. It was said that, if you were real quiet at night, you could hear your Vega rusting in your garage. It would eventually be recognized as the worst-quality car in GM history.

All three cars sold well initially but, as the Detroit executives predicted, at the expense of their larger cars. The anticipated "conquest" sales, the defection of an import owner to a domestic car, did not materialize. This new generation could not be counted on to buy their fathers' Oldsmobiles.

The new entries lacked one of the key features that differentiated

Honda — the front-wheel-drive configuration, paramount for a roomy small car. Detroit had made numerous attempts to build front-wheel-drive vehicles and had abandoned the concept. It was deemed too expensive to develop such a radical layout.

Sales of the Honda N600 rose to 9,500 units in 1971, still a blip on the 10 million car American market. In 1972 Honda introduced its first significant automobile in America: the 1973 Civic hatchback. The Civic's base price of $1,973 was a stroke of marketing genius and several hundred dollars less than Detroit offerings. It was a larger automobile than the one it replaced and featured a 1,240cc four-cylinder overhead cam engine mounted transversely for increased passenger room. The Civic was a grown-up car in a small package: comfortable, powerful, quiet, but still economical. The Environmental Protection Agency rated the Civic the highest-gas-mileage car sold in America, at 29 miles per gallon for in-city driving.

Though not quite ready to deem it a "real" automobile, the automotive press considered it the perfect urban car, lauding its ability to squirt through city traffic. *Motor Trend* magazine wrote, "once in each generation of new cars an automobile appears that is so right for its time and application that it's a wonder all cars that follow aren't carved . . . in its image. The Honda Civic is a revolution on wheels." *Road Test* magazine named it its Import Car of the Year, the first of scores of awards Honda automobiles would garner in the United States.

Honda changed advertising agencies after the ineffective N600 campaign and began an enduring marketing image with the Civic launch. Basically a copy of Volkswagen's brilliant advertising of the 1960s, the campaigns were simple, intelligent, and funny, Honda making its point without hip models or hyperbole. One magazine ad listed the gas mileage ratings for every car sold in America, the new Civic ranking first. The headline read: "Brought to you by the makers of the car at the top of the list. Partly as a public service." The tag line of "The Civic — What the World is Coming To" would be prophetic.

American Honda gained credibility with dealer candidates with the Civic — over 400 retailers signed up to sell Hondas by mid-1973. Honda did not have the product line or reputation to warrant dealers building facilities to handle Honda exclusively, so it sought out stores that would "dual" their showrooms, selling Hondas alongside their established makes. Honda concentrated on pitching dealers handling Volkswagen, Pontiac, and Oldsmobile, franchises with track records of selling to younger, upscale buyers. Detroit pressured their dealers not to add Japanese car lines to their stores, threatening to withhold hot-selling cars from those who dared. Some dealers were not interested in an import franchise. "Take your Jap car and get the hell off my lot," screamed an Alabama Oldsmobile dealer to a Honda field manager trying to recruit him. Fortunately, Honda would not have to actively enroll dealers for much longer.

Late 1973 brought the first in a series of perfectly timed world crises that benefited Honda and other small car makers — an Arab oil embargo sent gasoline prices skyrocketing. Predictions of fuel shortages and gasoline rationing were rampant. President Nixon requested that gas stations close between Saturday night and Monday morning and enacted the 55-miles-per-hour speed limit law. The average American car got only 13 miles per gallon of gas, whereas imports averaged over 20. Consumers scrambled to buy fuel-efficient automobiles, and demand for large domestic cars plummeted.

Customers purchased every Civic that Honda shipped to America in 1974, along with every leftover N600, for a total of 43,119 sales. The most significant impact of the oil shortage for Honda was that almost 800,000 people bought Pintos, Vegas, and Gremlins in 1974. By the time those consumers were ready to dump their junkers a few years later, they would consider a small import automobile for the first time.

The automobile business in the early 1970s was complicated by new U.S. government regulations designed to improve vehicle safety and to reduce tailpipe emissions. The required stronger bumpers and ill-conceived seat-belt interlock devices added precious weight and price to autos. An amendment to the Clean Air Act decreed that all cars sold in America must have substantially reduced exhaust emissions by 1975. Most automakers' answer to this law was to develop catalytic converters, after-the-fact devices hung on vehicle exhaust systems to clean the emissions. Catalytic converters sapped engine power, emitted the smell of rotten eggs, and had a tendency to clog. Detroit feared they would choke their small cars' already anemic four-cylinder engines.

Soichiro Honda did not see the emission challenge as merely meeting a government standard. He firmly believed in the need for reduced air pollution for the good of society. Honda's engineers had long studied the most basic principal of an engine, the efficiency of the burning of fuel in the combustion chamber. Initially, Honda's goal was to increase the horsepower of its motorcycles through more effective combustion, but the findings would lead it to an automobile emissions breakthrough.

In February of 1971 Honda announced the details of a new engine — the compound vortex controlled combustion (CVCC) — featuring an innovative precombustion chamber for each cylinder to better ignite the lean fuel mixture needed for low emissions. The motor met the new standards with only small sacrifices in power and economy and without the expensive unleaded gasoline required for catalytic converter–equipped autos. The American Society of Automotive Engineers praised the new technology, noting that Honda was the first automaker to meet the upcoming standards.

Improving gas mileage to meet the realities of the market and reducing tailpipe emissions at the same time was a Herculean task for Detroit. They fought the Clean Air Act to give themselves breathing room. In a hearing in Washington, domestic automakers demanded the government postpone the regulations for at least one year, saying more development time was needed. Honda was prepared for 1975 with the CVCC technology, and a Honda official told the congressional committee, "We do not intend to apply for a qualified extension of time which certain automobile manufacturers have asked of the EPA administrators because we are capable of meeting those standards in 1975 and we consider it our obligation to do so." American automaker executives sat in humiliated silence.

The introduction of the 1975 Civic with the CVCC engine was a defining moment for Honda — it had bewildered Detroit and established itself as a technologically innovative company. American mainstream media applauded Honda's breakthrough.

Ford chairman Lee Iacocca was one of the first Detroit executives to see the light. Honda's engine quality and experience with front-wheel-drive technology impressed him. Iacocca decided to throw some money at Honda to purchase its engines for the Fiesta, the 1977 vehicle being readied as Ford's first small front-wheel-drive car. Iacocca flew to Japan in late 1974 without informing Henry Ford II of his agenda — Ford's president was against further development of small autos, often referring to Japanese cars as "little shitboxes."

Soichiro Honda invited Lee Iacocca to his home and threw him a giant party. The two men worked out an agreement for Ford to buy 300,000 Honda CVCC engines and transmissions for $711 per set, a tremendous bargain for Ford. With this drivetrain, Ford could save hundreds of millions in engineering and production costs and come to market quickly with its new car. An excited Iacocca returned to Detroit with the news, but the shortsighted Mr. Ford nixed the idea, saying, "No car with my name on the hood is going to have a Jap engine inside!" Ford Motor Company would have been hailed as forward thinking had it consummated the Honda deal, but the whims of Henry Ford II ruled the corporation. Iacocca and Ford's disagreements over small cars would be the beginning of their protracted battles, ending in Ford's firing of Iacocca in 1978.

It was uncharacteristic of Soichiro Honda to have made such a deal, one that might have sacrificed his company's independence. Iacocca claims Honda struck the engine deal because of uncertainty about his company's future selling automobiles in the United States. A more likely explanation is that Honda's admiration of Ford, along with the persuasiveness of consummate salesman Iacocca, convinced him to commit.

The arrangement would have altered Honda's fortunes in America. Honda having to compete with a Honda-powered Ford meant vying for the same customer. Its fledgling dealer network would have been up against 5,600 Ford dealers and Ford's plentiful marketing money. Ford would likely have pressed Honda for more than just drivetrains, and American Honda's growth would have slowed as it became a slave to Ford Motor Company.

American Honda executives stunned their Tokyo counterparts with the request of 150,000 cars for 1975, but production capacity was limited. Honda sold 102,383 Civic CVCCs in 1975 in the United States, including a new four-door station wagon model.

Detroit was feeling good in late 1975. Though none of the domestic companies had yet to develop an efficient four-cylinder car to challenge the Japanese, they were not concerned. The pesky energy crisis was over. Sales had picked up on their full-sized vehicles. The more smug of the executives predicted that the days of small autos were numbered. Detroit had only to look in their rearview mirrors to see a steamroller called Congress and a new Honda both about to blow their doors off — and change forever how they would build cars.

In December 1975 the government enacted the Corporate Average Fuel Economy (CAFE) law, a measure designed to save gasoline. The law required carmakers to produce vehicles with a gas mileage average of 20 miles per gallon by 1980 or face stiff penalties. American cars' average had crept up to 16 miles per gallon because of their increased mix of small automobiles, but the new law meant sweeping changes in product development. Detroit deemed the legislation anti-American, since Honda and other Japanese carmakers were already in compliance. Like their previous battles against government regulations, the American firms would whine but not win. The CAFE law forced them to get serious about building small automobiles.

The Civic alone could not carry Honda. Many consumers were put off by the bite-sized N600 and still equated Honda with "small," a perception not helped by the Civic. "From the outside, prospects arbitrarily decide that the Civic is small, so they can't use it," said Honda's 1970s sales chief Cliff Schmillen. "Dealers tell us all they have to do is get people in and they're sold." Honda's next car would bury the size misconception.

In May 1976 Honda introduced the automobile that would forever define its success: the Accord. One of the most significant cars in American history, the Accord eventually ranked alongside three other cars that created new high-volume markets and a loyal following: the Ford Model T, the Mustang, and the Volkswagen Beetle. The Accord was a stunning achievement, the first luxurious small car. It was the first movement by a Japanese automaker toward larger car territory, the sacred ground of Detroit.

The Accord was a step forward in quality, drivability, and creature comforts. An aerodynamic three-door hatchback, the Accord was two inches wider than most of the competitors, could accommodate four adults comfortably, and most importantly did not look small. It featured four-wheel independent suspension and was powered by a 1,600cc CVCC motor, Honda's largest offering to date. The car came equipped with thoughtful touches such as a carpeted coin box, side window defrosters, electric rear wiper/washer, a remote hatchback release, and instruments that told the driver of doors ajar and burned-out taillights.

Soichiro Honda's engineering expertise and attention to detail differentiated the Accord from the rest. Honda built a drivetrain with efficiency and smoothness unmatched by the competition, even other Japanese manufacturers. When pushed to the limit, an American four-cylinder motor sounded like a garbage disposal full of forks, while the Accord's power plant purred. The five-speed transmission snicked through shifts like butter. Each of the perfectly placed controls and switches moved solidly, the paint quality was equal to the best in the world, and the doors closed with a solid thunk. The Accord was quieter at highway speeds than many full-size American cars.

Moving upscale did not mean a loss in efficiency — the Accord's fuel economy was rated 31 miles per gallon in city driving and 44 on the highway. Sticker-priced at $3,995, the Accord cost less than most domestic small cars. Accord buyers' only choices were deciding on one of three colors and automatic or five-speed transmission. Fewer options was a foreign concept to Detroit, which offered over 300 models that could be ordered in thousands of permutations depending on customer preference. Honda's limited offerings stemmed from having to ship finished cars from Japan and the obvious fact that building the autos identically meant more expeditious production and fewer defects.

The Accord was Japanese precision, German quality, and American luxury all integrated into a handsome package. The reviews were orgasmic. "The difference between the Accord and everybody else's small car is considerable," wrote *Car & Driver* magazine. "The Honda seems more thorough, more complete, more intricate and more capable in more situations. For most types of driving, it's probably the finest small car built." *Motor Trend* magazine named the 1976 Accord its Import Car of the Year.

Honda's marketing efforts for the Accord continued its savvy strategy. They avoided showing young models fawning over the automobile, as was Detroit's advertising habit. The marketing campaign was launched with a clever three-page print ad. On the first page was a Civic with the message "The Bigger Little Car From Honda. The Civic." Turning the page revealed a two-page-wide shot of the Accord with the headline "A Little Bigger Car From Honda. The Accord." Television spots were simple, quirky, and funny. The marketing included the first use of what would become Honda's trademark tag line—"We Make It Simple."

The stampede was on. Customers literally stood in line to buy the little jewel of a car. Many dealers did not keep an Accord on hand for consumers to test-drive, much less to look at, but that only served to fan the frenzy. People followed transport trucks into the dealerships to catch a glimpse of an Accord. A Honda salesman recalls, "I had one guy follow me into the bathroom and ask, can you please sell me an Accord?" The wait for an Accord averaged three months nationwide and over a year on portions of the West and East Coasts. Dealers jacked up the Accord's price by adding high-markup items such as pinstripes and paint and fabric protectors ("mop and glow" in dealer parlance). Dealers with no experience selling imports added vinyl roofs and whitewall tires—the "Full Cleveland" package—demonstrating their lack of understanding of the new-age consumer. The less imaginative dealers simply marked the Accord's price up, calling it "Additional Dealer Profit." Even selling over sticker, the Accord was a better value than any competitor. American Honda grumbled about the price gouging, but its philosophy of not interfering in its dealers' business prevented it from taking action.

Behind all the hoopla, two product glitches developed that could have proven fatal to the neophyte automaker. Civics developed rusted fenders after two or three years on the streets. An alarming number of CVCC engines blew head gaskets. Honda told dealers to fix both problems, no questions asked, even if the car was past its 12-month/12,000-mile warranty. Dealers were shocked. One service manager remarked, "You won't find the Detroit car companies like GM or Ford doing this. I've seen (Honda) pick up the bill on blown engines on cars with over 30,000 miles." It was consistent with Honda's long-term policy of keeping customers happy whatever the cost, knowing word of mouth could make or break the company. Said one Honda executive, "While many companies debate over costs versus customer satisfaction, Honda will never conserve at the expense of our customers." Every carmaker has spoken such rhetoric, but Honda was one of the few to walk the talk.

Honda spent over $40 million to fix both the head gasket and rust problems, a significant portion of its American profits for those years. The company was in it for the long haul — it swallowed a short-term loss knowing the move would pay dividends down the road. To the U.S. automakers, whose credo was that they were in the business to make money — not to build cars or satisfy customers — such an expense would have been unthinkable.

Enough people traded Civics for Accords that Honda was ranked first in import owner loyalty by R. L. Polk and Company in 1978 — a position that Honda would hold throughout the 1980s. In 1978 Honda passed the fading Volkswagen, whose Beetle-replacing Rabbit was not selling well, as the number-three seller of imported cars in America. Honda now trailed only Toyota and Datsun.

In January 1979 the overthrow of the Shah of Iran started Energy Crisis II, which in turn doubled gasoline prices and plunged the U.S. economy into recession. Within five months the small car segment's share of the market jumped from 43 percent to 58 percent. With remarkable timing once again, in 1979, Honda first offered a full line of automobiles. It introduced the four-door Accord, the Prelude sport coupe, and an all-new Civic, all to the usual kudos from the press and public. The 1980 Civic marked the last time it would take Honda more than four years to completely redesign and reengineer a car. A four-year product cycle was an anomaly in the automobile business — Detroit typically milked a model for 8 to 12 years before a redesign. Honda's lack of bureaucracy, the R&D engineers' independence from other departments, and Fujisawa's legacy of keeping products fresh made lightning-fast development possible.

Honda was now the hottest auto franchise going. American Honda was flooded with applications for dealerships. Word spread among dealers that a Honda outlet was a car man's dream: the products were in demand and profitable, the factory stood behind the cars, and the customers were not mooches — the educated professional buyers having the wherewithal to buy cars. Dealers were amazed at Honda's policy of not shipping vehicles with known problems — a common Detroit trick. A recall was one thing, but knowing a car was defective and still selling it to a dealer was another — and not Honda's style.

Honda had signed up 740 U.S. dealers by the end of the decade, while Toyota and Datsun each had just under 1,100 outlets. Since the latter two had set up American operations in 1958, they were able to establish stores before the onslaught of early 1970s dealer-sponsored state franchise laws that restricted the placement of new dealerships. Neighboring Honda retailers could protest any new franchises proposed by Honda to dealer-friendly state motor vehicle commission boards. Impasses between manufacturer and commission meant going to court. Knowing the competition had the jump on them, Honda officials wanted to add more retailers and were distressed that it was difficult to do so. The state laws, along with the Japanese officials' litigation-shy nature, hindered expansion.

The 1970s marked the establishment of the Japanese automakers as major forces in America. Their market share rose from 5 percent in 1970 to over 21 percent by 1979. Shipments of Japanese vehicles to the United States soared from 400,000 to more than 2 million annually during this decade. Though helped by the gasoline shortages, it was the superiority of their products and the failure by Detroit to recognize the values of a new generation of buyers that propelled the growth of Japanese carmakers. The domestics' blundering response to the demand for fuel-efficient cars, capped by General Motors' late-1970s full-size automobiles with defect-riddled diesel engines, had tarnished their reputation. Detroit's rush to lighten vehicles to improve fuel economy resulted in declining quality during the 1970s and would later be recognized by industry analysts as the decade of the worst-built American cars in history. A 1978 survey revealed that a majority of consumers rated Japanese automobiles higher in quality and value than American cars.

The Japanese responded better than did Detroit to the flood of new government regulations in the 1970s — after dealing with the stranglehold MITI held on companies in Japan, American requirements were a breeze. "I found doing business much easier in the United States than in Japan," said Soichiro Honda.

Honda's American sales increased every year during the 1970s and it finished the decade by selling 353,291 cars in 1979, capturing 4 percent of the market. It was a remarkable first ten years, but Honda was only beginning.

Executives from domestic manufacturers flocked to Honda. The lure of the opportunity to mold the policies of an exciting young company was irresistible. Honda looked like the place to be.

The accepting of cash and gifts by American Honda executives has wrongly been tied to the notion that the business world in Japan is rife with corruption, that some sort of tacit approval for such activities was exported to America on the boat carrying the first load of Super Cubs. That is not the case. There is little difference in the prevalence of corruption between the two nations.

The Orient Pacific Century corporation of Malaysia annually ranks countries by the amount of perceived corrupt activities by their public and private officials. Acknowledging that accurate measurement of bribery is impossible, it relies on subjective input from ten international business study institutes. Its 1996 survey placed the United States 15th and Japan 17th in the least amount of corruption out of 54 nations. (New Zealand and Scandinavian countries were ranked as the most corrupt free, while China and several Asian and African nations were perceived as being the dirtiest.) Prior studies dating back to 1980 reveal similar rankings for both Japan and the United States.

The exchanging of gifts between officials of companies in Japan is a time-honored tradition done with the blessing of the corporation. Such gifts rarely exceed a couple of hundred dollars in value. Honda Motor of Japan's practice of limiting interaction with outside vendors, preferring to develop its own technology whenever possible, meant that its executives had less opportunity for contact with other companies and subsequent temptations for large-scale kickbacks. The independent Honda was also never part of a traditional *keiretsu* network of Japanese corporations, in which the companies are tied together by interlocking ownership and directors, a situation tempting executives to pass money under the table.

There is no evidence to suggest that Honda Motor Company officials engaged in corrupt activities or that American Honda Motor Company executives were following a Japanese cultural tradition. The scandal was fueled by a bunch of money-grubbing American cowboys given free rein to set up a dealer network and distribution system for Honda automobiles.

The first such American Honda executive was Jack Billmyer. Meeting in 1975 with a Georgia dealer wanting a Honda franchise, Billmyer reviewed the requirements to secure the deal: proper experience, capitalization, and facility for Honda — and a pile of money and a new car for Billmyer.

"Nobody really loves you but your momma, and everybody else got to pay a little cash up front," Jack Billmyer told the dealer.

CHAPTER 4

Lean and Mean

> We are committed to fostering the initiative and creativity of our employees.
>
> — American Honda philosophy

JACK BILLMYER hated driving Hondas. While stationed as a sales rep far away from Honda's California headquarters, he piloted a Lincoln or Chevrolet sedan on dealer calls in his southeast territories. When promoted to national sales manager and reassigned from New Jersey to California in 1980, he had to cool it with the Detroit iron, at least in his commute to the office where he would be relegated to driving an Accord. Billmyer figured a black BMW sedan would be an appropriate side ride in import-car-crazy Los Angeles — dealer supplied, of course.

Billmyer's disdain for piloting his company's products did not prevent him from becoming the Godfather of Graft at American Honda, the first executive to shake down dealers for cash and gifts, the man who paved the way for others to follow. Billmyer tried to teach his underlings the right way to steal and conceal, but they would not listen.

Billmyer was the black sheep of a well-to-do North Carolina family. His older brother earned a Ph.D. degree and frowned upon Jack, the renegade working in the lowly car business. After a brief career at Ford Motor Company in the mid-1960s, Billmyer opened a Ford dealership in Greenville, North Carolina. The store soon went bankrupt because Billmyer spent more time pursuing his enthusiasm for auto racing than he did being a businessman. The closing was a blow to Billmyer. "He felt like a failure after losing the Ford store," recalls a friend. "He still felt inferior to his brother."

Billmyer's career with American Honda began in 1970 as North Carolina district sales manager at age 40. The beefy 6′4″ Billmyer could not fit into Honda's early cars. He had a surprisingly high-pitched voice, curly gray hair, a ruddy complexion, and huge ears that protruded from his head like Prelude doors. When a technical glitch at a national dealer meeting caused a live shot of Billmyer's face to suddenly flash rather than fade onto a 30-foot-high screen, the audience gasped and recoiled.

The plain-speaking Billmyer was a man true to his southern roots — a lover of automobile racing and beer drinking. He eventually lived a redneck's wet dream: co-owning both a Budweiser beer distributorship and a NASCAR stock car race team, thanks to the side money he earned peddling shiny new Hondas to grateful dealers.

Billmyer was lauded for his understanding of the automobile business, from both the factory and retail sides, and his natural instinct for dealer relations. He was one of only a few Honda execs whom one could picture selling cars on a showroom floor, toe-to-toe with a customer. Billmyer worked hard and expected the same from his people. Field sales reps learned the Billmyer adage that "you work all day and drive all night because that's why there are headlights on company cars." Billmyer managed by intimidation, transferring managers he disliked or felt were too old to out-of-the-way regions. When a district sales manager made an off-handed remark to Billmyer, unaware of whom he was speaking to, he was jettisoned from California to the lowly Louisiana territory. The rep resigned from Honda shortly thereafter, knowing his career was over.

"As a district manager, there was a very small likelihood you could advance your career by tailing around with Jack," says one Honda veteran, "and there was a very high likelihood that you could probably destroy it. I made it a point not to get in his way."

Not making the millions he had expected by being a car dealer, Billmyer turned to graft in his early positions at Honda. He toured the South recruiting dealers and trying to spot applicants who would pay him for a Honda franchise. Billmyer foresaw the upcoming introduction of the Accord transforming the fledgling franchise into a sought-after concern: the time was right to squeeze some dealers.

Bob Foster was a successful Honda motorcycle dealer in Athens, Georgia, and applied for the Honda automobile franchise in 1975. He was granted tentative approval, but the official notification had yet to arrive. He took out a $157,000 mortgage on his house to fund the expansion of his dealership to carry Honda cars. He canceled his MG and Triumph automobile franchises to concentrate on the upstart brand. Enter district sales manager Billmyer, who recognized that Foster was too far along in his plans to turn back — the perfect candidate for a bribe. Billmyer, after mentioning how little money he made at Honda — about $1,700 per month — informed Foster he wanted $20,000 cash and a Ford station wagon to finalize the deal. Foster refused to pay and threw him out of his store.

"You don't know a good deal when you see one," said Billmyer on his way out the door. "You'll live to regret this."

A few weeks later, the Athens Honda point was awarded to someone else. Foster called the Japanese director of American Honda's motorcycle division and reported the attempted extortion by Billmyer. The executive did nothing about the information — the first of many times Honda higher-ups would ignore the corruption.

Billmyer joined a company in the process of developing a structure and culture different from other automakers in America, domestic or import. It stemmed from Soichiro Honda's vision of decentralization and individualism, a system granting employees vast amounts of responsibility and freedom in their positions. The corporation also followed Takeo Fujisawa's philosophy of lean management staffing, the better to weather cash flow crunches. Former executives of Detroit carmakers stepped into a different world when they joined American Honda. It was a fast-moving company with an even faster-moving product. The cars, customers, and dealers came first at Honda, a simple and logical concept to the new recruits.

Honda possessed an ideal corporate climate for people to advance quickly and to be given decision-making authority from day one. "The company's policy is to give people a lot of latitude to run their operation the way they see fit," says current Honda executive vice president Tom Elliott. "It puts a lot of trust in the individual to run their operation and to do it in a professional manner. I probably have, myself, more latitude than I would ever have had working for another company."

Many new hires had endured the stifling bureaucracy of a Ford or General Motors, where internal politics was more important in the decision-making process than building a quality car or addressing the needs of the consumer.

"There was no comparison in management style," remembers 1979 recruit Bob Rivers, a veteran of Ford Motor Company. "Ford was very structured; lots of policies and procedures, lots of levels of management, lots of red tape, and a much more rigidly run organization. Honda, on the other hand, was a very lean organization, very few levels of management. At Ford, I was there for eight years and never, not once, did I ever meet or address personally a vice president. The very first day that I was brought up there for an interview I met a vice president at Honda. It was a much more casual, much more loosely-run organization." Over at Chrysler Corporation, if you were a junior executive and actually got to meet chairman Lee Iacocca, you would get his autograph as proof that you had actually seen the isolated mogul.

New employees gave up a lot of perks when leaving a domestic automaker to join Honda — no private offices or dining room, no corporate jet, no chauffeur, no country club memberships, no stock options or million-dollar retirement plan — not to mention a hefty pay cut. All to work for the little company from Japan and have more responsibility and freedom than they had ever dreamed of.

American Honda's executive offices in Torrance, California, could not be more different from General Motors' fabled Fourteenth Floor, where GM officials enjoy sumptuous offices and an executive dining room. There are no private offices at Honda. Most employees sit in 8′ by 10′ cubicles separated by 42″ tall panels. A handful of top executives are granted slightly larger cubes. Based on Honda's offices in Japan, the intent is to foster communication and promote the egalitarian environment. The reality is that you have to hunker down to get any privacy. Computer-generated white noise keeps sound levels down, but any sudden racket causes rows of heads to pop up over their cubes, like a human prairie dog town. Honda executives retreat to conference rooms to work undisturbed.

Some foreign automakers setting up shop in America used native-born employees to interact with dealers and vendors, which created language barriers and feelings that the company did not truly understand America. At Honda, the Japanese executives let the American officials run the sales department. This setup was agreeable to Billmyer, who mentioned to confidants how he hated the Japanese officials. He particularly did not trust his boss, Koichi Amemiya, the executive vice president of automobile operations, who would become American Honda's president in 1989. The mistrust was mutual. Says Jim Cardiges, Billmyer's eventual successor as national sales manager: "Amemiya, like many of the Japanese, was secretive, and socialized with other Japanese and did not appear to trust either Americans and/or dealers."

The Japanese and American officials ran in separate circles. "The only thing I knew about the Japanese was how heavy their luggage was," recalls one former executive. The president and other top Japanese managers spent a great deal of time in Japan, often one to two weeks per month away from Torrance. The Japanese officials emanated from world headquarters in Japan, some after a tour of duty in Honda's European or Canadian operations. Most had engineering or manufacturing backgrounds and dealt with long-term product plans and were not attuned to sales and marketing tactics. The only Americans who had substantial interaction with the Japanese were those working in product planning and accounting.

For a company founded on the philosophy of open communication, the lack of contact between the Japanese executives and the American sales officials was more than paradoxical. The Japanese were certainly intimidated by the Americans, particularly Billmyer, but the cars were selling too quickly to rock the boat by challenging the sales officials. "Billmyer had the Japanese snowed that he was the key guy, so they left him alone," says one executive. Honda automobiles had never flown off the showroom in Japan as they did in America, so the Japanese were content to concentrate on their core business of developing superior automobiles and left the sales and distribution responsibilities to the American officials.

"I can recall giving presentations to Japanese management maybe once a year on the objectives and goals of the division," remarks Cardiges. "I do not recall Japanese management ever coming to me and telling me what to do on a monthly, weekly, quarterly or yearly basis. It was up to myself when I was in that position and Mr. Billmyer when he was in that position to run the sales division. We had very little interference by the Japanese management."

Late-1980s president Yoshihide Munekuni once reflected on his job description: "I really don't have a job because the people beneath me are the ones who run the company. All I have to do is make sure that the results are good." In other words, sell the cars and don't tell me how you do it.

The American officials, although finding their jobs at Honda rewarding, did not have the level of corporate commitment displayed by the Japanese, who were married to Honda for life. "The Japanese management and executives had a much higher level of loyalty to Honda than the American management and executives did," says Cardiges. "Our loyalty was to the individuals that we were surrounded by, American management, myself, Mr. Billmyer, and our loyalty was split between us and the dealers."

In keeping with the firm's philosophy of autonomy, each division did its own recruiting, with the human relations department playing no role in who was hired, other than to process the paperwork. This practice gave questionable hires opportunity to slip through the cracks: Two Honda sales executives were heavily rumored to have been fired from a domestic automaker for accepting gifts from dealers. Two others falsely claimed on their resumes to have college degrees. All would become players in the corrupt game at Honda.

American Honda employs about 2,300 white-collar workers, including those in the motorcycle and the lawn mower and generator divisions. Add about 7,000 more employees in Japan responsible for product development and engineering and it totals up to the leanest automaker selling cars in the United States. The structure and head count of Honda's American arm changed very little between the late 1970s and early 1990s, despite annual sales booming from 200,000 cars to over 700,000. Each Detroit automaker employed tens of thousands of white-collar employees, even after several rounds of layoffs during the 1980s. Chrysler Corporation cut its white-collar workforce from 40,000 to 22,000 during the early 1980s. General Motors entered the 1990s with more than 100,000 white-collar workers, less than half its total in 1980. The competitors closest in size to American Honda were the U.S. arms of Toyota and Nissan, each with about two to three times as many employees as Honda.

American Honda's sales division employs about 120 employees versus approximately 2,000 in each of the Detroit giants. Honda's sales hierarchy is simple. Below the national sales manager/senior vice president are Eastern and Western regional sales managers, positions similar to that of the vice president of the Unites States: an abeyance between the two factions of power. The ten zone sales managers responsible for geographic territories around the nation held the true authority, connected to both the national sales manager and to the dealers. Reporting to each of them was an assistant zone sales manager and five to seven district sales managers, the people responsible for day-to-day contact with the dealers. A field clerical staff of 30 and a dozen headquarters employees rounded out the hierarchy. Above the national sales manager were two Japanese managers: the president and the executive vice president of the automobile division. Support staff was minimal: only the president and a few select others had private secretaries.

The lean structure was a source of pride to Honda. It enjoyed a reputation within the industry for making quick decisions and sticking to them. There were no layers of managers to call rounds of mind-numbing meetings to ponder minutia and fight for political positions, as was the case in Detroit. When a decision was needed on a sales division issue, the top people consulted with the zone sales managers and, if the matter affected the dealers, surveyed 30 or 40 of the retailers and reached a consensus that day. A customer writing the president of American Honda would actually receive a response.

The lack of head count may have aided Honda's success, but it also stifled employees. Its market representation department, entrusted with determining new dealership locations and qualified dealer candidates, employed a staff of 5 employees, whereas Toyota's had 48 and Nissan's 36, both including managers in each field office, the better to watch the markets. As with those of other department heads, market representation manager Jim Moynihan's pleas to the personnel department for additional staffing went unheard. His division was also responsible for determining annual operating budgets for the zone offices and recapping sales figures, duties unrelated to the department's core mission. "We had three times the amount of work as the other (Japanese) companies, with one-fifth the people," says Moynihan.

The understaffed market representation department had to acquiesce to the zone sales managers when it came to picking new dealers. "Rather than market rep finding where Honda should put dealers," explains Moynihan, "we were checking the viability of locations that the field was asking us about, so that worked beautifully in their favor." When Moynihan balked at some of the strange new points and dealer operators proposed by the field sales staff, he was overruled by Billmyer or Cardiges. A market representation department with adequate staffing would have been able to proactively pursue dealer appointments that were in the best interest of Honda. That simple oversight might have prevented dealerships being awarded solely on the basis of how much cash was slipped to Honda executives.

Honda did not pay its overworked staff competitively. The tightwad Japanese executives who controlled American Honda's purse strings were still living in the 1950s, when Honda Motor Company was often on the financial ropes. Funding was readily available for product research and development but little else. Honda's miserly employee compensation plans were the most glaring example of its cheapness and would become a central issue of the scandal.

Whether from the retail automobile business or another automaker, new hires suffered a cut in salary to work for Honda. Although being paid poorly does not excuse taking bribes, the devil often dances in empty pockets. In 1985 an *Automotive News* survey of the compensation of 170 of the top domestic automaker executives revealed an average annual salary of $620,000. The median of the top echelon at Honda was about $60,000. Hundreds of domestic automaker managers earned more than the president of American Honda, who pocketed around $200,000 per year. As senior vice president and national sales manager, Billmyer made $165,000 in his final full year at Honda in 1987, less than the sales managers of some high-volume Honda dealerships. Cardiges topped out at $181,000 in 1991.

The pair were the only Honda marketing officials ever to earn more than $100,000 annually. Detroit executives' compensation figures did not include their lucrative retirement plans, stock options, or other perks, benefits Honda did not provide. Domestic car company officials were overpaid, and Honda execs were underpaid. Other Japanese automakers in America paid significantly more than Honda, though nowhere near the going rates of the domestics.

Honda's human resources department exuded confidence that its compensation packages were competitive. It rationalized its position by claiming that other automakers' officials earned more money because they had greater responsibilities than their counterparts at Honda. Nothing could be further from the truth. At the lean Honda, managers had tremendous decision-making authority and responsibility on their shoulders, far more than their peers in Detroit. Human resources also pointed out that domestic firms sold more cars than Honda, thus the need for higher compensation for their managers — another theory that did not wash. In reality, upwards of half of the domestics' sales were automatic: they were fleet sales. These vehicles "sold" to rental car companies owned by the automakers constituted a transaction that took little effort by marketing executives. Over 98 percent of Honda's sales were through the dealer network to individual customers, the true measure of an automaker's sales.

In 1991 American Honda sold more cars than Chrysler Corporation's combined total of fleet and retail sales, while Chrysler's national sales manager was earning 20 times more than Honda sales chief Cardiges. That same year, Chrysler chairman Lee Iacocca made $4.6 million while his company was losing $795 million. Iacocca spent $2 million of his company's dollars to remodel its corporate suite at the Waldorf Towers in Manhattan, a sum that would have paid the salaries for half of Honda's sales division managers. The Honda officials knew they were doing a better job than their counterparts in Detroit and were well aware of the disparities in compensation.

Honda did not provide cost-of-living salary adjustments when employees were transferred to expensive markets like Los Angeles. Honda's cost-of-living policy paid an employee one month's additional salary upon relocation, in effect an 8.3 percent raise for one year only. Other large corporations offered employees up to a 100 percent pay increase to transfer to Southern California. Midlevel Honda managers earning $2,500 per month could not afford to own houses in Los Angeles, where the average price was $280,000 in the mid-1980s, unless they were willing to commute four hours a day from remote desert communities with more affordable housing.

During national sales meetings, Honda's human resources department presented its annual two-step about how it was working to improve both salary and cost-of-living allowances, a promise the hostile crowd of executives had heard for years. California-based managers asked, how can we afford to buy a home? A personnel minion once responded by saying "Well, *I* own a house." He was booed out of the room. More than one sales division manager straddling the fence about taking payoffs made his decision after hearing that comment.

With a remarkably low employee turnover rate of less than 5 percent during the 1980s, and people clamoring to join Honda, the human resources department had no motivation to pursue with the bean counters any enhancement to the firm's compensation programs. Honda attracted people simply because it was a great place to work. The sterling reputation of the products and the stream of positive press and rising sales made for a stimulating work environment.

Employees resorted to unethical means to make up for Honda's tightwad internal policies. Top executives — both American and Japanese — winged around the country for free in jets owned by various Honda dealers, a corporate aircraft being a time-saving device that Honda desperately needed but never considered buying. One zone sales manager ordered his field people to obtain fax machines for their home offices and to have dealers pay for them. He had tried and failed to persuade Honda to purchase them. Sales reps' car phones, a necessity for those in the field in metropolitan areas, were also paid for, along with the monthly bills, by dealers, because Honda refused to provide them. It was embarrassing for the executives to ask dealers for these minor items, but the retailers were eager to comply, figuring it was good for extra cars in return.

Non-sales-division managers were not lucky enough to have benevolent Honda retailers to call on for their needs. A market research official, unable to procure a simple software program through normal company means, once inflated the price of a project to cover the purchase. He was caught, and his salary and bonus were reduced as punishment.

When a district sales manager was promoted from the field to become an assistant zone sales manager or an assistant manager at headquarters, a curious thing happened — Honda took away his company car. Getting promoted thus resulted in a pay cut. Honda's penny-pinching company car department wrongly assumed that managers at that level did not call on dealers and thus did not need cars. Every other sales division employee, above and below the assistant manager, drove a free automobile. The assistants in the field, even the clean ones, were forced to prevail upon dealers to supply them with vehicles. "It's crazy," says one. "We are a *car* company, aren't we? I was very uncomfortable with asking a dealer for a car, but could I do?" Assistant managers at Honda headquarters would be slipped an automobile by their bosses, often an older model that had been damaged during shipment and poorly repaired, unsellable to a dealer. In the Torrance parking lot after work, the sight of a battered Honda emitting a strange whistle and wobbling toward the exit meant an assistant manager was headed home.

The freedom in your job, the lack of interference by the Japanese executives, the huge sums of money being raked in by Honda dealers, the poor pay and inherent cheapness at Honda — all perfect ingredients to encourage a fellow to take a few bribes.

Every Honda sales division manager began his career at the bottom of the ladder, as a trainee or as a district sales manager (DSM), calling on a geographic territory of 20 or so Honda dealers. The primary responsibility of an automaker's sales staff is to sell, or "wholesale," vehicles to dealers. Because of the high demand for Honda automobiles throughout the 1980s, DSMs were not burdened by having to sell cars to the dealers like their brethren at other automakers. They never endured the humiliation of a Ford Motor Company "phone room," where district sales managers could not go home until they had pressured a dealer into buying more orange Pintos. On the downside, Honda DSMs had to allocate cars to the dealers by hand on a cumbersome worksheet, Honda not supplying computers for the task until 1989.

Without having to spend countless hours "cramming cars," Honda DSMs could concentrate on working with the dealers on furthering the sales division's simple core missions:

- Increase customer satisfaction.
- Increase market penetration.
- Encourage dealers to build new facilities.
- Encourage "dualed" dealers — those selling Honda alongside other brands in the same showroom — to build exclusive Honda dealerships.
- Keep the corporation out of lawsuits.

Working at Honda gave employees a well-rounded education about the car business. Without the local support personnel provided by other carmakers, Honda field salespeople would perform the duties of a half-dozen managers. There were no local market representation employees, so they would process the morass of paperwork needed for dealer buy/sells and open points themselves. They analyzed dealers' financial statements, another task reserved for accounting specialists at other car companies. They conferred with dealers on new facility plans. They called sales meetings. Each sales division manager acted as a management consultant, a sales manager, an accountant, an advertising and promotion specialist, and a market analyst—without a paycheck reflecting the various responsibilities.

Honda district sales managers enjoyed the freedom to simply allocate the cars, do the minimum amount of paperwork required, and go to lunch with the dealer principals. Or they could choose to go the extra mile, by assisting the dealer in developing business plans or doing a host of other management consulting-type services. Most chose the latter route, which resulted in Honda ranking highest for dealer satisfaction among all automakers during most of the 1980s. Clean or dirty, most Honda sales division managers worked their tails off, buoyed by the gratification of working for the industry leader.

Honda managers also commanded respect from the dealers simply because they represented Honda and the retailers felt their financial destiny was in the execs' hands. Dealer principals warned their personnel to be on their toes when Honda officials were due in their showrooms. "You're the best (district, zone, regional) sales manager that has ever called on me," the dealers all said, as they had told your predecessor and would later tell your replacement.

The job could be rewarding in other ways, too. The dealer gratuity program began with the introduction of the Accord in 1976 and slowly ballooned from the bottle of wine or $100 gift certificate at Christmas, gifts common in the industry. New hires were flown to Los Angeles to meet with Billmyer, who sometimes spelled out the underground program. A district sales manager hired in 1981 remembers Billmyer's talk: "He said that dealers are gonna provide you with gifts, and that's okay. He didn't become explicit . . . but that was, I think, my first introduction as to what I envisioned the culture was going to be." If not informed by Billmyer, a DSM would learn about the Honda program in his first few weeks with the company, often from his superior.

Newly hired district sales manager Bill Green remembers taking cover in a phone booth from a December wind howling through Stillwater, Oklahoma, to call his zone office in Denver. It was his first conversation with his new boss, zone sales manager Frank Pisano, who had just transferred into the position. Pisano was hopelessly indiscreet. He loved to brag about the gratuities he received from dealers and did not waste time trying to determine whether Green was a player, nonplayer, or potential whistleblower. He needed to learn the lay of the land in his new territory.

"What's Christmas like in Oklahoma?" asked Pisano.

"It gets pretty cold with a little snow sometimes," replied Green.

"No, you idiot," said Pisano, annoyed. "I mean what kind of gifts can I expect from the dealers at Christmas time?"

Welcome to Honda, Mr. Green.

Honda district sales manager Dave Pedersen recalled his initiation into the corrupt world of Honda. In December 1979, Pedersen had been with the company less than four months when he paid a visit to upstate New York Honda dealer Bill Lia. As Pedersen was leaving, Lia opened Pedersen's sport coat and stuffed an envelope containing three $100 bills in the pocket.

"Bill, if this is what I think it is," said Pedersen, "you're going to have to take it back. I cannot accept this." He returned the envelope to Lia. The dealer was taken aback — he had never seen a Honda employee turn down a gift before.

Pedersen told Lia he was going to report the attempted bribe to his boss, zone sales manager Bill Kutchera.

Lia chuckled, "Well, Dave, don't worry about that. We've already handled the zone."

Pedersen left the dealership without the envelope. He phoned Kutchera who sat next to Billmyer in Honda's New Jersey office. "Dave, it's okay," said Kutchera. "Tell Bill you can accept gift certificates in lieu of what you thought was in the envelope." After Pedersen called Lia and relayed Kutchera's recommendation, the dealer mailed a $300 Macy's gift certificate to Pedersen.

Kutchera later gave Pedersen the lowdown on the Rolex watches, furniture, and cruise he had received from various Honda dealers. Pedersen never hesitated again. He thus began a tainted career that would have a huge impact on the Honda scandal in later years.

Most of the payoffs to an entry-level Honda exec were initiated by the dealers. Few were victims of extortion by the Honda managers — no "if you don't pay me, I won't give you any cars" type of muscle. The gifts just appeared. A few hundred dollar bills pressed into your hand. A gift certificate to a clothing store. A night on the town with a female companion of low moral standards. An outrageously high price paid for a personal car. "Just be sure to take care of us," said the dealers. "If there is anything I can do for you, let me know," they all said.

Fledglings were advised not to insult a dealer by turning down a gift — but also never to promise anything in return. Says one manager, "We had been told all along that if you were in jeopardy of damaging your relationship with a dealer by turning down a gift taken in the spirit of exactly what it was, a gift, then you should go ahead and take it. However, if you thought that there were strings attached to it, and it was being offered in other than the spirits of exactly being a gift, then you should walk away from it. I gave those similar instructions to my district managers." Those who truly believed that the dealers had no expectations of something in return were either stupid or already in denial of the addictive powers of the greed syndrome.

It was during his initial contacts with the Honda retailers that a young DSM made the determination about which road he would take — to the promised land or to the poorhouse — in the Honda world. About half of the force chose to participate. Those uncomfortable with what was happening asked their superiors about the ethics of receiving gifts from dealers. The standard response from their zone sales managers would be: "We are making these dealers millionaires and they're just showing their appreciation. If you do it, just be very careful and don't tell anyone. The worst thing you want is to have another dealer find out about it." A Honda dealer discovering that another dealer was paying off Honda executives would mean a certain lawsuit, the resultant favoritism being in violation of state and federal franchise laws. No one had to be told that the issue was never to be discussed with the Japanese executives, Honda's personnel department, or Honda's law firm.

The retailers all rationalized their participation in the corruption. Said New Jersey dealer Rod Ryan, "It was important to make sure that the people at Honda knew who you were so you didn't lose any allocation, you didn't lose any cars, you didn't lose any ground. You just wanted to make sure you got what was coming to you." Others said they were just trying to "improve the business relationship" with the Honda executives by slipping them some cash. Many were convinced that other dealers were doing it. "I knew that was what was expected," says California dealer David Conant, "and I conferred with some other Honda dealers that I had close ties with, and they told me that they were doing essentially the same thing."

Some of the dealers were no virgins when it came to payola. "We'd buy a freezer full of steaks or a hooker for our Pontiac rep, no big deal," said one dealer. "With Honda reps, it was different. We made sure to take good care of them. Of course, we were making a hell of a lot more money with Honda than Pontiac."

Some dealers paid out of defense, some paid out of offense, and all paid with the goal of making more money from their hot franchise.

Like most large corporations, Honda had a Conflict of Interest and Business Ethics Policy. The policy stated that employees were prohibited from accepting gifts from a vendor or dealer valued at more than $25, later raised to $50 in the late 1980s. ("Nice $49 suit you got there," the execs ribbed each other.) The policy spelled out how employees were forbidden from having ownerships in Honda dealerships or vendors. Each employee was supposed to sign the document annually, acknowledging his or her understanding of the meat of the policy: that any violation was grounds for termination. However, Honda's personnel department never consistently enforced obtaining signatures on the conflict of interest policy. "There was a period of time when the signature wasn't required," says a Honda personnel manager. "There was some debate legally as to whether we at Honda could force somebody to sign something." Honda's fear of litigation prevented it from mandating an employee signature on a document commonplace in most businesses. Many employees report they never saw a copy of the policy. Vigorous enforcement of the conflict of interest policy signings would not have stopped the corruption, but it would have given pause to some.

It was hard to turn down the gifts. Your boss said it was okay, everyone on the fast track at Honda had a Rolex watch and an extra car in the garage, you never saw the memo telling you that it was wrong, and the dealers were stuffing envelopes in your pocket. No one told you not to do it. The Japanese managers know about it, said the whispers, and they don't care.

As a DSM you earned around $30,000 per year, 30 to 50 percent less than your peers at other carmakers. The top dealership salespeople commanded more than $80,000 annually. Dealership sales managers earning a paltry $70,000 whined to you about their poor pay and asked if you could talk to the owner about it. The dealer principals themselves made millions. It seemed like everyone was making the big bucks but you.

A district sales manager did not control the number of automobiles a dealer received but did determine which color and body styles of each model would be allocated each month. This power could have a huge impact on a dealer's bottom line, since a loaded green Accord coupe might bring twice the gross profit as a white Accord sedan equipped with a five-speed transmission. When the time came to distribute cars, a tainted DSM put the hotter Hondas into his buddies' showrooms.

A graft hierarchy slowly developed among Honda officials and retailers. A dirty dealer paid off his district sales manager for the right mix of cars, the zone sales manager for extra shipments of cars, and a combination of the zone sales manager, regional sales manager, and Billmyer or Cardiges for an additional Honda franchise. The peripheral players, such as the traffic assistants (the field office employees who coordinated the physical distribution of the cars) and the assistant zone sales manager, received occasional gifts.

Every year during the 1980s Honda sold more cars, the dealers made more money, and the gifts to Honda executives grew bigger and better.

Honda is a secretive company. Its executives have been the least visible of any of the Japanese importers' American officials. They are rarely allowed to speak with the press, and most media inquiries are referred to Honda's public relations department.

The corporation's penchant for privacy stemmed from its practice of closely guarding new product plans. The Honda test track in California's Mojave Desert features the same "hideaway huts" as its Japanese facilities: small structures stationed around the track for cars to duck underneath in case aircraft — that might be carrying photographers from competitors or car magazines — are spotted. Real-world testing of upcoming automobiles is done at night in highly disguised prototypes. When a secret new car is moved outdoors at the Torrance complex, spotters watch for low-flying planes or the pesky Goodyear blimp, which is moored two miles away. If suspicious aircraft are seen, the automobiles are immediately covered up. Heads rolled in 1993 when Honda's service division accidentally mailed a technician training video about the all-new 1994 Accord to dealers a month before the car's introduction, blowing the cover off the new model.

"Honda was a little more reclusive than the other Japanese companies," says *Automotive News* reporter Lindsay Chappell, "sometimes to the point of absurdity. Honda would fight and deny things until the last minute, like when introducing a new automobile."

It was not just paranoia or the fear of a competitor stealing a Honda secret: The company's marketing savvy said that if consumers knew a new Honda was in the pipeline, they might not buy a car today. Detroit automakers routinely unveil future vehicles at press conferences months or even years before their introduction, costing themselves sales in the interim because customers delay their purchases until the new machine hits the showroom.

But the biggest secret Honda would ever keep was about the corruption between its executives and the Honda dealers.

CHAPTER 5

Jack and Jim

That's Latin, isn't it?

—Jim Cardiges, upon hearing the phrase *quid pro quo*

ROD RYAN was wising up. The owner of a New Jersey Honda dealership clutched the brown manila envelope containing $25,000 in $50 and $100 bills as his flight took off for Los Angeles. Ryan was heading for the 1984 Summer Olympic Games and his first meeting with Honda sales chief Jack Billmyer. Ryan had ambitions to attain additional Honda franchises and finally, hopefully, knew what to do. His Honda zone sales manager, John Conway, was a silent partner in Ryan's organization. Conway told him what was expected. Ryan's application for a new Honda dealership had fallen on Billmyer's deaf, albeit large, ears. Conway, the son of a New York police officer, mentioned to Ryan that a little cash would cure Billmyer's hearing problem. Honda executives were especially happy when their peers were secret owners of Honda stores, since they could tutor their partners on how to play the corrupt game.

It was all beginning to make sense to Ryan. The gossip he had heard at dealer gatherings of the need to bribe Honda executives to get ahead was true. In his early days as a dealer, Ryan was solicited by a Honda official for $500 per car for extra Hondas. He refused and watched his allocations evaporate. It was common knowledge in Jersey that many Philadelphia Honda dealers were playing the game. They were getting cars that the factory was diverting from New Jersey, where most of the dealers were either too dumb or too honest to bribe Honda executives—ironic for businessmen in a state notorious for corruption. Ryan's first step of putting Conway in his pocket by giving him co-ownership in his operations had not brought forth the increased number of cars he had expected. Greasing the head guy seemed to be the next logical step. This $25,000 just might get me more automobiles in addition to another franchise, Ryan figured. Still, he was uncomfortable — he did not even tell his wife about the scheme.

Ryan had called Billmyer the week before to arrange the meeting. Neither party discussed specifics, but both knew the agenda. The morning after his arrival in Los Angeles, Ryan found himself sitting alone in a dingy, out-of-the-way coffee shop that Billmyer had designated for the rendezvous.

"I didn't feel very good about the whole situation," says Ryan. "It was the first time I would ever really meet Billmyer and I was going to hand him $25,000. It was a very peculiar situation. I didn't know the man. What if he didn't take the money?" Ryan had hidden the stuffed envelope in a section of the *Los Angeles Times* on the seat next to him.

Billmyer walked in, and the pair exchanged pleasantries. Ryan mentioned his desire for a new Honda franchise. After an awkward silence, the embarrassed dealer made his move. "I simply put the envelope on the table," recalls Ryan. "I said: This is for you, and pushed it across the table. He didn't seemed surprised. He didn't seem anything." Billmyer did not open the envelope — like an old gambler, he never counted his money while sitting at the table. As with most of the tainted transactions, it was accomplished without ceremony or discussion of the particulars, no agreement to grant the franchise, no quid pro quo. The meeting took less than ten minutes.

Thus was Ryan's initiation into the highest level of the Honda underground. His application for the new dealership was approved by Billmyer 12 days later, and Ryan was now officially a player. Members of his organization would later forward another $150,000 to Billmyer, shower Jim Cardiges with tens of thousands of dollars, and pay for a boat, a backyard deck, and landscaping for their local Honda reps. Ryan and his partners would eventually own 13 Honda and Acura dealerships and build personal net worths of between $4 and $15 million each. A few hundred thousand well-placed dollars was a good investment.

Jack Billmyer quickly climbed the Honda ladder. Like most employees who started with Honda in the 1970s, Billmyer's career advanced rapidly as Honda expanded its operations. He was promoted to Eastern regional sales manager in 1977, responsible for sales activities in the eastern half of the United States, at a salary of $2,300 per month. He moved to California to become assistant vice president and national sales manager in 1980 and just three years later would be upgraded to senior vice president.

Billmyer differed from his underlings in his expertise at being secretive about his corrupt activities. The number-one adage that he imposed on the others was: "Never take a check from a dealer." At national sales meetings, Billmyer held a separate gathering with the regional and zone sales managers, away from the Japanese officials. "If you've got a close relationship with a dealer, don't be obvious about it," Billmyer would preach. "If it is above and beyond the call of duty, you don't want other dealers to know about it. You need to be discreet." It was yet another signal to the unwashed that it was okay to take gifts from dealers, as long as no one (i.e., the Japanese officials or any non-sales-department employees) found out.

Some did not listen to Billmyer. The ultimate sin was informing a dealer of the gifts you received from another Honda dealer. Jim Olmstead manages First Texas Honda in Austin and recalled a violation of this mandate. His Honda district sales manager, Carl Jensen, had the reputation of being the rare arm-twister, aggressive with his demands of dealers, vindictive to those who did not play. Jensen invited Olmstead into his home to see his "gun room." The Honda rep proudly showed off the room, but Olmstead noticed something odd — there were no firearms on display.

"Where are your guns?" asked Olmstead.

"You don't understand," said Jensen. "This is not a gun, G-U-N, room. This is my Gunn room, G-U-N-N, as in Gunn Honda." Jensen was referring to a San Antonio dealer. "Gunn Honda furnished it," said Jensen. "I'm giving you the opportunity to build a First Texas Honda room." Olmstead declined the offer.

Billmyer constantly looked over his shoulder. He was paranoid about Honda's head of security, Tony Piazza, a former Federal Drug Enforcement Agent, seeing the dealer-provided BMWs parked in his driveway. Billmyer installed a device on his telephone to alert him if the line was bugged. He once spotted someone snapping pictures of his house, likely the busybody Piazza, who tried unsuccessfully to persuade the Japanese officials to investigate the goings-on among sales division managers.

One item Billmyer was not discreet about was his Rolex watch. If the corrupt boys' club had a coat of arms it would be a Honda dealer new car sticker, noting a $2,000 markup over list price, surrounded by a wreath of Rolex watches. The high-dollar timepiece was the stamp on the wrist that gained admittance to the club. "What dealer name is engraved on your watch?" the execs kidded each other. The Rolex served as a wink to fellow club members and a reminder to others that they were the ones — those in the sales division — running the "real" show at Honda. A district sales manager aspiring to climb the ladder would buy or bribe for a "Rolex Starter," the least-expensive, $2,000 stainless steel model, hoping to catch the eye of his superiors and let them know he was a player. The unwashed thought it odd that someone would spend several months' salary for a watch, unaware that the Honda Dealer Rolex Real-Easy Finance Plan featured No Payments for Life.

Billmyer collected Rolexes like stamps. He received his first one, a $12,000 diamond-bezel President model, from a New Jersey dealer in 1979, the first of three or four he would receive annually. Billmyer wore a Rolex constantly, once being spotted in grubby clothes cleaning his house with the President strapped to his wrist. He toted a half-dozen Rolexes and other jewelry to annual dealer meetings in an 8″ by 12″ Louis Vuitton box, complete with handle. He changed suits and watches for each meeting during the two-day get-together, being sure to sport the right Rolex around the corresponding dealer.

Dealers called Jack Billmyer "The Pope." They would name his protégé, Stanley James Cardiges, "Jim Car-Jesus," the God of the Hondas.

Image was everything to Cardiges, a laid-back, handsome man of Greek descent, with an easy smile and silky voice. "He was very status- and image-conscious," says a friend. "For him, what he drove and what he wore were very important. You knew that just from listening to his conversations about what (he did) with his money." Cardiges was always impeccably groomed: every strand of sandy-brown hair in place, the corporate-blue suit, his trademark collar pin, and the unscuffed Johnston & Murphy shoes. He had a commanding yet down-to-earth charisma that mesmerized employees and dealers alike.

Raised in Baltimore, Cardiges worked part-time as a radio disk jockey during college at Towson State University, a job that helped him develop his voice to disguise a barely noticeable lisp. After graduating with a psychology degree, he taught junior high school for one year and then joined IBM as a sales rep. The regimented white-shirt world of IBM fit the fastidious Cardiges well. He sold computers in the Baltimore area for two years before being hired by Ford Motor Company in 1971. While calling on Maryland Ford dealers, the 27-year-old Cardiges got his first taste of payola, albeit minor gifts like a bottle of wine or some firewood. He accepted them eagerly.

"I didn't have the intestinal fortitude to stand up and say what was happening was wrong," said Cardiges later. "My sense of right and wrong went right out the window during my first year in the automobile business."

Like many carmaker executives, Cardiges perceived that being an automobile dealer was an easy road to riches. In 1975 Cardiges resigned from Ford to become 25 percent owner of Glenmont Chrysler-Plymouth in Wheaton, Maryland, in partnership with his father's brother, Peter Cardiges. His motivation to work for his uncle was not merely his desire to make a pile of money, though. Cardiges wanted to be near his uncle's young wife, Effie, a delicate, beautiful, dark-haired woman four years older than Jim. Effie had lived on an island in Greece before Peter brought her over to America to become his bride.

Peddling Plymouth Valiants and Chrysler New Yorkers during the late 1970s was difficult. "We did not have what you would call a quality product," remembers Cardiges. "You'd try to show a car to a customer and the damn thing wouldn't start." Chrysler also lacked a small automobile to offer to consumers screaming for high-gas-mileage vehicles. The company introduced the industry's first-ever consumer rebates in 1977 to help dealers move vehicles, but it was spinning toward bankruptcy and a government bailout. More than 1,600 Chrysler dealers, nearly 27 percent of its dealer network, closed their doors during the 1970s. Jim and Peter Cardiges bailed out of their bleeding dealership in 1977, each losing their investment.

Peter Cardiges also lost his wife to Jim Cardiges, shortly after he caught Jim and Effie in the act of . . . well, doing what car dealers are accused of doing to customers. Effie and Peter divorced. Jim and his wife divorced.

Jim Cardiges then married his Aunt Effie.

He adopted his four cousins to be his children. To add to the confusion, the couple now had two sons named George among their combined six offspring. They would later have one son of their own. The meticulous pair shared an aspiration for the finer things in life. Effie's favorite television show was "Lifestyles of the Rich and Famous." Wags called the perfectly dressed and coifed pair "Ken and Barbie."

In September 1977 Cardiges answered an ad for a district sales manager position with American Honda, covering the Baltimore and Washington, D.C., territory. He was the perfect candidate for Honda, possessing the odd combination of a college degree and retail automobile experience. Cardiges was hired by Billmyer, Honda's Eastern regional sales manager at the time, at a starting salary of $18,000 per year. Cardiges joined the company flat broke and money hungry, a feeling intensified by the need to support a bigger family and a high-maintenance wife. Fortunately for him, his timing was good—Honda was on fire with the recent introduction of the Accord.

That December, Cardiges was disappointed to open his first Christmas bonus check from Honda, only $75. He mentioned that fact to the owner of a Baltimore Honda dealership, who promptly took Cardiges on a free shopping expedition at a men's clothing store. Though only grabbing $200 worth of underwear and ties, despite the dealer egging him on, Cardiges read between the lines: A lot of goodies were available to him, and all he had to do was ask.

Cardiges soon got on the gift program in a serious way. Within a year he had his first dealer-supplied Rolex watch. In 1978 Maryland dealer William Schuiling, grateful for Cardiges's help in obtaining a Honda franchise, began paying some of Cardiges's personal bills. The dealer later put Cardiges on his company's books as a "consultant," eventually paying Cardiges $400,000 over the years.

In 1979 Cardiges received his first warning from Billmyer about the need for discretion. A New Jersey dealer principal handed Cardiges two checks, drawn on a small Jersey bank, for $5,000 apiece, Christmas "bonuses" for Cardiges and Billmyer. Cardiges personally delivered the present to Billmyer at Honda's New Jersey zone office. Billmyer was miffed that Cardiges had created a possible paper trail by not asking for cash and admonished Cardiges to be more careful, though noting that, "at least they'll never be able to find this bank." *They* of course meant the outsiders — the Japanese executives, Honda's personnel department, or any clean Jersey Honda dealers.

Most times when Billmyer was promoted, Cardiges took his place. When Cardiges became California zone sales manager in 1981, the pair often commuted to work together. The ruddy redneck and the suave urbanite made an odd couple, linked by their devotion to their employer and their need for greed.

The 1980s dawned with more good fortune for both American Honda and its sinister executives. The U.S. government was under pressure from Detroit automakers and the United Auto Workers (UAW) union to restrict the number of Japanese automobiles imported to America. Unable to understand the demands of a new quality-conscience consumer or to build competitive small cars to combat the invasion from the East, the American entities turned their attention to competing through legislation. The four Detroit companies were in financial trouble — they had lost a total of $4 billion in 1980, and both Chrysler and Ford were teetering on the verge of bankruptcy. Chrysler subsequently received $1.5 billion in loan guarantees from the U.S. government, saving it from extinction.

Detroit automakers' small cars still lagged far behind the competitors from Japan. The Ford Escort, introduced in 1981, was a decent effort but still nowhere near the quality or performance of the Japanese autos. General Motors was hopelessly lost, introducing automobiles even funnier than its small cars of the 1970s. GM poured lemonade on a fruitcake when it dropped an impotent and unreliable diesel engine into the 1981 Chevrolet Chevette. GM's full-sized cars were getting weird, too — the company trotted out the Cadillac V-8-6-4 "variable displacement" motor, a powerplant designed to improve fuel economy by having two or four cylinders shut down at different speeds. What typically happened was all eight cylinders giving up the ghost. It did save on gasoline, though, since Cadillacs got good mileage while being towed.

Worst of all were General Motors' so-called J-cars — named for their chassis designation, not the fact that beating Japanese automakers was their objective. The J-cars were GM's first serious attempt at building small, front-wheel-drive automobiles. Like with nearly every small or mid-sized car introduced during the 1980s by Detroit, the announced target of the J-cars was the Honda Accord. It was quickly apparent to industry analysts, however, that the autos were little more than crude copies of the Japanese competitors. The J-cars were nearly identical in size to an Accord, but the similarity ended there. They weighed 400 pounds more than an Accord. Their styling was boxy and boring. Their balky engines delivered worse performance and worse gas mileage than an Accord. They lacked features that Honda owners were accustomed to: an independent rear suspension, overhead camshaft engine, and even a standard tachometer. They were priced almost $2,000 more than a comparably equipped Accord. Honda dealers could charge $4,000 over sticker price for an Accord and still be offering a better value than a General Motors J-car.

Detroit had to blame someone for their problems. They chose the Japanese automakers.

The carmakers screamed about how Japan's lower wages were the reason the Japanese grabbed 21 percent of the American car market in 1980. They are using their cost advantage to exploit our market, Detroit whined, they are not playing fair. The Michigan giants did not mention how they had succumbed to the UAW's blackmail over the years and paid their factory workers salaries and benefits 50 percent higher than those in other industries — and gotten nothing in return in terms of increased productivity or quality. Nor did the domestics talk about their labyrinth of white-collar workers and million-dollar bonus programs for their top executives. No, their declining market share was all Japan's fault.

Beneath the rhetoric was a fact that Detroit was slowly beginning to realize but would not dare admit publicly: that the Japanese automakers built a superior automobile.

Detroit had ignored the threat from Japan for over a decade and now promised Congress they could get their act together in only three years if they could get relief from the "unfair" Japanese. Auto industry supporters bashed Japan to sway the public into persuading Congress to enact a restriction on the number of Japanese automobiles imported. Michigan Representative John Dingall, head of the House Commerce Committee and the leading quota-backer, called the Japanese "little yellow people" and blamed them for Detroit's dropping market share. The public in Michigan responded. Japanese automobiles parked in the wrong parts of town—like near UAW hangouts—were subjected to smashed windshields and other acts of vandalism.

In early 1981 Japan's Ministry of International Trade and Industry, Soichiro Honda's old foe, agreed with U.S. trade representatives to enact the Voluntary Restraint Agreement (VRA), in which Japan would "voluntarily" limit the number of automobiles exported to America to 1.68 million units annually, an 8 percent reduction from 1980 figures. The VRA allocated the number of cars exported among each manufacturer based on 1980 U.S. sales. Toyota and Datsun (soon to be renamed Nissan in the United States) were outselling Honda, so their share of the pie was larger: Toyota was granted a limit of 550,000 cars, Datsun 470,000, and Honda 350,000.

The VRA slowly rose to 2.3 million units by 1985, but the damage to the consumer was irreversible: this artificial shortage of Japanese automobiles sent prices soaring. The shortsighted Detroit carmakers increased prices on their vehicles accordingly. Honda dealers increased their additional markup to the consumer, and their profits began to skyrocket in 1981. With the number of cars limited, the psychological effect on the consumer was predictable: people want what they think they cannot have. The showroom frenzy intensified. Retailers of other Japanese cars began mimicking Honda dealers and adding "addendum" window stickers to their vehicles to boost prices. American consumers paid $5 billion annually in higher automobile prices during the 1980s because of the effects of the Voluntary Restraint Agreement.

The enactment of the VRA was a sonic boon for the crooked Honda officials. Dealer endowments to the executives shot up exponentially. A bottle of wine became a case. A free round of golf included a new set of clubs. A $100 bill became $1,000. The loan of a car to an executive's wife now came with the pink slip (ownership title). The under-the-table fee for a franchise soared. Representative Dingall should have been made an honorary member of the Honda boys' club.

Other Japanese automakers went ballistic over the enactment of the VRA, but not Honda. It would not be as stifled as its competitors because Honda was already busy with a bold step: the building of an American factory to produce automobiles. It had broken ground in November 1980, just months before the VRA commenced. Honda could not have foreseen the trade restrictions, but its timing was once again fortuitous. The move to U.S. production had been planned since 1974, all part of Soichiro Honda's global vision of building products in the markets where they are sold. America was Honda's most important market, since the automaker was too much of a latecomer in Japan to ever pose a threat to giants Toyota and Nissan in their homeland.

In 1979, with an eye toward building automobiles, Honda had set up a motorcycle factory in rural Marysville, Ohio, 30 miles northwest of Columbus. The plant's location was far enough south from UAW strongholds, Honda not wanting to hire any ex-UAW members, but still in close proximity to key parts suppliers. Honda's announcement of its plans to build an automobile factory next door to the motorcycle facility was met with derision by Detroit. Said one domestic carmaker executive, "After Honda announced its first factory in the United States, I suggested that (we) . . . should be looking at the impending invasion, because if Honda is coming, then others are going to come. The response I was met with was, 'Oh, don't worry about those little yellow Japs. They will never make a go of it in the United States. They are going to have to contend with high costs and they are going to have to contend with the UAW, and it's simply not going to work.'"

Construction of Honda's $250 million Marysville automobile plant, modeled after Honda's production facilities in Japan, was finished in 1982. There is no mysterious Oriental magic inside the facility, but it hums with common sense. Although Honda imported its machinery and production techniques from Japan, its philosophy said that assembly-line workers were the key to success in producing good cars. The Marysville plant is an egalitarian orgasm with no division between workers and management. The employees are not treated as mindless zombies who need to be controlled as they perform their tasks by rote but rather as thinking human beings able to offer ideas and help the company improve. Any worker can stop the assembly line if a problem is spotted, and all are encouraged to make recommendations to improve product quality. The plant is a tribute to teamwork, with none of the adversarial relationship between management and labor found in other U.S. automobile factories.

The UAW was delighted that Honda was coming to America. The union had watched its membership erode as Detroit closed factories and laid off workers. The number of UAW members declined from 1.5 million in 1974 to less than a million in 1982. The union figured that Honda's new factory would mean thousands of new members. It was wrong — Honda's workers kept the union at bay. They were treated well by Honda management and saw no reason to organize. While the UAW demanded that Detroit guarantee workers have a job for life, Honda told its people that building a quality automobile was the best job security. The UAW's job-classification system, dating back to the 1920s, would have strangled Honda. The UAW decreed that auto plants have more than 100 separate job descriptions, while Honda had only two: assembly and maintenance. The lack of this UAW "it's not my job" environment was paramount to Honda's philosophy of fast and flexible production. Honda executives would never say publicly what the company truly believed — that the United Auto Workers union would have ruined Honda.

In November 1982, 18 months after the enactment of the Voluntary Restraint Agreement, the first Honda Accord — a burgundy sedan — rolled off the Marysville assembly line. (Ironically, that car is now on display at the Henry Ford Museum in Detroit.) Automobile magazines quickly lined up comparison tests between American- and Japanese-built Accords and could find no appreciable differences in quality between the two.

Soon after, Detroit car companies began scrambling to hook up with Japanese automakers. They still supported restrictions on Japanese imports but began to realize they needed help from the Japanese automakers if they wanted to build a competitive small car and do it profitably. Honda was becoming an American car company as fast as the domestic automakers were becoming Japanese. Ford bought 25 percent of Mazda, and together they began planning a factory in Michigan. General Motors began negotiating with Toyota to launch a joint-production venture in California. Chrysler chairman Lee Iacocca continued to rage against the "unfair" Japanese, even though his company had been saved from bankruptcy in part due to its partnership with Japanese conglomerate Mitsubishi, which supplied Chrysler cars and engines. Chrysler and Mitsubishi started formulating plans for a joint factory in Illinois. Toyota, Nissan, Subaru, and Isuzu also announced plans to follow Honda's lead and build automobiles in the United States.

In 1987 Honda surpassed American Motors (soon to be purchased by Chrysler Corporation) as America's fourth-largest car builder and had its eyes fixed on number-three Chrysler. Marysville enjoyed the lowest absenteeism rate — 2 percent — of any U.S. auto factory. The plant stunned the car manufacturing world by completing a model change for a totally new 1986 Accord with no assembly-line shutdown; Detroit factories typically close for two to four weeks for a model changeover. Honda became the first Japanese auto producer to open an engine plant, building a facility in Anna, Ohio, in 1985. It established a research and development center in Marysville and was finalizing plans for two more North American production facilities. Honda was streaking toward its goals of building 500,000 cars annually in North America by 1990 and becoming a totally self-sufficient American car company. Marysville was the most productive and efficient automobile factory in America, turning out 1,330 Accords and Civics per day with a workforce of 3,500 employees. Just 170 miles to the northwest, in Hamtramck, Michigan, 960 Cadillac Eldorados, Buick Rivieras, and Oldsmobile Toronados were produced daily at General Motors' newest factory by 5,800 UAW members — on days when the plant did not have to shut down because of high absenteeism. Honda gladly opened its doors for Detroit executives to tour its Ohio plant, knowing the domestics could never duplicate it.

Honda had shown the competition the way once again by establishing American factories — and provided its crooked sales executives with 500,000 more opportunities a year to make some extra cash.

Honda's sales, dealers' profits, and the corruption took off during the early VRA era. Managers from all levels of Honda's sales hierarchy received increasingly larger gifts from Honda dealers. From a time-line standpoint, this was still your basic automaker bribery case. Previous auto industry scandals had followed the same pattern: a year or two of spreading payola, followed by warning signals or evidence prompting the company to take action and put a stop to the nonsense. But Honda was different.

In 1981 a Virginia Honda dealer wrote American Honda vice president Yoshihide Munekuni to complain about the goings-on:

> I have never been a Foreign car dealer before — so I know things are different. It's that I keep hearing that Honda Franchises are awarded to people (who) have *Honda employees* as partners. . . . Also my car allocation is not being done fairly. I was promised lots of cars (and) its not happening. . . . please keep my name out of this.

Munekuni did not respond.

James David Power is the founder of J. D. Power and Associates, the esteemed automobile business research company. His firm's surveys of customers about the cars they buy are the score sheets for automakers to measure product quality and customer service. Around 1980, Power began hearing rumors that Honda executives were granting favorable allocations of cars and awarding franchises to dealers in exchange for under-the-table payments. After his speaking engagements to dealer groups, Honda retailers would sidle up to Power and complain about the corrupt practice. Some of the dealers had been shaken down themselves, some had heard fellow dealers bragging about paying off Honda officials, and some were just repeating the rampant rumors. The dealers implored Power to speak to someone at Honda about the problems.

Over a two-year period Power had several conversations with Honda officials about the situation and felt no progress was being made to curb the corruption. In March 1983 Power outlined his concerns in a letter to Munekuni, head of the Honda automobile division:

> As you probably know, I have had conversations with both Mr. Fujita and Mr. Schmillen concerning a far ranging problem existing in the distribution of Honda automobiles throughout the United States.
>
> The matter of financial irregularities and personal favors in the allocation of Honda automobiles first came to my attention three or four years ago. And I dismissed them as minor indiscretions that occur in all automotive distribution companies. However, in the past few months I have heard from a variety of sources that the Honda system is rampant with inequitable distribution policies, inviting dealers to "pay" extra for more favorable allocations.
>
> It is with the best wishes for Honda's continued success and my personal concern that these unethical and illegal practices be stopped that I am approaching you with this information. I would hate to see the wonderful Honda image tarnished by a broad scale scandal attributable to a flaw in management control.

Power met with Munekuni and executive vice president Cliff Schmillen, Billmyer's predecessor as Honda's national sales manager. Power detailed the dealers' allegations. The retailers had requested anonymity, so Power did not name names. "Munekuni was obviously disturbed by what he heard," recalls Power. "He was embarrassed by the situation." Schmillen, himself a hidden partner in two Honda dealerships, told Power that there had been indiscretions in the past but that the people involved had been terminated. He was exaggerating, of course. Honda fired one district sales manager in 1978 for pocketing $20,000 from a San Diego dealer, but only because he was so overt in demanding cash that a dealership employee complained to Honda's human resources department.

Munekuni turned the Power matter over to Roland "Bud" Smoot, a partner in Honda's lead law firm, Lyon & Lyon, an old-line Los Angeles firm specializing in patent law. Smoot, a genial sort in his mid-60s, was the principal attorney assigned to handle disputes between Honda and the dealers and a member of the American Honda board of directors. Smoot knew the program. He was aware of Schmillen's co-ownership of a California Honda dealership, a violation of Honda's conflict of interest policy. In 1979 Schmillen had asked a Lyon & Lyon lawyer if he could accept the dealer's offer. Yes, just do not tell anyone about it was the attorney's response. Schmillen does not remember the lawyer's name but thinks it might have been Smoot.

Smoot asked Power to gather evidence from the dealers, confident that none would come forward. Power contacted 50 complaining dealers and requested documentation about their accusations. All refused, fearing retaliation from Honda.

"(The dealers) felt that everyone in the organization was involved in the kickback scheme," said Power. "Therefore they were liable to lose their franchise and their allocation of vehicles if they came forward to complain." Northeast retailers were also leery of implicating the Honda dealers reputed to have organized-crime connections.

Honda took no action. No investigation, no meeting with the sales executives, no memos reminding employees of the conflict of interest policy, no notifying the human resources department of the alleged problems. The matter was dropped — it was all only a rumor, the officials said later. Honda's most significant opportunity of the 1980s to take action and put a stop to the payoffs was lost.

Soon afterwards, Munekuni timidly confronted Billmyer about the dealer allegations Power had brought forward. Billmyer cut him off.

"You can go try to hire people with what I have to pay them," said Billmyer. "If you don't like the way I am running this company, you can get yourself another boy!"

Munekuni backed off.

In June 1984, California dealer Bob Estes obtained tentative approval for a new Honda franchise in Beverly Hills, where he was a successful

Volkswagen dealer. The paperwork was complete, Honda's zone sales manager had approved Estes's showroom, and everything seemed to be proceeding smoothly. Estes was feeling good until he received a phone call from a North Carolina dealer who was tight with Billmyer. The retailer wanted to initiate outsider Estes into the reality of being a Honda dealer, possibly at Billmyer's request.

After congratulating Estes on his appointment as a Honda retailer, the dealer said he needed to explain one item. "Well, this is kind of a touchy subject," he said. "There is something that is going to be important if you're going to be a Honda dealer. There is a little fund that all the dealers contribute to that goes to some of the officials . . . (for) getting cars directed to their dealerships." He indicated that $150 for every car allocated was the current kickback rate.

Estes was steamed: "I had never paid for a dealership under such circumstances in my life, and I was absolutely not interested in any such arrangement." Estes told the dealer to relay a message to the Honda execs: "kiss off."

Shortly thereafter, Estes called Honda headquarters in Tokyo and asked to speak to Soichiro Honda. He was informed that Mr. Honda had retired and was referred to president Kiyoshi Kawashima. When Estes told him of the proposed graft, Kawashima replied that he knew nothing about any corruption between American Honda executives and dealers. The president of Honda took no action.

Two months later the rights to Beverly Hills were quietly taken from Estes and given to Peter Epsteen — a dealer who had paid for the installation of a swimming pool at Billmyer's home and also "loaned" the sales boss a Rolls Royce automobile. The spurned Estes had committed to Honda a modern dealership facility with an enormous amount of square footage, rare in pricey Beverly Hills. Epsteen's hodgepodge Honda operation was a fraction of the size of Estes's and included a dank, off-site, underground service department, described by one Honda service division manager as "the worst I've ever seen, and I've been to hundreds of Honda dealers." Honda would have been better represented in Beverly Hills by Estes, but Epsteen was chosen because he played the game.

"I did the wrong thing," Estes now says. "I should have taken the deal and then operated it for a couple of months and then squealed on them."

Epsteen thanked Billmyer for Beverly Hills by forwarding him $200,000.

Non-Honda dealers who complained that a franchise was awarded in exchange for financial consideration would receive a response from Billmyer. A dealer principal named J. H. Thomas was passed over for a

Honda dealership in Decatur, Alabama, in 1984, which was bequeathed to a buddy of Billmyer's. Thomas wrote to American Honda president Tetsuo Chino, accusing Honda officials of receiving money in exchange for awarding the Decatur rights. The allegations were true, but Chino did not want to hear about it. He handed the letter to Billmyer.

Establishing a dealership in Decatur had been particularly arduous for Billmyer. His first overture was made to California Honda dealer Lathrop Hoffman. The car business was in Hoffman's blood. His father was the former president of the star-crossed Studebaker Automobile Corporation of South Bend, Indiana, which ceased operations in 1963. The only payola problems the inept Studebaker company might have had were its dealers bribing executives to *not* give them extra cars or franchises, so Hoffman grew up in a business world devoid of graft.

One of Hoffman's employees was an Alabama native, and Hoffman agreed to bankroll him in applying for the Decatur Honda point. The pair flew to Atlanta to meet with then–Eastern regional sales manager Billmyer. The blunt Billmyer reviewed their application and asked, "Is there room for anybody else in this deal?" Translation: can you cut me in? Hoffman was shocked — he did not do business that way.

"No, we can handle the store fine," replied Hoffman.

"Not even ten per cent?"

"No. I don't do that type of thing."

Billmyer stood up and said good-bye, leaving their paperwork lying on the table. Application for Decatur denied.

It took Billmyer another year to find a player for Decatur, prompting spurned dealer J. H. Thomas to write to president Chino. Billmyer wrote a standard response to Thomas's letter:

> Your letter of July 8, 1984, to Mr. Chino has been referred to me since I am responsible for Honda field operations.
>
> It has been and continues to be our policy to appoint dealers who in *our* opinion are the best qualified prospects for a particular open point. That is precisely what we did in Decatur, Alabama. We do not care to comment on the erroneous information and innuendo contained in your correspondence. There is one area that I would like to clear up. There is no fee involved in securing a Honda franchise!
>
> We cannot comply with your request to reverse our decision on the candidate chosen for Decatur, Alabama.

When any current Honda dealer threatened to expose the schemes, he would find his dealership flooded with Hondas or, if particularly menacing, be offered a new dealership — standard practices for shutting up a wayward Honda dealer.

If anyone should have understood the legal ramifications of American Honda executives trading cars and franchises for cash, Lyon & Lyon should have. The attorneys had the responsibility of telling Honda: The corruption must stop. If the information becomes public, it could lead to federal charges for the people involved and bad publicity for the company. Dealers who did not participate could sue you, the lawyers should have implored Honda. Instead, Lyon & Lyon's own fear of the possible liability may have motivated the firm to squelch the information. It may have been simply following the orders of Honda's Japanese executives, who loathed the American legal system. Whatever the reason, Lyon & Lyon did not act in the best interests of its client. Instead, the law firm became an active co-conspirator in a cover-up.

Matters of alleged corruption by Honda executives were referred to Honda's human resources department — unless the managers in question were employed by the sales division. In those cases, the information was handed over to Billmyer, Cardiges, or Lyon & Lyon. By involving the law firm, Honda assured that the information could not be used in a court of law, since it would be subject to client-attorney privilege, the legal right mandating confidentiality of conversations and information shared between client and attorney. This twisted unwritten corporate policy guaranteed that if a Honda dealer ever sued the corporation because a neighboring dealer received preferential treatment for paying off Honda execs, the plaintiffs could not access information about similar activities known to the corporation. Including Smoot in the conversation with Power allowed Honda officials to store the allegations in Lyon & Lyon's client-attorney privilege "vault." What was right or wrong was not as important to Honda as preventing litigation.

Lyon & Lyon developed other sinister tactics when it came to serving Honda. "There was a term that (Smoot) and subsequently others eventually did adopt and used on many occasions with me," says Cardiges. "Smoot told me that if I got on the stand and said something that was not exactly the truth, that a bolt of lightning wasn't going to come out of the sky and strike me dead." In legal terms, such activities are called suborning perjury, coaching someone to lie. Lawyers can be disbarred for engaging in the practice, but Lyon & Lyon had yet to be caught.

At annual meetings of the Honda sales division, Lyon & Lyon attorneys gave presentations about their lightning bolt concept. It made no sense to tell the entire sales staff, most of whom would never appear on a witness stand, about the firm's unethical ways. The attorneys also coached the group to never document anything of substance in a contact report — the summary recapping a meeting with a Honda dealer. "Never write something you don't want to hear read back to you in a court of law," they admonished. You could observe salespeople tying up customers and pouring motor oil down their throats until they agreed to buy a car, but all you were allowed to note was "reviewed customer satisfaction survey with dealer principal." Telling an owner that his store was doing a good or bad job could have an impact on future litigation, said the paranoid Lyon & Lyon. Based on this information, field people wondered why contact reports were necessary, and some began submitting "Ed Temple" reports — photocopies of previous generic contact reports with the date and dealership's name changed — a technique pioneered by The Master.

Lyon & Lyon lawyers informed the managers that, if they ever won the lottery or inherited a large amount of money, they should notify the law firm so they would be prepared if anyone became suspicious about the source of the funds. Only the government has the power to investigate bank accounts, and it had never looked into anyone at Honda, but the attorneys were preparing the officials for that possibility.

Consider the three main points Lyon & Lyon stressed to the Honda executives:

- It is permissible to not tell the truth.
- Do not document anything.
- It is suspicious to have large sums of money moving through your bank account.

Was there a hidden message here? The law firm was talking about how to conduct yourself in the Honda world, but it sounded more like Billmyer telling you how to cover your graft.

Lyon & Lyon lawyers never said to the assembled sales executives: If you are involved in receiving gifts from Honda dealers, you need to stop now or face severe consequences. Chrysler Corporation confronted its top officials in such a manner in 1959 and halted the underground relationships between executives and suppliers. Instead, Lyon & Lyon attorneys gave a purposely vague speech about not compromising one's integrity — a clever tap dance around the forbidden subject.

Lyon & Lyon attorney J. Donald McCarthy once stood before the Honda sales staff and inadvertently revealed his knowledge of the payola during the portion of his presentation on bank accounts. A poor ad-libber,

McCarthy tried to spice up his speech and said out loud — in front of a crowd that included the Japanese executives — what everybody knew.

"After a new dealership goes in," McCarthy joked, "maybe we should check the zone manager's bank account." Nobody laughed. McCarthy had just committed the worst sin of all: talking about the corruption in public.

Lyon & Lyon attorneys were up to their briefs in covering up the corruption by their client's officials. Honda employees nicknamed the law firm "Lying & Lying."

Like the corrupt executives, Honda retailers struck the VRA jackpot. Most became instant multimillionaires. Each year during the mid-to-late 1980s, the average Honda dealership sold 650 new automobiles and profited over $640,000. Add to that a token salary of about $100,000 taken by the dealer principal, plus his personal expenses that were hidden on the financial statement, and each owner was pocketing around $800,000 a year. Not bad for a family-owned business employing 30 people in a medium-size market. Honda dealers in large metropolitan areas who were not making a million dollars a year were simply not trying. The top Honda stores on the import-car-crazy East and West Coasts were moving over 4,000 cars a year and profiting up to $5 million annually. The only automotive franchisees earning more money than Honda dealers were those selling Mercedes-Benz.

Domestic franchises were lucky to profit one-third of a Honda dealership's total, with far more effort and aggravation for the owners. Toyota and Nissan dealerships were doing well but not generating the money of a Honda store. Both lacked a strong competitor for the Accord, a car for the booming "large small-family car" segment of the market that Honda dominated during the 1980s.

Honda dealership profits lived and died on new automobiles sales — over half of a dealer's earnings were generated by the new car department. During the mid-1980s, the increased availability of new Hondas, thanks to the Marysville factory, caused Honda prices to drop to "only" MSRP. The average Honda went over the curb with a fat $1,700 gross profit for the dealer, with Accord sedans and Preludes averaging more than $2,000 per unit. It was not uncommon for some dealers to squeeze $2,500 per car out of hungry Honda shoppers, with an occasional "home run" of up to $5,000 on a particular vehicle. Any gross profits over $700 per car flowed straight to the bottom line. Dealers' spending on advertising was minimal, since word of mouth among customers was selling Hondas. Dealers' floorplan costs — the interest paid on loans to purchase cars from the factory — were also low, because Hondas rarely sat on the lot for long. Non-Honda dealers grossed only about $950 profit per automobile, on units that required far more spending on advertising and floorplan expenses than did Honda cars.

It was not only profits that the dealers danced about — a Honda dealership attracted the cream of the consumer crop. Most possessed the income and credit history to qualify for a car loan. Honda dealership finance managers did not have to fight lending institutions to get the rare marginal consumer's loan approved. If problems arose, the dealer could simply sell the car to the next panting customer. According to lending institutions, the Honda "paper" was the best in the business, a group of customers who repaid loans even better than those buying high-dollar luxury cars. The repo man rarely hooked a Honda.

Honda cars seldom broke down. When they did, Honda did anything to keep the customer happy, even footing the bill for repairs not covered under warranty, much to the amazement of dealers accustomed to the domestic factories not backing up their automobiles. Honda dealers did not need to employ an army of mechanics, because there was little warranty work needed on the reliable cars and relatively few units on the streets.

The headaches of being a Honda dealer were inconsiderable — never having enough cars topping the list. Customers whining about not being able to test-drive a Honda or having to pay dealer markup were other annoyances. Hey, if you don't buy it, someone else will, was the dealers' response. Next. This classic dealer short-term mentality led to Honda having one of the lowest dealer loyalty rankings among consumers, despite being tops in overall owner retention. A license plate frame popular with Honda owners in Los Angeles read, "Great Car . . . Terrible Dealer." The outstanding Honda operators, those with true consumer focus, became hyper-rich as they developed hundreds of lifelong customers.

It was Honda heaven. The franchise was profitable and easy to operate. Many dealer principals spent more time at their domestic dealerships or on the golf course than they did at their Honda cash cows. After years of fighting the Detroit factories and struggling through the cyclical nature of the business, the dealers felt they deserved to finally make some serious cash. "I now have more money than I could ever spend," declared one dealer in 1987. His multifranchise operations anchored by two Honda dealerships once profited over $1 million in a single month. Both dirty and clean Honda dealers became rich. Dozens of dealers built individual net worths of over $50 million.

The freewheeling Honda retailers spent their money wildly — private jets, yachts, race cars, second and third homes, second and third wives. Several became co-owners of professional sports franchises. Some chose a lifestyle of hookers, cocaine, and trips to Las Vegas, the favorite playground for the American car dealer. Indeed, a pair of Honda dealers once tried to purchase the Tropicana Hotel and Casino in Vegas. Every morning, a Los Angeles dealer flew 100 miles to work in his $2 million Aerocommander from his castle at Big Bear Lake. Another purchased the Aspen, Colorado, airport and, in true Honda dealer fashion, immediately jacked up the price of the landing fees. One dealer principal purchased an $8 million ship that was featured on the cover of *Yachting* magazine. His six-member crew sailed the ship to Monte Carlo each year, where the dealer hosted top Honda officials from Japan during the Monaco Formula One Grand Prix race.

The wild spending by dealers was not always for selfish means. Most automobile dealers have a philanthropic side that would surprise the public. One of Honda's most successful dealers donated $8 million to build a cancer wing for a Los Angeles hospital.

Honda dealers had seen their other franchises go through hot periods, but they had never seen anything like Honda, which kept going and going and going.

CHAPTER 6

Good Ol' Boys

Power tends to corrupt and absolute power corrupts absolutely.

—Lord Acton, 1887

Power corrupts. Absolute power is kind of neat.

—John Lehman (Secretary of the US Navy 1981–1987)

THE TRUCK driver was lost. His flatbed car hauler strained under the weight of a brand-new Mercedes-Benz 500SL convertible. He negotiated the "mixmaster" in downtown Dallas, where Interstates 30, 35, and 45 collide, and headed northwest on I-35, bound for Jim McNatt Honda in suburban Lewisville. Passing the Dallas Cowboys football stadium, he thought it strange that his directions did not mention that landmark. A few miles later, he should have spotted the dealership. He did not notice that the highway sign now read Texas State 114, and not I-35, the route to his destination.

The $89,000 German luxury car was a gift to Jim Cardiges from McNatt, on its way from a dealer in Georgia to Texas. McNatt was going to drive it to California and deliver it personally. The dealer had recently opened a Honda store in De Soto, Texas, and this was his penance to the Car-Jesus for granting him the franchise. De Soto was not a prime market, which may explain why McNatt only leased the Mercedes-Benz for Cardiges for one year, rather than stepping up to the pump and giving it to him, like a dedicated dirty dealer would have. The lease cost McNatt $1,822 per month, a pittance to the wealthy Honda retailer.

The truck driver was relieved to see a giant red HONDA sign on a beige building ahead on the right, forgetting that his directions said Jim McNatt Honda was on the left side of the freeway. He exited and headed toward the sign. The building did not resemble any car dealer he had ever seen. He parked his rig and walked into the Texas zone office of American Honda Motor Company.

"I have a delivery for Jim," said the driver.

"Jim who?" asked the receptionist.

"Jim Cardiges. It's a Mercedes." Not knowing Cardiges, she thumbed through her employee directory and found him listed under "auto field sales." She called back to the sales division. A sales exec came out to the lobby and, trying to suppress his laughter, gave the driver directions to Jim McNatt Honda, five miles to the north. Thank God no one from parts or service saw this, he thought, they might have blown the whistle.

He should not have been concerned. The ignored warnings about the corruption during the early 1980s proved that if Honda brass had learned about the Mercedes-Benz, they would have ignored it—unless McNatt had driven it through the plate-glass doors of American Honda's national headquarters, hung a left, and parked it in the employee cafeteria. At which point they would have dismissed the incident as only a rumor.

It was all in the cars. Like clockwork, Honda completely redesigned each automobile every four years, while plodding Detroit stretched a model run out for ten years or more, making only occasional cosmetic changes. Buick produced the same Century sedan from 1982 through 1997—a cost-saving strategy benefiting GM's shareholders but not in tune with consumers' changing needs. The average customer traded cars every four years, so Honda was ready to sell its loyal owners a completely new automobile at the right time. It was an expensive strategy, the cost of developing a new vehicle running upwards of $200 million. Honda was one of the few car companies quick enough on its feet to pull off a four-year product cycle, and it paid off by developing customer retention.

Honda anticipated the needs of the baby boom generation throughout the 1980s. Each new Accord, Civic, and Prelude was bigger, faster, quieter, and more refined than the last—and got better gas mileage to boot. The amazing smoothness and efficiency of a Honda four-cylinder motor was still unequaled by any other company. Honda introduced a flood of technical innovations, such as the double-wishbone suspension, a system that balances ride and handling and allows for a low, sleek hood line. Little ergonomic touches showed that Honda listened to the American consumer: a gas cap holder on the filler door, childproof door locks, and the "valet" keys that denied outsiders access to the trunk or glove box.

The bullet-shaped two-seat Civic CRX coupe was introduced in 1983, designed by Honda's expanding U.S. research and development arm. The CRX was a rarity, a car so unique that it created its own market segment. It was available as either a high-performance sports car or the highest-gas-mileage car sold in America. The stunning third-generation Accord, introduced in 1986, was a styling *tour de force* featuring hidden head lamps and a racy profile, far ahead of all other sedans on the market.

The 1988 Prelude was the first car in the world available with four-wheel steering, more a symbol of Honda's creative engineering than a useful feature for the consumer. The free publicity generated by the innovation was priceless. Honda could do no wrong.

Honda's advertising strategy has been lauded as a textbook example on brand management. Its advertising during the 1980s continued the consistent theme developed in the 1970s, not jumping from concept to concept like Detroit carmakers' campaigns. All Honda ads featured the same "We Make it Simple" tag line and the same humorous voice of actor Burgess Meredith. Wildly creative, yet simple, funny, and understated, Honda's print and television ads featured the car as the star and stressed how Honda's advanced technology benefited the consumer.

Honda resisted falling into the weary wasteland that is automobile advertising. No offending the intelligence of the consumers by screaming at them. No comparing of Hondas to other cars, proven in focus groups to cheapen the Honda brand image in the eyes of the customers. No insulting of female prospects by showing doe-eyed women hanging on the arm of a guy driving his new car. Honda was praised by Gloria Steinem, the publisher of the women's magazine, *Ms.*, for advertising the same message in female publications as in men's. More than half of Honda's buyers were women.

Honda was good at advertising but not so good at marketing, the discipline that encompasses all the ingredients that persuade and assist a consumer in buying a product.

The key ingredient in a solid automobile marketing program is a strong captive finance arm, essentially a bank wholly owned by the corporation. Ford Motor Company's captive finance company is Ford Motor Credit. If Ford needs to boost sales, the company rings up Ford Motor Credit and orders a subsidized lease program or a temporary loosening of consumer credit standards needed to qualify for a car loan. Beginning in the late 1980s, Ford's finance arm encouraged dealers to sell two-year leases as part of the corporation's strategy to encourage customers to buy new cars more often. The program was wildly successful, boosting both Ford's owner loyalty and dealer profitability. At the same time, Honda sales division executives were begging the elderly Japanese bean counters at Honda Finance to offer any sort of lease program.

Honda Finance did not offer nationwide retail financing for customers until 1990. Once available, few dealers utilized the loan programs because Honda Finance would only work with customers with impeccable credit. Honda Finance offered no extended service contracts, a tool lengthening the manufacturer's warranty for up to five years. Jim Cardiges would announce at annual dealer meetings that "we have too much respect for our dealers to offer them. We believe our dealers should choose their own extended service contract companies." The retailers loved Cardiges's proclamation because it meant more money in their pockets. A manufacturer-supported service contract program required dealers to adhere to a specific selling price, eliminating their chance to gouge a customer for $800 or $900 on a contract worth $395. Dealers chose vendors offering the least-expensive contract available, regardless of the provider's reputation for customer service. Some dealers started their own insurance companies to provide service contracts.

Why would Honda's top execs say they wanted their customers to have a service contract from a fly-by-night company rather than one associated with the Honda name? Because they were covering for the stubborn Honda Finance, which was loath to hire the additional people necessary to develop a service contract division.

The mid-1980s found consumers demanding better treatment on the showroom floor. Some automakers bribed dealers to take care of the customer by offering cash incentives tied to satisfactory customer satisfaction index (CSI) scores. Some required attendance in seminars to teach salespeople how to interact like human beings. Some even canceled the franchises of dealers whose CSI ratings were below par. Honda did nothing, other than to simply encourage its dealers to do better. We have too much respect for our dealers to tell them what to do, repeated the old company saw. Dealers left to their own devices will inevitably fall back on their high-pressure selling ways, the tradition of the American retail car business. Refusing to give a price without a commitment from the customer to buy. Marching a platoon of closers into the booth to berate buyers into submission. Giving shoppers lowball prices that no other dealer can beat, prices the sales reps have no intention of honoring when the pigeon returns. Whatallittake to put you in a car today? Honda rushed to assist dealers to take care of customers in the back end — the service and parts departments — but essentially ignored the needs of the consumer on the sales floor.

In the late 1980s, J. D. Power and Associates, the consulting firm that measures customer satisfaction among car buyers, began to survey consumer attitudes about the car shopping process. Honda dealers were ranked in the bottom half among all carmakers' retailers and would begin a slow sink to the bottom quarter as customers began to expect better treatment. (To be fair, Toyota and Nissan also suffered from poor sales satisfaction rankings, indicating to some Japanese automaker executives that pleasing a large number of educated consumers was impossible.) When General Motors established Saturn in the late 1980s, it demonstrated that a mediocre car combined with exemplary handling of buyers could be as effective as the Honda approach to the car business. Saturn did not meekly suggest that its dealers be nice to customers, it mandated good treatment of car buyers. Saturn dealers were required to sell every vehicle for the window sticker price, eliminating the humiliating haggling process.

Honda did have some sound strategies in the marketing of its vehicles. The company did not undermine its dealer body by selling cars to fleet accounts and rental car companies, as did Detroit automakers. The approach had two benefits: It appeased Honda's dealers, who bemoaned the fact that other manufacturers sold cars to rental outfits at discounted prices, companies not required to meet any of the standards to which dealers had to adhere. Honda also understood the potential long-term damage caused by massive fleet sales. Domestic carmakers' practice of dumping 30 to 40 percent of their automobiles into fleet and rental companies depressed used car values of those units when they returned to the market. Honda knew the vaunted high resale values of its cars, both a major selling point in the showroom and a key figure in achieving low consumer lease payments, would suffer if the company initiated fleet sales. Honda wanted its cars in the hands of the consumer, a long-term strategy benefiting both factory and dealer. It was yet another reason Honda dealers loved the factory and the people who represented them.

When Honda resorted to cash incentives to help move cars beginning in the late 1980s, it wisely avoided a key marketing mistake of the competition. Other automakers offered cash directly to customers — commonly called rebates — and used them as advertising hooks. This sent a mixed message to consumers: here is our great new car and here is the money we will pay you if you buy one. Honda's incentives were given only to its dealers and were never publicized. The company was fiercely protective of its strong brand image, and consumer rebates would have eroded a reputation that had taken years to build. Honda told dealers to use the additional funds to bolster their advertising and merchandising efforts, but the dealers did what they knew Honda really wanted with the incentives and lowered the prices of the automobiles.

Knowing how to build a great car but lacking in marketing acumen is a better scenario than the other way around. There was no reason for Honda to put money into developing strong marketing tools during the 1980s while the cars were selling themselves. Besides, the company had other issues to (not) deal with.

Jack Billmyer wallowed in the kickbacks from the Honda retailers. New Jersey dealer Marty Lustgarten spent $40,000 to pay for the wedding of Billmyer's son, Jerry, who was employed at one of Lustgarten's dealerships as a lot boy. He also gave Jerry Billmyer 20 percent ownership in a Honda store. The friendly folks at Dah Chong Hong handed Billmyer over $200,000 in cash and gifts. A Tennessee dealer gave him 20 percent interest in a Budweiser distributorship, from which he earned about $80,000 per year in profit sharing. Billmyer received annual Christmas gifts of $5,000 to $10,000 each from countless dealers. Others forwarded large-screen TVs, a hot tub, jewelry, Waterford crystal, and gift certificates to Nieman Marcus. And, of course, innumerable luxury automobiles and Rolex watches.

Those dealers were mere pikers next to Rick Hendrick.

Rick Hendrick and Jack Billmyer would make each other multimillionaires. Thanks to Billmyer, and later Jim Cardiges, Hendrick would own far more Honda franchises than any other dealer in America and enjoy a pipeline to an unlimited number of scarce Honda cars. All it took was a few gifts.

Hendrick had grown up the son of a North Carolina tobacco farmer. He first met Billmyer while a teenager racing hot rods on local dirt tracks. Later, as a college student, Hendrick mowed the lawn at Billmyer's home. When Hendrick started his automotive career as a used car salesperson in Raleigh, Billmyer promised him a Honda franchise if he could first establish himself as a dealer. In 1975 the 26-year-old Hendrick opened a Chevrolet dealership in Bennetsville, South Carolina, becoming the youngest Chevy dealer in the nation. Two years later, Billmyer followed through on his word and granted Hendrick a Honda franchise for Bennetsville.

As the years passed, Hendrick was granted more and more Honda franchises. He obtained a dozen more Honda stores in the Carolinas, as well as franchises in New York, Georgia, Florida, Texas, and California. Most manufacturers have policies restricting the number of franchises a dealer principal can own because of the possibility of one retailer controlling the sale of too many cars and thus being prone to exert too much influence on the automaker. It is also contrary to the spirit of automakers' franchise agreements, which require an owner with financial interest to be present in the dealership. In addition, the scenario of a megadealer filing for bankruptcy also gives automakers cause to limit the number of dealerships held by one individual, a number most set at between six and ten.

Honda did not have such a policy, but Billmyer took no chances, fearing the Japanese would question either Hendrick's holdings or Billmyer's relationship with him. At Billmyer's recommendation, Hendrick's true ownership interests in many of the dealerships are not reflected in any Honda records. Hendrick Honda stores were established in the name of the store's general manager, a maze of holding companies, or Hendrick's brother, John.

There were only so many new Honda points or existing Honda dealerships for sale, but Hendrick's Honda pals found ways for him to obtain more franchises. The easiest way was to lower a dealer's allocations of automobiles down to the point where the dealer could no longer make money. The sympathetic executives at Honda would then strongly recommend he sell the store to Hendrick.

William Van Dalsem owned such a dealership in Corona, California. He was a good operator, having won numerous awards from Honda for having superior customer satisfaction rankings. In 1983 the Los Angeles market was the hottest in the country for Honda. Hendrick indicated to Billmyer that he wanted a Honda store in Southern California. Soon after Billmyer became Honda's national sales manager, Van Dalsem watched his allocations slowly shrivel to 20 cars per month, half of what he needed to be profitable. He agreed to sell his dealership to Hendrick.

Less than a week after the buy/sell between Van Dalsem and Hendrick closed, the former owner drove by his old store to discover the dealership crammed with over 100 new Honda automobiles. Hendrick was in business. "I just wondered 'where the hell did he get all those cars?'" said Van Dalsem. Hendrick later built an office at the Corona store for Billmyer's use.

Whatever dealership Hendrick wanted, he got. South Carolina Honda dealer Dick Young was granted permission to build a new dealership in Aiken, South Carolina, and submitted his facility plans to Honda. Enter Hendrick, who made it clear to Honda officials that he was upset that someone other than him could be granted a Carolina dealership. The gang scrambled to eliminate Young. Suddenly, Young's building plans were too extravagant for the Aiken market. The executives told Young to scale back his building. He resubmitted his plans to Honda and was told that his proposed facility was now too small and that Hendrick had been granted the franchise.

Hendrick was different from most of the retailers who paid off Honda officials—he was actually a good automobile dealer. With Hendrick, Honda was not represented by dealers with poor facilities and abysmal customer handling, two by-products of the short-term mentality of dealer principals who preferred to bribe rather than work their way to success. Hendrick's spotless stores are the model of organization, with professional management practices and sophisticated record keeping, items too often missing in modern car dealerships.

One of the fascinations of the retail car business is that a dealership's people and procedures always reflect the personality of the dealer principal himself. A good factory man can walk into a dealership and immediately sense the character of the owner. The energy of an agency owned by a dealer who plays golf every day is lackadaisical. The tightwad dealer who delights in cutting salespeople's pay plans finds his customers squeezed to the point of being as unhappy as his employees.

The Hendrick dealerships reflect Rick Hendrick—friendly, organized, shrewd businessman, tough competitor, and family-oriented Southern gentleman. Not to mention generous. Hendrick's stores are liberal with customers on the service drive, willing to pay for fixes that are out of manufacturers' warranty periods, all in the name of taking care of your neighbor and developing a lifelong customer. "We won't replace an engine for someone who ran it without oil," says Hendrick, "but good service means good customers who come back." All dealers feed the factory that rhetoric, but Hendrick lived it.

Hendrick is known for helping out employees and friends in need. He once provided a car and house for a family that had sold most of its belongings to pay medical bills for a family member stricken with multiple sclerosis.

True to form, Hendrick was the most generous gift giver of all the dealers when it came to Honda executives.

Hendrick provided Billmyer with BMW sedans to drive in Los Angeles, replacing the Chevrolet Caprice he had loaned to Billmyer in the Carolinas. He hired another of Billmyer's sons, Stephen, to work in one of his dealerships. Billmyer was rumored to have secret ownership in several Hendrick corporations, but it has never been proven, his discretion making it difficult to ascertain. The holding companies that own Honda stores on Hendrick's behalf probably hide Billmyer's ownership as well. Commemorative Acura rain jackets given to dealers featured the Hendrick Sportswear logo, further fueling speculation about the relationship between Hendrick and Billmyer.

Hendrick became the ultimate Santa Claus when he started buying luxury homes for Honda executives. In 1986 he purchased a sprawling Palm Springs, California, vacation house for Billmyer. Hendrick arranged a $280,000 mortgage for the home through the NCNB bank in Charlotte, personally guaranteeing the note. A notation on a closing document noted that there would be no need for an appraisal on the property because, "Mr. Billmyer, as the top man for Honda in the U.S., remains an excellent credit risk." Particularly since Hendrick made Billmyer's house payments for him each month, paying the bank out of his personal account. The shrewd Hendrick kept his name on the loan papers, protection in case Honda automobiles ever stopped selling.

It was at this house, sitting around the pool that dealer Peter Epsteen had paid for, that Billmyer uttered his famous line: "At American Honda they don't pay you a million dollars, but you can live like a millionaire." The statement was the rallying cry of the Honda gang.

Everyone knew about Billmyer's house and how he had obtained it. When a group of Honda managers were riding a shuttle bus to a Palm Springs hotel in 1988, the driver pointed out the estates of singer Frank Sinatra, former president Gerald Ford, and other celebrities. Pointing to comedian Bob Hope's mammoth castle, he said, "That home belongs to . . ."

"Jack Billmyer!" yelled an executive as the crowd cracked up.

Hendrick also financed a home for Stephen Billmyer. Stephen's house payments, like those of his father, were made by Hendrick, who also paid for the younger Billmyer's boat.

Rick Hendrick was on his way to owning 26 Honda and Acura stores, twice as many as the next largest megadealer. Hendrick earned over $100 million from those dealerships during the 1980s, a good return on the gifts he had donated to his friends at Honda. By 1995, the 46-year-old Hendrick would be the largest car dealer in America, with 67 dealerships totaling sales of over $2 billion annually. Hendrick was as discreet as Billmyer, and "only" $825,000 worth of cash and gifts that he bestowed upon Honda officials would ever be discovered.

Billmyer and Hendrick shared a passion for the South's favorite sport: NASCAR stock car racing. Billmyer granted Honda franchises to a half-dozen NASCAR drivers, including Darrell Waltrip and Cale Yarborough, as well as IndyCar drivers A. J. Foyt and Bobby Rahal and race car owner Roger Penske. Hendrick's wealth gained from the automobile business led him to become stock car racing's most powerful team owner and a celebrity in the Carolinas. He hung out with actors Paul Newman and Tom Cruise and was the technical adviser on Cruise's film about NASCAR racing, *Days of Thunder.* Randy Quaid's role in the movie as Cruise's car owner was patterned after Hendrick, right down to his owning a dealership named City Chevrolet, the name of a Hendrick store.

Billmyer schemed to combine his love of racing with his corrupt ways. The sales chief distanced himself from Hendrick's stock car teams, not wanting rumors racing around about his relationship with Hendrick. Instead, Billmyer invested in a struggling NASCAR team owned by a Honda dealer named Junie Donlavey. In 1987 the race team was in need of a new crew chief, the person who directs the team's operations. Billmyer made overtures to a crew chief named Doug Richert, who agreed to sign up for a salary of $1,000 per week. The low-budget team was strapped for cash, but Billmyer handled it the same way he took care of other personal needs — he prevailed upon a Honda dealer for the money. Billmyer contacted John Orsini, owner of a Connecticut Honda dealership, and a man clamoring for one of Honda's new Acura luxury-car franchises. Orsini was no rookie in the Honda game — he had previously given cash and automobiles to two other Honda executives.

The pair met in September during the Honda New Car Show, the company's annual national dealer gathering, in Billmyer's suite at Bally's Hotel and Casino in Las Vegas. Orsini was among a string of dealers invited one by one into Billmyer's and other Honda officials' hotel rooms during these get-togethers. More cash changed hands in these clandestine meetings during New Car Shows than in the casino downstairs. Billmyer told Orsini that Acura for Nanuet, New York, was available, with one catch — Orsini had to put a fellow named Doug Richert on Executive Honda's payroll, at a salary of $1,000 per week. Orsini agreed, and Billmyer supplied him with Richert's social security number and home address. Billmyer had his new crew chief handled. A few weeks later Orsini was granted the Acura franchise.

It was a relatively minor deal for Billmyer, but one that would later become significant. Besides reeking of quid pro quo, a rarity for Billmyer, the Richert deal left a paper trail, the one thing Billmyer had always warned the others about.

Another bunch of blabbers surfaced during the mid-1980s, trying to get someone to put a stop to the rapidly spreading corruption between Honda executives and Honda dealers. They were summarily dismissed.

Everyone, from a Honda Motor Company official in Japan to numerous top "clean" American Honda executives — both American and Japanese —

as well as Honda's law firm, was by now aware that Honda sales employees were on the take. The opportunity to put an end to the pandemic payola presented itself to the officials time and again, but they repeatedly looked the other way. For every documented case of key Honda personnel being told about the problems, there are likely dozens more that were swept under the rug.

Few Honda dealers were brave enough to confront the factory executives about the corruption. Most had seen their personal net worth soar after obtaining a Honda outlet and saw no reason to rock the boat. One who did was Ron Tonkin of Portland, Oregon, who called Cardiges after hearing from a Honda dealer who was being squeezed for $100,000 in exchange for a franchise.

Cardiges's response to Tonkin was predictable: "Ron, I hope this is misunderstanding. We don't do business this way."

There were sound reasons why clean sales division employees did not turn in their dishonest peers. It was feared that members of the clique were ruthless enough to do anything to keep the cash rolling. The chance of physical harm to a bean spiller was very real. The thought of being jettisoned to the motorcycle division for being labeled a troublemaker also gave executives pause. However, the biggest reason for the silence was simply that Honda was a great place to work. In referring to toiling under the sinister California zone sales manager Dennis Josleyn, district sales manager Tony Graziano said, "We had good jobs. We were fairly independent being in the field. Honda was the best thing going. Why would we want to screw it up (by turning Josleyn in?)" There was also no one to turn to. The Japanese were too distant, Lyon & Lyon did not care, and the personnel department was trusted by very few. Within the sales ranks, one ran a risk of telling the wrong person, someone in the greased group. Some managers aspired to become junior members of the boys' club and were certainly not going to blow their chances by squealing.

For most, business hours at Honda were consumed by activities other than gossiping about who did what. The corruption was something you shook your head over and then went about your business.

Honda's human resources department managers never knew they were being kept in the dark about the really good stuff, the J. D. Power allegations or other tidbits that had been directed to the Lyon & Lyon vault. The personnel department was always ready to pull the trigger on employees caught with their hands in the corrupt cookie jar: The department terminated a half-dozen executives during the 1980s for various kickback incidents. They fired a parts division employee for accepting a leather jacket from a supplier. They booted a lawnmower division vice president for taking a vacation trip from a vendor. National advertising manager Eric Conn had his pay and bonus frozen for one year for accepting tickets to the 1985 Super Bowl. Personnel could never seem to get its hands around any allegations about sales division officials, though, despite having several opportunities.

Just before Christmas of 1984, soon after Cardiges was promoted to vice president of automobile sales, someone tried to trip him up. An anonymous person, claiming to be a neighbor of Cardiges's, called Honda personnel director Don English. The caller claimed to be upset about the conga line of delivery trucks arriving at Cardiges's Irvine home and blocking the entrance to the neighborhood. English summoned Cardiges to his office. He questioned Cardiges about the allegation and about the always-swirling whispers about sales division managers receiving gratuities from dealers. Cardiges replied that it was crazy to listen to the rumors. He said he told sales reps "all the time" not to accept gifts. He assured English he would check with his wife, Effie, about the delivery trucks.

English then asked about Cardiges's gold Rolex Presidential watch. Cardiges responded calmly, saying that Effie came from a wealthy family and had given him the watch as a gift. English asked to see it and noted the inscription on the back: "To Jim. Love, Effie." Apparently because it did not say "To Jim. Thanks for the Cars. Love, Joe Honda Dealer" English was satisfied that Cardiges was clean.

Another anonymous caller tipped off English to a briefcase phone received by Billmyer. English confronted the sales boss, who said it was a "bullshit" gift and that he was too clumsy to use it. He offered it to English. English told him to return the phone.

Whoever was trying to ratfink on Cardiges and Billmyer, likely a clean Honda executive or a disgruntled dealer, was never identified.

In 1985 Honda's head of security, Tony Piazza, the man whom Billmyer was convinced was spying on him, alerted American Honda president Tetsuo Chino that Billmyer was likely taking bribes from dealers. Piazza and English were told of Billmyer receiving $100,000 in cash in a paper bag from a dealer in exchange for the rights to a new dealership. They also had vague information that Billmyer held secret ownerships in several Honda stores. Chino agreed to meet with English and Piazza and invited Bud "Lightning Bolt" Smoot of Lyon & Lyon to attend (and thus put the conversation under the cloak of client-attorney privilege). The president decided to take no action — the risk for litigation would be too great if other dealers found out about Billmyer's business. Likely tipped off by Chino, Billmyer later confronted Piazza and told him to call off his dogs.

Sometime in 1986, American Honda vice president Chet Hale and finance chief Doug Divall both spoke to Chino about the problems. Hale tried to explain to Chino that such gift giving is not acceptable in the American business world, as it is in Japan. Divall asked Chino if he could initiate an investigation. Chino said no. Around the same time, an indiscreet California Honda dealer wrote Cardiges a letter, offering him free use of a $40,000 BMW sedan. The dealer mailed the letter to Cardiges at Honda's headquarters, where it accidentally fell into Chino's hands. Still, Chino took no action.

In 1987 a midlevel Honda purchasing manager named Cecil Proulx began a crusade to stop the immoral activities, having been informed by Piazza about his own attempts in that direction. Proulx came upon a suspicious relationship between Billmyer and a vendor, Events Unlimited, a Nashville-based corporate events planning company. The firm was headed by Patsy Bruce, a former songwriter who wrote the Willie Nelson hit country song "Mamas, Don't Let Your Babies Grow Up to Be Cowboys." Bruce was just Billmyer's type. He awarded Events Unlimited a contract to produce Honda's multimillion-dollar annual dealer meetings, starting in 1987. He did not obtain competitive bids from other vendors. Events Unlimited responded in kind by hosting some Honda executives' wives on all-expenses-paid shopping trips. When Proulx attempted to force Billmyer to adhere to corporate policy regarding selection of future suppliers, Billmyer refused.

Proulx spoke with Michiaki Shinkai, a Japanese vice president of administration who controlled the purse strings at Honda and reported directly to Chino. Proulx said that he felt Billmyer was taking payoffs from Events Unlimited. Shinkai told Proulx to back off of Billmyer, informing the tattler that kickbacks were a form of compensation at American Honda.

"We can't afford to pay our sales executives what Ford and GM and Chrysler pay them," explained Shinkai, "so we look the other way."

When that stunning comment was revealed years later, it confirmed employees' suspicions: that taking bribes was considered an employee fringe benefit that saved the corporation money. The human resources department was under Shinkai's jurisdiction, so they likely were directed to establish employee compensation plans with that philosophy in mind. Shinkai also rejected personnel's attempts to establish cost-of-living allowances for employees transferring to Los Angeles and other expensive markets. Maybe he calculated a higher graft factor for Los Angeles because of its profitable and generous dealer network and figured sales execs received the equivalent of a raise when moving to Southern California.

Frustrated with the lack of response from Shinkai, Cecil Proulx turned to Lyon & Lyon's Smoot. In June 1987 Smoot received a hand-delivered letter from Proulx. In it, the purchasing manager outlined his concerns about the graft and the inactivity by Honda management to curtail it:

> The casualness with which seemingly credible information (internal and external) is passed around concerning vendor gifts, far in excess of $25 in value, to highly-placed individuals concerns me. . . . Executive management does not want to hear about it and nothing is done when they are told. I think that's a dangerous situation: the perceived permissive attitude . . . verbiage to the contrary, the actions and inactions of executive management, the "body language" of this company, seems to send a message that loose practices are okay. It's a permissive attitude. The point is, I think it is asking for trouble to ignore the situation. It's foolish, in my opinion, for a company to subject itself to such unnecessary exposure.

Smoot met with Proulx but took no action. Said Proulx, "The only thing that changed ultimately was my responsibilities being curtailed. Whether there was any cause-effect, I don't know. . . . It's very difficult. You love the company. You love the people. Even the people that are supposed to be the bad guys, they've got things you like about them. And you just wish to hell somebody would do something."

When Proulx resigned a few years later, Honda paid him $250,000 to keep his mouth shut, fearing his knowledge about the extent of the cover-up. Honda in-house attorney Mark Brooks warned Proulx to never talk about the corruption or details of the settlement.

"Look, if you ever want to find out how mean we can be, just open your mouth about this," threatened Brooks. "We once settled with a paraplegic woman and she had talked about it and we got every bit of the settlement back."

The reluctance by Honda officials to take action during 1986 and 1987 to stop the corruption was probably spurred by two highly publicized legal battles that hit close to home. Both the all-terrain vehicles (ATVs) fiasco and the runaway Audi mania reinforced to the Japanese executives that the twisted American tort system was unpredictable. Firing one of its executives for being corrupt might lead to dealer lawsuits.

Honda and four other manufacturers had been producing three- and four-wheeled ATVs since the late 1970s. Comprising little more than an engine, a seat, and huge balloonlike tires, the machines were designed for young adults to ride off-road. Honda dominated the ATV market, selling almost 65 percent of the total 2.3 million units purchased by consumers by 1985.

The three-wheeled versions of ATVs began to attract government and media attention in the mid-1980s. Between 1982 and 1986 approximately 400 people were killed while riding three-wheeled ATVs, and another 150,000 were injured. The majority of the accidents involved the absence of common sense: the riders were either drunk or not wearing a helmet or were children whose parents had allowed them to pilot the powerful vehicles. A group of attorneys representing ATV accident victims banded together to form the ATV Litigation Group. More than 300 lawsuits were filed against the manufacturers, all citing the machines as dangerous and the companies negligent for not properly warning consumers about the hazards. The Consumer Product Safety Commission proposed a ban on three-wheeled ATVs. "Killer Tricycles!" screamed the media. In April 1987 the television news program "60 Minutes" aired a biased segment laying blame for the deaths and injuries on the ATV manufacturers and dealers.

One particular ATV lawsuit in San Diego landed the biggest blow to Honda. In 1982 a nine-year-old boy suffered severe injuries when he fell off a Honda three-wheeled ATV that was being driven by an eight-year-old friend. Tetsuo Chino, by now the president of Honda North America, was called to testify in October 1987 in a lawsuit filed against the corporation by the boy's parents. Honda fought efforts by the plaintiff's attorneys to obtain Chino's testimony. The company took the matter all the way to the California Supreme Court but was ultimately overruled.

In a courtroom packed with lawyers and representatives of consumer groups, the short, bespectacled Chino took the stand, the highest-ranking Japanese officer of a major corporation ever to testify in an American product liability suit. Chino made a horrible witness. He admitted that he had refused requests to meet with officials from the Consumer Product Safety Commission. He cried when shown a list of the people who had died while riding ATVs. Chino claimed that Honda did not have this problem in other countries in the world, a subtle indictment of the U.S. legal system. A Honda internal memo was produced, claiming that more people died in 1984 in the United States from hunger and neglect than from ATV accidents, an anti-American statement bordering on racism.

Worst of all, Chino cited an internal investigation that concluded that the riders were at fault. "There is no problem with the machine," Chino stated. "The problem is with the rider." That was the truth, of course, but saying it publicly was the worst thing a corporate executive could do. Few will sympathize with a large company when it appears to be discrediting the consumers who buy its products, people the media portray as victims of the evil company's merchandise.

Honda prevailed in the San Diego case but was forced to settle dozens of others. In December 1987 a Washington, D.C., federal court banned further sales of three-wheeled ATVs. It was only a small financial blow to Honda, since automobile sales constituted the lion's share of the company's profits, but it was a gigantic public embarrassment.

Could the same thing happen to automobiles, the Honda executives wondered, as they watched a similar scenario unfold at Audi of America, the domestic arm of the German luxury carmaker. Arguments can be made about the possible danger in riding a three-wheeled ATV, but there was nothing wrong with an Audi 5000 sedan until a few lawyers and the media came along.

In a tragic accident in Ohio in 1986, a six-year-old boy was opening the garage door for his mother when her Audi 5000 suddenly shot forward and fatally crushed him against the rear wall of the garage. The distraught woman told police that her foot had slipped off the brake pedal and onto the accelerator. When she later changed her story to say that the car had roared away on its own, and that the brakes could not stop the vehicle, the term *sudden acceleration* was born. The woman and her husband filed suit against Audi, and the news went nationwide. Other people who had been in accidents in their Audis suddenly decided that they too must have been the victims of demon runaway automobiles. They formed an advocate group called the Audi Victims Network. The organization deemed the Audi 5000 "a notorious killer car." Dozens of lawsuits were filed. The Center for Auto Safety, a consumer group heavily funded by trial lawyers eager to sue car companies, demanded a recall of all Audi 5000s.

The National Highway Traffic Safety Administration refused to order a recall and began an investigation of Audi. Unintended acceleration as described in the accidents involving Audi cars was a scientific impossibility. An automobile's braking system can easily override an engine, even one running at full throttle. Inspection of the cars in question found no mechanical defects in either the accelerator or the brakes.

Audi's public posture was that the drivers were in error, that they were accidentally pressing on the gas pedal instead of the brake. Audi should have had the confidence to keep its mouth shut until the government completed its inquiry. Instead, the company was vilified for blaming consumers for the accidents.

Like in the ATV case, the death blow to Audi came from "60 Minutes." In a November 1986 episode, the television show rigged the transmission of an Audi 5000 to induce it to perform as the producers wanted. They disabled several pressure-relief valves in the transmission and pumped compressed air into it, causing the motor's throttle to open slightly. None of the mechanical manipulations were mentioned on the program. All viewers saw was an Audi 5000 mysteriously driving itself down the road. The sudden acceleration hysteria reached full bloom after the segment aired, and more lawsuits were filed, many from owners of cars other than Audis.

The trial lawyers, the "safety" groups, and the media had throttled a bewildered Audi. Though in 1989 the National Highway Traffic Safety Administration concluded that the unintended acceleration cases were due to driver error, Audi was already dead. Its annual U.S. sales had plummeted from 74,000 automobiles in 1985 to 23,000 in 1988.

Both the ATV and Audi cases were likely on the minds of Japanese executives at American Honda when they decided not to investigate the allegations of corruption within their ranks. Product liability lawsuits are far removed from an automobile dealer suing American Honda because another dealer received preferential treatment in return for kickbacks. But to the Japanese officials it was all the same, the suits having confirmed that the U.S. legal system was treacherous and to be avoided at all costs. Exposing one of their own for taking bribes could only lead to the courthouse and to bad publicity from an anti–big business American media. The safest strategy was to continue to look the other way.

As the Japanese fiddled, the corruption by the Honda executives grew more aggressive and more innovative.

CHAPTER 7

Top Speed

> Order us another drink, Billy Clyde. I'll go ask those girls what color cars they want.
>
> — Shake Tiller, from the Dan Jenkins novel *Life Its Ownself*

JIM CARDIGES rarely talked — he gave speeches. On this day in 1989, he climbed onto a tall stool in front of his ten zone sales managers and two regional sales managers at a meeting at Honda headquarters in Torrance. The overgrown fraternity boys in the blue suits who made up Cardiges's crew milled around, laughing heartily and cross-preening as Cardiges called them to order.

The Japanese executives had finished their presentations and left the room, and the atmosphere formerly thick with boredom and tension had eased. Cardiges could now speak frankly. Today, he wanted to talk about his favorite subject: image.

"How's your attitude?" he asked the group.

"Great!" the trained throng called out in unison, correctly answering the signature Cardiges greeting.

"Well, all right," said Cardiges. "You guys look great. It's super to get you all together like this. I wish we could do it more often."

"I want to talk about where you guys are in your lives. We have the best cars, the best ratings by the dealers and you guys are the best sales team in the industry. You have to carry yourselves like the leaders you are. Have you got your second house yet? No? Whose got one? What kind of sports car are you driving? Why haven't you gotten these things handled? If you can't get that kind of stuff handled, you don't need to be in your position." He grilled the managers one by one, asking what they were driving and what vacation homes they had purchased, dismissing Corvettes and $200,000 houses as "not good enough." The lightweights in the room —

the few men who never asked for gifts, thus limiting their annual dealer take to around $50,000 — squirmed in their seats. This was not a lighthearted discussion — one audience member recalls Cardiges being "serious as hell."

It was a subtle message to the waffling members of the corruption club: start working the kickback program or get out. Be like me or else. It was dangerous to the welfare of the boys' club to have any nonplayers — they were a threat to security, those most likely to squeal if squeezed. While Jack Billmyer did not care if his underlings chose to receive dealer gifts, as long as they were discreet, Cardiges demanded the practice, veiled in the guise of upgrading one's image. Cardiges also took the corruption in new and ingenious directions.

The men had heard it all before, but listening to Cardiges speak was always enthralling. He had replaced Billmyer as the head of American Honda's sales division in 1988, at age 42, when the elder statesman retired. Cardiges's annual performance as host of the business meeting at Honda New Car Shows was the stuff of legends.

New district sales managers heard a different Cardiges speech than the one he had given to the heart of the club. He stressed the importance of setting goals and "crystallizing" your thinking, standard how-to-succeed schtick. His recommendation of never selling your home in California, in order to take advantage of rising real estate values, was galling to those not playing the game and unable to afford Los Angeles houses on Honda salaries. "The closest I ever came to having a house in L.A.," says one clean California manager, "was when a dealer said he'd rent me one for free."

Cardiges told the rookies how he and his wife, Effie, wrote down their annual financial goals and plans to achieve them. Some wondered how they established such objectives with Jim supposedly on a fixed income. Maybe the couple pledged: "Jim to extort minimum of $2 million from Honda dealers this year."

Most of Jack Billmyer's time starting in 1984 was devoted to the startup of Honda's new Acura luxury car division, so Cardiges was unofficially in charge of the Honda sales division during the mid-to-late 1980s, the peak years for product demand and dealer profitability. He gathered his crew, promoting to zone sales managers the men who fit the Cardiges image. They all began to dress and talk like Cardiges. One said he would "would run through a wall for Jim."

The managers worked long days for their beloved company. They each happily juggled the demands of 100 Honda dealers, their understaffed field office, and the whims of headquarters. They took dealers' calls at all hours. Their devotion to Honda can be interpreted another way: being the first one in the office in the morning, and the last one to leave at night, has been identified as a common characteristic of white-collar criminals. It's called paranoia.

Nonplayers of the extracurricular games faced careers on hold permanently. An assistant zone sales manager watched for years as members of the gang whizzed by him on their way to the top. He complained to his boss, Bob Mazzitelli, about his stalled career. "You've got to understand how you get ahead in this company," Mazzitelli responded. "You have to start playing the game." Mazzitelli, a former elementary school teacher, knew well the perks of joining the crew. Cardiges had little use for him until he became a player, at which point other managers noticed that Cardiges was suddenly singing Mazzitelli's praises instead of condemning him.

Cardiges had little patience for officials who complained about Honda's substandard pay plans. Mazzitelli once asked him about the possibilities of raises for his struggling district sales managers, explaining how they were all young, raising families, and dead broke.

"They're all big boys now," said Cardiges. "Tell them to get on the program."

"Jim, you gotta understand," said Mazzitelli. "Some of these guys work in areas of the zone where that just doesn't happen."

"Well, they got to figure it out themselves," was Cardiges's only advice.

Mazzitelli subsequently decided to funnel some of his ill-gotten kickbacks to his district sales managers in the form of bonuses.

The Cardiges command introduced the practice of ignoring all business sense when establishing new Honda dealerships. Although Billmyer received compensation for helping Hendrick and others obtain franchises, dealer selection under the Billmyer watch was based on standard industry predictors of success: experience, capital, reputation, and proposed location and facility. Dealers were established in spots in which market studies showed a need for a Honda dealership. There were a few exceptions, but Billmyer generally kept Honda's best interests at heart.

With Cardiges behind the wheel, new Honda stores were granted to enrich the executives first and foremost, regardless of the impact on Honda's presence in the marketplace. With Cardiges's most-trusted lieutenant, about-to-resign California zone sales manager Ed Temple, as the point man, the Cardiges crew hit fast and hard. The rules were simple:

Issue the letter of intent to a cooperating straw dealer and then flip it fast to a real dealer for big bucks. If selling the rights directly to the eventual dealer, push him to get established quickly, regardless of location or facility. While Billmyer's rewards for granting franchises seemingly came at random, Cardiges's boys spelled out the selling prices up front. The most lucrative open point deals began in 1988, soon after Cardiges was promoted to replace Billmyer. At that point dealers were beginning to balk at paying for extra shipments of cars, Honda's increased production having eased supply problems. Selling the rights to new dealerships looked like the only remaining source of extra income for the men.

A Honda store established in Moreno Valley, California, in July 1988 yielded the biggest jackpot of the scandal, paying out $750,000 to Cardiges, Temple, and Texas zone sales manager Fred Meis, the latter supplying a friend to be the temporary dealer. A point in Folsom, California, was good for $500,000 for Cardiges, Temple, and new California zone sales manager Dennis Josleyn. The Folsom dealer originally had agreed to pay $1 million to the trio but negotiated the figure downward after encountering financial difficulties. A new store in Auburn, New York, yielded $250,000 for Cardiges and New England assistant zone sales manager Mark Benson. A third Honda dealership was established in Austin, Texas, despite Honda being the best-selling imported car in town, the key measure of the need for a new store; $150,000 was split by Cardiges, Temple, and Meis. The infamous Santa Paula Honda paid out $400,000, as did a San Diego point. Dozens of deals forwarded millions of dollars to the executives during the Cardiges era. And Honda's Japanese officials, including the president, approved every new dealership, even those established in decayed buildings or in backwoods burgs. They did not question their sales chief.

One of the zone sales managers refused to play. New York sales chief Roger Novelly, a former Detroit police officer, was at odds with Cardiges over the seemingly random placement of dealerships in his territory. Novelly received a call from Cardiges one day, informing him that a man named David Trainer had been issued a letter of intent to open a Honda store in a remote Philadelphia suburb. Novelly and Trainer drove out to the proposed site, a location Novelly couldn't believe.

"It made absolutely no sense whatsoever," recalls Novelly, "because there were no other dealerships around. I don't even believe there was a grocery store around."

Novelly told Cardiges that the site was ludicrous. He called area dealers and told them to raise hell with Cardiges about the proposed dealership. The point never went in. Novelly also resisted Cardiges's attempt to establish two new stores in Pittsburgh, a market where Honda already handily outsold both Toyota and Nissan.

A zone sales manager trying to block Cardiges from opening new points was committing the ultimate career buster. Cardiges could not afford the risk of having a rebel in the ranks. He began pressuring Novelly to resign from the company or transfer out of the Honda division. Novelly secretly invested in a Honda dealership, knowing his departure was inevitable.

Cardiges became best known to the dealers for his yearly performance at the Honda New Car Show. The annual autumn event was held to introduce the dealers to the upcoming year's new automobiles and marketing plans. Typically held in Las Vegas, New Orleans, or other locales popular with car dealers, the show consisted of two days of extravagant parties sandwiched around the dazzling, multimedia business meeting emceed by the smooth-talking Cardiges. During the early 1980s he had shared the stage with Billmyer, but his predecessor was not the polished public speaker that Cardiges was, so Cardiges did most of the talking. The hour-and-a-half business meeting took two months of preparation and rehearsal, all to achieve that spontaneous Cardiges feel.

Cardiges's superb presentations were constantly interrupted by thunderous applause as he bragged about Honda's rising sales and never-ending accolades. He urged the retailers to strengthen the Honda "family" by taking better care of customers. He was an evangelist urging automobile dealers to heal thy evil ways.

Cardiges repeated the Big Lies, the Honda dealer policies born out of the corporation's cheapness, but translated by Cardiges into being enacted at the request of the dealers. Honda will not offer extended service contracts. Honda will not tell you how to run your businesses. Honda will never have as many dealers as Toyota and Nissan. The dealers cheered.

"We hope there'll never be enough cars," said Cardiges at one show. "Many dealers have commented that they enjoy having the demand higher than the supply, for obvious reasons." Obvious to Cardiges, too. The dealers stood and cheered.

Most Honda employees were convinced that Honda's Japanese officials did not participate in the dealer gift program. The Japanese had only limited contact with dealers, and the thought of them and a retailer discussing an arrangement was too far-fetched. Rumors often floated around Honda about Japanese officials receiving unsolicited gifts of golf clubs or paintings, though. The only dealer bequest they actively sought was the free use of Honda dealers' airplanes for business trips, the corporation being too tight to buy one. A California dealer once even arranged for Honda's president to use entertainer Frank Sinatra's jet, the *Lady Barbara.*

At least one of Honda's Japanese executives got swept away by the graft gale. Koichi Amemiya was Billmyer and Cardiges's boss while executive vice president of the automobile division starting in 1987 and would be promoted to president of American Honda in 1989. A tall, bespectacled, gray-haired man, Amemiya was a nondrinker who liked to scour swap meets looking for antique cameras. He referred to the American officials who dragged themselves into work after a long night or missed sales objectives as his "bad boys."

Amemiya likely knew of the underground program at Honda but probably had no idea of its extent. He once joked to Cardiges as he handed him a bonus check that "you don't need this." Amemiya had seen gift giving between businesspeople in Japan and was seeing it among the Americans at Honda, only this time on a much larger scale.

Amemiya loved old Mercedes-Benz automobiles and mentioned that fact to various Honda dealers. Some took Amemiya's Mercedes mention as a signal to ante up, a Pavlov-like response they had learned from Billmyer's hints about Rolex watches. In 1988 Northern California dealer Ted Stevens, a man with a strong track record of paying off Honda execs, called Amemiya with the news that he had come into possession of a classic early 1970s Mercedes-Benz 280SL convertible. It's yours, said Stevens. Amemiya initially resisted Stevens's offer but eventually accepted it as just an American-sized gift from a business associate.

Amemiya visited Honda dealers more often than his predecessors had. His presence made the gang nervous, fearing Amemiya would discuss issues about car allocations or new franchises, potentially messing up the executives' under-the-table activities in those markets. Like the time former American Honda president Tetsuo Chino visited Texas.

In early 1985 Fort Worth, Texas, Honda dealer Bill McDavid had just finished building a new dealership, and the Honda head honchos were coming to visit. McDavid's new store, a spectacular blending of neon and glass highlighted by Honda-blue trim, had set him back over $2 million. Chino, along with Billmyer and Cardiges, were flying in to inspect the new facility and give McDavid some "attaboys." Unbeknownst to McDavid, the trio were winging their way to Fort Worth on his rival brother David's Learjet. The siblings had been partners in a half-dozen Houston and Dallas dealerships until a bitter breakup in 1983.

The executives toured the dealership and were pleased with the new

Bill McDavid Honda. The dealer reviewed his operating philosophies, including a staff devoted to contacting all customers who visited any department of the dealership to ensure they were happy with how they were treated. The dealership's commitment to customer satisfaction would earn Bill McDavid Honda recognition as one of Honda's top 40 dealers nationwide for taking care of the consumer.

As the group stood outside the building, Chino pointed to an adjoining piece of land that McDavid owned and said, "A perfect place for an Acura store, don't you think?" Chino indicated that McDavid should submit a proposal to Honda's luxury car division. McDavid was overjoyed — he had wanted to build an Acura store in Fort Worth, but Acura officials had denied him the location. The president of American Honda just gave me the Acura franchise for Fort Worth, thought McDavid. He noticed that Billmyer and Cardiges had suddenly grown quiet.

The Honda executives spent less than an hour with McDavid. Twenty minutes after they left the dealership, McDavid was startled to see Billmyer and Cardiges standing in the doorway of his office — without Chino.

"Look, we need to talk to you," said Billmyer. "You can forget what Mr. Chino said. We give out the Acura points, not him." Billmyer made it clear that McDavid would have to go through "the system" to be granted the franchise.

The two highest-ranking Americans at Honda had become so swollen with power that they forgot the Japanese were still in charge, but they had additional agendas: a dealership awarded by Chino meant several hundred thousand dollars in kickbacks down the drain. They also did not want to annoy David McDavid by granting his brother another franchise. The scheming duo knew Bill McDavid would not play but had yet to find another dealer who would pay top dollar to become the Fort Worth Acura dealer.

The following year, McDavid built his Acura store on the piece of land that Chino had recommended. Chino's word to McDavid was good. He made a decision that day about dealer placement, rare for any of the Japanese officials. It was the nightmare the corrupt American executives feared whenever either of their two Japanese bosses visited a Honda dealership.

Under Cardiges the officials hit upon a new way to moonlight. True to the industry axiom that "what sells good new will sell good used," preowned Honda automobiles were in high demand. Most dealers wondered why Honda, unlike other automakers, never made used company cars available to them. Honda did have a pool of used cars at each zone office, a mixed bag of executive-driven vehicles, lease returns, and cars used to train service technicians. Unlike other manufacturers, though, Honda did not sell these autos to dealers through auctions — that would have required the hiring of additional personnel to oversee the vehicle distribution. Instead, Honda bequeathed the responsibility of disposing of the used cars to the zone sales managers.

The right to sell the used cars was a graft gift from heaven to the already filthy executives. Honda's company car department's policy on the sale of the vehicles dictated that the zone sales managers were to give all area Honda dealers the opportunity to bid on the units, with cars going to the highest bidder. Instead of following that practice, the opportunistic officials set up a shady system that guaranteed predetermined winners. They directed favored dealers to submit bids of $1,000 to $2,000 below the wholesale value of the automobiles, with the agreement that the dealers kickback several hundred dollars per unit to them. Some zone sales managers prepared phony bids from dealers on forged stationery, which verified to headquarters that other dealers had participated. The less imaginative tipped their friend off on others dealers' bids, so he could offer a couple bucks more and be assured the units — but this meant the prices were not as appealing as those from the fake bid method. Honda's company car department did not have a clue as to the market value of the vehicles and blindly accepted whatever prices the managers procured as the highest possible.

The happy Honda dealer sold the vehicles for profits of up to $2,000 apiece — even after deducting the amount of the kickback — a figure higher than the average gross profit on a new Honda. For the executives, selling the company cars was a more discreet transaction than taking gifts for new automobiles — nosy dealers would not be able to detect it without effort, as they could when a load of scarce new Hondas appeared on the front line of a competing dealer. While the monetary loss that Honda may have suffered because of an executive receiving cash for a franchise or extra new cars cannot be quantified, selling used cars for below market value is easily measured. The corporation was being defrauded of the true value of the used cars: The officials were stealing from Honda in this scam, though it was only a crumb of embezzlement compared to schemes they would later concoct.

The biggest buyer of the used vehicles was Norm Reeves Honda, a store located in the Los Angeles suburb of Cerritos, a dealership that in 1992 would overtake Dah Chong Hong's Gardena Honda as the number-one-volume Honda dealer in America. Honda's headquarters had the largest share of company cars for sale, and the responsibility for moving them fell to California zone sales manager Dennis Josleyn. He targeted Norm Reeves Honda as the perfect candidate for a little graft. Josleyn had monitored the dealership's financial statements and knew the enormous amount of profit it generated. Dave Conant, the dealership's co-owner and general manager, was not your typical car man. A sensitive, intelligent man, Conant bore an uncanny resemblance and demeanor to bookish 1960s TV journeyman Wally Cox. Josleyn was aware of the Honda CRX and Ford Bronco that Conant had given to Cardiges. He wanted Conant to pay to play with him, too, but was wary of asking him for a kickback. Rather then spell out what was required up front, Josleyn decided to hammer Conant after the deal was done, figuring the timid Conant would not stand up to him at that point.

Conant was delighted when Josleyn told him in mid-1990 that he could bid on a batch of cars. But he was skeptical about Josleyn's instructions to submit offers $2,000 below market value, figuring other dealers would pay more.

"Dennis, if we bid them two grand light," said Conant, "we won't get these cars."

"Don't worry," laughed Josleyn. "You'll get the cars."

Conant and his used car manager inspected the vehicles and submitted their offers as directed. Conant did not know it, but the fix was in — he was the only dealer in the game. Josleyn had prepared the phony paperwork to document Norm Reeves Honda as the winner. The day after the first go-round, where Norm Reeves Honda was high bidder on all 64 cars available, Conant learned about the hidden agenda. The vehicles were still parked at Honda headquarters when Josleyn showed up unannounced on Conant's showroom floor.

"He handed me an envelope," remembers Conant. "He said, I have a little invoice for you. I didn't ask him what it meant. I just shook his hand and said thank you, and went back up to my office to open the envelope." In the envelope was an invoice for $64,000, payable to Garey and Associates, an advertising firm owned by Josleyn and his brother, Gary. The amount represented $1,000 for each auto the dealership had just purchased, Josleyn not being content to make $300 to $500 per car like other zone sales managers. He had just pulled the equivalent of the 1950s car dealer trick of throwing customers' car keys on the roof of the showroom, holding them hostage until they agreed to buy at the dealers' terms. To Conant, the unspoken message from Josleyn was clear: pay the money or

64 sets of keys will disappear—and I won't be agreeable to helping you get extra new Hondas, either. It was flat-out extortion, rare in the Honda scandal.

Conant paid up. "I believed I had no choice," he says. "If hadn't paid the amount, I would have incurred the wrath of Dennis Josleyn and possibly some of the other Honda gods, and I believe they would have taken our store down." Conant may have been intimidated, but not enough to prevent him from buying (and selling for a hefty profit) 377 more used cars in this manner in 1990 and 1991. He lined Josleyn's pockets with a total of $441,000.

In the grand tradition of the car business, Josleyn and the crew were "curbing" used cars, a technique they had learned on the used car lots of America.

Jim and Effie Cardiges were devoted to each other. Her pet name for her nephew-turned-husband was "Daddy." More than one Honda executive remembers taking his wife to dinner with the Cardigeses and hearing the inevitable question Jim would ask: "Isn't Effie the most beautiful woman in this room?" Mazzitelli recalls the aftermath of his answering in the affirmative: "My wife's kicking me under the table. I was thinking, 'What the hell is my wife, second fiddle?' Afterwards, she said, 'if you ever make me go to dinner with them again. . . .'" Better to offend your wife than the man who holds your career in his hands.

The Cardigeses struggled with one son with a drug problem and another who could not hold a job, even at a Honda dealership, but their life was good in general. Effie spent her days shopping and working out. Jim volunteered at his church and the local YMCA and donated to the Republican National Party. But the Cardigeses' life was really all about image and the money needed to sustain that image.

Jim Cardiges raked it in like none of the others. Cash-filled envelopes from dozens of dealers. Checks as part of Cardiges's split on open point deals. Annual profit disbursements from the Honda dealerships in which he owned a stake. A box stuffed with $250,000 cash from a Washington dealer. Another $250,000 in cash from a Jersey dealer. Christmas presents of up to $50,000 in cash and gift certificates from scores of dealers.

It was not all money. Cardiges's personal needs and his whims to own toys were met by eager dealers. The legal fees for the adoption of his cousins were handled by an East Coast Honda dealer. (The same retailer also paid for the divorces of three other Honda executives.) Dozens of $1,000 suits. Tens of thousands of dollars in home furnishings. All-terrain vehicles. A restored 1965 Mustang. A Porsche 911. A Mitsubishi sports car for Jim and Effie's only son by their marriage, James.

"I only had to wish for something and it was there," says Cardiges.

A few dealers grumbled about Cardiges being demanding when it came to requesting gifts, but all still ponied up. Marty Lustgarten provided the couple with a red Mercedes-Benz 450SL convertible, a car that Effie boldly told Lustgarten's wife to buy for her. Lustgarten wrote a check for $25,000 so the Cardigeses could make a down payment on a Big Bear Lake, California, vacation home. He gave a Honda Civic to one of Jim's daughters. When Cardiges asked him to pay for two $80 rugs during a shopping spree, Lustgarten reached his boiling point. He quietly complied with the sales chief's request but later complained to his wife that Cardiges had become "a goddamn pig."

Cardiges directed a variety of East Coast dealers to give automobiles to his relatives. Uncle Peter Cardiges, Effie's former husband, received a free Honda. Even Cardiges's philanthropic nature was an excuse to hit up dealers for gifts — he directed a Los Angeles dealer to donate an Accord to his Greek Orthodox Church every year.

Jim and Effie made an annual Christmas shopping trek to New York City. Arriving at the Carlisle Hotel toting several empty suitcases, they would visit a few Honda dealers to collect $80,000 or so in cash and then proceed to vacuum up and down Fifth Avenue. They considered buying a condominium in Manhattan for just such occasions.

Effie Cardiges lived the lifestyle she had always dreamed of. Her husband was not allowed to be famous, but at least he was rich. Effie received another Mercedes-Benz, fur coats, and jewelry from various Honda dealers. One retailer gave her $45,000 worth of clothing. The true insiders knew Effie's birthday and forwarded lavish gifts.

Cardiges received more Rolex watches than he could count. He secured so many cars that he had to lease a remote Trabuco Canyon garage to store a dozen of them. He kept $100,000 in greenbacks stored in a paper sack in one of his unrented condominiums. Cardiges was making over $1 million a year beyond his Honda paycheck. He purchased an $850,000 shopping center in Arizona and a dozen Southern California rental properties.

Cardiges's home in Laguna Hills was the ultimate in gifts, so expensive that it took more than one Honda dealer to pay for it.

When Cardiges was promoted to Los Angeles in 1981 to become California zone sales manager, dealer Lustgarten purchased his New Jersey home for $170,000, about $70,000 more than its market value. Cardiges leased a home in Irvine, an hour south of Honda headquarters. In 1983 he mentioned to Honda megadealer Rick Hendrick that he was unable to afford a house in the expensive Southern California market. The remark was made soon after Cardiges helped steer Hendrick toward purchasing the Honda dealership in Corona, California.

Hendrick wasted no time, knowing that Cardiges would someday be the heir apparent to Billmyer. He offered to buy Cardiges's rented home and eventually sell it to him for the original price. Hendrick purchased the house for $305,000 in 1983 and leased it to Cardiges for $1,100 a month, far below Hendrick's mortgage payments. In 1985 Hendrick sold the home back to Cardiges for $305,000, though the value of the home was closer to $400,000 at the time, thanks to skyrocketing California real estate prices. Between the appreciation on the home and the reduced rent, Cardiges gained about $150,000, a rather complicated deal to hide a relatively small gratuity. He would sell the home in 1989 for $515,000.

Over lunch one day Billmyer told Cardiges that it was "stupid" for him to have such an arrangement with Hendrick, a deal the management at Honda, as well as other dealers, could easily discover through a search of real estate records. Billmyer's way was better: his name was on the deed of the house and Hendrick made the payments directly to the NCNB bank in Charlotte. Billmyer again instructed Cardiges to be more discreet in his arrangements with dealers. Cardiges had never listened to Billmyer's warnings before, and he was not about to start now. He had no intention of living in Irvine much longer, anyway — it did not fit his image.

Enter Cardiges's good friend, David Trainer, the owner of Honda and Acura dealerships on the East Coast. Trainer was a player, having slipped Cardiges about $250,000 over the years. He was also a friend of Peter Cardiges. Uncle Peter had been demanding money and harassing Jim and Effie ever since the divorce years earlier. Cardiges once instructed Trainer to contact his uncle and persuade him to leave the couple alone.

Trainer spent several months of the year in California and decided to purchase a second home there. He built a house in Laguna Hills, located in Orange County, the rich-but-dull Los Angeles bedroom community. Trainer's neighborhood was called Nellie Gail, an enclave of homes valued from $500,000 to $1.5 million. Shortly after the home was completed in 1987, Cardiges approached Trainer and mentioned that Effie really liked the home and wanted to buy it. Effie was used to getting whatever she desired, and now she wanted their friend's brand-new home on Buckskin Lane. Trainer agreed to sell it to the couple.

Cardiges bought the home in the summer of 1988, a few months after being promoted to replace the retired Billmyer. The purchase price was

$760,000, the same amount Trainer had paid the year before, giving Cardiges a gain of about $80,000 due to appreciation. As thanks, Cardiges gave Trainer a Mercedes-Benz sedan from his collection of cars hidden away in his storage garage, a vehicle given to Cardiges by another dealer.

Cardiges had recently sold a rental property for a $200,000 profit, enough for a down payment on the home. It was time to call the Rick Hendrick EZ-Payment Mortgage Company. By now, Hendrick had leveraged the extraordinary favoritism he was shown into becoming Honda's biggest dealer, owning 16 Honda and Acura stores. His personal net worth was estimated at over $100 million. Cardiges told Hendrick of his plans to buy the home.

"Can I get any assistance?" asked Cardiges.

"Assistance?" said Hendrick. "Hell, I'll buy the house for you. I know how to handle it because I did the same thing for the Pope."

Hendrick arranged a $528,000 commercial loan to Cardiges through the NCNB bank of Charlotte. He told Cardiges that he would take care of the payments on the note. Evidently deciding that his direct settlements with the bank for house payments, as he had done for Billmyer, could raise suspicion, Hendrick devised a different strategy for Cardiges's note.

Every 90 days for the next four years, Hendrick forwarded an overnight package stuffed with between $15,000 and $20,000 in cash to Cardiges's home. Cardiges deposited the cash, never in individual transactions over $9,999, to avoid the federal cash transaction disclosure law, and mailed his mortgage check to the NCNB bank. During that time, Hendrick acquired ten more Honda and Acura dealerships.

Cardiges preached to his employees the importance of living in the right neighborhood in the right house, and now he was walking the talk. Sitting on an elevated one-third-acre lot behind a gated entrance, the 7,600-square-foot brick English Tudor home featured a domed, octagonal turret, prompting neighborhood children to dub the home "The Castle." Cardiges boasted that the home was worth $1.2 million. Visitors were dragged on a mandatory tour by Jim and Effie, as they showed off the air-conditioned garage and the expensive antiques and paintings. "It looked like a damn museum," said one of Cardiges's friends. Like the hair on their heads, nothing was ever out of place in Jim and Effie's home.

Few possessions in the household had not been purchased by Honda dealers. The exquisite furniture. A black baby grand piano. Closets full of expensive clothing. A karaoke machine. Cardiges prevailed upon Ted Stevens, the dealer who gave the Mercedes-Benz to Amemiya, to spend $103,000 to install a pool, spa, and landscaping at the house. The same retailer had previously shelled out $25,000 for improvements on Cardiges's Irvine home.

Cardiges's Laguna Hills house was the preeminent dealer gift, the monument to all that was wrong inside American Honda. The home was not the largest individual transaction in the scandal, but it was the most visible.

The purchase of a lavish residence is usually the biggest mistake made by a corrupt corporate or government official. Countless cases have been broken by coworkers wondering how one of their peers could afford such a home. Cardiges was officially earning about $140,000 per year but was unconcerned about Honda employees ever seeing his Laguna Hills estate and questioning the source of his finances. The easy anonymity of living in sprawling Los Angeles helped hide his excesses, since Honda people were scattered all over the Southland, many living hours from each other. Honda's human resources department knew Cardiges's address but was clueless about the implications of him living in the bucks-up Orange County community.

Two other desirable Los Angeles neighborhoods had been rejected by Cardiges. High-dollar Beverly Hills might have raised too many eyebrows. Palos Verdes, overlooking the Pacific Ocean and convenient to Honda headquarters, would have been ideal, but American Honda's president lived there in one of several company-owned homes provided for top Japanese executives. Cardiges could not go for a coastline cruise in his Mercedes-Benz with Koichi Amemiya living nearby. And Amemiya would have had the same problem if he had lived near the American officials. Living "behind the Orange Curtain" made the most sense to the sales executives.

Cardiges's non-Honda acquaintances believed a man in his position could afford the Nellie Gail estate. Indeed, had Honda paid him competitively, he could have purchased the house on his salary alone. The only Honda people who knew of Cardiges's home were fellow sales department executives. Honda's Orange County district sales manager made an annual pilgrimage to Laguna Hills—it was his responsibility to rent a truck and pick up Cardiges's Christmas gifts from the Dah Chong Hong dealer group, usually Oriental vases and rugs, that were shipped to Long Beach Harbor from Hong Kong.

The Cardiges home was an annual stop on a "Showcase of Homes" tour by a local charity. The biggest event in the neighborhood was Effie Cardiges's annual yard sale. Neighbors scored great deals on television sets, videocassette recorders, and other duplicate dealer gifts, all still in their unopened boxes. The same people who had grumbled about the Cardigeses purchasing their home for a below-market price, thus lowering the values of their own houses, loved the pristine couple on Buckskin Lane.

Jim and Effie's house and lifestyle was pure excess, in keeping with the image of the 1980s. Cardiges never thought he was doing anything wrong, that it was all just gifts from friends who loved him. Those friends were really only enamored with the cars produced by a band of engineers following the legacy of an eccentric Japanese genius. Most of the dealers could not have cared less about Cardiges, as he would later learn.

If Cardiges's house was the most conspicuous dealer gift, the annual Hong Kong trip was the most blatant payola party.

Most years during the 1980s, American Honda hosted the Holiday in Japan trip, an all-expenses-paid sojourn to Tokyo and Hong Kong for a group of 50 U.S. Honda dealers and their wives. The outing was designed to honor retailers with high customer satisfaction ratings, but the selection process was based more on the generosity of the dealers. Billmyer and Cardiges were careful not to invite more than one dirty dealer from the same market, so as not to create any conflicts.

Billmyer and Cardiges, along with a half-dozen zone and regional sales managers, hosted the dealers and their spouses. The group spent a week in Japan, touring both the Honda factories and local tourist spots, sometimes accompanied by the then-retired Soichiro Honda. The American contingent said good-bye to Honda's Japanese executives at a farewell dinner party and then flew to Hong Kong, where the real soiree commenced. Wives of the officials were forbidden by the Japanese from attending company functions, so the executives had dealers spring for their spouses' airfares to join them in Hong Kong.

With no pesky Japanese bosses around, a band of cash-laden dealers, and the duty-free Hong Kong stores, the holiday was a Honda executive's dream. One dealer wore a money belt stuffed with $100,000 in cash to spend on the gang. The Dah Chong Hong dealer group was on its home turf and knew where to spend the $25,000 it had allocated each trip for Cardiges and Billmyer. Dealers earmarked a lesser amount to spend on their zone sales managers than for the top duo. The executives carefully scheduled the retailers: roam the stores with one dealer, return to the hotel to drop off the booty, and then hook up with another dealer. One retailer's method made the process easier—he would hand over his credit card and tell the execs to go have fun. The take included the usual assortment of gifts: Rolex watches, clothing, vases, artwork, and sometimes just good old cash.

Shopping by day and partying by night, the Honda officials were on top of the world. The dozens of reminders the week before, so apparent during the tours of Honda's plants and research and development departments, of the real reason why the executives were being treated like kings were forgotten.

Yee-Honda! We had too much fun at American Honda during the Decade of Greed. Even if you did not gather gifts from Honda dealers, it was still a "euphoric atmosphere," as our leader Car-Jesus liked to say. The smiling worker bees in our farmland factory in Ohio cranked out the best-quality cars in America. Customers and dealers begged for more Hondas. People traded in automobiles impulsively, and it seemed they all wanted new Accords or Civics in their driveways. It did not hurt that the 1980s was the biggest decade for automobile sales in U.S. history. Honda's sales in America nearly doubled between 1980 and 1990.

Ours was a company with a focused vision. As Detroit automakers turned their profits into acquiring nonautomotive businesses, we reinvested in product and factories. We exported Ohio-built Accords back to Japan, yet another move to be copied by other "transplant" Japanese automakers.

The press did a ten-year-long swoon. Industry analyst Maryann Keller told *Fortune* magazine in 1985, "I can't think of anything that will stop Honda's momentum." One journalist deemed the spirit at American Honda headquarters as being akin to that of the Kennedy White House. Maybe, but the skullduggery was pure Nixon.

The awards came in caps. R. L. Polk and Company said Honda was Number One in Owner Loyalty. J. D. Power and Associates said Honda was Number One in Customer Satisfaction. Honda automobiles captured the *Motor Trend* magazine Import Car of the Year Award three times. Hondas dominated *Car and Driver* magazine's annual Ten Best Cars in the World list. The Honda Accord became the Best-Selling Car in America in 1989, an accomplishment never before achieved by a car outside of the Detroit circle.

Best of all, the dealers, the God-blessed Honda retailers of America, were Kissing Our Royal Butts.

It was intoxicating. Honda was no place for the insecure or the morally or financially bankrupt. Some overlooked the fact that the automobiles were the true keys to Honda's success. I personally made you rich, Mr. Millionaire Honda Dealer, so you had better bow down, we thought. We'd stroll onto a showroom floor and be greeted like a customer paying cash for three Accords. Dealer principals who hid from their Buick reps rolled out the red carpet for us; if we had been representing any other automaker, the same dealer would not have given us the time of day. Or the Rolex.

We were myopic, believing the Honda world was perfect. Dealers asked: why doesn't Honda build pickups? Our college-educated clientele will never buy trucks, we laughed. What about sport-utility vehicles? Just a fad. Minivans? We're going to build an Accord station wagon. Collapse of the dollar? We have the Marysville plant. Detroit catching us? Get a clue. The market changing? No way. (Japanese execs firing us for our shenanigans? Get real. They know the score and they don't care.)

We snickered about the unwashed dealers whose Christmas presents to us were a bottle of wine or a canned ham. Ed Temple once received a large fruit basket from a dealer and in disgust gave it to his next-door neighbor. The man knocked on Temple's door the next morning and said: Ed, we can't accept this gift, we hardly know you. Temple had missed the video camera concealed beneath the fruit. The number of $100 bills hidden below the bottom layer of candy that were thrown out by Honda executives may never be known. We did not write thank-you notes, after all.

We did compare notes, though. The clothes. The watches. The cars. We were treated to meals in the finest restaurants. We never had to pay for a round of golf. We never rented cars while on vacation, since a dealer at our destination would supply us with a Honda.

The rumor mill cranked: Two delivery trucks bearing gifts collided in front of Cardiges's house. . . . Pisano got a Porsche Cabriolet. . . . Novelly wrecked a speedboat given to him by a dealer. . . . To cover for an accident caused by a drunken Honda executive, a Chicago dealer repaired two smashed cars for free. . . . Cocaine and Kruggerands are the favored gifts in Florida. . . . Most of the whispers turned out to be true.

We aspired to become zone sales managers, men with the power to grant new franchises and sell the company's used cars. Men who scored the equivalent of a year's salary in Christmas gifts without even asking. Men who traveled to the Far East for the dealer-paid shopping extravaganza. Men who lived by a Billmyer slogan: "Honda doesn't pay us enough and the dealers pay us too much."

We worked the program. We knew the buzz phrases: The G and C

Account. He's a player. How is Christmas in your territory? What dealer number is on your Corvette? Nice $49 suit you got there. Have a dealer handle it.

Live like a millionaire.

We were the envy of other automobile companies. The customers loved their Hondas. The Honda dealers loved us. Anything we wanted was ours for the asking.

God, it was a wonderful time

We only had one problem. We did not know exactly how many cars we were selling.

CHAPTER 8

Flushing the Cards

> You gotta know when to hold 'em and know when to fold 'em.
>
> —Poker players' adage

SOMEWHERE OVER Waco, I broke the law at the urging of American Honda. Flying from San Antonio to Dallas on a warm Friday afternoon in early 1984, I prepared the precious package for delivery to the Honda zone office in suburban Irving. The Honda dealership where I worked knew its future depended on my delivering the goods. It had to arrive by 5:00 P.M. or our profits would plummet and I would be relegated to washing used cars come Monday. I was nervous, this being my first task in the world of Honda espionage. My plane landed at Dallas Love Field at 4:00 P.M. and I hailed a cab. By the time we passed Dallas/Fort Worth airport at 4:30, I knew we had a problem—the driver was lost. Several U-turns later, I spotted a Honda Accord with dealer license plates rolling rapidly in the opposite direction. We turned around and the Honda led us to the zone office, where its passenger and I jumped out to deliver our wares.

An envelope stuffed with $100 bills for the zone sales manager? Plane tickets to Aruba for Jim Cardiges? No, my cargo was 60 falsified retail delivery registration (RDR) cards, worth their weight in Accords. These RDR cards, also known as sales cards or warranty cards, were the documents that notified American Honda of the sale of a vehicle. The 3″ by 8″ forms included pertinent information on both the vehicle and the purchasing customer. Since the Hondas in question were still parked on our lot, I filled out the cards with names and addresses of friends, family members, and phonies from the phone book. We were informed of an impending allocation of cars by our Honda district sales manager and were told to falsify, or "burn," our cards. An allocation was the key part of Honda's car distribution system, the day designated for calculating the number and models of cars a dealer would receive the following month. Any reported deliveries would increase our sales history, or "travel rate," and any cars showing in our inventory would count against us and lower our allotment. The faster you sold cars, the more cars you would be allocated, referred to in the industry as "turn and earn." At Honda, it was more like burn and earn.

Submitting dummy sales cards was part of the monthly allocation dance, where our dealership earned more hot-selling Hondas and made more money — and Honda could report inflated sales figures to the press. Only consumers would lose, since their cars' warranty clocks began ticking when the bogus cards were submitted, before they actually bought their automobiles. Customers also would not receive important recall notices. The practice was a violation of a myriad of state and federal consumer laws. Falsifying RDR cards may not have been corrupt, but it was another symptom of a company out of control. Other automakers encourage the practice periodically, but, like the kickback activities, nobody did it longer or better than Honda.

It was more of the lawless Honda world: Burn the cards, beat up the customers, and bribe the corrupt. Anything goes.

The number-one priority of Honda's Japanese officials was achieving retail sales objectives. The corporation made money only on the "wholesale" transactions — when Honda sold automobiles to the dealers — but the number of cars retailed by the dealers determined bragging rights. Honda wanted to be able to announce another record sales month or year, to boast about the Accord's race to become the best-selling car in America, and to keep pressure on the Japanese government to ease the Voluntary Restraint Agreement. So we cheated.

Card burning began in the early 1980s, when Honda suffered some soft sales months and began to encourage dealers to "prereport" sales, by filling out RDR cards with the names of customers who had committed to buying a particular car but had yet to take delivery. The prereporting was done just prior to the end of a month, because Honda reported sales figures to Tokyo headquarters and to the media on the first day of each month. Card burning slowly became flat-out cheating by dealers, who discovered that by submitting phony cards, they would receive more scarce Honda automobiles and bolster their profits. Honda started encouraging the practice by scheduling allocations just before month's end, so dealers would input bogus sales to increase their allotments. The cars will sell to somebody in a few days anyway, the Honda officials rationalized. By the mid-1980s, Honda's actual deliveries had fallen about 25,000 units behind its cumulative "official" sales figures as measured by RDR cards. Each month, Honda was robbing Peter to pay Paul.

Like the Japanese officials, our futures were determined by our territory's sales numbers. The pressure on us to force dealers to report false sales was tremendous. A district or zone sales manager could hit his annual sales objective and still not be considered for promotion. What mattered was consistently coercing dealers to falsify sales on the days the Japanese executives said "go," always at month end, often at the end of the industry's ten-day sales reporting periods, and sometimes on seemingly random days.

We snapped our fingers and sales numbers skyrocketed. American Honda president Koichi Amemiya would walk into Jim Cardiges's cube and say: "It's time to get on the golden telephones," his way of hinting that we need a good sales day. Thus would begin the Japanese fire drill. The word passed from national to regional to zone sales managers that dealers needed to report sales immediately. As a district sales manager, it was my responsibility to pass the message to the dealers, just as word had come down to me when I worked at Honda dealerships. We were warned to never explicitly tell a retailer to falsify RDR cards, but instead to hint, to talk about impending allocations, anything to say it without really saying it. "Keep those cards and letters coming," was the popular code phrase passed to the dealers. But when time was short to notify 20 dealers, the district sales manager's message was more succinct: "Burn 'em!"

We were breaking the law and creating havoc in the dealerships. Errol Dauenhauer manages the sales department of a Mississippi Honda dealer and remembers the frantic days Honda would ring the bell. "We would always have a truckload of cars arrive late in the day," he says. "I would climb up onto the greasy transporter in my three-piece suit, rip the RDR cards off the window stickers of the cars, run to my office, fill them out with whatever names I could think of, and rush to Federal Express. It was insane." Some rural dealers chartered airplanes to deliver the paperwork directly to their Honda zone offices. Dealers were forced to implement complicated inventory systems to assure that they first sold cars whose sales had already been reported, as opposed to the standard dealership practice of selling the oldest units first. Honda's reported sales for the first half of a month were dismal, as dealers were only moving vehicles with "burned" cards. Sales during the final week of a month would often total 70 percent of the month's tally, as the monthly allocation was imminent and the bonfires were lit.

Sometimes the dealers went overboard and reported 80,000 sales in one month, smashing Honda's all-time monthly sales record and perhaps representing 20,000 more than reality. In those instances, we backed down the publicly announced number to one from the 28th or 29th of the month, so as not to arouse suspicion within the industry.

Creative retailers used the RDR card system to intercept Honda's customer satisfaction surveys, which measured buyers' experiences with the selling dealer. By filling out the forms that had been mailed to bogus customers, the dealers saved the expense of bribing real customers with $20 bills or free oil changes to return the blank survey to the dealership, as many dealers did. The retailer would then post near-perfect scores for customer handling. They would thus become eligible for factory-sponsored trips and, more importantly, not have to listen to Honda officials grind on them about improving their customer handling skills. In the short-term, shortcut dealer mentality of the 1980s, it was more important to make Honda think you were treating customers well than actually doing it.

The acknowledged King of the Cards, wily Southern California dealership manager John Gritter, claims to have created the phony-customer survey response scheme, as well as the practice of renting post office boxes to use as addresses of the nonexistent buyers. "Honda could never figure out what we were doing," says Gritter.

The chaos all this caused in dealerships eased in 1985, when Honda established a dealer communication network called Hondanet. Honda was the last major carmaker to implement a computerized linkup with its retailers. The dealers could now sit at computer terminals and dump warranty cards. Honda's distribution managers were overjoyed — they previously had to manually enter thousands of sales on card-burning days. Overnight delivery services reported a drop in revenue.

The most outrageous component of prereported sales was the Honda policy that required us to perform audits on dealers' sales records to ensure they were not cheating. We had the power to punish: we could decrease a dealer's allocation one car for each violation we found. This audit policy was instituted to cover our rears if the cards ever hit the fan with a government agency.

On the one hand we instructed dealers to falsify sales, and on the other we could penalize them for doing just that. Dealers thought we were nuts. They hid their unsold "sold" cars on remote lots on audit days, fearful of us "catching" them. We were directed to document one or two false registrations per dealer per audit, so Honda could prove it was monitoring dealers uniformly in case of a lawsuit. I know of few instances of a dealer actually being charged back cars on an allocation as the result of our audits.

My audits were training sessions showing dealers how to cook the books. My years in the retail Honda business made me an expert on how to deal with the RDRs. We kept two sets of sales records at the Honda stores I worked at, one that was accurate and one for Honda's audits. We composed complex folders with detailed information on each ghost customer to fool our Honda rep. The dealers I called on soon learned the right way to falsify sales records. The Southern California dealer who once registered Mickey Mouse and Donald Duck as proud owners of new Accords on RDR cards clearly did not have the proper tutoring from his factory representative on the subtleties of cheating properly.

The Honda system allowed the dealers to officially cover their tracks by submitting a customer update form to Honda when a previously falsified auto was actually delivered. Few dealers bothered to do that paperwork, so many Honda buyers never received information on recalls or other pertinent information from the factory.

Honda dealers were not the only ones shuffling papers to perpetuate this policy. Since Honda's computerized sales reports were worthless, on the first day of each month Honda district sales managers had to contact dealers and do a "Sales and Inventory Report"—we called it the "How Many Cars Did You Really Sell Last Month and How Many Cars Do You Really Have Report." The paperwork was instituted by the Japanese officials, who kept close watch on the number of "gray cars," their euphemism for unsold units with burned sales cards.

When the market for Hondas softened in the early 1990s, Honda dealers began to carry an industry-average 60 days' supply of cars, but no one besides the sales executives had any idea exactly how many that was. Regional fluctuations in demand for particular models could not be identified. The Honda personnel who needed sales and inventory figures the most, those in product planning and production, did not have a clue that things were changing, as sales execs closely guarded the "real" numbers. Instead, they relied on the limited information available from figures provided by R. L. Polk and Company, the firm that tracks automobile registrations nationwide. Those numbers were not available until 90 days after a particular month, an eternity in the fast-changing car business.

In 1989 I devised a document for Honda of Hollywood to counter confusion caused by the card-burning practice. The California dealer was one of the first to sign up for floorplanning from Honda's fledgling finance arm, American Honda Finance Corporation. Floorplanning, or "flooring," is the money a bank loans a dealer to buy automobiles from the factory. When a dealer sells a car, he is required to immediately pay off the loan on that particular unit from the proceeds of the sale. Failure to do so places the dealer "out of trust," the car business equivalent of defaulting on a loan. Being Honda's captive finance arm, Honda Finance is the only financial institution with access to Honda's sales records. When it noticed Honda of Hollywood had reported the sale of 50 cars and had not reimbursed the company, Honda Finance canceled the dealer's credit line and any further shipments of automobiles. Of course, the dealership had falsified the RDRs as it had been doing for years. Dealer principal Bill Robertson was furious, knowing an interruption in the flow of Hondas meant decreased profits. I explained the realities of Honda's sales division policies to Honda Finance and worked out an arrangement where the dealer would fax the subsidiary a list of cars with falsified sales cards.

In 1990 the state of California, at the urging of San Francisco area Honda dealer William Shepherd, threatened to initiate an investigation into Honda dealers falsifying warranty registrations. Shepherd did not participate in the card burning and had watched his allocations evaporate. The state considered taking action against Honda and any dealers who participated in the scheme. My boss, California zone sales manager Dennis Josleyn, informed me and the other six district sales managers of the state's inquiry. Our first thought was, thank God, we can finally stop playing this stupid game. The elation lasted about ten seconds.

"I don't give a shit about the California district attorney or anyone else," said Josleyn. "I can win a trip to Japan as the zone manager who hits the highest percent of his sales objective, and I *will* win it. We have over 5,000 cars not reported sold. I want you to call every one of your dealers and have them report every car sold by tonight." When we asked about possible resistance from dealers concerned about the state taking action if they complied, Josleyn retorted, "That's a risk they'll have to take. Them not receiving any cars because they wouldn't play along is a bigger risk."

After Josleyn left the room, assistant zone sales manager Jim Mortimer remarked, "If we ever get caught, we're all going to jail for this." Honda dealers in California sold 5,000 cars that day, about 11 times more than on an average day. Josleyn was happy.

By 1990 Honda was averaging approximately 30,000 "gray cars" on dealers' lots on most days. On the first day of a month, the count could be as high as 60,000 — more than half of the actual number of cars on the ground and a figure higher than an entire month's sales. The Honda service division personnel, who administered warranty claims, would usually pay any claim that fell in the gray area — the typical one- to four-week period after the expiration of the car's warranty, a time frame corresponding with the delay between the date the car was reported sold and the date a customer actually bought it. Fortunately, Honda automobiles rarely suffered major calamities during their three-year warranty period. As the market weakened, some "gray cars" began to sit unsold for six months or more, creating a larger warranty shortage for consumers. Honda's service people began to balk. The threat from the state of California and the clambering from the service division forced the sales division to fix the problem.

Dealers were skeptical when informed that we were cleaning up the sales reporting system in 1991. At the time, they had their biggest carrot ever to falsify sales: cash. Honda's sales were slipping that year, and it instituted its most lucrative series of dealer cash incentives ever, up to $1,000 for each car reported sold. The incentives changed monthly and dealers never knew what the next program would bring, so they continued to burn RDR cards to earn money, a hedge against the incentive dollars dropping.

The cleanup began with zone offices receiving monthly objectives from the Japanese executives for reducing the number of "gray cars" on dealer's lots. Armed with R. L. Polk registration reports, we audited the dealers and compared names on the cards to the actual owners of the cars. Under penalty of chargebacks of incentives already paid, most dealers took us seriously and stopped falsifying sales cards. The fact that the demand for Hondas was softening, and dealers were no longer screaming for cars, helped the transition. By the end of 1991 the system was about 90 percent purified.

American Honda had to pay a public relations penalty, though. In 20 years of selling automobiles in the United States, Honda's sales increased every year except for 1 percent dips in both 1981 and 1982, due to the Voluntary Restraint Agreement, and a 2 percent drop in 1986. Calendar-year sales for 1991, based on dealer-reported warranty cards, totaled 659,659 cars, an 8 percent decrease from the record 716,495 vehicles sold in 1990. The sales drop was noted by the press as a sign of the end of the Honda Halo. However, with car sales nationwide plunging 12 percent in the war- and recession-marred year, Honda still looked good. In reality, Honda's true 1991 sales, based on R. L. Polk registrations and dealers' financial statements, were approximately 685,000 units. The 25,000 car differential over the official sales figure represented the cars falsely reported as sold in late 1990 and actually delivered in 1991, a number equal to the average number of "gray cars" on dealers' lots at any one time during 1990.

The transition period from bogus to truthful sales reporting gave the mercenary Honda officials another opportunity to snare more pocket change. A few favored dealers were granted unspoken exemptions from punitive action as the result of discrepancies found in the audits. They could still char RDR cards and reap the financial benefits of Honda's incentive money. Honda executives notified friendly dealers of impending cash programs and to "hold their cards," or not report legitimate sales, until the incentives started. The dealers responded in kind to their benevolent zone sales managers.

The changing market conditions signaled the end to the most common corrupt transaction between Honda official and dealer — the zone manager "selling" extra cars to his favorite retailers through the manipulation of Honda's automobile allocation system. Honda had no written agreement with its dealers about the distribution of automobiles. The only stipulation in the Sales and Service Agreement, the franchise compact between Honda and the dealers, stated that Honda "reserves full discretion in accepting orders and allocating and distributing Honda Products, and its judgment and decision in such matters will be final." The document stated that Honda had an obligation to distribute cars in a "fair and reasonable manner," the only caveat to Honda having total control over the process. An explanation of the system was available to dealers, but few took the time to educate themselves and many were cynical about the integrity of the procedures. Dealers could not order cars from Honda — they were at the mercy of the allocation system and the Honda execs.

A dealer could be made or broken through manipulation of the allocation system. In 1987 Norm Reeves Honda of Cerritos, California, made the mistake of filing a protest with the California Department of Motor Vehicles over Honda attempting to relocate a dealership to neighboring Downey. Said Norm Reeves's co-owner David Conant, "Ultimately Honda began taking the store down, and the sales records and allocation records show that Honda's allocation to Norm Reeves was systematically reduced over a period of about fifteen months, and the decline was nearly 50 percent." It took Norm Reeves Honda two years to recover from the punitive action. It later became Honda's number-one-volume dealership, but the memory of Honda's actions haunted Conant and led him to join in on the bribery, including paying Josleyn for Honda company cars.

"The allocation system was wrought with fraud. It was useless," says former Honda executive Roger Novelly. With dealers reporting all their cars sold prior to an allocation, it was difficult for a dealer to earn more cars and increase his sales volume. His piece of the zone's car pie would remain constant. An influx of additional Hondas would mean instant profits today and more cars tomorrow, since the chosen dealer's sales rate would increase.

Dealers' allocations rose and fell through the manipulation by Honda executives of the distribution of "port cars," a component of the allocation system. Honda's ten zone sales territories each had a varying number of cars to distribute each month, based on Japan and Ohio plant production. The zone allocated 85 percent of these autos, based on computer calculations of dealers' sales rates and inventories, with the result of each dealer being allocated an equal days' supply of product. The zone offices held back 15 percent of these cars to be distributed at the zone sales manager's discretion. These so-called port cars were supposed to be sent to dealers who built new facilities, had inventory levels below the zone's average, or were superior dealers, but Honda brass found other justification.

Port car payola was the mainstay of a semicrooked Honda executive's corruption, for those who did not sell franchises. There were always extra automobiles to distribute and dealers who would pay for them. As in most of the graft transactions, there was no quid pro quo to determine the chosen gifts from dealer to executive, no promise of "I will give you $500 for each extra car you allocate to me." A steady stream of random presents to the official, or one expensive Christmas gift, would buy the right for a dealer to receive port cars upon request. Every dealer pleaded for extra Hondas, but the corrupt dealers were taken care of first. A dealer who rarely received bonus cars would watch his allocations shrink.

Megadealer Rick Hendrick's buying homes for Honda officials theoretically meant an unlimited supply of port cars whenever he desired, but Hendrick took no chances. Concerned that paying off the top people was not enough insurance, Hendrick also bribed Honda's clerical help. Each zone employed a traffic assistant responsible for converting the allocation into the actual shipments of cars by working with the trucking and rail companies. Hendrick's brother and partner, John, paid Honda's North Carolina zone traffic assistant Bonnie Sikora over $120,000 in exchange for her slipping their dealerships additional automobiles. The Hendrick dealer organization was one of the few to grease the entire Honda hierarchy, from national sales manager to clerk.

It was not always the raw number of cars that mattered in the port distribution. When the market slowed, whatever was hot selling, say a green Accord coupe, would be the car of choice by the favored dealer. Being able to call Honda and order specific cars was a dealer's dream, and some had that opportunity.

Honda inadvertently developed a second distribution channel for its automobiles due to the inequities in the allocation system. If a dealer did not earn enough cars through the system, he would have to turn to automobile brokers, who bought Hondas from oversupplied dealers. Many desperate retailers bought cars directly from favored dealers, paying from $300 to $1,000 over invoice and without the RDR card, so they could not increase their allocations. "We would have our trucks sitting at (a dirty New York Honda dealer)," says one New England dealer principal. "They would unload the cars from the Honda car carriers and reload them onto ours." For consumers in markets where the distribution was influenced by the bribery, it was an inconvenience to find a Honda dealer with a good selection of automobiles — but that was generally the case during the 1980s anyway.

Most retailers were convinced that their neighboring dealers were in bed with Honda officials when it came to getting more and better models of cars. One favorite pastime of such owners was cruising other Honda dealerships' lots at night to count their cars. Sometimes the slighted dealer was correct about his suspicions, particularly when the evidence was obvious. When my San Antonio store and our cross-town rival both had a two-month waiting list for cars in 1983, a Houston Honda dealer had 300 vehicles parked on his lot. It was a clear display of Honda's problems and no amount of "they sell more cars and thus they earn more" rhetoric from the factory could appease us. The distribution system was supposed to give all retailers a near-equal days' supply of cars, meaning we should have had 60 Hondas in stock to correspond with the Houston dealer's inventory. We had zero. All we could do was pray that our customers in abeyance did not visit Houston.

A dealer howling that a nearby store was receiving preferential treatment would be quickly gagged. "Give him some cars to shut him up," was the Honda kickback club's slogan. A wily zone sales manager would fool such a "whiner" by distributing port cars to him just prior to an allocation, so the autos could not arrive in time for the dealer to sell them before the allocation. Under Honda's curious system, these cars still in transit lowered a dealer's allotment the same as unsold cars, negating any increase in the dealer's travel rate. By making that move, the factory man exploited the dealer's inherent short-term thinking. The dealer would be happy, since he could make some fast cash, not knowing he had actually fallen behind and would earn fewer cars in the next allocation.

With the debut of a new Honda model, zone sales managers salivated at the prospect of some extra payola and would distribute the cars accordingly. When Honda introduced the Accord wagon in January 1991, it and the dealers were convinced the car would be a sales smash, despite the fact that families were buying minivans in record numbers. Dennis Josleyn seized the opportunity by allocating the first Accord wagons at will, giving most retailers in California one each and divvying up the rest among his buddies, 8 to 16 apiece to those who had paid him off. This blatant action literally had dealers screaming at me and the other district sales managers — the heat shields for our boss, Josleyn. The clean dealers had the last laugh when it became clear that the public had little interest in the Accord wagon. It took some of Josleyn's beneficiaries over six months to unload their wagons, most at a deep discount. Unfortunately for those dealers, there was no money-back guarantee on Josleyn's graft.

Industry observers wondered whether Honda's practice of prereporting its sales influenced the corporation's crowning triumph of the 1980s: the Accord becoming the best-selling car in America in 1989.

Sales of the Accord totaled 362,707 units in 1989, unseating the Ford Escort, the top-selling car in 1987 and 1988, and beating the Ford Taurus by 15,000 units. The 1989 registration figures verified Accord's top spot, the numbers being close to what Honda had reported to the press. The 30,000 Accord sales cards that Honda falsified in late 1989 were balanced by the 30,000 Accords delivered in early 1989 but reported as sold in late 1988. The Accord truly was number one.

It was a stunning achievement for Honda, the first time a "foreign" car had been the best-selling automobile in the United States. Honda's understated advertising campaign thanked Honda customers and dealers for making the Accord number one and reminded the public that over 60 percent of the Accords sold were built in Marysville, Ohio. The Accord's crown stuck in Detroit's craw — one week after the announcement, Chrysler Corporation chairman Ben Bidwell accused Japan of being an economic aggressor bent on eroding America's industrial base. It was more finger-pointing from a corporation that was watching American Honda's automobile sales close in on its own.

Achieving the sales award for the Accord was never a corporate objective. It happened as much due to Honda's model management as to the car's popularity. Automakers sold every car they built during the 1980s, so it came down to which manufacturer built the most numbers of one single model. The proliferation of domestic models paved the way for a Japanese automaker to boost one of its cars to the top. With Honda's lineup consisting of only three models — the Accord, Civic, and Prelude — as opposed to Toyota's seven and Nissan's six, Honda cruised to an easy victory. If Toyota or Nissan had devoted 60 percent of its production to one vehicle, as Honda did with the Accord, that auto might have become the top-selling car in America.

Honda dedicating so much if its production to one model was a huge risk. If the Accord had suffered a major recall to fix a safety-related defect, or come under attack from one of the trial lawyer–funded "safety" agencies or consumer publications, Honda and its dealers would have been in deep trouble. The corporation profited about $3,000 for each Accord sold to a dealer, while Civics only brought around $1,000 apiece. Certainly Honda would have been able to quickly develop a new vehicle if the Accord stumbled, but the loss of momentum and profits would have been staggering.

The Accord reigned as the best-selling car in America for three years, until the Ford Taurus wrestled the crown away in 1992. By dumping 50 percent of its Tauruses into fleet and rental car companies at subsidized prices, and providing a heavy burst of year-end customer incentives, Ford basically bought the sales achievement. Sales of the Taurus roared from 299,659 units in 1991 to 409,751 in 1992, besting the Accord by 16,000 cars. The Accord had crushed the Taurus by almost 100,000 units in each of the previous two years. More than twice as many Accords as Tauruses were purchased by consumers in 1992, but Ford now owned the bragging rights. When retail registration figures released in March showed that the Accord remained the number-one-selling car to individual customers, Honda officials declined to brag about it in their advertising. It would sound like sour grapes, they said.

Ford may have also used an old Honda trick to boost Taurus sales. "I just found out that I 'bought' a Taurus in December," confided a grinning Ford executive during the hoopla launched by Ford to crow about the Taurus beating the Accord, "but it's not exactly in my driveway yet."

Sales figures based on bogus warranty card registrations was not the only fib we spread in the automotive world.

One of American Honda's primary objectives during the 1980s was to increase the number of exclusive Honda dealerships. We wanted the dealers to concentrate on Honda and not be distracted by the demands of other, usually inferior, franchises under the same roof. Honda customers on the service drive watching an Oldsmobile owner screaming about his or her car's mechanical woes and the dealer's inability to fix them would not further the image of our dealerships. Dealers with Honda and another brand sharing the showroom were pushed to move the other franchise elsewhere or to build a new dealership devoted exclusively to Honda.

Nearly every Honda franchise established before 1980 had begun as a so-called "dual" dealership, and most had made the move to exclusive

Honda buildings by the mid-1980s. Despite the fact that the exclusive requirement was not on Honda's franchise agreement with the dealers, since it was in violation of some state laws, new Honda points granted during the 1980s would not be approved if the dealer proposed a dual showroom. Even Honda executives who granted franchises in exchange for cash followed that mandate.

We did not provide assistance to dealers building new facilities, as did other automakers. We offered no architectural help, no financial backing, nothing but the promise of an injection of several loads of new Hondas upon opening. We had no standardized facility plans for dealers to adhere to. Approving building plans was the responsibility of the overworked sales division executives, because Honda lacked a dealership development department (with experts in facility design and construction), standard for other automakers. Without guidelines to follow, some Honda dealers built truly outstanding new facilities and others erected dumps.

We took better care of dealers who spent several million dollars on exclusive facilities, those who were totally committed to Honda. Favoring one dealer over another for any reason was against numerous franchise laws, so it was done quietly. A better selection of cars and more timely information on Honda programs would go to the exclusive dealers. Phone calls would be returned quicker. Go call Pontiac, we would tell a dual dealer screaming for cars. The few exclusive Honda dealers who suffered financial problems and considered adding another brand to their dealerships were given veiled threats about decreased allocations of cars.

Honda was lauded by trade publications for having the highest exclusivity rate in the industry among volume franchises, 80 percent, the number we supplied to the press in the late 1980s. It was a badge of honor in the car business, an indication of dealers' confidence in the factory. Jim Cardiges bragged about the number at dealer meetings, displaying a chart of Honda dealers' progress at becoming exclusive.

In reality, we were not being truthful about the percentage of exclusive Honda dealerships. The number was only about 70 percent, still not a bad accomplishment. We had scores of dualed dealerships that we claimed sold only Hondas. Exclusive facilities were extremely important to the Japanese officials at Honda, and the sales division executives did not want them to know the truth: part of their job evaluations were based on the number of Honda-dedicated dealerships within their territories.

When I questioned why a suburban Los Angeles dealer was on the exclusive list, despite selling two other makes of automobiles from his Honda showroom, I was told to never mention that fact to anybody. The dealer principal in question was tight with Cardiges, and his store had been granted exclusive status. It was another benefit to being a dirty dealer and a way for Honda to inflate the exclusivity numbers, both to brag to the media and to pressure other dealers to build separate Honda facilities. I never brought up the subject of the two other dual stores in my territory that were also listed as exclusive.

The issue of exclusive dealerships was just another little secret in the Honda world, but it would take center stage at Acura, the new luxury car division established by American Honda in 1986.

CHAPTER 9

The Acura Disaster

Don't get above your raisings

— Country saying

IT SEEMED like another bold move by American Honda. With the 1986 rollout of the Acura automobile division, Honda created another market segment all to itself to sell a luxury line of Japanese cars in America. It was just part of a heady year for Honda. The company dominated the circuits in its return to international Formula One auto racing. J. D. Power and Associates ranked Honda the top automobile for customer satisfaction. Honda's corporate profits were at an all-time high. American Honda's sales were soaring and would rise 16 percent in 1986, led by a stylish new Accord. Honda had overtaken Nissan as the number-two-selling imported car in America and was closing in on leader Toyota. Slack-jawed Detroit automaker executives toured Honda's Marysville, Ohio, plant, realizing they could never reproduce Honda's atmosphere or production efficiency in their own factories. Other Japanese carmakers were scrambling to follow Honda's lead and build plants in America. Everyone was chasing Honda, and it seemed the new Acura division would be another runaway success.

Unfortunately, the evil that lurked inside American Honda headquarters and some strategic errors caused Acura to be a rare failure for Honda. The concept was brilliant, the execution bumbling.

With the Ohio plant building automobiles that did not count against the Voluntary Restraint Agreement, Honda had the flexibility to shift production in Japan to a new line of cars. Honda's allotment under the VRA had risen to 429,000 cars by 1986, while Toyota was allowed to import 621,000 and Nissan 548,000. The Ohio facility was building 220,000 cars annually and was two years away from full capacity of 360,000 units.

Honda was finishing construction of an engine plant in Anna, Ohio, and a factory in Ontario to supply Civics to both Canada and America. Plans were being finalized for a second auto factory in East Liberty, Ohio. Honda predicted production capacity and imports totaling nearly 1 million automobiles per year for America by 1989. Part of the plan to move these cars was to develop a larger distribution channel, so the Acura division was born.

The Japanese automakers had awakened Detroit in the 1970s, and now the haughty European companies could hear the alarm clock ringing. Acura's strategy was to market upscale automobiles to Honda's older and more affluent customers, those trading in their Accords for European brands, and to conquest current owners of luxury imports. Selling cars in the luxury category meant more than building a good product — such buyers desire a car with image and prestige, something to impress the neighbors. They tolerated the dubious quality and outrageous repair costs of their BMWs and Jaguars so they could pull up to the country club in the latest trendy machines. Acura's plan was to offer these consumers a luxury automobile with anvil-like reliability at a price $10,000 less than an entry-level Mercedes-Benz — and hopefully one with a prestigious image. The American carmakers had no product to counter Acura — just as they had had none to compete with Honda in the 1970s — and few prospects in this segment would consider a domestic automobile anyway.

The two cars developed for Acura's 1986 debut were Honda-terrific. The flagship was the luxurious Legend four-door sedan, powered by a silky-smooth 24-valve V-6 engine and a car a foot longer than an Accord. The Legend was the largest and most expensive car ever to come from Japan. It possessed the tightness and performance of the target German cars. Curiously, the Legend had no leather interior available the first year, a glaring omission for a luxury automobile. The Civic-sized Integra was available in both two- and four-door models and was powered by a high-performance four-cylinder engine. Its zippy acceleration and sporty image placed it in competition with the Honda Prelude, much to the dismay of Honda dealers. Acura was also developing a Legend two-door coupe to be introduced in early 1987, a challenge to the expensive European luxury coupes but for half their price.

Establishing an image from scrap meant Acura needed to divorce itself from the utilitarian Honda. Acura developing a reputation as an expensive Honda would not do. The key component of this strategy was to establish a separate dealer network to sell Acuras. "We felt that Honda can't be all things to all people," said Honda executive vice president Tom Elliott.

"The potential buyer of a deluxe car such as a Mercedes-Benz feels uneasy about making an expensive purchase from a company that also makes a $7,000 car."

Establishing a separate distribution channel for Acura was deemed by industry analysts as both innovative and risky, but Honda was simply following the legacy of its founders. Takeo Fujisawa had created separate dealership networks for both the motorcycle and automobile divisions in Japan. His tactics stemmed from a cash flow problem in the early 1950s — Honda motorcycle dealers refused to buy new products while they still stocked old units, so new dealers would provide Honda with the means to keep money flowing in. With automobiles, Fujisawa faced the opposite problem — that dealers stopped selling older vehicles if they knew something fresh was in the pipeline — so Honda established three separate automobile dealer channels in Japan. If dealers did not have access to the entire product lineup, they had to concentrate on their established line to survive. In America, Honda dealers would have killed to get the Integra, but then Prelude and Accord sales would have suffered.

The Honda division's mission was to sell "low to medium-priced vehicles, with the emphasis on economy, comfort, and value for the money," read an Acura press release. "The Acura division will market medium to high-priced vehicles with the emphasis on performance and luxury. These vehicles will be different in concept, styling, and drivetrain from Honda division products."

The Acura distribution channel was unique to America. In other countries, Legends and Integras were sold as Hondas in existing Honda showrooms, but expansion in America, the world's largest car market, was critical to Honda. An automaker's primary mission is to sell automobiles to dealers. Honda was constrained in expanding its U.S. dealer count and thus its volume of sales. Honda dealers were running at full steam, leading the industry in sales per outlet. The Japanese executives were loath to tackle the dealer-instigated litigation that surely would have preceded the establishment of badly needed new Honda outlets. A Honda attorney noted that creating 300 new Honda dealerships would cost upwards of $300 million in litigation fees to fight dealers' protests to state motor vehicle commissions, an amount nearly large enough to develop two new automobiles. Acura dealers would not fight the establishment of other Acura stores, because they believed Acura's sales projections and were thrilled to have the franchise.

Privately, Honda executives conceded that if the new luxury cars did not sell, they would at least have set up several hundred new dealers, many of which could be converted into Honda stores or used to sell rebadged Honda automobiles under the Acura name. The latter scenario is similar to how domestic manufacturers market their products, such as the Ford Taurus being sold through Lincoln-Mercury dealerships as the Mercury Sable.

Marketing myopia marked the Acura division's sales plan. Acura's announced objective of selling 300,000 cars through a dealer network of 600 outlets by 1990 was wildly optimistic. At the time, the Honda division was selling 550,000 cars through 860 dealerships. Honda automobiles competed in market segments — the small and midsize sedan categories — that made up 70 percent of new car sales. The luxury car segment was a growing but still small portion of the industry. Honda overestimated both the expansion of the segment and its projection of being able to capture 18 percent of the competitive market. The only way Acura dealers could sell 300,000 automobiles was if most of the cars were Honda-priced vehicles. Because every other Honda sales projection had come true, few dealers doubted the corporation's ambitious plans.

The Acura division's strategy and products were unveiled to Honda dealers in 1984, since the first 100 Acura franchises were to be granted to existing Honda retailers. Convincing dealers to invest in an Acura franchise was easy, despite the $2 million-plus needed to erect a facility. At the time, Honda dealerships' net profits were nearing an all-time high — an average of $640,000 for both 1984 and 1985. Few dealers were concerned that an Acura dealership would have little parts or service business for several years, other than some low-profit warranty work. Honda dealers were also poor used car marketers, the best insulation from a weak new car product or one in short supply. Still, the Acura concept caused dollar signs to dance in Honda dealers' heads. Each Honda automobile sold was profiting about $1,700 to the dealers. A quick calculation, based on Legends bringing $4,000 profit per car and Integras $2,000 each, yielded a money machine better than a Honda store. Most Honda dealers wanted a shot at an Acura dealership, and over 2,500 non-Honda dealers also applied.

From the beginning, the Acura division suffered from internal organizational and personnel problems. Ed Taylor was plucked from a middle-management Honda division position by the Japanese to be Acura's national sales manager. He was regarded as a man of little personality and an ineffectual leader. Taylor was also an enemy of the kickback camp because of his frequent grumbling about the crew's unethical activities. He may have griped, but he did not squeal. In 1987 an Acura district sales manager forwarded him a document revealing that Delaware dealer David Trainer, the man who would later sell Jim Cardiges his Laguna Hills home for a below-market price, had given Cardiges a check for $35,000. Taylor kept the information to himself.

Jack Billmyer and Cardiges's loyal following of Honda managers had no desire to transfer to Acura, in part because the pair reminded their flock that Honda was still the place to be. The Acura division became the dumping ground for Honda sales division employees who were screwing up. Or were too clean for comfort. "Billmyer sent Acura the dregs of Honda," recalls one manager. Your boss transferring you to Acura meant your career with Honda was stalled—better the lawnmower division than Acura was the saying.

The establishing of a new franchise gave American Honda a dream opportunity: to start with a clean slate, select the best operators, and write a dealer agreement with teeth. That strategy would later lead to great success by other new brands, such as General Motors' Saturn division, but Acura chose another path. Honda dealers were rated poorly in industry surveys about treatment of customers during the car buying process, in part due to the Honda division's lack of commitment to require dealers to take care of the showroom customer. With the first batch of Acura franchises granted to Honda dealers, Acura was doomed to have the same problem. Customer-handling requirements should have been part of the Acura franchise agreement. At the very least, Acura should have selected candidates based on their Honda Customer Satisfaction Index scores, the surveys of customers' experiences with the dealerships.

Instead, the number-one requirement to become an Acura dealer in many cases was how much graft you had already paid, or were willing to pay, to Honda executives. If you were a player, you became an Acura dealer. Some of the chosen dirty dealers ran excellent operations, but many were marginal ones who succeeded solely by taking the shortcut of greasing Honda officials.

Billmyer was named temporary head of the Acura division, in addition to his responsibilities on the Honda side. While Taylor looked on helplessly, Billmyer and Cardiges chaired the Acura dealer selection committee and dictated the placement of the initial batch of 50 retailers. The first honorees were among the best players on the corruption team. Dah Chong Hong. David Trainer. Rod Ryan and silent partner John Conway, Honda's New York zone sales manager. Peter Epsteen, who had paid for Billmyer's swimming pool. John Orsini, Billmyer's NASCAR payroller. Rick Hendrick received the first two Acura franchises in North Carolina. Cardiges granted a Maryland point to dealer pal George Poling, in exchange for Cardiges receiving 42 percent ownership in the store. The execs awarded a California location to a man who had lost his Ohio dealer license for rolling back odometers on used cars but who was also good at rolling out the dough. They granted a Florida franchise to a retailer regarded as one of Honda's worst operators. The chosen dealers reciprocated to their friends at Honda.

Acura's market representation department was charged with quickly establishing 600 dealers, and their decisions often conflicted with those of the boys. A clean California Honda dealer was approved by Acura's market representation department for a franchise in a prime suburb of Los Angeles. His sales manager returned from visiting the Honda dealer in the market they were to build Acura and reported that the dealer principal, a notorious player, was doing a war dance in his showroom, celebrating his receiving the Acura franchise for that city. A screaming Mr. Clean Dealer called Acura and was told by an Acura executive that they had no record of his tentative approval and, yes, the other dealer had received the Acura point. Billmyer and Cardiges probably disposed of the clean dealer's paperwork when their friend declared his desire for the point. Later agreeing it had "misplaced" his application, Acura offered the first dealer the rights to a franchise in the San Joaquin Valley, California, towns of Modesto or Merced — markets that might be lucrative if Acura built farm tractors.

Some Honda dealers were not eligible to become Acura dealers due to some curious guidelines. To ensure that dealers kept their Honda and Acura operations separate, owners were required to build their Acura dealerships a minimum of ten miles away from their Honda stores. This requirement was a small annoyance to metropolitan dealers, but it was a knife in the back to operators in small- to medium-size markets. Those dealers were typically pillars of their communities, high in customer satisfaction, and the logical choice in markets that could support only one Acura store. Acura dealer placement became a multimillion-dollar game of musical chairs, as dealers were forced to establish stores in markets they were unfamiliar with, while outsiders opened Acura dealers in their communities. Acura's plan left it with dozens of absentee dealer principals, opposite of normal dealer selection processes in which manufacturers mandate that dealerships have an owner on the premises. Some dealers applied for Acura franchises in their sons' or daughters' names, so they could keep the operations local, incurring the wrath of those who played by the rules.

Acura's biggest challenge came from the free-falling dollar. For once, Honda's timing as it related to U.S. economic conditions was awful. In September 1985, as the first Acura stores were breaking ground, finance ministers and bankers from the United States, Japan, and Europe agreed to reduce the value of the dollar in an effort to trim America's mounting trade deficit. The resultant drop of the dollar pushed up the cost of importing Japanese products. The value of the yen rose 40 percent over the course of the next year. In the six months preceding Acura's debut, the price of Honda and other Japanese automobiles had risen by over 10 percent. Fortunately for the Japanese automakers, Detroit companies took the opportunity to raise prices on their own cars, rather than using the situation to regain market share from the foreigners.

American Honda's bean counters panicked because of the rising yen. They decided to trim the head count of the already understaffed corporation. A voluntary separation program was offered to any employee willing to resign. In response to president Tetsuo Chino's memo announcing the program, company cynics circulated a parody of the 1960s song "The Letter":

They say you're secure in a Japan company
But the dollar to yen ain't what it used to be
Gravy days are gone
I'm being sent home
Ol' Chino, he wrote me a letter.

Few employees took Honda up on the offer. Coworkers of those who departed found their workloads increased to overwhelming levels.

Honda's increased Ohio production protected it somewhat from the fluctuating currency, but Acura automobiles were all built in Japan. Acura officials promised that Legend prices would start around $18,000, but the dropping dollar played havoc with their plans. When the first 58 Acura dealerships opened in March 1986, the Legend's base price was $19,298. With automatic transmission and a dealer-installed leather interior, the price topped $21,000, making it the first Japanese car to sell for more than $20,000 in America.

Nevertheless, the Acura franchise got off to a hot start. The automotive press loved the cars. The Integra was embraced as the high-performance small car that Honda should have been building for years. The Legend coupe was hailed as *Motor Trend*'s Import Car of the Year before it even hit the showroom in early 1987. People traded in low-end luxury makes such as Volvo, Audi, Saab, and BMW 3-series for the Legend, though Honda Accords were the cars most often swapped.

Acura did not require a standardized facility or signage for the new dealerships, a curious move in light of the hodgepodge of buildings housing Honda stores. A standardized, recognizable look was paramount when establishing consumer awareness of a new brand. Some dealers built mausoleums and others simply hung Acura shingles on dilapidated structures. One of the most costly stores was Acura 101 West in Calabasas, California, a city wedged between Los Angeles's San Fernando Valley and moneyed Thousand Oaks. The dealership was owned by first-time dealer principal Lee Froelich, a man with a successful track record of operating a high-volume Honda store. Acura 101 West cost more than $6.5 million to build and featured marble floors and an employee gym. Located on the congested 101 freeway, it was the most visible Acura dealership in the nation. Acura 101 West had become Acura's second-highest-volume dealership by 1988 — behind only Tustin (California) Acura, a dealership owned by the payola philanthropics of Dah Chong Hong.

Acura 101 West's success was soon to be hampered by the overabundance of Acura stores popping up around Calabasas. By 1989 in Southern California there was nearly one Acura store for each Honda dealership. From Calabasas, consumers could travel six miles into Thousand Oaks and buy an Acura from Al Piano's store, which occupied a rundown rental car building, or drive to seven other Acura dealerships within 25 minutes. "You can't put that many dealers in and expect to survive," said Froelich. "Those were the days that you didn't piss (Honda) people off, so we did not protest the new stores." Nonplayer Froelich also had a feeling that lesser dealers were being allocated a better mix of cars than he was. Acura 101 West's sales began to nosedive.

The dealership was bleeding heavily by late 1989. Froelich sought help from Acura officials. Acura had approved Froelich's ambitious building plans and should have shared in the responsibility with a man who had sacrificed his life's savings for the company. Instead, Acura refused to let Froelich add another franchise and did not offer any solutions to his dilemma. "We were scrambling to stay alive. We were out of trust. I was in deep trouble," recalls Froelich. He ran into Cardiges at a new car show and asked his advice. "The best thing you can do is just let it go, Lee," said Cardiges. "We all have things like this happen to us. I went bankrupt in my Chrysler store back in Maryland. You should just cut your losses and get out." Froelich was disheartened to hear the usually optimistic Cardiges telling him to quit.

Acura 101 West filed for bankruptcy in early 1990. Froelich had tried to do the right thing for Acura and had represented it well, but Acura let his store die. American Honda had no choice but to take an unprecedented step and purchase Acura 101 West's facility — it could not afford the adverse publicity of one of its biggest stores closing. The dealership sat empty for three weeks as Acura scrambled to find a new owner.

What happened next was a bigger blow to Froelich than losing his dealership. The Acura division decided to subsidize the lease for a new operator. The lucky recipient was a player named Angelo Falconi, owner of Las Vegas Honda and a half-dozen other Honda and Acura dealerships. In return for them granting him additional Honda franchises, Falconi had split the profits of his operations with Cardiges and Honda Western regional sales manager Bob Rivers. Cardiges alone received over $700,000 from Falconi. The money was distributed out of a holding company boldly titled JAAB, short for "Jim, Angelo, and Bob." Falconi also bought a Beechcraft airplane for the use of the executives, with Billmyer and Cardiges handling the details of the purchase — including the redecoration of the plane's cabin.

Falconi paid $25,000 per month to lease Acura 101 West, far less than Froelich's mortgage of $90,000 per month — a sweet deal for Falconi and another reward for his benevolence. Froelich realized that Cardiges had encouraged him to bail out so the generous Falconi could take over. "What upsets me the most is what Acura did for Falconi that they wouldn't do for me," Froelich now says. "Three weeks after I closed, here's Falconi with a subsidized lease. I would still be in business if Acura had done that for me." Even when faced with the crisis of an important Acura store closing, American Honda officials found a way to take care of a favored dealer.

From the start, Acura required that every dealer be exclusive, that they carry no other lines of cars. In 1988 Acura allowed a dealer in Ocala, Florida, to build a dual Honda and Acura dealership as an "experiment," with separate showrooms for each brand but sharing parts and service departments. Despite this move, Acura still required its other dealers to remain exclusive, a policy that was unenforceable because of many states' dealer franchise laws forbidding such a mandate. Dealers went ballistic upon learning about the Ocala deal. Most were losing money in their Acura stores and had every right to add another franchise to stay alive, but Acura clung to the exclusive dealership clause. Some dealers thumbed their noses at Acura. By 1989 a dozen Acura dealerships had quietly added other makes to their showrooms.

Elmer Brown of Amarillo was one of the first Honda dealers in Texas. With its nearest dealership located 300 miles away, Acura allowed Brown's Southwest Honda to perform warranty work on Acura automobiles in 1986, with the understanding that once Acura was ready to establish an Amarillo outlet it would be awarded to Brown. It was not to be. When the time came three year later, Brown offered to erect a new sales showroom for Acura and combine parts and service operations with his Honda store, à la Ocala. Brown's plan was realistic for the domestic vehicle–oriented Amarillo market, where Acura projected sales of only 15 cars per month. Demanding an exclusive dealership, Acura officials turned down Brown's proposal and awarded the point to the local Cadillac dealer. An angry Elmer Brown started turning away Acura owners looking for service, leaving them in the lurch until the new Acura store opened.

American Honda moved quickly and established 300 Acura outlets by 1988. To its credit, the company instituted a moratorium on new dealership placement in 1989 to mollify the grumbling dealer principals and help them shore up their stores' profitability. In 1987 an industry survey revealed that 67 percent of Acura dealers rated the franchise as "good." By 1989 that figure had plummeted to 32 percent.

Most Acura dealers marketed the cars the same way they did Hondas, unfamiliar with how to establish a prestigious image for their brand. Discount advertising appeared within a few weeks of Acura's opening. The hands-off Acura division took no step to prevent "The Boss Is Outta Town and We're Going Crazy!" sales events advertised by its supposedly upscale dealer body. Luxury European automakers' U.S. dealers understand the potential erosion of a product's brand image through fire-sale advertising and most refrain.

The discount advertising and numerous price increases due to the falling dollar combined to push the gross profit per Acura car to barely more than that of Honda automobiles. It was apparent that an Acura dealership was not going to be the money machine many dealer principals had envisioned.

The rising yen and uneven factory policy aside, the worst setback to the Acura division arrived in late 1989. Toyota's Lexus and Nissan's Infiniti automobiles came along and blew Acura's doors off. The Lexus LS400 and Infiniti Q45 sedans were rear-wheel-drive, V-8–powered machines priced between $35,000 and $38,000. The following year's second-generation Legend was priced just under $30,000 and still powered by a V-6 engine, despite Acura's 1988 commitment that the car would feature a V-8. It did not matter that a V-6–powered Legend was quicker than a V-8 Lexus and got better gas mileage — a V-8 meant prestige and performance to the consumer. Front-wheel drive and gas mileage were of little concern to high-end buyers. The Lexus LS400 became the standard for Japanese luxury sedans.

Unlike Acura, Lexus and Infiniti required dealers to invest in the proper facilities to welcome upscale consumers. Infiniti assisted the retailers with construction financing. Both brands mandated that dealers offer exemplary sales and service customer-handling policies. While Acura merely suggested that its dealers institute value-added services such as free loaner cars, Lexus and Infiniti required it. Both newcomers instituted complimentary 24-hour roadside service, a program the tight-fisted Acura would not offer until 1995. The new duo selected retailers with track records of high customer satisfaction, regardless of whether they were current Toyota or Nissan dealers. Lexus and Infiniti were perceived by consumers as true luxury automobiles, with the added touch of superb customer handling. Most importantly, the two automakers wanted their dealers to be profitable — they each established half the number of dealers Acura had. In 1992 sales of the Lexus 400 series passed those of the Acura Legend, despite their higher price. By then Acura was offering dealer incentives of up to $3,000 per car on Legends.

In the 1991 J. D. Power and Associates survey measuring customer satisfaction during the purchasing process and first year of ownership, Lexus and Infiniti each scored a record 170 points, tying for first and bettering Acura's 1989 high score of 154. Acura slid to fourth in 1990, with a score of 146, one point behind Mercedes-Benz. Being deadlocked at the top of the prestigious survey gave both manufacturers something to brag about in their advertising — and the public began to forget about Acura, winner of the three previous surveys. The late 1980s saw a rise in consumer awareness, and dealers' 1950s method of selling cars no longer worked. Product reliability alone would no longer satisfy consumers' expectations. Honda may have been number one in customer satisfaction in 1986, and Acura for the next three years, but that ranking was based on the strength of the cars' quality overcoming poor showroom customer-handling ratings.

Acura endured both disasters and delights with new products. It introduced the ground-pounding NSX sports car in 1990 as a challenge to Ferrari and Porsche's stranglehold on the high-performance market. The gorgeous mid-engine, aluminum-bodied two seater was the showcase of Honda's performance-oriented engineering. The handcrafted NSX could rip from 0 to 60 miles per hour in a shade over five seconds, top out at over 160 miles per hour, yet get an astounding 24 miles per gallon on the highway. Best of all, the NSX was an exotic car without the driver-defying ergonomics, frequent dealer visits, or astronomical repair costs of competing brands. The NSX stickered for $61,000, though enterprising dealers, true to their Honda roots, sold the first ones for $20,000 to $30,000 above MSRP and demanded deposits from customers to test-drive the car. One prospective NSX buyer wrote to Acura complaining that his local dealer priced an NSX at $150,000. We don't tell our dealers what to do, replied Acura.

The low-volume NSX created a positive "halo" effect for the entire Acura lineup, one the brand sorely needed. In 1992 Acura introduced the strange Vigor sedan, a bland-looking car built on an Accord chassis and featuring a buzzy five-cylinder motor. It was the automotive equivalent of a three-legged dog—American buyers are wary of cars whose motors have an odd number of pistons. The Vigor did not provide added business for Acura dealers, since it stole sales from the Legend and the Accord.

Acura's product lineup now included two Honda-segment cars—the Integra and Vigor—one high-line sports car in the NSX, but only one true luxury machine in the Legend, a car overshadowed by its new competitors.

Acura never came close to the 300,000 annual sales projected at the outset. Acura deliveries peaked at 143,708 cars in 1991, followed by a steady drop to 97,151 cars in 1995. Another round of the sinking dollar hurt the luxury car market in the early 1990s, as did the 1990 federal luxury tax. Luxury car buyers began a defection to sport-utility vehicles. The German automakers came roaring back with more aggressive pricing due to slashed production costs. The least-expensive Mercedes model was almost $9,000 less than a Legend by 1994—exactly the Legend's price advantage over Mercedes in 1986. Legend sales tumbled from 65,000 in 1991 to fewer than 19,000 units by 1995.

Rumors surface periodically that the Acura division will fold into Honda someday, perhaps in the fallback plan the executives had originally envisioned. The Honda-priced Integra accounted for 70 percent of Acura's sales by 1995. The theory that Acura was headed toward being a second outlet for Honda-segment cars was apparent with the 1996 introduction of the car replacing the Legend coupe: the Acura CL, built on a Honda Accord chassis with a standard four-cylinder engine and priced less than a top-of-the-line Accord.

1996 also found Acura struggling with a confused brand image. It renamed its automobiles with alphanumeric monikers, in keeping with the Japanese and German luxury cars, to focus more attention on the Acura name. At the same time, Acura consumer research found that Legend owners referred to their cars as Legends, rather than Acuras, to divorce themselves from the low-priced image of the Integra. The redesigned third-generation Legend, still V-6 powered, became the Acura RL. Canceling the brand equity and customer recognition of the Legend name was a huge risk for Acura. Part of the Honda division's strong brand awareness stems from the fact that its cars' names have remained the same for so long: Civic since 1973, Accord since 1976, and Prelude since 1979. Changing the names of Acura automobiles was a short-term, copycat fix for the problem of the public not understanding what an Acura was, an issue better addressed by product than by a superficial name change.

Acura mercifully dropped its snooty "Some Things Are Worth the Price" advertising theme, one suggesting to customers that Acura automobiles were overpriced. Acura had bounced from slogan to slogan, none capturing the public's imagination. In October 1996 Acura terminated its original advertising agency and hired a new one.

Half of all Acura dealerships are consistently in the red, the biggest problem facing the Acura division. The competition from the overabundance of Acura dealers made it impossible for some to be profitable. Dealers not making a profit are loath to spend money to take care of their customers. In the 1996 J. D. Power and Associates survey that measures how consumers were treated during the buying process only, Acura earned the lowest score of any luxury car brand.

The underqualified Acura managers could not coerce kickbacks with the same creativity as their Honda division counterparts. During the original NSX madness, when customers stood in line for the low-slung rockets and dealers profited $30,000 on each one, some Acura zone sales managers developed a scheme to grab some money. They required dealers to provide them with proof of a customer deposit before they would ship the dealer an NSX. The corrupt executives then forwarded that customer's name to a favored Acura store in exchange for cash or other gratuities and would route an appropriate car to that dealership. When customers anxious for their cars received a call from the second dealer informing them that an NSX was available, they would usually not question how the retailer knew of their order. They would just be pleased their wait was over, even if it meant forking over a few thousand dollars more. Unless, of course, they were friends of the dealer principal at the first store.

Said one Acura dealership owner, after his personal physician had received such a call, "The (Acura) zone sales manager denied giving out his name, he just said maybe he left a deposit at the other store, too. The son-of-a-bitch shut up when I told him I've known this guy for 30 years. He suddenly came up with an NSX for my friend, though."

Acura's Chicago zone sales manager Leo Stec pulled a stunt that cost him his job. When an Acura was heavily damaged during shipping and subsequently repaired, it was Stec's job to sell the car to a dealer. He arranged for a friendly Acura dealer to be low bidder on the unit and then had the dealer sell the car back to him personally. Stec resold it to another Acura dealer for a $5,000 profit, failing to mention the car's damage history. When the retail buyer of the car, an attorney, discovered the undisclosed damage on the vehicle that had been represented to him as an Acura company car, he threatened to sue American Honda. Stec was fired.

Those two scams placed Acura customers in the thick of the executives' actions, and each involved two different dealers — unfathomable to those in the Honda division.

A Southern California company named Garey and Associates was hired to produce and publish the Acura parts and accessories brochures, a huge account for the fledgling advertising firm. It complied with the two Acura parts division officials who shook them down for cash, wanting to keep the business. The vendor supplied credit cards for the Acura executives' free use and hired one of their sons. When Honda president Tetsuo Chino asked Garey and Associates to make a $10,000 donation to his favorite charity, the Los Angeles Music Center, the advertising firm did so without complaint. Unbeknownst to Chino, Garey and Associates was owned by the brother of Honda zone sales manager Dennis Josleyn.

Acura's inconsistent application of dealership exclusivity guidelines, a Honda-ejected Acura official, and Garey and Associates would all later figure heavily into the Honda scandal.

The establishment of the Acura division was Jack Billmyer's last hurrah. In March 1988, the 58-year-old national sales manager retired from American Honda. He had wanted to depart in 1986 but was dissuaded by Honda's Japanese officials, who were insistent that he remain to oversee the start-up of Acura. Upon retirement, Billmyer was appointed to American Honda's board of directors.

Billmyer left a legacy of having built Honda's dealer network. Whether dirty or clean, the retailers chosen during the his regime were among the industry's best. There were a few notable exceptions, particularly among some of his NASCAR buddies, but most dealers chosen by Billmyer represented Honda well. He may have taken bribes, but Billmyer was unwavering in his commitment to his company and its long-term health. The dubious dealer appointments made by his successor Jim Cardiges would have abhorred Billmyer.

Billmyer deferred some dealer payoffs until after he was gone from Honda. Dah Chong Hong paid him $115,000 in "consulting" fees after he retired. Rick Hendrick and Peter Epsteen also forwarded delayed gratuities. Billmyer accepted the moneys by check, feeling he no longer had to be glancing over his shoulder.

In a letter to dealers announcing his retirement, Billmyer said that he was returning to his native North Carolina but would be keeping his Palm Springs home. During his exit interview, Billmyer told new Honda vice president of human resources Sherry Cameron that he was financially prepared for his golden years. In an uncharacteristic revelation about his personal life, he informed Cameron that he owned several Hardee's restaurants and an Alabama Budweiser beer distributorship. The only business more lucrative than owning a Honda dealership is likely being a Bud distributor in the South, and ownership of such an enterprise does not come cheap.

Those tidbits should have set off a lightbulb in Cameron's head, but she apparently did not give them a second thought. Or maybe she did not want to hear about them.

American Honda's record of ignoring and covering up the corruption by its sales executives was about to be put to its most severe test.

CHAPTER 10

Christiaan and the Lions

But love is bigger than a Honda.

—Bruce Springsteen, *Pink Cadillac*

PRESIDENT BILL CLINTON can warn you about the hazards of having affairs with Arkansas women. American Honda executive Christiaan Walker's Little Rock romance with a Honda dealership office manager led him to evidence that some Honda officials had received money in exchange for awarding a franchise. Walker got the goods on Jim Cardiges, Ed Temple, and (maybe) one other official and decided to do something about it. Like Clinton with his concubines, Walker now wishes it had all never happened.

A Houston native, the lanky, dark-haired Walker possessed the good looks and enthusiasm requisite for a successful career at Honda, traits that also furthered his reputation as a womanizer. He once enjoyed a fling with movie star Jennifer O'Neill. Friends say Walker had an insatiable need for attention, that he loved the sound of his own name. Despite a tendency toward indecisiveness, Walker was sure of one thing: he wanted to work for Honda.

In August 1986 the 25-year-old Walker impersonated a newspaper reporter in order to meet Honda vice president of operations Tom Elliott and ask for a job. "I always like to go to the top," says Walker. Elliott was amused by Walker's brashness, especially since he himself had pestered Honda until he was hired. Elliott directed his secretary to keep Walker supplied with information on job openings. Two months later Walker was hired as a sales analyst, an entry-level position in Honda's California zone sales office. His supervisors were zone sales manager Ed Temple and his assistant Fred Meis.

One year later Walker was promoted to district service manager in

Honda's Arkansas/Mississippi territory, and he moved to Little Rock. Walker was disappointed that he had not been awarded a district sales manager position but was willing to endure the lowly service division for awhile, dealing with warranty claims and the occasional irate customer, until a sales department slot opened up.

Soon after the promotion Walker observed some odd occurrences. "I noticed that a dealer's service and performance did not always go hand-in-hand with his ability to earn cars from Honda," recalls Walker. Referring to Honda's two Jackson, Mississippi, dealers, Walker said, "I saw Patty Peck Honda getting 150 Hondas per month and Paul Moak Honda getting 20. It wasn't fair." Walker heard the murmurs about corruption among Honda sales division officials.

In late 1987 Walker was notified of the impending establishment of a new Honda dealership in Conway, Arkansas, a burg 25 miles northwest of Little Rock. Conway is home to the annual Toad Suck Festival, one of the state's biggest bashes. An Arkansas highway sign alerts motorists to the exit for Toad Suck Park, likely the only municipal sign in America featuring the word *suck*, excluding those decorated with spray paint.

Conway's most important attribute was that it was far enough from Little Rock that no Honda dealer could protest to the state motor vehicle commission about any new dealership placed there. It was a mute point that Honda enjoyed outstanding market penetration in central Arkansas, thanks to customer-friendly Little Rock dealer Russell Honda. The Conway deal was about Temple and Cardiges making some dough, not about American Honda having a sound business reason to open a store there.

The rights to the Conway franchise were going to Cliff Peck, a 73-year-old Little Rock Chevrolet dealer and a buddy of Temple's. Temple was Honda's California zone sales manager at the time, but that did not prevent him from working transactions elsewhere, utilizing his myriad of connections. If the local zone sales manager did not have the *huevos* to put deals together, Temple figured the territory was fair game. Ed was everywhere.

Temple had called on Peck when the former was Honda's Arkansas district sales manager during the early 1980s. Peck previously had procured the Jackson, Mississippi, open point for his daughter, Patty — one of ten dealerships the Peck family owned in Arkansas and Mississippi — and he knew how to play the Honda game. Peck had no interest in acquiring another dealership — he just wanted to make some quick cash — so he and Temple struck a deal for the Conway point. They agreed that in exchange for Honda issuing Peck the Conway letter of intent, Peck would establish the dealership, quickly sell it, and pay both Temple and Cardiges 12.5 percent of the profits from the sale. Temple told Cardiges of the deal, mentioning that "there'll be something in it for you." Cardiges did not ask how much because Temple had proven himself a man the national sales manager could trust and, more importantly, as a man who delivered.

Cardiges signed off on the paperwork awarding Peck the Conway letter of intent in October 1987. Peck leased a makeshift facility, one that would do until he could find a buyer. A one-story warehouse on an empty street in an industrial park became Cliff Peck Honda. Peck knocked out a wall to create a showroom window. Customers drove up a loading dock to enter the service department. As with other new Honda dealers established with payola in mind, the Conway facility and location would have been rejected by any other automobile manufacturer.

"From the highway, it looked like a Honda dealership sitting all by itself in the middle of a field," remembers Danny Watson, the store's general manager. "Actually, that's what it was." The store did well during Peck's ownership, selling about 90 cars per month, thanks in part to Honda officials' generosity with allocations to the new dealership.

Six months later, Cliff Peck sold the dealership to a group headed by Winthrop Paul Rockefeller, the 40-year-old great-grandson of America's first billionaire, John D. Rockefeller, founder of Standard Oil Company. Winthrop Rockefeller was heir to an estate worth an estimated $850 million. He was Temple's target from the start — the magnate had recently purchased two other Arkansas Honda stores and paid way too much for them. Rockefeller gave a staggering $4.5 million "blue sky" — the amount of money beyond the value of the assets — for Richards Honda in Little Rock, one of the highest prices ever paid for a Honda dealership. High-volume Los Angeles and New York Honda dealers rarely commanded such a figure. Rockefeller then paid $1.1 million blue sky for a 15-car-per-month Honda dealership in tiny Hot Springs, four times more than its true worth. Rockefeller was on a buying binge to satisfy a stipulation of his father's will: that he increase his assets. In other words, he had to be employed to keep the inheritance cash flowing. And he thought being a car dealer might be fun.

Rockefeller's consortium paid for the assets of Cliff Peck Honda plus $1.3 million blue sky. The sale price was a disappointment to Temple, but he obviously could not be involved in the negotiations between Rockefeller and Peck. Rockefeller renamed the dealership Honda World and made plans to build a real Honda facility on Conway's main thoroughfare.

In August 1988 Peck forwarded Temple a check for $325,000, representing Temple and Cardiges's combined 25 percent share of the $1.3 million sale price, telling Temple to split the money with Cardiges. This was not in the plan, the careful Temple having asked Peck for separate checks. He was not about to take the entire fall if the impossible ever happened: somebody discovering the payoffs. Temple returned the check to Peck and directed him to issue two new drafts, one for him and one for Cardiges, each for $162,500. Peck complied, and the deal was done.

Peck grumbled that the greedy executives wanted him to pay the taxes on the capital gains from the sale, but overall he was pleased with the deal. He and his investors walked away with $1 million, the Honda officials got their slice, and Rockefeller got another toy to play with. Everyone was happy. It was another classic Honda dealership flip. The scheme was executed dozens of times by the executives, but this time the story would have a different ending.

The conspirators were unaware that Christiaan Walker was dating a woman named Michelle Bregard, who was Peck's office manager and the person who had cut the checks to Temple and Cardiges.

She told Walker that day: you would not believe what I did. Mr. Peck had me write some big checks to some Honda guys. Walker instantly saw a golden opportunity — he was going to become a hero and stop the corruption. And maybe get a promotion to the sales division to boot. Walker pressed Bregard to obtain copies of the checks. The next day, she gave him copies of the drafts made out to Cardiges and Temple, drawn on Peck's account at the First National Bank of Conway. At the bottom of each $162,500 check was typed a notation: "12.5% interest in Honda World, Conway, Arkansas." Walker could now blow down the Honda house of cards.

Walker denies that his motivation to squeal was self-promotion or revenge against Temple for being moved to the service division but rather it was a sense of duty born out of his loyalty to Honda. The Peck checks became the O. J. Simpson bloody glove of the Honda case, the key piece of irrefutable evidence brought forward against the executives. Walker was the Mark Fuhrman of the Honda case — like the accusations of planting evidence against the Los Angeles Police Department detective who investigated the Simpson murder case, Walker found the bloody glove at the crime scene, but he may have tried to take things one step too far.

What happened next is a bit blurry, but three things are clear: (1) After receiving the Cardiges and Temple drafts, Walker directed Bregard to collect copies of all the checks she had issued as payouts for the sale of Cliff Peck Honda. (2) One of the checks was in the amount of $100,000, payable to an investor named Arnold Creekmore. (3) Somebody then altered the Creekmore check to show the payee as Honda executive Fred Meis.

Someone was trying to frame Meis, who had recently been promoted to Texas zone sales manager. Was Walker the culprit? He had opportunity and motive. As Temple's former assistant in California, Meis was Walker's direct supervisor, and the two had butted heads during their stint together in Torrance. Walker had once infuriated Meis by fulfilling a routine request from Honda Finance, which wanted stats on how many Hondas had been sold in California the previous month. Walker's giving them the sales reports threatened to unveil the sales division's practice of falsifying warranty registrations to inflate sales numbers. Meis railed at Walker and ordered him to retrieve the reports.

Walker also asked too many questions and was told by Meis that "you are standing on the outside of a circle, looking in. We are in here and you are out there"—a telling characterization of the corrupt Honda crew's view of other employees.

Meis was also instrumental in Walker's downgrade to the ignoble service division.

Fred Meis was a natural target for this frame-job: he was known as a player, Arkansas was within his territory and he was instrumental in processing the Conway paperwork, and he was a major suck-up to Cardiges. Setting up Meis as not making as much money on the deal as Cardiges and Temple also made sense. Whoever did the deed was very savvy.

Walker vehemently denies he altered the Creekmore check. He fingers Bregard as the forger. "It was just one of the checks she gave to me," says Walker. "I don't know why she dummied the Meis check." Bregard had never met Meis. (Ironically, Meis would later receive a Porsche 930, a Jaguar sedan, and $50,000 cash from the Rockefeller organization, but he was not paid off by Peck.)

Walker added the Meis check to his collection. It was time to crank up the bus.

One month later in New Orleans, Honda held its annual self-congratulatory meeting, the New Car Show, jokingly referred to as the Rolex Convention. The national dealer gathering consists of a multimedia business meeting emceed by Cardiges, followed by an enormous party. Honda enlisted the aid of a half-dozen sports and entertainment celebrities for that year's business meeting, highlighted by Los Angeles Lakers basketball coach Pat Riley giving a *Reader's Digest* version of one of his motivational speeches. Riley and the rest were mere backup for the smooth Cardiges. He was the star now. Jack Billmyer had retired in March, so Cardiges no longer had to share the stage with him.

Before the Fall: American Honda's Sales Hierarchy in 1991/Their Fates

Key: NSM = National Sales Manager
RSM = Regional Sales Manager
ZSM = Zone Sales Manager
DSM = District Sales Manager

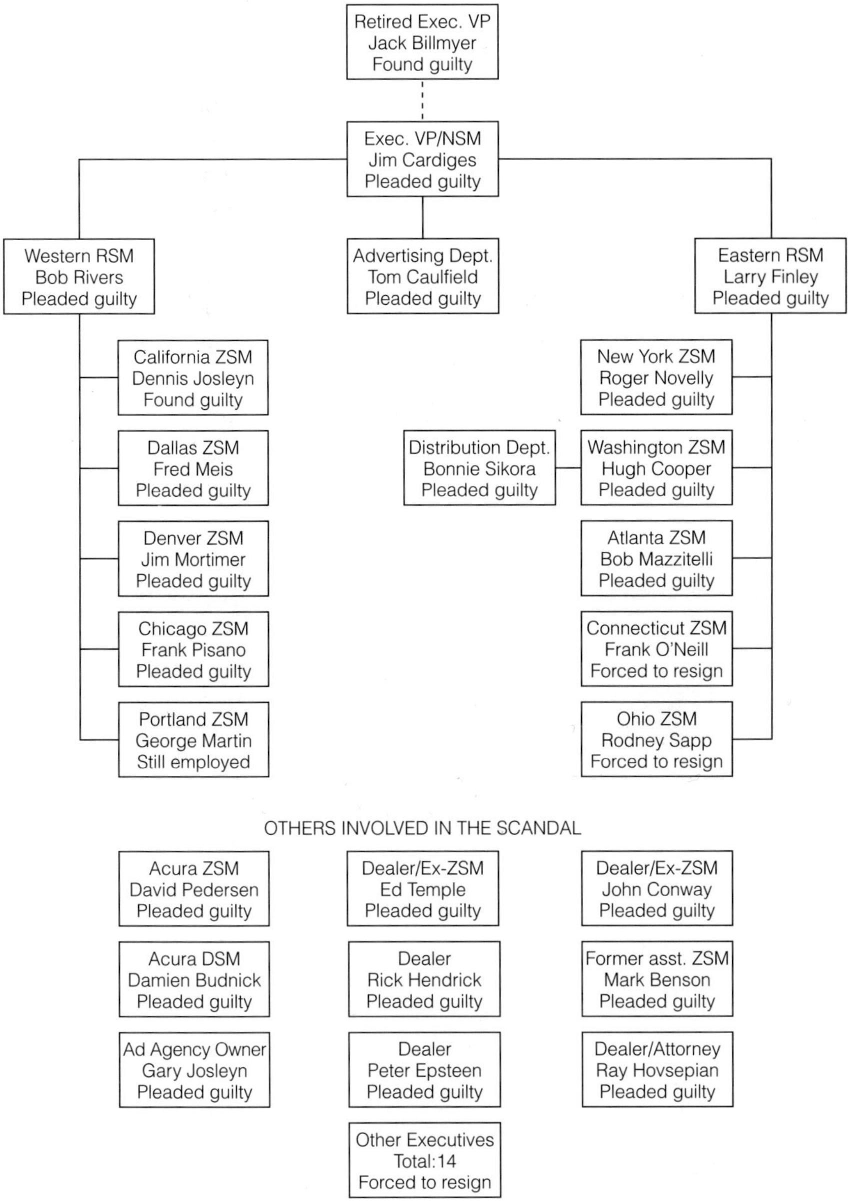

Marcia Curtis

John W. 'Jack' Billmyer was the patriarch of payola at American Honda, the first executive to shake down dealers for cash and gifts.

Stanley James 'Jim' Cardiges replaced Billmyer as American Honda's national sales manager in 1988, at age 42. He demanded that his followers play the corrupt game.

Jim Cardiges's Laguna Hills home was so expensive, it took more than one dealer to pay for it.

Howard DeCruyenaere

North Carolina dealer Rick Hendrick was granted 26 Honda and Acura franchises, more than anyone else. He made the payments on Cardiges's house, as well as on that of Jack Billmyer's.

Automotive News

Ed Temple was Cardiges's most-trusted lieutenant. He made more money from dealers after he departed American Honda.

Beverly Moore-Gorss

The former home of Santa Paula (California) Honda, photographed in 1997 while undergoing renovation. Of all the odd Honda dealerships established with payola in mind, Temple's Santa Paula Honda was the most bizarre, housed in a tiny building on a back street of a nowhere community.

Honda service division executive Christiaan Walker stumbled upon the "Peck checks." (Below) He tried to blow the whistle on Cardiges and Temple, but his motives and methods would be questioned.

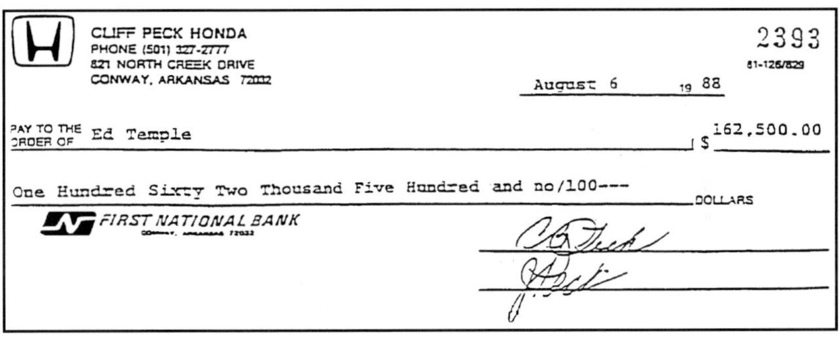

CLIFF PECK HONDA
PHONE (501) 327-2777
821 NORTH CREEK DRIVE
CONWAY, ARKANSAS 72032

2393
81-126/829

August 6 19 88

PAY TO THE ORDER OF Ed Temple $ 162,500.00

One Hundred Sixty Two Thousand Five Hundred and no/100--- DOLLARS

FIRST NATIONAL BANK

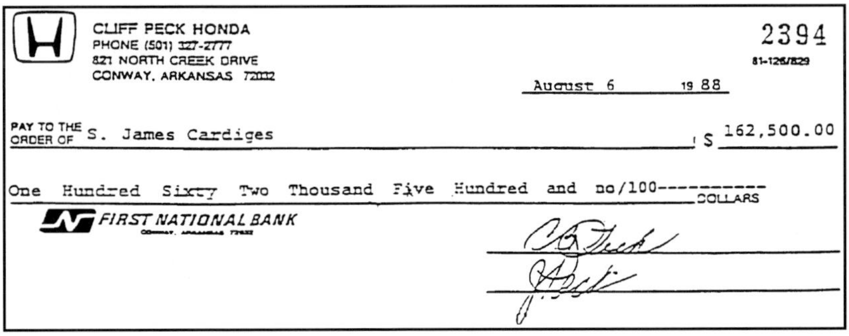

CLIFF PECK HONDA
PHONE (501) 327-2777
821 NORTH CREEK DRIVE
CONWAY, ARKANSAS 72032

2394
81-126/829

August 6 19 88

PAY TO THE ORDER OF S. James Cardiges $ 162,500.00

One Hundred Sixty Two Thousand Five Hundred and no/100---------- DOLLARS

FIRST NATIONAL BANK

Did they know or didn't they? Current American Honda president Koichi Amemiya (left), and executive vice-president Tom Elliott. Both were accused of hiding their knowledge of the rampant corruption.

Lyon and Lyon attorney J. Donald McCarthy's controversial handling of a civil suit led to the FBI investigation of Honda.

Mid-1980s American Honda president Tetsuo Chino declined several opportunities to investigate the activities.

Honda's California zone sales manager Dennis Josleyn led the sea change from bribery to embezzlement.

Cardiges and Josleyn at the 1991 Honda New Car Show in Reno, six months before they would be forced to resign from Honda. As Honda's U.S. sales plunged for the first time, the pair was busy stealing from the corporation.

Jean Cleverly

New Hampshire attorney Paul Twomey represented Dennis Josleyn in federal court. He accused Honda's Japanese executives of condoning the corruption.

Assistant U.S. Attorney Michael Connolly, here receiving the John Marshall award from U.S. Attorney General Janet Reno for his work in the trial of Jack Billmyer and Dennis Josleyn, was in charge of the federal investigation of Honda. Connolly had doors slammed in his face during the first three months of his probe.

That evening's $2 million gala in the Superdome is remembered as Honda's most lavish affair ever. The stadium is home to the New Orleans Saints NFL football team, which is owned by megadealer Tom Benson, a man who counts two Honda franchises among his holdings.

Artificial bayous filled with live alligators greeted the 3,000 guests at the entrance to the Honda party, as the Saints' cheerleaders performed a "Gimme an H, Gimme an O, Gimme an N, etc." yell. Inside the dome Honda had erected a remarkable replica of the French Quarter — the only thing missing was the stench of dried vomit. Staffs of the top New Orleans bars and restaurants served up their Creole specialties from exact duplicates of their buildings. Dealers listened to blues singer B. B. King, rode in horse-drawn carriages, and caught beads thrown from floats in a Mardi Gras–like parade. The evening was capped off by the first fireworks display ever staged inside the Superdome.

The Honda retailers were in a great state of mind as they partied the night away. The "Niece Indicator" — the number of dealer principals whose dates were 25-year-old babes instead of their wives — was high, a sign of a prosperous dealer body. Cardiges strolled through the throng, dealers tugging at his sleeves. With Billmyer gone, the dealers were cozying up to him exclusively. The month before, Cardiges had closed the deal to buy the ostentatious Laguna Hills mansion. He was on top of the world.

The New Orleans party marked the peak of Cardiges and Honda dealers' profitability — and of the bribery. It was all about to slowly fall apart.

Cardiges talked to the dealers about a recent *Business Week* magazine cover story detailing American Honda's myriad of successes. The issue also contained an article about the niceties of the federal minimum-security prison in Lompoc, California. Little did Cardiges know that, a mile from the Superdome inside a dark French Quarter dive called the 2121 St. Charles, Christiaan Walker was about to take action that would eventually make the Lompoc lockup Cardiges's next new home.

Walker and fellow manager Dan Zeid left the bash early for a night of barhopping. Walker's confidence was waning about his next step — he was suddenly scared and confused about the situation. "He wanted to do the right thing," says a friend of Walker's. "He just needed someone to tell him what to do." Unsure of his next move, Walker sought out Zeid's advice. Over his trademark bar drink that always drew attention — a glass of milk — Walker told Zeid about the Peck checks. In his naïveté, Walker did not realize that sales division managers would stonewall the information. Or maybe that was his plan.

Zeid said he would talk to Western regional sales manager Bob Rivers, the number-two man to Cardiges, when they got back to California. The

42-year-old Rivers was a short, blond man with a constant smile and a reputation as a hard drinker. Knee-deep in the boys' club himself, Rivers had converted his graft dollars into two Colorado vacation homes and property in Arizona, in addition to his lavish Irvine, California, residence.

Rivers panicked when Zeid told him that Walker had the checks. For a moment, he considered using the information to squeal on his pals, a move that might result in him replacing Cardiges as the top American ("Head Round-Eye") at Honda. Meis and Temple getting axed would be nice, too, thought Rivers, since they both are after my job. "Temple was always trying to cut my legs off," Rivers recalls. He rejected his fantasies, remembering his own involvement in the bribery. Cardiges and Temple had just left for the annual shopping soiree in Hong Kong with a group of dealers. Rivers had to get control of Christiaan Walker until the pair returned to Torrance.

"Jesus Christ!" Rivers swore at Zeid. "Tell him not to do anything or say anything until I talk to him. Give him my home number."

Walker called Rivers. "Walker was extremely nervous," remembers Rivers. "I think at that point he was probably sorry that he had ever seen the checks. He said that he had contacted his father and his father's attorney to inform him because he was very nervous about the consequences. For some reason he didn't feel that Temple and Meis liked him very much, so he was concerned about something possibly negative happening to himself. So I attempted to calm him down, assured him that nothing like that would happen." The indecisive Walker was realizing that threatening someone's multimillion-dollar empire might lead to trouble.

Rivers asked Walker for copies of the checks and told him to not tell anyone about their existence. Walker overnighted them to Rivers's home. Rivers recognized the signatures of Cardiges and Temple on the endorsements, but was not sure of Meis's.

Rivers's worst fear was realized — an "outsider" had come forward with hard evidence, an inevitability always in the back of Honda executives' minds.

Cardiges arrived home from the Orient the following Sunday, where he was greeted by Rivers and the copies of the Peck checks. The normally Zenlike-calm Cardiges was stunned. Rivers remembers that Cardiges "nearly broke up." Cardiges's first instinct was to fire Walker, but that thought conjured up visions of Walker going to the media. Cardiges was puzzled about the check to Meis but more worried about saving his own hide.

"Jim, he's making noises about going to the Japanese," said Rivers.

"Obviously, we can't have that happen," Cardiges replied. "You have to help me cover this thing up. How well do you know this guy?"

"Not very well at all. I've only met him a couple of occasions."

"We have to keep a lid on this thing. We can't let the Japanese find out about this."

Cardiges got on the phone to The Master. Ed Temple drove to Cardiges's house, and the pair decided to draw up a bogus promissory note between them and Peck. "There is a notation of '12.5%' at the bottom of the check," said Cardiges. "If this ever gets out, our note can say that it was a loan from Peck at 12.5% interest. We're covered." Cardiges produced a fake promissory note he had drawn up for a previous transaction and used it as a model. Temple recommended they create a clause that stipulated that, in the event of the death of Peck, the debt would be forgiven. They added a notation that Cardiges had never solicited the funds from Peck, did not receive them directly from him, and never spoke with Peck about the arrangement, all true. The document stated that Cardiges agreed to pay off the loan. Temple drove to a local secretarial service with a rough draft of the note and returned with the finished document.

Cardiges was in full self-protection mode. "Call Peck and tell him about this note," he told Temple. "Don't tell him I am involved in the cover-up. This is something you decided to do on your own." Cardiges knew Temple was thinking about leaving American Honda, and he recommended that he do so immediately, so that Cardiges was somewhat protected if Honda ever found the Peck checks. Eliminating the link between me and Peck might save my job, thought Cardiges. The obedient Temple agreed to resign. He spent his final four months at Honda scooping up millions of dollars for himself and Cardiges by establishing dubious new Honda stores in California, including the senseless Santa Paula Honda.

In March 1989 Temple resigned from Honda, saying his wife had suddenly inherited $1 million and that he was moving to Hilton Head Island, South Carolina, to open a Honda dealership. American Honda president Koichi Amemiya approved Temple's letter of intent for Hilton Head and, as a bonus golden parachute, one for Fernandina Beach, Florida.

Meis went crazy over the charge that he had received $100,000 from Cliff Peck. He told Cardiges that he had never seen a dime from the Conway deal. Cardiges admitted to Meis that he had received money from Peck. When Meis pressed Cardiges for more details, Cardiges simply said "end of subject."

Walker and Cardiges spoke by telephone about the Peck checks. Walker indicated that he wanted to be promoted to the sales division, so Cardiges quickly arranged for him to become Tennessee district sales manager. Blackmailing Cardiges to further his career, Honda would later claim, was Walker's real motivation for squealing.

Walker got his promotion, but there was a price to pay. The venal executives could not fire Walker, so they tried to force him to self-destruct and resign. Walker was placed on double-secret probation. Cardiges told Walker's new boss to keep him quiet and to start "building a file" on him. The message came down to Walker's superiors that "every time he takes too long to take a shit, write it down." Walker was summoned to make an 800-mile round-trip drive to Atlanta for a ten-minute meeting. He watched his performance reviews go south. Word spread among the executives: we have a rat in our ranks.

A few months later, Walker called Rivers to find out what action had been taken. Rivers said that Temple had resigned because of the checks and that Meis had denied receiving the money. His voice dripping with sarcasm, Rivers added: "Jim wants to know if you think he should give the money back." The message was clear: you have messed with the wrong bunch.

"I was beginning to think I had made a mistake by coming forward," said Walker. "From the moment I first reported the information about the bribe and kickback schemes, I was harassed, threatened and ostracized." He began to fear for his life.

Walker remained silent for the next two years, and the execs figured the Peck issue was dead. They were wrong. In early 1991 Walker met with Atlanta zone sales manager Bob Mazzitelli to complain that his peers were being promoted faster than he was. Both men knew Walker's career was dead — none of the executives wanted a squealer as an employee.

"Why would anyone want to promote you when you got this job through blackmail?" asked Mazzitelli. "They're gonna think you're crazy. My advice to you is to throw the checks away, get your head screwed on right, and sell cars. Then I will try to get you promoted." Walker told Mazzitelli he was going to call Tom Elliott about his career situation and maybe mention the Peck checks, too. Walker will literally get killed, thought Mazzitelli.

Executive vice president Elliott was the man Walker had duped into a meeting years earlier. It was no surprise that Cardiges and Rivers had tried to cover up the Peck checks, but Elliott was perceived to be on the other side of the fence, apart from the shenanigans of the sales officials. A career Honda employee, the 49-year-old Elliott bore an amazing resemblance to children's television show host Captain Kangaroo. He was in charge of marketing, distribution, and product planning for Honda automobiles and worked more closely with the top Japanese officials than any other American executive. Surely he would understand, thought Walker.

On April 11, Walker called Elliott and told him of the evidence implicating Cardiges, Temple, and Meis. Elliott did not want to hear about it. He referred Walker to Lyon & Lyon, the customary procedure for hiding allegations of wrongdoing between Honda executives and the dealers.

If Elliott had referred Walker to Honda's human resources department, Cardiges would have been toast within a few days. Human resources rarely encountered a case involving the Honda automobile sales division, the department generating 75 percent of the company's profits. That information usually ended up in the Lyon & Lyon vault.

Walker called the law firm and spoke with attorney Don McCarthy about the Peck checks. McCarthy transferred Walker to attorney Bud Smoot. Walker spilled everything to Smoot: the Peck deal, the payoffs to Honda executives for extra automobiles, and other allegations about the "bulletproof gang," as Walker referred to the officials.

And by the way, said Walker, I just got passed over for the Denver district sales manager position and I'm frustrated being stuck in Nashville.

Smoot told Walker to forward him copies of the checks and not to talk to anyone about them. He advised Walker that the information was probably insignificant and that there were numerous reasons why the executives may have received the money. Walker sent the checks by overnight delivery, arriving at Lyon & Lyon on April 15.

Lyon & Lyon contacted Amemiya and informed him about the checks. Amemiya either did not grasp or chose to ignore the implications of his top executives being on the take, and no action was taken to confront Cardiges or Meis.

Amemiya did not say anything to Cardiges. Instead, he called Mazzitelli and told him to get control of Walker.

"We must calm him down," said Amemiya. "We will help you to handle him. If Cardiges finds out that we or I know about this, he might resign, and we don't want that to happen." Amemiya wanted to protect his favorite "bad boy."

Shortly thereafter, in one of the most baffling moves of the entire scandal, Amemiya approved Temple to be the new Honda dealer for Costa Mesa, California, despite knowing that Temple was involved in the Peck deal. Costa Mesa Honda was purchased by Temple and his partner, a Houston Honda dealer. Temple had visited Honda headquarters a few months before, and he and Amemiya had embraced like brothers, raising the eyebrows of employees, who had never before seen Amemiya hug anyone.

Temple was back in California. He made sure to pay off his old buddies at Honda to get extra cars allocated to his dealership.

Missing the action, Temple had sold his Hilton Head Honda store the previous year and was running around the country sniffing out open point deals for him and Cardiges when he came upon the opportunity in Costa Mesa. Honda insiders referred to Temple as the "Eleventh Zone Manager," the freelance broker with the connections and savvy to make deals happen. "Ed became the National Letter of Intent Broker," remembers one Honda official. "If you wanted a dealership, you went to Ed." Temple positioned himself to dealers as a middle man, a friend of the right people at Honda. He put together a dozen deals in 1990 and 1991, making millions for himself, Cardiges, and several zone sales managers. Temple's attorney helped Honda executives set up "consulting" companies to shelter income gained from their share of the deals.

Temple added a twist to the establishing of new Honda stores. He had gotten away from the burdensome task of setting up new dealerships and then selling them for profit; he was now concentrating on obtaining the letters of intent. Instead of supplying Honda with a genuine car dealer to be the recipient of the document assigning a Honda franchise, before the letter was sold to the eventual dealer, Temple developed an easier plan: just use any acquaintance as the original applicant. He arranged for a man named Paul Stephens to be issued the letter of intent to become Honda's new dealer in Warrenton, Virginia.

Paul Stephens was an Illinois soybean farmer. He brought true meaning to the term *straw dealer*.

Stephens was a childhood friend of Temple's payola prodigy Mark Benson, an ex–Honda assistant zone sales manager. Benson, a former Eagle Scout and the son of a minister, left the company to become general manager of Temple's Costa Mesa Honda. Stephens was among a string of non-car-business buddies of Temple and Benson who were approved to become Honda dealers during the early 1990s. Temple loaned the straw dealers enough capital to be approved by Honda. He filled out phony dealer applications on their behalf. He then alerted Cardiges as to the inbound paperwork requiring his signature. Temple slipped the dummy dealers a few bucks and then prospected for real dealers willing to buy the letter of intent. Having the document in his hand allowed Temple to start bidding wars that drove his and other executives' "consultant fees" skyward.

Ed Temple was now both a Honda dealer and a Honda dealmaker, a banker and a broker. He was playing offense, defense, and coaching — The Master was in his element. In the late 1980s and early 1990s, more decisions about who would become Honda dealers were made by Temple than by American Honda.

Amemiya may have been trying to keep Temple happy by approving him to become the dealer in Costa Mesa — added insurance that Temple would not blab about the Peck checks. Allowing Temple to buy Costa Mesa Honda was another poor dealer appointment by Honda, since he did not have a sterling track record as a dealer and spent more time working deals than selling Hondas.

Tom Elliott spoke to Jim Cardiges and Bob Rivers about his conversation with Christiaan Walker regarding the Peck payoffs. Both men told Elliott that Walker was trying to blackmail Honda for a better job, that he had no evidence of wrongdoing, and that there was no financial arrangement between Cardiges and Peck or any other Honda dealer. Walker is a crackpot, they said, we will handle him. Elliott took no further action.

The Peck checks were in Honda hyperspace. American Honda's president, executive vice president, and the firm's legal counsel all turned their backs on the evidence. They trusted that the sales division crew would make the problem go away, as it had done in the past.

Cardiges wasted no time. Angry that the Peck issue had resurfaced, he decided to meet with Walker face-to-face. He flew to Atlanta on megadealer Rick Hendrick's personal jet, which was at his disposal 24 hours a day. Walker was summoned from Nashville to Atlanta, where he and Cardiges met in a conference room in the zone office.

After an awkward discussion about Honda's Tennessee market penetration, Cardiges blurted out, "Christiaan, what are your intentions? What do you plan to do?"

"I don't know what to do," stammered Walker. "I've got copies of the checks in a safe deposit box because I'm afraid of someone harming me."

"Nobody is going to hurt you, Christiaan. But, you have to do what you think is right," said Cardiges, his eyes boring into Walker's. When the top dog at Honda tells you to follow your heart, you had better do what *he* thinks is right

"Look, things are not always as they appear," said Cardiges. "Sometimes dealers give people things even if they don't ask for them. If you destroy the checks, I will make sure you get promoted." Walker said he would think about it.

Walker called Bud Smoot of Lyon & Lyon and relayed the details of his conversation with Cardiges. Smoot told him to keep quiet about it.

Unfazed by his meeting with Walker, Cardiges walked into the next conference room to arrange a payoff from Atlanta district sales manager Barry Alexander. Alexander wanted to leave Honda and open a dealership, and he knew how to play the game. He and his partners had plans to establish a Honda store in the affluent Atlanta suburb of Woodstock. Alexander presented Cardiges and Bob Mazzitelli with a handwritten memo outlining why he should be awarded the dealership:

> At some point in time, the Japs may get involved in dealer selection or start doing it by committee, the way most companies do it, especially since CSI (customer satisfaction) is getting more attention. (The dealership) could be awarded with nobody being taken care of. . . . If somebody like Hendrick gets it, they wouldn't be as generous as I would be!

The memo spelled out a dozen gratuities that Alexander would pay Cardiges and Mazzitelli if he were granted the dealership, including $70,000 cash up front, $10,000 to $20,000 every Christmas, no-show jobs for their family members, use of credit cards and limousines, and "nice birthday presents." Despite the problem the Peck paper trail was creating, Cardiges did not have a problem with Alexander putting his intentions in writing.

The Alexander memo to Cardiges and Mazzitelli was one of the few written quid pro quo agreements of the entire Honda scandal. It was definitely the only one left on a copying machine in a Honda office. Cardiges was getting sloppy.

Cardiges agreed to grant Alexander the rights to open a Honda dealership in Woodstock. He directed Alexander to submit his application under the name of a straw dealer so as not to arouse suspicion. Alexander chose a chiropractor friend to be the faux dealership owner.

Cardiges got back on the jet and flew to Charlotte to visit Rick Hendrick, the man who was paying the mortgage on his Laguna Hills home. He wondered how to tell Hendrick that the megadealer was not going to receive a Honda dealership in Woodstock.

Shortly thereafter, Walker was promoted to district sales manager in Portland, Oregon, regarded as a desirable territory because of Honda's excellent market penetration there. He hung on to the Peck checks. Had Walker once again blackmailed his way to a better position? Walker says no, he was only attempting to persuade Honda to take action against the executives.

Walker's promotions were not enough to silence him. He was still underfoot, ready to mention the Peck checks when he did not get his way. The gang decided to attempt a permanent solution to the Walker problem.

The week before his departure for Oregon, Walker was in the Atlanta office reviewing the Tennessee market with the manager assigned to replace him. Mazzitelli invited the pair to lunch. As they exited the car at the restaurant, Mazzitelli yelled, "Hey, look! There's Ed!" Walking across the lot came a grinning Ed Temple. Mazzitelli and Temple had set up this "accidental" meeting. For the first time since Walker had come forward with the Peck checks three years earlier, he was in the presence of the man whose departure from Honda he had caused. "I was scared shitless," says Walker, knowing that Temple not being a Honda employee meant he did not have to handle Walker with kid gloves. Mazzitelli invited Temple to dine with them.

Walker picked at his food, wondering what was going on. "I was sitting there with the enemy," recalls Walker. "I had the appetite of a gnat." After lunch Temple said to Mazzitelli, "Bob, I'm going to take Christiaan back to the zone office. Christiaan, you don't have a problem with that, do you?" Mazzitelli answered for him, "Go ahead, Christiaan. We'll see you back at the office."

Walker climbed into the passenger seat of Temple's silver Porsche 928, and the pair headed for Honda. "Did Rivers pressure you for the checks?" asked Temple, convinced that his other nemesis had forced the Peck revelations.

"Yes," said Walker. "I hope you are not angry with me."

"Look, don't worry about me," Temple replied. "It hasn't been so bad on me."

"Christiaan, I know this whole thing has been very difficult for you. I have an opportunity for you that I think may help. I want you to pick five cities that you would like to live in, and we will find a Honda dealership for you in one of them." Temple proposed to arrange a letter of intent for a new Honda store that Walker could either sell for $500,000 and walk away or find a partner and open the dealership. Either outcome would quiet Walker forever, Temple figured.

Not wanting to become affiliated with the gang, Walker turned down Temple's offer. The bribe that had worked so well to shut up whining Honda dealers did not sway Walker. He climbed out of Temple's car, thankful to be alive.

In January 1992 Amemiya spoke to Bob Rivers about the Peck checks. "I know about the kickbacks," said Amemiya. "I don't care about that stuff right now. We have to concentrate on sales now. Please don't tell Jim (Cardiges) about this conversation. I don't want him upset because we have a sales job to do." Amemiya pointed to a photograph of Walker on an organizational chart of Honda sales officials. "Continue to keep him quiet," urged the president of American Honda.

If Koichi Amemiya, Tom Elliott, or Lyon & Lyon had taken action on the Peck checks, Honda might have stopped the executives' unethical activities in early 1991. Instead, 1991 will be remembered as the year the gang started raiding the corporate coffers.

CHAPTER 11

A Bribe Too Small to Keep

None of us could ever run for political office.

—Jim Cardiges

AN UNDERSIZED bribe from a Honda dealer persuaded Dennis Josleyn to start stealing from American Honda.

In March 1989 the 42-year-old Josleyn replaced Ed Temple as Honda's California zone sales manager. He was promoted from the Washington, D.C., office and immediately set out on a path of corruption unmatched by any other zone sales manager. Josleyn's first act in California was his attempted shakedown of Steve Shuken in return for granting him permission to relocate his Honda dealership out of Santa Paula — hardly a transaction worth paying a bribe. Josleyn did not miss a trick.

I toiled under Josleyn as a district sales manager in California. An intimidating, arrogant autocrat with a reputation of not promoting his people, Josleyn was a man cast from the Jack Billmyer mold: a beefy, chain-smoking Southern guy. His towering frame was capped by a thick pompadour of hair that periodically changed color between black and gray. Josleyn's eyes looked past you, as if searching for someone better to talk to. The son of a Tennessee Baptist preacher, Josleyn was the most conceited of a conceited bunch, perpetually amused by his own wit, punctuating most sentences with a low chuckle. Josleyn fancied himself a country singer and "good ol' boy," hanging out with the stringy-haired and missing-hubcap crowd. Soichiro Honda would have liked that about Dennis Josleyn.

The corrupt executives looked after Honda's best interests most of the time, but not Josleyn. When a California Honda dealer informed Josleyn that he was about to sell his store due to his father's terminal illness, he learned how ruthless Josleyn could be. The sale would have been a boon for Honda — the proposed buyer would provide Honda with a new facility, stronger capitalization, and better customer satisfaction ratings than the selling operator.

Josleyn met with the seller and threatened not to approve the buy/sell — he was miffed about not being informed of the transaction and thus the opportunity to earn some side money by steering the seller to a buddy. Denied that chance, Josleyn took a shot at shaking down the retailer.

"I tried to tell (Josleyn) that this wasn't for me," explains the dealer principal. "This deal was for my parents. My father was very sick and we needed the money. Dennis was relentless. He kept saying, 'I won't sign off on it. I won't sign off on it,' but he wouldn't say why." Josleyn was throwing out the bait for the dealer to pony up some cash to ease his writer's cramp, but the dealer did not bite. By the time the buy/sell was finalized, Josleyn would be gone from Honda.

Josleyn was a mystery man to his employees. He would disappear for weeks, only surfacing to threaten to fire us for not burning enough sales cards. On the other hand he was generous with his money, sympathetic to the plights of district sales managers struggling to survive in California on a Honda salary. He once reached into his own pocket to sponsor a December sales contest for us, complete with cash prizes and a boat cruise on Newport Harbor, an event the cheap corporation would never consider sponsoring. Josleyn also tipped the clerical help for their assistance in processing the paperwork on the used cars he was selling to various Honda dealers, from whom he received kickbacks.

Between Josleyn's chatty personal secretary, his own big mouth, and a lack of discretion in his ways, we learned how he worked his dark deals. He even told me the story of the Piano man.

In December 1990 Josleyn received a phone call from Al Piano, the owner of three California Honda dealerships. A round, jovial Italian man in his late 60s, Piano maintained a kitchen in his office so he could cook pasta for his guests. He reveled in the incorrect rumors of him having Mafia ties and was a favorite with the Honda brass, particularly Jim Cardiges.

Piano had a Christmas present for Josleyn. As was the tradition, Piano did not use those words in his phone call. Instead he said, "Dennis, sweetheart, you gotta come see me before Christmas. Come down to Indio, we'll have lunch."

As Josleyn drove from his home in Los Angeles toward Piano's dealership in the desert town of Indio, he was curious about being summoned by Piano. He knew of Piano's ties to his superiors but had yet to receive any gifts from Piano himself. Piano was the only operator to have Honda dealerships in contiguous markets in Los Angeles, located in Thousand Oaks and Simi Valley. This practice is normally frowned upon by manufacturers, because of the potential for illegal price-fixing. To be awarded neighboring stores in the Honda-crazy Los Angeles area is the equivalent of the Academy Award for graft. Piano was a player.

Josleyn thought that Piano had finally figured out that, when it came to cars, Josleyn was the man. Piano only had to drive the 11 miles from Indio to Palm Springs and pass Fred Smith Honda to see who was being allocated the hottest Hondas. Since Fred Smith and Piano were former partners and now bitter rivals, Josleyn thought that it must kill Piano that he took care of Smith. Josleyn's close relationship with Smith was well-known, but he was not above playing both sides of the fence.

Josleyn imagined Piano would have at least $5,000 in cash for him and the requisite plea to "take good care of me, okay?" That would be a start — it would mean Josleyn could begin calling Piano with a shopping list later. Josleyn was hallucinating — he did not know that the biggest individual gift that Piano had given Cardiges was only $1,000.

Indio, California, sweltered in the low desert as Josleyn turned his black Accord into Al Piano's Honda Automobiles of Indio. He had forgotten what a dilapidated facility Piano owned. Piano's Honda operations would not have been tolerated by any other automaker. An inadequate building and poor customer relations were made up for by Piano knowing how to get the cars he wanted. One of the side benefits of being in bed with Honda officials was immunity from enforcement of Honda's few dealership operating standards.

The meeting between Josleyn and Piano was brief. Piano was not feeling well and begged off the lunch. He handed Josleyn an envelope and mentioned he was short on Accords. "Don't worry about it, partner," said Josleyn. They shook hands.

Josleyn left Al Piano Honda, envelope in his coat pocket. His heart was racing. It was still the best rush there was: The excitement of people handing you cash as they kissed your ass could not be beat. Josleyn had the discipline to drive two miles down Highway 111 before pulling into a parking lot. He had to see. He tore the envelope open and discovered not $5,000 but $200 — the equivalent of a slap in the face. Dennis was livid. "200 bucks! Can you imagine?" he said. "I almost turned around and took it back to the son-of-a bitch! I guess Fred Smith will keep getting all the good cars." The image of Josleyn doing a U-turn in the desert and taking the money back to Piano was too funny: "Sorry, Al, but I just can't accept this payoff. It is not enough."

Josleyn did not know if Piano was trying to send a message or was just plain stupid. Maybe the other zone sales managers were right, he thought, maybe things are changing. It had been another spectacular year for Honda in 1990, but not so for the crooked executives. Honda had enjoyed another record sales year, finally achieving its goal of outselling Toyota to become the number-one-selling import-brand car in America. Honda had edged Toyota by a scant 821 automobiles, 716,495 to 715,674, after Honda reported a flurry of bogus sales during the final days of the month. Combined sales of Honda and Acura automobiles were only 6,000 units less than those of Chrysler Corporation.

But there was trouble in payola-dice. Production from Honda's second Ohio plant was increasing. The dealers were carrying an industry-average 60 days' supply of new Hondas, and gross profits per car were plummeting as consumers were price shopping dealers hard. Los Angeles Honda dealers were beginning to turn down portions of their allocations, a first in California. Dealers could procure as many Hondas as they wanted from the factory. There was no longer any reason for them to pay off Honda executives for more product. With this level playing field of car availability, Josleyn knew the days of dealer endowments were just about extinct. The party was not quite over, but the host was yawning and the booze had been drunk.

Against this backdrop, Josleyn and the boys set out in 1991 on a series of scams far more pernicious than accepting gifts from dealers. It all occurred during Honda's toughest year ever in America. The Gulf War and an uncertain American economy slowed automobile sales. The California economy began a nosedive that would cause sales of Hondas to plunge 35 percent over the next two years in its highest-volume state.

The current Accord, introduced in 1990, was being criticized for its boring, derivative styling. No longer sleek and racy-looking like its 1986–1989 incarnation, the new version resembled a bloated 1982 Accord. Honda's intuitive advertising agency took one look at the car and scrambled to develop a defensive strategy — they produced a launch campaign to encourage skeptics to test-drive the car: "You Have to Drive It to Believe It." In other words, "It May Look Ho-Hum, But it is Still a Honda." The new Accord wagon, introduced in January, completely missed the market as consumers were flocking to minivans, vehicles with more interior room and power than traditional station wagons. Dealer incentives on the Accord rose to a record $900 per car.

In reaction to the softening market, Honda cut production for the first time ever at the Marysville plant, trimming 5,000 Accords in the first quarter of 1991, as well as reducing imports by 15,000 units. The company rented space at an Ohio Army depot to store vehicles that dealers would not buy. Honda's reported sales figures were abysmal due to the cleansing of the warranty card system, and the press finally had a chance to pounce on Honda. "Did a decade of success sap (Honda's) strength?" asked an *Automotive News* headline. The competition was catching Honda, and automakers building sport-utility vehicles and minivans would soon be lauded for having Honda-like foresight.

Worst of all, Soichiro Honda passed away in August at age 84. He died without knowing of the cancer inside his U.S. sales arm.

Jim Cardiges was asked by a zone sales manager whether the time had come to curtail their activities. "No, we are going to continue to play the game," said Cardiges, "but we'll play with a select number of dealers we can trust." That number was shrinking fast.

Cardiges suffered a frightening experience in the autumn of 1990 that shaped his attitude about the changes going on around him. He became ill with what appeared to be the flu, but he felt worse as several days went by, until one night he could barely move and was becoming irrational. Concerned about what the neighbors might think of an ambulance pulling up to the Cardiges estate, Effie instead loaded Jim into her Mercedes-Benz and rushed him to the hospital. She also did not want to make a scene at the hospital's emergency entrance, so she dragged her wobbly husband in from the parking lot.

Cardiges had come down with a rare strain of toxic shock syndrome, the fast-moving, often fatal disease normally contracted by women. The doctors said he would have died within 24 hours had he not sought treatment. Bob Rivers and Ed Temple hustled to the hospital and stood watch outside Cardiges's hospital room the first night, concerned about someone tape-recording his delirious rantings about his wealth. Cardiges's old friend, Virginia dealer William Schuiling, flew a toxic shock specialist to Los Angeles to monitor Cardiges's condition. Cardiges lost a great deal of weight and was out of action for several weeks but then recovered fully.

The episode convinced Cardiges it was time to slow down. Always the one to present what he thought was the right image — even a worn-out, stereotyped one — he returned to Honda and announced how the illness had changed his outlook on life. Material thing are no longer important to me, he said, the near-death experience has made me appreciate my life and my family more. He dropped hints that he might retire. Privately, Cardiges decided to throw caution to the wind in his attempts to grab more cash. He was establishing his own company, Worldwide Dyve, a manufacturer of casual clothing for scuba-diving enthusiasts, and the capital required for start-up was enormous.

Cardiges realized that the Big Secret was going to come out someday, probably sooner than later. The black cloud of the Peck checks had been hanging over his head for more than two years. The wife of multi-Honda dealer Don Carlton had recently called Cardiges and threatened to tell president Koichi Amemiya about the box stuffed with $250,000 cash that she had witnessed her soon-to-be-ex-husband hand Cardiges in exchange for a dealership in Washington state. Cardiges had to scramble and produce a bogus promissory note to cover the transaction, like the one he had fashioned to hide the Peck deal. He did not need these headaches any longer.

For Cardiges, it was time to score and to score fast. He and the gang had to draw up some new scams — and Josleyn became the playmaker.

The most lucrative source of zone manager moonlighting money — shaking down dealers for the rights to new Honda franchises — had also dried up in California, thanks to Ed Temple, Josleyn's predecessor. Temple had established Honda dealers in towns that could barely support a stoplight. Dealers would still gladly pay for a franchise, but there were few viable locations available that did not violate the state's ten-mile rule.

Josleyn did manage to get his hands on one new point. Honda was under pressure from the National Association for the Advancement of Colored People (NAACP) to increase its number of minority-owned dealerships, which accounted for less than 2 percent of its dealer network. In 1988 Honda had run afoul of the Equal Opportunity Employment Commission in a case involving the Marysville, Ohio, plant. Honda's policy of hiring people who lived within a 20-mile radius of the factory was deemed racist because it excluded minority neighborhoods in Columbus. The company was ordered to pay $6 million to African-Americans and women denied employment at the facility. Fearing another EOE inquiry, Honda decided to move swiftly on the minority dealer issue.

The mandate came down to the zone sales managers to quickly find qualified minority dealer principals and to award them any open markets. Josleyn was more than happy to engage in color-blind bribing. He called a friend from his General Motors days, an African-American man named Joe Pope, who now owned a Chevrolet dealership in Modesto, California. All you have to do, Josleyn told Pope, is to find some sort of facility, pay me $150,000, and you will become the Honda dealer in Elk Grove, a suburb of Sacramento.

Pope was nervous about Josleyn's request that the transaction be in cash. "Being black and going to the bank for $150,000," said Pope, "they might think I was dealing dope." He asked if he could write a check, and Josleyn reluctantly agreed, requesting that it be made out to Garey and Associates, the advertising company owned by Josleyn and his brother, Gary. In June 1991 Pope handed Josleyn a $150,000 check, which Josleyn dutifully split with Cardiges, in exchange for the Honda letter of intent for Elk Grove. Josleyn had just violated Billmyer's Rule about always taking your graft in greenbacks, an occurrence becoming increasingly more common under the whirlwind Cardiges regime.

Pope's proposed dealership would have marked a milestone in Honda kickback history — it would have topped Temple's Santa Paula Honda as the one in the silliest facility, no small feat. Pope was approved to operate out of a tiny storefront in a strip mall, wedged between a floor covering store and a Jack-in-the Box restaurant training center. This was not a case of Pope being cut some slack because he was black, just standard operating procedure for the greed-driven executives. Honda president Amemiya would have approved the building even if Pope had not been a minority — he rarely stood in the way of the dubious deals his "bad boys" made. Josleyn and Cardiges were always ready with their, "don't worry, it's only a temporary building" rationale if Amemiya balked at Pope's facility. (After the tainted officials departed, the new Honda sales division managers deemed Pope's proposed dealership "an embarrassment" and canceled the deal.)

Other zone sales managers tried to throw together minority-owned dealerships. There were plenty of successful minority dealer principals who could have been awarded Honda franchises. Instead, the managers called upon dealers who had paid them off in the past, instructing them to find minority candidates and to put their names on the paperwork. The candidates would then receive a Honda point — for the usual kickback to the backers, of course. Favored dealers Cliff Peck, Rick Hendrick, and Jim McNatt produced some rather questionable candidates. One Southern dealership owner used his African-American car wash porter as the straw dealer. None of the deals were ever consummated. Honda allowed the minority dealer project to die off, much to the chagrin of the corrupt executives. To truly commit to developing a minority dealer development program, Honda would have had to add additional employees, the big no-no at the lean machine.

Shortly after the Joe Pope transaction, Josleyn suffered yet another setback to his secondary income. He was the distributor of several hundred used Honda company cars annually in California, using a rigged bidding process with area dealers. This practice was putting $1,000 per car in his pocket in kickbacks from the chosen Honda dealers, who would gladly buy these units for $2,000 below wholesale book price. Dealer profit on the cars was higher than those on new Hondas, the market taking its toll on the margins on new car sales.

Norm Reeves Honda in Los Angeles had purchased 441 used cars from Josleyn during the previous year, forwarding over $400,000 to him in the process. In mid-1991 the dealership's thoughtful co-owner Dave Conant suddenly got religion. "It was making me sick," he says of the kickbacks. "I was throwing up every morning. I was losing a lot of sleep and (when) I was out doing my morning runs and stopping at my little lookout point that I've always enjoyed, I would say a lot of prayers." He decided to call Josleyn and try to cancel the deal.

"Dennis, I'm uncomfortable with our arrangement and I don't want to continue buying the cars," said Conant.

"You're the only dealer with deep enough pockets to take them all," Josleyn responded. "I am going to sell every goddamn one of them to you, and you are going to take them." Josleyn hung up the phone.

Conant then boldly approached Honda executive vice president Tom Elliott about the situation. He suggested to Elliott that Honda might want to consider selling the cars at auction like other automakers do. Conant did not mention anything about the payoffs.

Here was Conant, profiting hundreds of thousands of dollars from selling Honda's used cars, telling a Honda executive that he did not want to make that money anymore. No dealer in his right mind would do such a thing, but Elliott did not see anything unusual in Conant's recommendation, just as he had not been phased by the revelations about the Peck checks three months earlier.

Soon after, Conant was saved by Honda's company car department. Likely prompted by Elliott, they reviewed the sale prices of the used cars. Vehicles that should have been commanding more money in Honda-crazy Los Angeles than the rest of the nation were bringing thousands less when Josleyn sold them. They found it odd that Josleyn had sold some of the California cars to Temple's South Carolina Honda dealership. Deciding to sell a batch of company cars at auction, they were astonished by how much more they fetched than when Josleyn sold them, to the tune of about $2,000 per unit.

The company car department canceled Josleyn's right to sell the used cars, concluding that Josleyn was not attuned to the market. He was the only zone sales manager to lose such privileges at the time. Honda sent subsequent automobiles through the auction, where all California Honda dealers could bid on them. Dennis Josleyn had pushed it too far. Other zone sales managers conducting the same scam were content to squeeze $300 to $500 per car from the dealers, but Josleyn's need for greed had tripped him up.

Amazingly, it did not occur to the company car department or to Elliott that Josleyn might be receiving kickbacks on the deal. Elliott knew about Temple's involvement in the Peck deal, a clue that should have sent up a red flag when Temple's name surfaced as one of the used car buyers. Instead, Elliott and the company car department were just happy to brag to the Japanese execs about the additional money they would be generating for the company. Just as they had the Peck checks, Honda officials missed another opportunity to instigate an investigation and put the brakes on the corruption carousel.

Josleyn racked his brain to mastermind a fresh scheme to funnel money back into his and Cardiges's pockets. He winced when recalling their first feeble attempt a few months prior. The pair did profit—but at the expense of Honda's credibility with its dealer body. The sales training seminars scam of 1990 had been a catastrophe.

Honda was asked by its National Dealer Council—an advisory board of ten Honda dealers—to offer sales training to dealership salespeople. The request was in reaction to the softening market and to the fact that such seminars were common practice for other automakers. Cardiges spoke to Amemiya, and he agreed it would be a good idea—as long as Honda did not have to pay for it. Honda could hire an appropriate trainer, but the dealers would have to ante up. Honda would bill the dealers through their open parts accounts—a monthly computerized transaction system—and forward payment to the chosen vendor.

When Cardiges announced to the zone sales managers his intentions to offer Honda's first-ever salespeople training seminars, Josleyn's eyes lit up. He pulled Cardiges aside and proposed that one of his and his brother's companies could act as middleman between Honda and a sales training corporation, and the two executives could split the profits. Cardiges said to go for it.

The Josleyns' advertising firm, Garey and Associates, hired a sales trainer named Bob Davies. A college football coach turned high-energy motivational speaker, Davies was a self-described "recovering exercise bulimia obsessive-compulsive." He exercised six to eight hours a day so he could stuff himself with food, doing sit-ups instead of throw-ups to purge the calories.

Garey and Associates did not want to receive checks directly from Honda, so it set up a subsidiary called Sales Training Technologies (STT) and forged Davies's signature as president. Davies had pitched his day-long seminars to various automobile dealers in the Los Angeles area with little success. The hefty cost of $185 per salesperson was the biggest obstacle to his marketing effort. Said one Honda dealer, "At that price, we simply did not see the value in it."

Josleyn's plan was to sell the seminars for $395 per salesperson.

"The fee is way too high," Davies told Josleyn. "Why are we charging so much?"

"Don't worry about it," said Josleyn. "If dealers don't send their people, we won't send them any cars." Holding the big Honda hammer over dealers' heads was Josleyn's way of selling the program. Davies was handed a lucrative nationwide contract, so he did not ask further questions.

We all flew to San Francisco to see a run-through of Davies's seminar, entitled "Breaking the Sales Barrier." It was awful. The program was a stale power-of-the-mind performance-enhancement show. The lowlight was the glazed-eyed Davies hypnotizing a salesman to lie across two chairs, as Davies stood on his stomach and exhorted him to remain "straight and stiff as a steel rod, straight and stiff as a steel rod," the crowd tittering at his choice of words. Davies handed out cassette tapes of Baroque music, which supposedly have a mystical power that enhances learning and memory. We were instructed to record mantras of our personal and professional goals (e.g., "I love salad. I will eat more salad") over the music bed and listen to them daily. In the back of the room, zone sales manager Frank Pisano could be heard muttering into his tape recorder "I will get laid. I will get laid."

We knew the dealers would hate it. Offering each salesperson $395 in cash would have better motivated them to sell more Hondas. Most of the zone sales managers smelled a rat and did not push the program like we did in California. The following week, Josleyn held a conference call with me and the other California district sales managers. He politely suggested we might want to shoot for 100 percent participation by the dealers.

"At General Motors, we had to sell programs like this all the time," Josleyn told us. "It will mean 60 days of hell and a bad review if you don't get it done. I could always get some girls to come in and do your jobs." Maybe Josleyn should have been the motivational speaker.

It was hard to explain to a dealer why he had to spend $395 per salesperson, plus buy a series of follow-up tapes for $895, particularly to those who had turned down Davies at $185 per person. There was no sense trying to sell the dealers on the merits of the seminars. We begged, coerced, made promises, apologized, blamed Josleyn — anything we could think of to enroll the retailers. One of my peers told dealers that he would be fired if they did not comply. We signed up over 1,000 salespeople in California, and more than 6,000 attended nationwide.

Pushing this program was the worst task I performed during my career at American Honda. Looking the dealers' employees in the eyes at the meetings was tough. Many skipped the afternoon sessions and went back to their stores. My largest dealer, Robertson Honda of North Hollywood, spent over $14,000 on the seminar, and dealer principal Jack Robertson attended personally. "It was a rip-off," he said, a comment echoed by other dealers. One dealer joked that "someone at Honda must be making money on this thing."

Cardiges did not agree with the dealers' dissent, saying later, "I would have supported this program even if I was not receiving a kickback." The seminars were everything that Cardiges himself embodied: the high-tone image, the flash, the handsome motivational speaker, the lack of substance.

More than $2.8 million was collected from Honda dealers nationwide, funneled through Honda's accounting department, and forwarded to Sales Training Technologies. Bob Davies estimated that the program made a $1.8 million profit for Garey and Associates. In May the company paid Davies his $180,000 fee and forwarded checks to three Honda officials: $100,000 to Cardiges, $50,000 to Western regional sales manager Bob Rivers, and $30,000 to Josleyn.

For a program that generated so much money, I have always wondered about the payout. Josleyn would not walk across the room for $30,000. The seminars involved too much work and exposure for the relatively small sum of money paid to the officials. Two incidents support my feeling that more cash was divvied up. A Honda manager spotted Dennis and Gary Josleyn high-rolling at the craps tables in Las Vegas the weekend after the seminars were held in California. And soon after, Josleyn bought a $500,000 home in the Nellie Gail subdivision of Laguna Hills, three doors down from Cardiges's mansion — not bad for a guy officially making $83,000 annually. Josleyn and Cardiges's homes were the only ones in the neighborhood surrounded by security fences.

Josleyn's relocation cemented his place in line to succeed Cardiges as national sales manager. Whom Cardiges would choose to take his place if he retired had been unclear since the obvious heir apparent, Ed Temple, had left the company the previous year. Though the two regional sales managers outranked Josleyn, neither was going to get the head job. Eastern boss Larry Finley had already served a stint in California and did not want to go back. Western chief Bob Rivers was perceived as being a playboy and not committed to the company. Worse, he was short, blond, and balding; no way would Cardiges pick someone not in his own image to represent American Honda.

Soon after moving in, Josleyn walked over to Cardiges's house and handed him an envelope containing $10,000 in cash, a gift not tied to any specific deal.

"Thanks for taking care of me," said Josleyn.

Josleyn and Cardiges had to invent a better money trap. They could not propose another sales seminar, fearing a dealer revolt. The pair decided to turn their attention to Honda's dealer advertising association funds. They had dabbled in this money for a few months but decided to turn up the heat in early 1991.

Honda relied on dealer advertising associations to support local markets. These groups of dealers hired their own advertising agencies and operated independently of Honda. The creative executions of their television commercials were not always in keeping with Honda's strong brand image — they often resembled the "if you ain't yelling, you ain't selling" philosophy of individual dealer advertising. From exploding Toyotas to screaming spokespeople, most Honda association commercials made Cal Worthington spots look like public service announcements. The antiquated advertising system also prevented Honda from having a presence in markets where the dealers chose not to form an ad group, shutting their market out from receiving any Honda funds.

Cardiges and Josleyn undertook a scam that could work only at Honda, with its lean staffing and resultant inadequate systems of checks and balances. Honda contributed to the 80 Honda dealer advertising associations with $40 million of direct funding annually. The administration of this money was not as strict as convenience stores protecting $20 bills. The Japanese officials' faith in Cardiges meant he and the zone sales managers could direct the marketing money at will. The absence of paperwork to back up funding of these proposed advertising campaigns by the criminals was laughable. All it took was a minimal proposal from a zone manager and two signatures — one from advertising association manager Tom

Caulfield and one from Cardiges. Million-dollar-check requests would be rubber-stamped by the Japanese executives.

Josleyn and the gang directed advertising associations to contract with Bergmann and Associates, another of the corporations owned by Josleyn and his brother. The firm was named for Gary and Patti Bergmann, old friends of Josleyn's, a couple recently hired due to the burgeoning business being done by the Josleyn empire. Gary was a former truck driver and Patti a secretary, a pair whom Josleyn figured would not grasp the company's true mission. Indeed, when a Honda field office secretary called the firm to ask a question about STT, she was told by Patti Bergmann that "Mr. Josleyn is not in," causing the secretary's boss, a dirty zone sales manager, to scramble to convince her that it was a mere coincidence that the vendor had an employee with the same last name as Honda's California zone sales manager.

Bergmann and Associates' medium of choice was direct mail, targeting current and potential Honda owners with flyers offering free prizes and special deals at their local dealers. Unlike television or newspaper ads, direct mail pieces were impossible to track by the dealer groups, the only support documentation being provided by the executives' front company — and easily faked. The checks from Honda were made out to the associations, so the name Bergmann and Associates did not appear in Honda's records. The associations in turn paid Bergmann, and the profits from the campaigns flowed back into the Honda officials' pockets.

This game was a turning point for the Honda scandal. With the dealer advertising associations acting as conduits, the executives were now embezzling money directly from American Honda.

The 28-year-old Tom Caulfield was the only non-sales-division employee involved in the shenanigans. He had to be carefully recruited into the fold, since his conversion to the dark side was critical to the scheme — his signature on the checks was the key to the $40 million vault. Caulfield worked for advertising manager Eric Conn, a long-time Honda employee with a prize corner cubicle, a man who often confessed to not knowing what his employees did all day. Though Conn was on the other side of the fence, tight with the Japanese officials and Tom Elliott, and thus a potential whistle-blower, Cardiges correctly figured that Conn would never realize what was happening.

Cardiges engaged in a little reverse schmoozing, playing to young Caulfield's burning ambition to get ahead. He told his impressionable understudy, "You are the son I never had. Grab onto my coattails." We all looked up to Cardiges, but Caulfield began to idolize him. "Tom was Cardiges's trained Labrador puppy, wagging his tail and licking his boots," recalls one Honda official.

Cardiges outlined the scheme to Caulfield. "There'll be something in it for you, too," Cardiges added.

"Is what we are doing illegal in any way?" asked Caulfield.

"Don't worry about it," said Cardiges. "I've checked with my lawyer. The worst case scenario is that it is a possible conflict of interest."

A few months later, Josleyn laid a $100,000 check on Caulfield's desk, erasing Caulfield's fears and cementing his participation and loyalty in the plot. Receiving twice your annual salary in one transaction can do that to you.

Cardiges and his crew thus had their vendor in place and had gained control of the advertising funds. Caulfield became the point man and recruited the zone sales managers to participate and share in the proceeds. The scam divided the crew. Said Larry Finley: "I can understand giving friends dealerships, but now they've got their hands in the company pocketbook." Only four of ten zone sales managers joined in. One who refused was Ohio manager Rodney Sapp, who recalled a late-night meeting with Caulfield in Detroit.

"Tom said some of the guys had figured out a way to get money out of the ad fund," said Sapp. "He asked if I wanted to join in. I said no way. It was amazing. They just assumed we were all crooks."

The Cardiges cadre also could not convince New York zone sales manager Roger Novelly of the merits of the program. Novelly traveled in his own circle at Honda, accepting the occasional gratuity from a dealer, but he drew the line at stealing money from his employer. His high-volume territory included New York City and Philadelphia and received a huge chunk of the advertising money, thus providing a potentially lucrative market for the gang. Caulfield turned up the heat on Novelly, intimating that he would cut off advertising funds for Novelly's markets if he did not play along. Cardiges was still stinging from Novelly's earlier refusal to push the sales training seminars and his resistance to Cardiges's attempts to establish three dubious Honda stores in Pennsylvania.

Cardiges was furious that Novelly would not endorse the direct mail scam. He told Novelly that he was not being a team player and threatened, "You either get out of the company or else we're going to move you to Lower Slabovia, or do whatever we want to do with you." Novelly held his ground and further infuriated the brotherhood by contacting his dealers who were presidents of advertising associations and instructing them to rebuff any overtures from his bosses about using Bergmann and Associates' programs. When Caulfield subsequently attended a Pittsburgh association meeting, the dealers heeded Novelly's warning and turned a deaf ear to Caulfield's pitch.

"I kept Jim Cardiges and his friends out of my zone as long as I could," said Novelly.

Cardiges gave one of his "life philosophy" speeches to Denver zone sales manager Jim Mortimer to convince him to endorse the advertising scheme. Cardiges made it clear to the meek Mortimer that his recent promotion was based on his agreeing to force his dealer associations to use Bergmann and Associates, but Mortimer was balking. After a meeting in Torrance, Cardiges called Mortimer into his cubicle to expound on the importance of a college education, knowing that Mortimer had a child on the way. You have to prepare for the future today, advised Cardiges, you've got to put at least $80,000 in the bank now if you want your child to attend a good university. Cardiges ended the meeting by telling Mortimer to let him know if he had a problem selling the promotions to his dealer groups.

Most of the zone sales managers passionately pitched the benefits of the direct mail program and the designated vendor to the dealer associations, implying that Bergmann and Associates was an approved Honda supplier. Josleyn, however, would bulldoze his plan through a dealer advertising group, announcing to the dealers and their agency: "If you want this money, you must do a direct mail campaign and do it with the company I recommend. If you don't like it, I will take the money elsewhere." He also hinted that Amemiya supported the marketing plan, dealers being unaware that American Honda's president had no clue about the use of the advertising funds. Josleyn offered the groups up to $1 million each in extra support, so they were compelled to acquiesce. Dealers grumbled among themselves about the direct mail strategy, but since it was found money, no one complained.

Josleyn designed some of the mailers himself on his home computer, though most of the creative and production work was farmed out. Garey and Associates had done legitimate advertising work in the past, so it supplied the contacts for its Bergmann subsidiary. When a mailer was completed, Josleyn determined the splits for his peers after he and his brother had each grabbed a chunk of the profits for their personal expenses. Josleyn instructed Patti Bergmann to list the other execs as consultants on the books. Josleyn mailed the checks to the field managers and hand-delivered them to Caulfield and Cardiges — except for the time Gary Bergmann met Caulfield in Honda's lobby and handed him one for $150,000. That transaction occurred 50 feet from Honda's personnel department.

Honda's regional marketing decisions were affected by the embezzlement. Nonplayer Novelly's key markets, New York City and Philadelphia, saw a cutback in association advertising funds, all because he refused to steal from Honda. When additional money was authorized for dealer ad groups, regardless of whether it was earmarked for Bergmann, Cardiges and Caulfield helped the territories of the cooperative zone sales managers first. An association with one or more dealers who were individual contributors to the executives would also receive a disproportionate share of the ad money. Although the tough 1991 economy demanded more precise marketing efforts in major cities, the country was still a giant Monopoly board to the Honda executives.

In earlier efforts, Bergmann fulfilled its contracts with the associations, and only the profits were split with the tainted executives. In mid-1991 Josleyn and Cardiges decided to push the direct mail envelope even further: they would contract for several hundred thousand piece mailers but only produce and mail half the amount promised. The fewer pieces mailed, the more money in the conspirators' pockets. They were now ripping off both Honda and the dealer advertising associations.

It was a natural progression to their final coup de graft.

The scheme reached its zenith in December 1991. By this time, Josleyn was desperate — the ad scam was now his only source of outside income to support his lavish lifestyle. He had just spent $300,000 on a pool and landscaping for his new home, just as California real estate prices started to crash. Josleyn began arriving in the office at 4:00 A.M. and leaving by noon to head for Bergmann and Associates. His sour demeanor worsened.

Josleyn was busy masterminding the ultimate twist on the direct mail swindle: to commit a total of $2 million to all four California dealer advertising associations for a supposed 1-million-piece direct mailer but then produce and send only a few thousand pieces. Bergmann and Associates' previous profit margin had been almost 60 percent — this plan would raise it to 95 percent, a potential $1.9 million bonanza for the conspirators. Josleyn envisioned it being the biggest score ever for him and Cardiges. The scam would help him achieve his goal of having Cardiges promote him to the top sales job upon Cardiges's retirement, not to mention pay a few bills.

In an infamous Josleyn conference call he announced how the swindle would work.

"I have an assignment for you," Josleyn began his monologue to me and the other California district sales managers. "I want you to contact every dealer in your district and have them give you the names and addresses of every one of their employees. That includes the dealer principals themselves. Tell them that I personally need them this week. Make up anything you want, but just get them." He signed off with his usual ranting: if you guys can't get this assignment done, maybe you need to transfer to the parts or service division. He even posed the ultimate threat: to exile us to the black hole of lost Honda employees, the Acura division.

He did not explain it, but we knew what the deal was. By sending the direct mail pieces to dealership personnel only, Josleyn envisioned dealer principals coming to work one morning and having dozens of employees report that they had received the flyer. Josleyn assumed the dealers would be impressed at the reach of the mailer. Josleyn and Cardiges had become so convinced of their invincibility that it never occurred to them that we or the retailers would figure the scheme out.

We called the dealers to obtain the names and addresses. It was impossible to fabricate a good story as to why we needed the information. Consider it "franchise insurance," we said, the standard factory line used to pressure dealers. The dealers fought back — most knew that giving out the information was in violation of California employment privacy laws. Most refused, and every dealer asked what it was for, a question we dared not answer.

Three days later, assistant zone sales manager Jim Gilbreath held another conference call with us. Gilbreath was like the rest of us, simply following orders. He had a tendency to stammer like cartoon character Porky Pig when Josleyn was breathing down his neck, and we could barely understand him that morning. He said, "Guys, guys, look, Dennis really needs these names, he really needs them, you gotta get 'em, you just got to. He's not very happy." Several of my peers mentioned the resistance we were encountering from the dealers.

In dozens of previous Josleyn Conference Calls from Hell, San Francisco district sales manager Jim Sweeting and I were the only ones who dared to speak up and question these odd assignments. Josleyn would always quickly put us in our places. I could hear Sweeting cowering, so I figured it must be my turn this day. Besides, Josleyn was not on this call.

I pressed Gilbreath as to exactly why Josleyn needed the dealerships' employee rosters. You could feel Gilbreath vibrating. "Steve, Steve, you know Dennis needs them. Don't ask why, just don't ask," Gilbreath whined. Undaunted, I asked again. Come on guys, I thought, jump in here anytime and back me up. Two beats of silence were followed by the sonic boom of Dennis Josleyn's voice, "BECAUSE I FUCKIN' NEED THEM, OK, STEVE?" The paranoid Josleyn had secretly been monitoring the call.

My peers called afterwards to revive me. "We were right behind you,

Steve," said one, "I was just about to say something myself." Working for Josleyn was becoming so absurd that all we could do was laugh.

We were only able to provide Josleyn with a handful of names and addresses. The Los Angeles dealer group refused to participate and returned a $1 million check sent to them for the campaign. We never found out how many mailers were sent.

In the end, over $2.5 million in direct mail money ended up back in the pockets of the crooked executives in 1991. The figure is based on what authorities would later uncover, funds that changed hands via check. It likely totaled a lot more.

Cardiges received a 1099 federal tax form from Bergmann and Associates reflecting the $657,000 paid to him in 1991. He enjoyed an official income of $1.25 million that year, only $181,000 of which came from Honda, the rest supplied by the dealers and front companies that issued 1099s reflecting their payoffs to him. Add to that the cash and prizes that Cardiges did not report to the Internal Revenue Service, and his total take was close to $2 million — a good year.

Dennis Josleyn made a total of $688,000 in the advertising scam. Gary Josleyn used his split to purchase a $1 million home in Anaheim Hills. Tom Caulfield pocketed $816,000 and bought a $400,000 house and a Corvette. Patti and Gary Bergmann paid themselves $447,000. Zone sales managers Hugh Cooper and Bob Mazzitelli each profited about $100,000. And Jim Mortimer made $85,000, enough to start that college fund for his child.

Things were out of control at American Honda. Larry Finley, one of those who refused to embezzle from the corporation, tried to initiate a conversation with Tom Elliott about the actions of the graft-happy executives. While the two were driving to the Phoenix Formula One Grand Prix race, Finley took a deep breath and tried to choose his words carefully.

"Tom, things were pretty tough when Jack was here," said Finley. "Since Jim has taken over, this thing has really become a mess. Things are getting worse."

Elliott knew that Finley was not referring to the dropping sales numbers. He stared straight ahead for ten seconds before responding.

"Who do you think will win the race today?" asked Tom Elliott.

CHAPTER 12

Confessions

WE INTERRUPT this book to answer the burning question on your mind: Okay, Mr. Former Honda Executive, what about you? If you know so much, you must have played the game yourself, right?

I confess.

I was no choirboy during my career at Honda. While in retail in San Antonio, my stores took good care of our Honda reps, including Ed (Everywhere) Temple. While at American Honda, certain goods and services came my way, but I did not play favorites among the retailers I called on. My take during eight years at Honda was one-tenth of what Jim Cardiges could procure with one phone call. I rationalized the gifts as being normal fringe benefits one receives at such a level in the business world — my version of denial.

My Top Ten List of Booty:

10. Free excursion to the 1993 Super Bowl football game, provided by Honda's advertising agency. Eight years earlier, Honda advertising manager Eric Conn was punished for accepting the same trip, one of the few cases of "corruption" that Honda's blind human resources department uncovered during the 1980s. Perhaps that was why the bus met me, Conn, and 20 other executives in a remote corner of the Honda campus, far from any personnel Pecksniffs who might have been working that Sunday morning.
9. One trip on a Honda dealer's $2 million airplane. We flew to San Francisco. We ate hot dogs at the airport. We flew back to Los Angeles.
8. Loans of off-road motorcycles and transportation into desert for use thereof. One of the dealer/dirt bikers led me up a brutal mountain trail in remote central California and at the top threatened,

"I want a load of Accords or we are leaving you here." I thought he was joking, but I took no chances.

7. Four years worth of car phone bills while I was a district sales manager in Los Angeles, paid for by a dealer. Honda was too cheap to provide what was a necessity in L.A. Estimated cost: $7,000. The dealer received four extra Hondas a year in return — my old company cars with high miles, worn-out brakes, and a $500 discount — hardly a good deal.
6. Floor seats to Los Angeles Laker basketball games, provided by a dealer. The tickets' face value: $500 each. Dealer paid $1,200 each. We sat opposite actor Jack Nicholson, the cheerleaders at our feet.
5. Innumerable dinner, drinks, and debasement evenings. One occurred during my first week on the job: an $1,800 tab at a strip joint for me and six other Honda officials, provided by a Texas dealer.
4. Dah Chong Hong's Honda of Oxnard gave me an electronic organizer as a Christmas gift, two weeks before Temple stuck Santa Paula Honda in their backyard. They never gave me another present.
3. A Rick Hendrick dealership gave me a gift certificate to Nieman-Marcus and another loaned me an Accord while I was vacationing in South Carolina. Hendrick did not forget anyone at Honda.
2. Honda dealers supplied me with the use of various vehicles, for periods ranging from one weekend to several months. Acura NSXs and Chevy Suburbans were among my favorites. I always had to give them back.
1. A certain Honda dealer made a company car of mine disappear. Hopefully, after he replaced the tires and suspension. And repaired the body damage. And did not tell my boss. (All I will say is four-wheel steering screws up the ability of a Prelude to do a hit-the-handbrake 180-degree spin.)

Disappointed? Me, too. I was a lightweight. I never even received a Rolex watch. I turned down many items, including free rent on a $200,000 home, a trip to Hawaii, and an American Express card with no limit (and no bill). I could have asked for anything and gotten it, but that was not my style.

I did make a run at some interoffice bribery. If you were a departing zone sales manager and a member of the boys' club, the rights to a new Honda dealership would be granted gratis, in the market of your choice. It was Honda's golden parachute. You could build the store or simply sell the letter of intent for a half-million bucks. Below the zone manager level, you had to pay off your bosses like any prospective dealer, albeit at a reduced fee. Former district sales manager Dan Zeid and his partner paid Bob Rivers a mere $52,000 for the right to open a dealership in fast-growing Tempe, Arizona. (That discount price probably also guaranteed that Zeid would remain silent about his knowledge of Christiaan Walker and the Peck checks.) I proposed being granted a Honda franchise in Texas and was quoted $75,000, though my nondealer backer got cold feet and we never followed through on the deal.

Although I eventually replaced Tom Caulfield as manager of dealer association advertising, I had been given the opportunity to take the job before he did in 1988. I turned it down — the best career decision I ever made. I know what I would have done when Jim Cardiges, the man we all idolized, handed me a $100,000 check from Bergmann and Associates, like he did Caulfield.

Let's just say I would be writing this book in prison.

CHAPTER 13

Den of Denial

I didn't really quit my job. I got fired. But it was the same thing.

—Albert Brooks, from the film *Lost in America*

IN EARLY 1992 American Honda had to make a move. All hell was breaking loose as details and rumors of their sales executives' venal activities suddenly popped up everywhere. The company was paying the price for allowing the problems to fester for so long.

It began with three Concord jams. Preliminary hearings in a Concord, New Hampshire, lawsuit, accusing the Acura division of wrongfully terminating a franchise, uncovered gifts received by an Acura zone sales manager. The proceedings were placed under a protective order, but the judge was threatening to revoke it. A Concord, California, dealer filed a lawsuit accusing Honda of pressuring retailers to falsify sales reports. The ex-husband of Honda traffic assistant Bonnie Sikora wrote Honda headquarters detailing $120,000 in cash she had received from the Rick Hendrick organization in exchange for her boosting the allocations of their Concord, North Carolina, dealership.

A New Jersey dealer protested Honda's establishing a new dealership, claiming the dealer principal was awarded the franchise because he paid off Jim Cardiges and Roger Novelly. Motormouth Christiaan Walker told dozens of fellow Honda employees about the Cliff Peck kickbacks to Cardiges and Ed Temple and also mentioned that Honda higher-ups were stonewalling the information. Members of a California Honda dealer advertising association, convinced they had been shortchanged by Bergmann and Associates on a direct mail campaign, were making noises about demanding their money back from Honda. Dumpy new dealerships established by Honda attracted the attention of industry observers.

Worst of all, the press was snooping around. The secretive company's dirty money laundry was in danger of going public.

Nine years after J. D. Power had warned Honda executives about the bribery within their ranks, and nearly one full year after Walker informed Tom Elliott and Lyon & Lyon about the evidence on Cardiges and Temple, Honda finally decided to take action to stop the corruption that had permeated its executive offices since the 1970s. The lawsuits and the Peck checks had forced their hand. The party had to end — the only problem was in covering up the cover-up.

In February 1992 American Honda president Koichi Amemiya conferred with Lyon & Lyon attorneys and agreed that the time had come for heads to roll. Amemiya could no longer protect his "bad boys." It was time for him to cover his rear — the hell with Cardiges and the other expendable Americans. Amemiya would be the one blamed for any scandal. The American Honda presidency was a high honor — second only to being head of Honda Motor Company — and Amemiya did not want a slow boat ride back to Sayama. Amemiya always felt that once the information about the corruption was in danger of going public, it would be time to put a stop to it. He was firm in his decision that any violations of Honda's conflict of interest policy that were uncovered would mean termination for the offenders.

Amemiya had just completed Cardiges's annual performance review, giving the national sales manager his lowest score ever. He deemed Cardiges's 1991 job performance as merely "proficient" rather than the "exceptional" ratings of prior years. Cardiges's attainment of sales objectives, as measured by Honda's poor 1991 sales figures, and his leadership and sales management skills were ranked a 2 on a scale of 5. Amemiya commended Cardiges for the fact that 81 percent of Honda dealerships were exclusive, unaware that the figure had been inflated by the sales executives.

That Japanese officials' careers lived and died by sales numbers was not the only reason Amemiya burned Cardiges in his review. During that hectic year, Cardiges, distracted by his side deals, had offered no solutions as to how to get Honda moving again. "When cars weren't going away anymore, Jim did not know what to do," says one executive. "He did not have any ideas to improve sales." The years of Honda not developing a strong finance arm or showroom customer-handling programs had caught up to it. All Cardiges could do was beg the Japanese to keep the incentive money flowing to the dealers, an expensive, short-term approach to a long-term problem.

Amemiya's decision to confront Cardiges about the Peck checks would also handle what Amemiya perceived as a lack of strong leadership by his sales chief. The days of Amemiya sheltering Cardiges and winking at his indiscretions were over. It was time for a change.

Amemiya summoned Sherry Cameron, Honda vice president of human resources, to his cubicle. "We have some very serious information about some of our executives," said Amemiya. "I would like you to take care of this. Could you please meet with Mr. Bud Smoot at Lyon and Lyon and his partners, and they will give this information to you. It's very important that you handle it and handle it quickly. We must be sure to protect the company." Cameron was placed in charge of the internal investigation. There was no limit as to who she could scrutinize — except for president Amemiya, who answered only to Tokyo. The Mercedes-Benz convertible parked in his garage was safe for now.

Cameron was a tall, attractive 41-year-old woman with shoulder-length brown hair. She had risen to the top of her department in seven years and was the only female vice president in Honda's corporate offices. Like other Honda managers, her range of responsibilities was greater than it would have been at other companies. Besides her personnel duties, Cameron oversaw the planning and construction of Honda's 101-acre, $225 million Torrance national headquarters campus during the late 1980s. She was regarded as aloof and out of touch with employees, admittedly a common perception about personnel managers of large companies. Cameron had taken the brunt of sales division executives' complaints about substandard salaries and lack of cost-of-living allowances for years. If her Japanese superiors had kept pay plans low figuring the execs could make it up through payola, she was probably not aware of it.

Cameron also claimed to be unaware of allegations of corruption about any current Honda executive until the day she met with Amemiya. Maybe she didn't know, but she was surrounded by clues. She knew that Jack Billmyer had ownership in a Budweiser beer distributorship while employed at Honda. The addresses of the expensive homes owned by Cardiges, Dennis Josleyn, and Tom Caulfield sat in a file a few feet from her desk. She was aware that Honda security chief Tony Piazza had insisted for years that sales department managers were on the take. And she had seen the letter regarding Bonnie Sikora receiving cash from the Hendrick organization. Cameron should have realized that something was wrong.

Cameron met with Lyon & Lyon attorneys, who proceeded to open the vault. The lawyers, led by Bud Smoot, came clean, telling Cameron that the corruption among Honda sales division managers had been "widespread" for years and that the selling of franchises had been a common practice.

They provided her with copies of the checks from Cliff Peck Honda to Cardiges, Fred Meis, and the departed Temple. They supplied her with a wealth of other interred tidbits—from rumors about Josleyn's involvement in his brother's companies to former vice president Cliff Schmillen's co-ownership of a Honda dealership. Despite the law firm learning about the Schmillen deal in 1979, the attorneys told Cameron they had only recently been made aware of it. In her notes from the meeting, Cameron wrote that the information "raises suspicion all past rumors are true."

Cameron was assisted in her investigation by manager of employee relations Jim Quirk. The pair would spend 80 percent of their time over the next two years rooting out the rank. With the help of a private investigation firm, they developed a strategy for conducting the inquisition, focusing on how to confront and question the suspects. They proceeded to dig into the lives of the accused managers.

The human resources department started with Cardiges. Private investigators rooted though his trash, as well as that of other suspected employees. They photographed his home. State records revealed Cardiges's ownership in his outside businesses and a dozen Orange County properties. They were unable to probe further into Cardiges's holdings, Amemiya wanting the deed done quickly, but it was clear he was living way beyond his Honda paycheck.

Cameron prepared for the showdown. Walker flew to Torrance to reidentify the Peck checks and reiterate rumors he had heard about the officials. On April 13, almost one year to the day after Walker had forwarded the Peck evidence to Lyon & Lyon, Cardiges was summoned to a small, bare-walled conference room in the human resources department. He rode the elevator to the first floor, unsure of why they wanted to see him.

Cameron and Quirk were waiting. They opened the meeting on an intriguing note, one with possibly deeper implications. Cameron produced a copy of a handwritten note Cardiges had given to Amemiya two months before, on the day of his 1991 performance review:

> Mr. Amemiya:
> Please, *no* increase for me this year. As you already know, I was a "bad boy" a couple of years ago. I'm trying to be better!
> Jim
> P.S. Thanks for looking after me!

"Bad boy" indeed. Cameron asked Cardiges to explain the meaning of the note. Cardiges stated that Amemiya used the term *bad boy* to describe sales officials who were not working hard enough. He said that, because of the lower sales in the past few years, he was simply describing himself as a "bad boy." The note could be overanalyzed into implying that Amemiya knew about some other shady Cardiges activity "a couple years ago." And Cardiges's reply that sales had been dropping for a few years was not true — they had dropped only in the previous year. Enticing clues — but not enough to get fired over.

The meeting turned to a discussion of Cardiges's understanding of the company's conflict of interest policy. I understand it, said Cardiges, but I don't remember signing a copy of it.

Cameron got to the point: "Jim, we have a very serious matter to discuss and we expect your cooperation. There is an allegation we must look into. We are not saying you are guilty. We want you to look at this check," said Cameron, proffering a copy of the four-year-old $162,500 draft from Peck to Cardiges. "Can you tell us what this is?"

Cardiges was caught flat-footed. Goddamn Walker, he thought. He paused and said, "Yeah, I received it through the mail, but I don't know what it is."

"You don't know why you got it?"

"There was no letter attached to it," fumbled Cardiges. "I never spoke to Peck about it. I never did anything for it."

"What about this notation on the draft, saying 12½ percent interest in Honda World, Conway, Arkansas?" asked Cameron. "Is that a dealer paying for a dealer?"

"No, it is the interest rate on a loan to me from Peck."

Cameron and Quirk scribbled notes to document the mood of the meeting and Cardiges's demeanor. They noted how reserved the normally friendly Cardiges was acting.

"So, it was a loan?"

"Yes. He just gave me a loan for no reason."

"Do you have evidence that you've paid back that loan? You must have checks that you've written to Mr. Peck that you can show me that you have made an effort to pay that back."

"Why do you need proof?" asked Cardiges. He did not mention the bogus promissory note that he and Temple had drawn up in 1988 to cover the Peck checks. A loan from a dealer was also against Honda policy and grounds for termination. Cardiges told Cameron that it was an isolated incident and that he had never received money or loans from any other dealers.

There was no need prolonging this, Cardiges figured, they got me. The image of this moment had always been suppressed in the back of his mind. And now it was happening.

Cameron outlined how the check indicated a violation of Honda's conflict of interest policy and could be grounds for termination.

Cameron then asked Cardiges about his knowledge of the Sales Training Technologies dealer seminars. She was fishing—Walker had alerted her to the rumors that Cardiges and others had received kickbacks, but she had no evidence. Cardiges, who had profited $100,000 on the smoke-and-mirrors scam, denied that any Honda managers made money on the deal.

Cameron had discovered the sportswear manufacturer owned by Cardiges. "What is Worldwide Dyve?" she asked.

"It is simply a company I invest in," replied Cardiges. "It has nothing to do with Honda." This isn't just about Peck, Cardiges realized, they have actually investigated me.

"What is J. Car Real Estate and Development?" asked Cameron.

"It is a consulting company I own."

"What is the nature of the business?"

"I help dealers out with their financial statements, or looking at their business operations, none of them Honda dealers," Cardiges responded, his voice rising.

Cameron dropped another bombshell. She asked about Mid-Atlantic Cars, the Maryland partnership between Cardiges and Honda dealer William Schuiling, one of Cardiges's first benefactors and a man who split his dealerships' profits with Cardiges. The piece of information was yet another nugget that had been hidden in the Lyon & Lyon cave.

Cardiges's head was spinning. He admitted to doing consulting work for Schuiling and receiving $5,000 per month, adding that it had nothing to do with Schuiling's Honda dealerships. Cardiges was confessing one minute and lying the next.

"Look, what I do is my business," an indignant Cardiges blurted out. "But I do understand that the company has to do what they have to do. If Mr. Amemiya wants me to leave, I will. I haven't done anything wrong criminally, but I will leave to spare the company embarrassment; not to spare myself embarrassment because I haven't done anything wrong."

Cameron concluded the meeting by again showing him the "bad boy" note. Cardiges emphatically stated that it was not related to the Cliff Peck checks.

"Jim, we will have to make a decision regarding this matter based on the information we have," said Cameron. "We will let you know our decision. That is all."

Cardiges went back upstairs and spoke to his boss, Takeo Okusa, the number-two man to Amemiya.

"I did not do anything wrong," said Cardiges. "If this in anyway has hurt American Honda, I will resign."

"We'll see," said Okusa, turning and walking away.

Cameron reported her recommendation to Amemiya and Okusa: that Cardiges be terminated. Without hesitation, Amemiya told her to do it.

On April 22, the cold Cameron and the cool Cardiges squared off again. Cameron called corporate security, telling them to be prepared to escort Cardiges out of the building.

As he headed downstairs, Cardiges knew what was coming. He had spoken to his attorney, who recommended that Cardiges rescind his statement about receiving the Peck payment through the mail. The lawyer had told Cardiges that, in the unlikely event the government ever discovered the transaction, he could be prosecuted for mail fraud.

Cameron got to the point. "Based on all the facts that were presented in the interview and our investigation, you will be terminated from American Honda."

She pushed two documents across the table. "Jim, you have your choice. If you want to voluntarily resign, we'll allow you to do that. If not, you will be terminated for violation of our conflict of interest policy."

Cardiges studied the resignation document for a few moments, made a written notation saying that he had not received the Peck check in the mail, and signed it. His 15-year-long career with American Honda was over.

"We would like to have you leave the organization as soon as possible," directed Cameron. "If you'd like to go back to your office to pick up your briefcase or any personal items that you might have, you may. To avoid any embarrassment, it would be better if you come back on Saturday."

"Embarrassed?" replied an incredulous Cardiges. "Why would I be embarrassed?"

Under the watchful eye of security, Cardiges returned to his cubicle to type a farewell letter to Amemiya:

> I sincerely hope that you feel that I have helped to pave the road which will enable American Honda Motor Company, Inc. to transition into future direction with both competent and younger talent that will assist both the Honda dealers and the American Honda Motor Company, Inc. to achieve whatever goals are set forth. . . . Mr. Amemiya, I will miss you and the people with whom I work at American Honda Motor Company.

He handed the note to Amemiya and thanked him for his support over the years.

"I always had the impression that Mr. Amemiya looked after me," says Cardiges. "I think that Amemiya protected me up until human relations, Sherry Cameron, became aware of the Christiaan Walker/Cliff Peck incident."

Cardiges walked out of American Honda headquarters for the last time. The kingpin of kickback was going home. He held his head high, still certain he had done nothing wrong. Waiting at home were his final under-the-table payments gained while employed at Honda, a check for $9,000 from Las Vegas dealer Angelo Falconi and another for $15,000 from a Chicago dealer. Cardiges used to consider such minor gratuities as walking-around money, but this night he felt grateful.

At 9:51 that evening, as he sat at home pondering his future, a 6.1 magnitude earthquake rocked Southern California, shaking the foundation of Cardiges's mansion.

The public relations spin began the next day. Amemiya sent a letter to the dealers saying, "I accepted, with regret, the resignation of Mr. S. James Cardiges. . . . (He) has made many contributions to the success of both our company, and to Honda dealers. . . . I know you join all of us at American Honda in thanking Mr. Cardiges and in wishing him well in his new business ventures." Many dealers were unaware that the bribery extended all the way to the top of Honda's organization and were saddened to see Cardiges go. They felt they had lost a good "car man," a rarity among automaker executives. Tom Elliott, who assumed Cardiges's responsibilities until a replacement could be found, told *Automotive News:* "Jim's leaving was a surprise to all of us. You like to think you are prepared for something like this, but then when it happens, you realize you can't be totally prepared."

Japanese executives unaware of the corruption were dumbfounded when briefed about Cardiges's departure. Amemiya summed it up for them: "A man who would marry his aunt would do anything," explained the president of American Honda.

Most Honda sales division employees knew the real story, people in the automobile industry smiled when they learned of Cardiges's exit, but Honda did a terrific job of keeping the details of the "resignation" out of the press. Honda hinted to trade publications that Cardiges's departure was tied to the company's poor 1991 sales performance. The earthquake helped divert the attention locally. It was a victory for Honda's public relations staff: Cardiges was gone and nobody was the wiser.

Cardiges called some of the zone sales managers and told them he had been "sideswiped" by Cameron and Quirk and that he felt Honda might be on to them all. "You would not believe the stack of stuff they have," Cardiges told one. "They know everything. The quality of the information is real good. They know names, places and money." Members of the boys' club panicked. Some fretted about their own shenanigans being uncovered, while others were concerned about their career paths being in jeopardy, the Cardiges coattails having been cut. "I have 'Jim Cardiges' tattooed on my ass," moaned Fred Meis.

Despite rampant paranoia among the crew, all went about their normal business — except they put the brakes on the bribery. There was little opportunity left anyway; zone sales managers had projected that the tough 1992 year, with Honda sales and dealer profits dropping once again, was going to be worth only about $25,000 apiece to them in dealer gratuities.

Cardiges's forced resignation was fast and easy. It marked the end of the culture of complicity at American Honda. If the company had taken such action one, three, or ten years earlier, it would have stopped the activities before they had blossomed into the morass of bribery and embezzlement.

Mega-Honda dealer Rick Hendrick quickly halted his quarterly cash payments to Cardiges for the mortgage on the Laguna Hills house. Other dealers whom Cardiges considered his friends also stopped their disbursements to him. Cardiges was of no use to them anymore.

Cameron's investigation picked up steam as new information surfaced. With Cardiges gone, clean sales division employees suddenly had a lot to say about their corrupt peers — vindication for their careers being put on hold because they had refused to work the program. The apparent extent of the kickbacks and embezzlement stunned Cameron. Honda hired additional law firms and private investigators to assist in the inquest.

Cameron realized the limitations that were hampering the investigation. "You can only ask for so much and we don't have the power of the government to get information from employees," said Cameron. "Where the government can get a bank record, we can't. And if the employee doesn't cooperate, then we take that into consideration. And if someone is not cooperating with us and not trying to show us that their side of the story is true, then you have to take that into consideration and say, is this person dealing with you honestly or not. . . . Many times we just had a rumor and we take a rumor just as serious as if we had a copy of a check."

The day after Cardiges's departure, Cameron received an anonymous phone call from someone with a vendetta against Western regional sales manager Bob Rivers. Claiming to be the wife of a Honda executive, she told Cameron that her husband understood that Rivers was being investigated for the Sales Training Technologies scam. Her spouse claimed to have knowledge of Rivers depositing large amounts of money in an Irvine bank, supposedly kickbacks from the scheme. It was another rumor, but a good one.

Cameron then received an unsigned letter from someone claiming to be an employee of MCI Planners, a firm that had handled the administration of Honda's dealership salespeople cash incentive programs. The letter stated that the top people at MCI made monthly payments of $15,000 to an unknown Honda executive for the rights to continue to service the Honda account. The loot, always in $100 bills, was placed in a bag and delivered to the official at Honda headquarters in Torrance. Cameron knew that Rivers was the primary contact for MCI Planners.

Cameron and Quirk confronted Rivers. He denied involvement in the Sales Training Technologies scheme. He knew nothing about kickbacks from MCI Planners. He admitted that he had known about the Peck checks for several years and had not come forward, a violation of the conflict of interest policy. Cameron could not pin anything on Rivers this time, but the anonymous voice would call again.

Dennis Josleyn was next in the box. According to state records, Josleyn and his wife were part owners of Gary Josleyn's Garey and Associates and Bergmann and Associates, the vendors for the tainted sales seminars and direct mail programs. A motorhome registered to Dennis Josleyn was spied in the firms' parking lot. Cameron was told of kickbacks between Garey and Associates' subsidiary, Sales Training Technologies, and the Josleyn brothers, but she did not have any evidence. However, Josleyn's interest in an American Honda vendor was against the conflict of interest policy and grounds for termination, so she could at least nail him for that.

Josleyn was summoned to the human resources conference room. He acknowledged his understanding of the conflict of interest policy and that he had signed a copy of it. Cameron asked Josleyn to help her understand Honda's procedures for establishing new dealers. Could he explain it to her? Asking open-ended questions was the perfect strategy—Josleyn loved to spread his pearls of wisdom, even if it was to the lowlifes in personnel.

After a detailed speech about the Honda dealer placement policy, Josleyn talked about one specific deal as an example: the Joe Pope point in Sacramento in which he had collected $150,000 for himself and Cardiges in exchange for issuing the letter of intent. Josleyn did not mention the kickbacks. A good story to tell my pals later, thought Josleyn, I even talked about Pope to these idiots. Josleyn rattled on. He talked about his philosophies about the retailers ("Honda dealers are lazy"), which dealers were his friends, and which zone sales managers he hung out with. Cameron and Quirk wrote it all down.

Cameron slowly turned up the heat. "Have you seen any special favors granted to dealers?" she asked. Josleyn's response was a monologue on the legitimate business reasons to allocate extra cars to dealers.

"Have you ever received special favors from dealers yourself, like trips or cash?" asked Cameron.

"No," replied Josleyn, beginning to sweat. Cameron backed off for a moment, wanting to see what else he would reveal.

"What do you know about former Honda employees becoming Honda dealers?" she asked Josleyn. Josleyn talked about Ed Temple. He told how Temple had purchased Costa Mesa Honda, who Temple's partner was, where their vacation homes were, and why they had bought the dealership. He did not mention Temple's payola but nonetheless provided plenty for Cameron to investigate. "I wasn't aware of all this until he told me," she said later.

"What do you know about Cliff Peck and his dealership in Arkansas?" asked Cameron.

"Don't know anything about it," laughed Josleyn. Cameron noticed that he had laughed a little too hard and was sweating again.

She edged in for the kill. "Can you tell me about Sales Training Technologies?" she asked, knowing about the subsidiary of Garey and Associates that had administered the sales seminars. Josleyn obliged with a filibuster on the meetings, not mentioning the cash that he, Cardiges, and Rivers had made on the deal.

"Did you receive any kickbacks on STT?" she asked.

"No," he guffawed.

"Do you know who Garey and Associates is?"

"I've heard of them. I'm not sure who they are. They're an advertising company or something that does business with Honda."

"What is the relationship between Garey and Associates and STT?"

"I have no idea."

"Do you know anyone at Garey and Associates personally?"

"No. I think they are out of business lately."

"Who is Gary Don Josleyn?"

"My brother." Sweat poured down Josleyn's face.

"What is your response if I say to you that we have seen documents to say that your brother, Gary Don Josleyn, was president and officer of the company?"

"Your information is not correct," said Josleyn, fidgeting in his seat. "You know more information than I do."

"What is your response if I say I know that you and your wife are officers of Garey and Associates?"

"I got no connection to my brother," said Josleyn. "I never got money from him. You can see my tax returns if you want. My only income is from Honda and from bank interest."

"If Gary Don Josleyn does not own Garey and Associates, what does he do?"

"I have no idea. I think he's unemployed. He's an attorney but I don't know who he works for. Last time I saw him was at a funeral a year or so ago."

Cameron asked again about his brother.

"I've already answered that question!" yelled Josleyn, his shirt soaked with sweat.

Cameron had heard enough lies. She dismissed Josleyn. She wanted to find hard evidence on Josleyn's kickbacks, but Amemiya had told her to clean house quickly. As with Cardiges, Cameron suspected there was more to Josleyn's activities than she knew.

On April 29, Josleyn was summoned and presented with a choice: resign or be terminated for violating the conflict of interest policy for having hidden ownership in a vendor and for his lack of cooperation and candor. Josleyn resigned.

Temple had just mailed a $100,000 check to Josleyn to keep the right cars flowing to Costa Mesa Honda. He quickly stopped payment on it.

Temple and Josleyn met for lunch. Josleyn said he understood why Temple had halted the check to him. Josleyn figured that Rivers had ratted on him and Cardiges. He showed Temple a copy of the $50,000 check to Rivers from Sales Training Technologies and mentioned that he might use it to bust Rivers.

"Could I have a copy of that?" asked Temple.

The day of Josleyn's termination, Rivers was demoted for failing to report his knowledge of the Peck checks. He could have been fired for his silence, but Cameron was concerned about how the corporation could defend the balance of punishment between Rivers and Cardiges. Ironically, Rivers was assigned to monitor Honda's legal expenses for the brewing lawsuits — including cases accusing Honda execs of being on the take. Rivers went from number-two American in the sales division to being a clerk.

Honda's president tried to cheer him up. "Mr. Amemiya came up to me later that afternoon," recalls Rivers. "He said, in his broken English, that: Bob, we have a saying in Japan. You go down one side of the street and it's raining. If you just continue moving forward and turn the corner, the sunshine will be there again." Actually, around the corner for Rivers would be the same hurricane that had just blown away his two pals.

For those working for the oppressive Josleyn, the news of his resignation was cause for celebration. His reign of terror was over. The next three nights, Los Angeles burned—but it was not Josleyn's district sales managers running amok. Josleyn's termination came on the same day the Los Angeles Police Department officers were acquitted for beating motorist Rodney King, which sparked widespread rioting in L.A. Like on the night of Cardiges's firing, a disaster occurred in Los Angeles that helped deflect media attention away from Honda's purging of another top official.

Fred Meis was summoned to Torrance. Cameron showed him the $100,000 Peck check with his name on it, supposedly for his split of the Conway deal. The irony was apparent to the slippery Texas zone sales manager, a man who often flew to payoff meetings under an assumed name. Meis had received about $500,000 in cash on other open point deals but now was in danger of losing his job because of something he did not do. He denied receiving the check and agreed to help Cameron contact Peck's bank and straighten the matter out. Meis authorized Honda to investigate his personal bank account, knowing they would not find the Peck check or anything else, his loot being well-hidden. Cliff Peck granted access to his bank account to one of Honda's investigators, who discovered that someone had changed the name of the check's recipient from Arnold Creekmore to Fred Meis, the likely culprit being Christiaan Walker. Meis was cleared of participating in the Peck scheme. It would take Cameron two years to find out about Meis's real deals.

In July 1992 Cameron received evidence that the son of an Acura parts division executive worked for Garey and Associates. She prevailed upon the manager to provide information on who was being paid off by the Josleyn firms. He provided proof of kickbacks given years earlier to two Acura parts division executives, in exchange for them granting Garey and Associates the contract to print Acura accessory brochures. The two men were fired. The informant gave Cameron copies of checks reflecting the advertising association payoffs from Bergmann and Associates to Josleyn, Cardiges, and Tom Caulfield. The checks were among the last issued by the Bergmann/Garey companies before they had shut down operations the month before.

Caulfield was next. The former advertising manager had bolted from Honda soon after his mentor Cardiges was canned and was now working for Honda's advertising agency, Rubin Postaer and Associates. While at the agency he had received an $18,000 check from Bergmann, a copy of which Cameron now had. She was still unaware of Caulfield's and the others' total $2.5 million take from the advertising scam. Cameron conferred with Amemiya about Caulfield. Amemiya ordered the agency to terminate Caulfield.

By October 1992 the word among the fragmented club members was that the Japanese officials were satisfied with the termination of Cardiges, Josleyn and Caulfield, and that the probe was over. The company's sales division was rudderless with Elliott in charge, and a search was on for a new national sales manager. When Washington, D.C., zone sales manager Hugh Cooper was summoned by Quirk to fly to Torrance for an unspecified reason, he figured his ship had come in. Despite the fact that Josleyn had told Cooper that Honda was on to the direct mail scam, Cooper thought he was untouchable. He figured he was the man, that his trip to California meant an interview for the top sales slot. We are talking serious denial here.

"Cooper is sitting in the lobby," was the whisper on the executive-level third floor of Honda headquarters. Unless he had flown in to eat in the employee cafeteria or to visit the credit union or dry cleaner, the only other entities on the lobby level, Cooper was on his way to the human resources department. The lobby rumor would be repeated more frequently over the coming months, the first signal of another field sales executive about to bite the dust. Employees referred to Quirk as "Dr. Death," since a visit with him was usually terminal. Cameron became known as "Sherry Kevorkian," a reference to the 1990s "suicide doctor" Jack Kevorkian.

Cooper was ushered into the gas chamber. He bragged to Cameron and Quirk about the success of his regime while a zone sales manager. When Cameron turned the conversation to his role in the advertising association program, Cooper realized he was not going to be promoted. He denied receiving money from Bergmann and Associates but admitted to being compensated for "consulting" with Honda dealers, a violation of company policy. Cooper submitted his resignation and walked upstairs to speak with Amemiya.

"You know, Mr. Amemiya, this witch hunt must stop," said Cooper. "I know these problems need to be addressed, but there isn't anybody in this company that I know of that can stand to have people running around looking up their skirt, including you, Mr. Amemiya. We all have skeletons."

"Yes, we have no priests here," replied Amemiya.

Cooper said he wanted to become a Honda dealer, and Amemiya responded that he would be pleased if Cooper remained in the Honda family.

A woman named Maggie King was Dennis Josleyn's secretary, at both Honda and at his extracurricular companies. For several mornings, she had noticed two men sitting in a car outside her apartment. She told a friend that a stakeout was going on. "Little did I know, they were watching me," said King later. Honda's investigators photographed her entering Garey and Associates. Cameron came into possession of checks made out to King from the company. In October, Cameron confronted King with the photographs and checks and the fact that King's name was on the firm's signature card. King denied receiving the money. Cameron asked King to grant permission for Honda to see her bank account. King refused. Cameron gave her a choice: resign or be terminated. King resigned.

In 1991 Atlanta assistant zone sales manager Dave Katarski decided to bail out from the corporation and become a Honda dealer. He approached his boss, Bob Mazzitelli, and Jim Cardiges, and they said: sure, we will issue you a letter of intent for a dealership. We will even give you the employee discount — only $100,000. An angry Katarski refused to pay and never got the deal.

When the bodies started flying in 1992, Katarski saw his chance for revenge. He turned over records from Mazzitelli's money-hiding company, Monarch Consultants, to Cameron. Katarski also gave her a copy of the note from Atlanta dealer Barry Alexander to Mazzitelli and Cardiges, outlining the cash and gifts he would provide the two executives in exchange for them issuing him a letter of intent. Mazzitelli came into his office one morning in February 1993 to find Cameron and another executive waiting. "They started hammering on me," recalls Mazzitelli. "It was very chilling. I felt the best thing to do was to tell the truth. I knew they were going to fire me." Mazzitelli's 11-year-long career at Honda was over.

When word passed that Bill Green was sitting in the lobby one day in early 1993, people were surprised — the Colorado assistant zone sales manager was known as a clean exec. A Denver Honda dealer had complained that a competing dealer had supplied Green's wife with an Accord to drive, a violation of company policy. Like other Honda managers who lived off their salary exclusively, a car payment would have strapped Green. Receiving free use of dealers' cars was a hard perk to give up, even with the company on a rampage of firings. Cameron was poised for the kill until Green pointed out that she would have to terminate 30 other managers who had the same arrangement with dealers. Green escaped the gallows, and Honda issued a clemency memo to sales department managers, telling them if they returned the automobiles none would be punished. A few months earlier, Honda had not given that option to a Midwest district sales manager, terminating him for the same offense. It was not the last time Honda would display an inconsistency in its dealings with suspected employees.

Some Honda dealers, no longer making the big bucks and forgetting about the millions of dollars they had profited thanks to Honda, began to roll over on the Honda executives. The executives finally realized that the dealers had never been their friends.

A Honda dealership manager came forward with proof that Chicago zone sales manager Frank Pisano had received cash and jewelry from the manager's boss. The slick Pisano was a man who flaunted his graft and once insulted a dealer by trying to exchange a gift of a television set. He was summoned to Torrance.

"Have you ever received money or gifts from Honda dealers?" Cameron asked Pisano.

"Never," said Pisano. "No, wait, a dealer gave me a cheeseboard once. And a gift basket." The Porsche convertible must have slipped his mind.

Cameron produced receipts from the jewelry store and the shipping company that delivered the goods to Pisano's home.

"How do you explain this?" asked Cameron.

"I never received it," said Pisano. "I never asked for it. I don't have it. There is another Frank Pisano in Chicago that always gets my mail. Maybe it went to him. You're pointing fingers at me and I don't like it." Pisano was terminated.

A Long Island dealer telephoned zone sales manager Roger Novelly and threatened to expose Novelly's cozy relationship with other area dealers. Novelly decided not to wait for the inevitable phone call from human resources and submitted his resignation.

In the spring of 1993, Cameron was finally able to pop Bob Rivers. The former Western regional sales manager's name had surfaced in connection with numerous schemes, but no evidence had emerged. In March the confidential source who had contacted Cameron the year before, fingering

Rivers as having received money from Sales Training Technologies, called again. Rivers got a classic 1969 Mercedes-Benz from a dealer, said the voice, and his father got a sweet deal on an Acura Legend from another retailer. What about the $175,000 STT check to Rivers that I told you about before, asked the caller, why haven't you done anything about that?

Cameron confronted Rivers about the allegations. I paid for the Mercedes-Benz, said Rivers. I never received money from STT, I told you that before. My father got the $12,000 discount on the car because he referred people to the dealership, said Rivers. Cameron asked Rivers to produce his bank records. Rivers refused. Cameron was foiled again.

Rivers's name resurfaced. Honda audited invoices received from Events Unlimited, the company that produced Honda's dealer meeting extravaganzas. The audit showed that there was no detailed review of the multimillion-dollar bills, and there were likely severe overcharges. The person who had approved the invoices and was the primary contact with the vendor was Rivers. Cameron suspected him of receiving kickbacks from Events Unlimited, but she had the wrong man. Events Unlimited had been handed the lucrative account by Jack Billmyer, and the firm had treated Effie Cardiges to at least one shopping spree. Rivers had merely handled the paperwork on the account, but Cameron's suspicions intensified.

In March 1993, Honda finally received hard goods on Rivers. The wife of an Idaho dealer wrote Honda claiming that her husband had given 10 percent interests in the dealership to both Rivers and Oregon zone sales manager George Martin. The woman and her husband were embroiled in a divorce and were battling over the proceeds from the sale of the dealership. She provided Cameron with the agreement between her husband and the Honda executives, as well as tapes of telephone conversations about the matter. Cameron confronted Rivers and Martin, who denied any involvement.

Cameron had listened to Rivers disavow various allegations for over a year. The Idaho deal, along with Rivers's lack of cooperation, were enough ammunition for Cameron to fire Rivers, which she did. Honda mysteriously chose not to terminate Martin.

And then there was Christiaan Walker, the man who arguably had started it all.

Honda did not throw Walker a thank-you party for bringing the Peck checks forward. In a meeting with Amemiya and Okusa the day after Cardiges's termination, Cameron noted that Walker "caused too many problems" by his blowing the whistle and starting rumors in the company.

She said that Walker should have reported the information to human resources in the first place. They decided to closely monitor Walker's job performance as part of a strategy to cast doubt on his character. It was imperative that Honda be able to discredit him if the information ever went public about the company hiding the Peck checks — nobody knew more about the length of the inactivity than Walker. Honda's investigators had concluded that Walker had forged the Peck check to Fred Meis, which made him an easy target to tarnish. His deceptive initial meeting with Tom Elliott did not hurt their case either.

In June 1993 Honda offered to pay Walker six months' salary if he would resign and never say anything about Honda again. Walker refused. The company's scrutinization of Walker became worse than that mandated by the corrupt crew years earlier. He was stripped of his normal responsibilities and relegated to processing mundane paperwork. Cameron told him he would never be promoted from his current position as Oregon district sales manager. Walker was admonished for filling up his company car with premium gasoline, something that cost the company about $5 per month. His corporate telephone bills were suddenly too high. The paranoid Walker started tape-recording conversations with his superiors.

Walker hurt his own cause by refusing to heed Honda's request that he remain silent about the Peck payoffs. He continued to tell his tale to other Honda employees and bragged to several dealers that he "could bring the whole house down." In the ultimate act of disloyalty, Walker leaked information about the corruption to *Automotive News.* Walker fired off an e-mail to Amemiya and Honda Motor Company president Nobuhiko Kawamoto, saying, "My loyalty to Honda has been used against me. I came forward in good faith yet was ostracized by the company and the 'gang.' . . . I was left in an uncertain and dangerous position. . . . You must assume that all charges against American Honda are real and hold degrees of truth. . . . This crisis can no longer be concealed." Walker hired an attorney and threatened to sue Honda for harassment.

Out of the blue, Honda was handed some damning information about Walker's personal life, which they would use against him. Walker had begun a whirlwind romance with an Alaskan Airlines flight attendant in April 1993. The pair set a wedding date for July 4. ("She was forcing me to marry her," says Walker.) They applied for the marriage license. She bought a wedding gown. A week before the union, Walker got cold feet and backed out. The screaming stewardess called Honda headquarters and squealed on Walker. She told them of their afternoon liaisons when Walker was supposed to be calling on dealers. She said that Walker used cocaine, a charge he does not deny. She then left a message on Walker's answering machine: "I just called Honda and told them everything about you. I hope this rocks your world, babe." Honda's human resources department smiled at its good fortune and added the information to Walker's file.

Honda needed one monumental screwup by Walker to seal his fate. It came in September, when Walker faxed a threatening memo to the Oregon Honda dealers. Saying that those who had failed to complete a minor salesperson training assignment would not receive shipments of new 1994 Hondas, a crazed Walker wrote, "if it were up to me, I would not care if you were apes and ran your stores naked, but this is the 90s, customers expect more. You need to present a professional image. . . . I have been *LET DOWN,* you don't want to *LET ME DOWN,* do you? . . . I will not be given lip service again." The dealers complained about Walker's threat to withhold cars, knowing that it was against the law. This was all Honda needed.

On October 27, Walker's supervisor escorted him into a conference room in the Portland zone office and informed Walker that he was being demoted to the "boondocks"—Spokane, Washington—and any missteps in the next 120 days would mean termination. Walker could stand no more. One week later, he resigned. He received no severance compensation. Honda claims Walker stole records and documents from the Portland office before his departure.

Walker filed a lawsuit against Honda claiming wrongful termination and charging that Honda inflicted emotional distress on him.

In May 1994, Honda was able to successfully apply its strategy of portraying Walker as a malcontent. The *New York Times* was about to publish a piece about the corruption case and Walker's role in it. Honda's attorneys wrote the newspaper a threatening letter to stop the story. "Mr. Walker has repeatedly threatened to sue Honda for claims arising out of an employment dispute," said the letter. "Mr. Walker has continually sought money in 'settlement' from Honda. At one point, Mr. Walker demanded $1,500,000 in cash. We rejected Mr. Walker's patent attempts to be paid off." Honda noted that Walker was a "dubious source . . . because Walker is patently biased against Honda." And he was—his love for Honda had turned to disgust. The newspaper toned down its story.

Christiaan Walker remains an enigma. Was he an innocent rookie on a mission to clean up Honda or a conniving forger and blackmailer? Was he looking for justice or craving attention? He is a study in contradiction—a man who dabbles in cocaine yet rarely orders anything stronger than milk at the bar. He planned events to focus the spotlight on himself (turning in the executives, a marriage) but was too timid too follow through with them properly.

Regardless, Walker's disclosure of the Peck kickbacks to Cardiges and Temple should have made him a hero — it was a brave move that helped stop the corruption at American Honda. Instead, his knowledge of the company's cover-up of the Peck deal, and his refusal to keep his mouth shut, led to the harassment and his forced resignation. He was punished as severely as were the men who stole from the company.

In the first year after Honda's internal investigation began in early 1992, 12 sales division executives were forced to resign from the corporation. Most had been with the company more than ten years. The heart of the marketing department was decimated. All refused to divulge any information about their peers' activities — the boys' club stuck together to the end. Human resources continued digging, suspecting that about 20 more current and ex-employees were involved in the schemes. Every remaining sales division manager was a suspect, and many careers were placed on permanent hold, victims of guilt by association. Company morale plummeted.

With the sales division in a shambles, and with Honda offering its largest dealer cash incentive ever — up to $1,500 per car — during the summer of 1992 to combat slipping sales, Honda dealers resurrected old habits and began falsifying sales cards again. Toward the end of the year, the Japanese officials faced their second straight year of declining sales and began to demand the practice. Roger Novelly remembers driving through New York City with sales vice president Takeo Okusa in November 1992, and Okusa asking why a particular dealer had not reported many sales that month. "We are paying him to turn in cards, after all," said Okusa. Novelly asked Okusa if he wanted dealers to report unsold vehicles as being sold. Okusa said yes. The falsified sales cost Honda an estimated $17 million in dealer incentive money during 1992. Honda's reported sales in 1992 of 648,745 cars totaled approximately 20,000 more than the dealers had actually delivered.

In early 1993, Honda hired fiery retired Mazda sales chief Richard Colliver to replace Cardiges. Amemiya did not inform Colliver of the hornet's nest of problems he would be facing. The company recruited an army of former Mazda, Ford, and Mercedes-Benz managers to replace the fired executives, the first time non-entry-level Honda sales division positions had ever gone to outsiders. The new regime sneered at the remaining managers and set about saving the sinking Honda ship.

Colliver learned of the company's losses in 1992 due to dealers earning incentive money by falsifying sales cards. He threatened to invoice the dealers to recover the cash. The retailers howled, and Colliver backed off. He held a conference call with the zone sales managers that finally put an end to the storied Honda practice of encouraging dealers to dummy sales records.

"If it's determined by me," roared Colliver, "that anyone within American Honda advises a dealer to falsely report a sale, that they better be looking for a job because they're not going to have one."

The new management team canceled pending letters of intent for new dealerships, at least the ones they could locate. Cardiges had left a half-dozen dealers — those who had already paid him for the rights to open new stores — holding the bag when he departed Honda. The cancellations cost an Oklahoma dealer $225,000. One organized crime–connected East Coast dealer threatened revenge on Cardiges.

Colliver found a bogus Ed Temple deal in Georgia, the rights issued to a man named Brian Linnemeyer, another nondealer buddy of Temple crony Mark Benson. Colliver called Linnemeyer at his home in Indianola, Iowa. "I don't know how a boy from a small town in Iowa got himself involved in something like this," screamed Colliver, "but I think I'm going to give you some advice. You have about twenty minutes to fax me a letter of termination for that dealership. Or I'll have federal marshals on your doorstep in about twenty-five." Linnemeyer complied. The entire third floor heard Colliver yelling at Linnemeyer, Colliver not yet adjusted to the open layout of Honda headquarters "Everybody in the building dove for the floor," laughs Colliver.

A Louisiana Honda dealer tried to give Colliver an oil painting. He turned it down. It was the dawn of a new day at old Honda.

Honda's human resources department started enforcing employee signings of the conflict of interest policy. Honda continued to deny to *Automotive News* and other media outlets that an internal investigation was taking place.

The departed managers went their separate ways, most staying in the car business. Dennis Josleyn sold his Laguna Hills home for a $200,000 loss and moved to Northern California. He tried to put together a deal to become a Ford dealer in partnership with his buddy, Joe Pope, but to no avail.

Jim Cardiges dabbled in real estate, struggled to keep Worldwide Dyve afloat, took acting lessons with Effie, and grew his hair into a ponytail. In late 1992, Honda stopped paying his legal fees related to depositions in various lawsuits against the company. Cardiges filed suit against Honda to recover his expenses.

Bob Rivers moved to Palm Springs and entered the wholesale used car business. Tom Caulfield sold computerized payroll systems. In a delicious irony, Frank Pisano peddled direct mail advertising programs to automobile dealers.

Bob Mazzitelli went to work for Ed Temple at Costa Mesa Honda. Hugh Cooper was hired by a North Carolina Honda dealer. Roger Novelly became general manager of a Philadelphia Honda store. Other automobile companies would have taken the owners of those dealerships "out behind the body shop" and said: look, these people stole from us, we strongly recommend that you fire them. But not American Honda. The company did not want to create more waves. It was just happy the entire mess was almost over.

Wrong.

In early 1993 a four-year-old lawsuit in New Hampshire was about to boil over and make Honda's worst nightmare come true.

CHAPTER 14

Parallel Lies

An incompetent attorney can delay a trial for months or years. A competent attorney can delay one even longer.

—Evelle J. Younger

DRIVING NORTH on I-93 toward Concord, New Hampshire, one sees a highway department sign notifying motorists that the next rest area features more than just bathrooms and pay phones. There is also a liquor store on the premises. Late afternoons find its parking lot crammed with Subaru automobiles bearing the state's "Live Free or Die" license plates, as plaid shirt–clad commuters buy booze for the drive home.

Things are a little different in New Hampshire.

This is no news to American Honda. The New England region is the remotest outpost, both geographically and psychologically, from Honda's California headquarters. New England is an enigma to the automaker, a place where dealers and customers do not behave normally. For one, New Englanders are crazy about Subarus. The Japanese maker of quirky four-wheel-drive cars is a minor annoyance nationwide to Honda, but in the snowy northeast they often outsell both Honda and Toyota. In 1988 the Connecticut Consumer Protection Commission sued a pair of Subaru dealers who had falsified sales cards in their zeal to earn more cars from the factory.

New England Honda dealer principals are a testy bunch, with a history of suing Honda over the establishment of new dealerships. They have an open disdain for Honda factory people. Their rancor is not merely due to their stubborn New Englander nature — they just never seemed to get enough Hondas. Before 1985, when Honda opened a Connecticut zone office, the New England dealers' automobiles were distributed with those destined for New York City and New Jersey, home to dealerships owned by ten major players in the corrupt game. With those favored dealers receiving priority, few extra Hondas ended up in the hands of the generally clean bunch of New England dealers. Honda's New York/New England zone sales manager John Conway secretly owning a piece of Rod Ryan's four New Jersey dealerships also did not help the New Englanders' situation.

With New England Honda retailers not having enough product, and Subaru, Nissan, and Toyota dealers having plenty, Honda's New England market penetration was below its national average during most of the 1970s and 1980s, including in the Boston metro area, the eighth largest car market in the nation. New England is probably the only geographical region of the country where Honda's entire dealer network was adversely affected by the corruption. And the dealers knew it.

A great place for American Honda to challenge a dealer in court.

The road to the Concord courthouse began in 1986 during the frenzy that marked the early days of the Acura division, when the company was crowing about the 600 dealerships selling 300,000 upscale automobiles it would establish by 1990. Thousands of dealers applied for Acura franchises. One was Richard Nault, owner of the Honda dealership in Manchester, a city 20 miles south of Concord. Nault was one of the original Honda motorcycle dealers established in New England in the 1960s. He was one of the first New England retailers of Honda automobiles in the 1970s and rose to become the largest-volume Honda dealer in New Hampshire. And now he wanted to be that state's first Acura dealer.

Acura granted Nault a franchise. But due to its ten-mile rule, which prohibited Honda and Acura dealerships owned by the same person to be in close proximity to each other, Nault was told to locate the dealership in Concord, a town far enough away from his Manchester Honda store to abide by the regulation.

Concord, New Hampshire, is home to the state capital and little else. A typically quaint New England burg with red brick buildings and narrow streets, Concord boasted a population of 37,000 people during the mid-1980s; Manchester had almost 100,000, including twice as many Acura target consumers, those with four-year or advanced college degrees. Manchester was the logical market for an Acura dealership. But Acura sent Nault to Concord.

The placement of an Acura outlet in Concord also violated a car business premise about how consumers shop: they are drawn in the direction of the nearest metropolitan area, in this case toward Boston. Customers from Manchester would be more likely to drive 20 miles south to shop in Nashua, New Hampshire, and then on to Boston, rather than travel 20 miles north to Concord. And there was no metropolitan area north of Concord for Nault Acura to draw from.

Acura performed no market study on Concord — no measurement of the demographics, shopping patterns, and income of local consumers. Acura's rush to establish dealerships and its thin staff did not allow for a market analysis. Acura officials assured Nault that the Concord market could support sales of upwards of 800 Acuras annually, an outrageous prognostication that was higher than the volume of Nault's Honda store. This Acura market study method is called "Kentucky Windage" — licking one's finger and sticking it up in the air to measure how many Acuras could be sold in Concord.

Nault could be faulted for believing Acura's wild projections and ignoring his own instincts about the Concord market, but he had faith in the company that had done him well over the years. He opened Nault Acura in June 1987, investing $2.2 million in an impressive new facility, trimmed in the official silver and red Acura colors. Enamored with his new franchise, Nault named a business park he was developing in Concord "Legend Industrial Park" and one of its streets "Integra Drive."

The Concord demographics were revealed by which Acura automobiles consumers purchased from the dealership. The majority of the vehicles sold by Nault Acura were the Honda-priced Integra model, while other Acura dealers' sales were dominated by the more expensive, and higher profit, Legends. Not that it mattered which model Nault sold — he was allocated an average of 24 cars per month, despite Acura's agreement of triple that. Even if he been granted the promised shipments, Nault would have had to sell the vehicles to customers outside of Concord, because his market could not support the sale of more than 30 Acuras per month. And Nault's most likely prospects lived in Manchester, but they were heading south toward Nashua and Boston to buy Acuras.

Nault was in trouble. His Acura dealership lost over $500,000 during its first year of operation. Only four Acura dealers nationwide lost more money. His pleas to Acura officials for financial help went unanswered. In late 1988, Nault requested permission to relocate the dealership to Manchester. Acura said no.

But something else was bothering Nault. His late-night reconnaissance of Sunnyside Acura in Nashua revealed that dealer's lot overflowing with new Acura automobiles, and in desirable models and colors that Nault could not get from the factory.

Richard Nault felt something was not right.

No Honda division official ever allowed a lowly district sales manager to pick up large amounts of dealer cash for him. No Honda division official ever shortchanged another when splitting up the proceeds of a deal. And no Honda division official ever ratted on a partner in crime.

But this was not the Honda division. This was the Acura division, home to the corporation's Keystone Kops, managers unschooled in the techniques of operating a stealth business. And home to executives Damien Budnick and David Pedersen, a duo responsible for both Nault Acura and the honor code violations described previously.

David Pedersen was a former Cadillac dealership sales manager from Maine. He had joined Honda in 1979 as a district sales manager, where he tried to turn down the first dealer gift offered to him, $300 in cash from a New York retailer. He quickly got over his trepidation and joined the program. Pedersen transferred to the Acura division in 1985 at age 38, becoming the assistant zone sales manager in the New Jersey zone, a territory that included New England. One of his employees was 36-year-old Damien Budnick, an ex–Ford Motor Company official hired by Acura to be New England district sales manager.

Budnick and Pedersen worked the payola program during the four-year window of opportunity for Acura executives to squeeze dealers for gratuities, before the franchise began its tailspin. Pedersen received a Honda Civic, 50 percent ownership in an Acura dealership, and about $100,000 in miscellaneous gifts from various dealers. Budnick grabbed around $40,000 worth of gratuities. The handouts were not as plentiful as those on the Honda side, but they were not bad.

The two men did not like each other. Pedersen thought Budnick was a "loose cannon" and sloppy with his paperwork. Budnick thought Pedersen spent less time working than he did running around with his hand out. Despite their problems, the pair became uneasy partners in crime.

Pedersen and Budnick divvied up $80,000 for granting an Acura dealership in Connecticut. They split $4,000 from a dealer wanting an store in Salem, New Hampshire. They became co-owners of a construction company, steering new dealers to do business with the firm. The pair earned about $11,000 apiece in the enterprise, before it shut down after a dealer stiffed the company for $200,000. It would be the pair's last somewhat successful joint venture.

Pedersen's biggest benefactor was a man named Tom Bohlander, the owner of Honda dealerships in Detroit and Cleveland. Bohlander became friends with Pedersen when the Honda manager called on his Ohio store during the early 1980s. In 1986 Bohlander gave Pedersen an $11,000 Acura Integra.

Bohlander declared his desire for an Acura franchise in New England. Pedersen arranged for him to become the dealer in Nashua, New Hampshire, assigning Budnick to process the paperwork. Bohlander's Sunshine Acura opened in early 1988, 40 miles down the road from Richard Nault's six-month-old Concord Acura dealership.

Pedersen then asked for something else from Bohlander. Pedersen's son, Tim, was about to enter Gannon University, and the elder Pedersen asked Bohlander to pay his son's college tuition. Over the next two years, Bohlander paid a total of $17,107 directly to the school for Tim Pedersen's tuition.

Bohlander's Nashua dealership received plenty of new Acuras, as well as a written agreement from Acura that it would not allow Nault to relocate his dealership from Concord to Manchester. Bohlander bragged to other Acura dealers about his payoffs to Pedersen.

Budnick was miffed that the only gift he had received from Bohlander was a cheap radio, while his boss was being showered with favors from the dealer.

Pedersen and Budnick's alliance was about to go south. In May 1988 Pedersen was promoted to become Acura's Atlanta zone sales manager. He transferred Budnick into his territory to become the central Florida district sales manager. Pedersen still thought Budnick was a bad rep but a good bag man.

New Jersey dealer Frank Holtham wanted an Acura store in Cocoa Beach, Florida, and informed Budnick of his desire in mid-1989. Budnick contacted Pedersen and asked him how much to charge for the point. Pedersen suggested $25,000, to be split equally between them. Budnick told Holtham what was required, which didn't surprise Holtham—he had knowledge of Nissan Motor Company executives making demands similar to those of American Honda officials.

For the next few months, Budnick delayed processing the paperwork for Holtham's deal. When Holtham indicated a desire to dual the Acura store with another franchise, Budnick dropped hints that more money might be needed. He eventually ratcheted up the payoff price to $100,000.

In March 1990 Budnick and Holtham met at a pancake restaurant in Cocoa Beach to seal the deal. A gun-toting Holtham handed Budnick a briefcase containing $100,000 in cash. Budnick flew back to Atlanta and gave Pedersen $12,500, the amount his boss was expecting. It is unclear what happened to the remaining $87,500.

A few months later, Holtham mentioned to Pedersen that he had given Budnick $100,000. A furious Pedersen figured that Budnick had shortchanged him. He decided to retaliate. In late 1990 a Florida dealer principal complained that Budnick had forced him to sell an Acura NSX to Budnick at dealer invoice cost, a price about $30,000 below the market value of the hot-selling sports car. Budnick wrote a check for $49,800 for the car, then turned around and sold it to a friend for a $4,000 profit. Budnick had just violated a Honda policy that prohibited managers from "curbing" cars.

Pedersen found his chance to double-cross the double-crosser. He told Honda's human resources department about Budnick's NSX transaction, not thinking that Budnick might spill the beans right back on him.

Pedersen's tattling on Budnick ranks alongside Koichi Amemiya's granting a Honda dealership to a dirty Ed Temple as being the most inexplicable incidents of the entire scandal.

Honda's human resources department verified Pedersen's claim and fired Budnick in January 1991. Stunned by his termination, Budnick did not turn around and rat on Pedersen, figuring he would get revenge someday. His chance would come in the Nault case.

In March 1989 Richard Nault moved his struggling Acura franchise in with his Lincoln-Mercury dealership and closed the Acura building. The move was designed to cut overhead expenses; the Acura franchise was losing $40,000 per month. Nault was still committed to doing a good job selling Acura automobiles in Concord, and it seemed like the only alternative to closing the dealership.

Nault was now in violation of Acura's rule prohibiting dual dealerships, those selling Acuras alongside other makes, a regulation that Nault had agreed to in writing. Nault was unconcerned about Acura's reaction. He knew that a dozen Acura dealers nationwide had done the same thing without retribution from the factory. Despite this fact, Acura continued to brag to the industry press that all but one Acura store — the approved dual with Honda in Ocala, Florida — were exclusive dealerships. Acura could not reveal the truth, fearing other dealers would join the bandwagon.

A few weeks later, Acura terminated Nault's franchise, the decision being made by Acura market representation manager Dan Crowe. The company's case was simple: Nault had violated the stipulations of his letter of intent by dualing his dealership. He broke the rules. Canceling an auto dealer's franchise is a move normally reserved for the most desperate of situations, where a dealer principal is convicted of a felony or the dealership files for bankruptcy. American Honda had terminated only a handful of dealers over the years and only under such desperate circumstances.

The Acura division wanted to make an example out of Nault and serve notice to other Acura dealers who might dare to defy the factory and dual their dealerships. To hell with Acura owners in Concord who would now have to drive 40 miles to Tom Bohlander's Sunnyside Acura in Nashua for service. And to hell with Nault's investment.

"A total, absolute stupid screw-up by Acura," says a senior Honda division official about the Nault cancellation, an understatement of the highest order.

The termination of Nault Acura would become the biggest mistake American Honda would ever make.

A stunned Richard Nault had no choice then but to shut down his Acura showroom. The factory came and hauled off his Acura cars and parts inventory. Nault quickly filed suit in U.S. District Court in Concord, charging American Honda with bad faith and unreasonable conduct, for establishing a point in Concord, and for wrongful termination of his franchise. Despite Nault's suspicion about Bohlander's relationship with Acura officials, his lawsuit originally did not include accusations of favoritism influencing Acura's decision to terminate his dealership.

"The Nault case could be settled by a first-year law student," said Honda in-house attorney Mark Brooks. Honda would have been better off with a rookie barrister. Instead, the company sent in the law firm of Lyon & Lyon, led by attorney J. Donald McCarthy, the man who had once joked about the bribery during a meeting with Honda executives.

Don McCarthy was a flamboyant Harvard Law School graduate, famous for his daunting stare during depositions. He was proud that his firm had successfully defended Honda in every dealer lawsuit brought against the company, but that record is deceiving. The real attorneys in the Honda world had been the dirty executives. They kept dealers at bay by placating them with additional cars or franchises whenever one would threaten to sue or protest a new Honda point.

Nault's attorney was Richard McNamara, a member of the Manchester law firm Wiggin & Nourie, whose offices are housed in an old brick church. A former New Hampshire assistant attorney general, the 39-year-old McNamara was the author of three widely used textbooks on New Hampshire criminal procedure and was known as an honest, ethical lawyer. McNamara was entering a legal battle that would force him to do things he had sworn he would never do.

Lyon & Lyon's strategy was simple. The downtown Los Angeles law firm was going to blow into podunk New Hampshire and confound Nault and McNamara until they caved in. Using Honda's enormous resources, the attorneys planned to drag out the proceedings until the plaintiff went broke. It had worked before. Honda may not have liked litigation, but once engaged it became a bulldog.

The evidence-discovery phase of the case began. McNamara's first clue that he was in for a fight came when he wrote McCarthy with a simple request: List the number of Acura dealerships nationwide that are dualed with other franchises.

Three, wrote back Lyon & Lyon. This is known as literal litigation.

McNamara tried again: Why you didn't give me their names?

Because you asked for the number, said Lyon & Lyon. The law firm provided the names of the three retailers.

McNamara knew there were at least a dozen. What about the others, asked McNamara.

We were talking about "Acura-approved" duals, said Lyon & Lyon, we don't recognize any "unapproved" duals.

"American Honda, from the inception of the case," says McNamara, "demonstrated a hair-splitting approach to answering interrogatories. Honda's attorneys played fast and loose with the discovery rules."

The case plodded along, as Honda fought or delayed every request filed by McNamara to produce evidence. In the summer of 1990, McNamara heard from area Honda dealers about the rumors of Nashua dealer Tom Bohlander having paid off Acura executive David Pedersen. Bohlander is an outsider from Michigan, said one dealer, why do you think he got the point instead of one of us? Another retailer told McNamara that kickbacks had been rampant in the Honda world for years. McNamara knew that if he could prove the rapacious relationship between Pedersen and Bohlander, and that it adversely affected Nault's dealership, then Honda might settle the case rather than go to trial.

McNamara took a shot and wrote Lyon & Lyon, saying, "It is my personal understanding that bribery is pervasive within the American Honda organization and that on many occasions American Honda personnel have extorted motor vehicle dealers."

For the first time ever, the issue of Honda managers accepting gratuities from dealers was an issue in a court case. And McNamara's theory was neat: One market with two Acura dealers, one dirty and one clean.

Lyon & Lyon did not respond to McNamara's letter.

McNamara spent 43 days in California deposing Honda executives. "It was obvious to me," recalls McNamara, "that there was something going on between Honda management and Sunnyside Acura in Nashua and my client wasn't treated fairly. The records show that we couldn't get a straight answer from the Honda employees." McNamara did discover that Acura had never performed a Concord market study.

McNamara subpoenaed Damien Budnick for a deposition. Budnick is our "factual consultant" now, said McCarthy, you can't depose him. When McCarthy lost his appeal to block the deposition, he instructed Budnick not to appear. McNamara prevailed upon a magistrate court to order Budnick's deposition. Budnick testified that he knew nothing about any bribery.

McCarthy continued to thwart McNamara's attempts to obtain documents from Honda. The two attorneys refused to speak with one another outside of court, further complicating the discovery process. When in court, their fights over evidence deteriorated into glowering matches. McNamara was being driven over the edge.

McNamara asked for a copy of a deposition given by Budnick in another case. McCarthy did not produce it. McNamara petitioned the court to revoke Lyon & Lyon's right to represent Honda in the case and demanded that Honda hire local counsel to "get control of the defendant and make them play by the rules." McNamara had never sought sanctions against an opposing attorney before. Lyon & Lyon suddenly produced the requested evidence, claiming that the box of documents had been "accidentally" misplaced under a desk. Another box had been "accidentally" left in the trunk of a car, only to pop up after McNamara complained to the court.

"I've practiced law for sixteen years and I've never been in a case like this," McNamara told the court. "The discovery has been used by a wealthy party to make it impossible for a party which is not wealthy to prosecute its meritorious claims."

Federal Judge Norman Stahl recommended that the two sides sit down and work out a settlement. He admonished both attorneys, saying, "the degree of courtesy that counsel have been showing each other is less than exemplary, and I do not think that this reflects well on either the local or California bar." The judge told McCarthy to cease his delay tactics and made him promise to abide by the rules.

In April 1991 Pedersen decided he was not through with Budnick. He called McCarthy and said, did you know Budnick got $100,000 from Florida dealer Frank Holtham? McCarthy called Budnick and asked him about the allegation. Budnick denied it, telling McCarthy: "I'm about $100,000 light."

In early May, McNamara forwarded McCarthy a set of written questions in a discovery order entitled Interrogatory #22. The document demanded a list of every allegation and instance of American Honda executives accepting gratuities from dealers that were known to the corporation. Complete details on each instance were required.

McNamara was only groping and hoping that he could find evidence of corruption, but he had placed Honda in an awful bind. Honda's record of keeping things under wraps was now in danger.

Worse, two weeks before they had to answer Interrogatory #22, Lyon & Lyon and McCarthy received the overnight package from whistle-blower Christiaan Walker containing the copies of the Cliff Peck Honda checks made out to Honda executives Jim Cardiges and Ed Temple. Four days before that, McCarthy had received the call from Pedersen about the Holtham bribe.

Interrogatory #22 was a catch-22 for the law firm: Answer truthfully and risk dealer lawsuits and bad publicity for Honda. Tell a lie and risk being caught by the court. Either alternative could cause Honda to lose the Nault case.

Lyon & Lyon panicked. The attorneys asked for a court ruling that would limit the scope of the question to instances of corruption only by executives who were in the "chain of command" over Nault's dealership. The court agreed to the request.

On May 2, McCarthy responded to Interrogatory #22 by stating that "American Honda is unaware of any such instance or allegation." He added that there was an "unsubstantiated allegation" about Budnick receiving a gratuity. McCarthy did not reveal any details about the gift.

McCarthy had split hairs again. He did not mention anything about Jack Billmyer or Jim Cardiges. Billmyer had been in Nault's chain of command, having been Acura's sales chief when Nault was issued his franchise. McCarthy knew of the allegations over the years implicating Billmyer. Cardiges was in the loop, Nault having been one of the original Acura dealers appointed by a committee that included Cardiges. McCarthy knew about Cardiges and the Peck checks. With Billmyer retired, and Cardiges having only briefly been officially involved with Acura, McCarthy was confident that McNamara would never link them to Nault.

Lyon & Lyon had just saved American Honda. For now.

In July, McNamara summoned David Pedersen to give a deposition in Atlanta. He also tried to contact Tom Bohlander. Pedersen called Bohlander and pleaded with him not to tell Nault's attorneys about the Acura Integra and college tuition.

Lyon & Lyon attorneys switched strategies for coaching Pedersen in preparation for the deposition. Rather than teaching their fabled "a bolt of lightning will not strike you down if you don't tell the truth" line, the attorneys now espoused the "I don't know" method of dodging questions. As an example, they told Pedersen, if asked where he was born, to answer "I don't know," because technically you really do not know. There are only three things that you know, said the attorneys, your name, your address, and your age. If you don't like the wording of a question, answer "No," or "I don't know," or "I don't remember." Do not give any opinions, the lawyers cautioned.

Pedersen was a willing student because he had plenty to hide. Richard McNamara was still trying to verify the rumors about Bohlander's payment of the college tuition of Pedersen's son. McNamara fired questions at Pedersen:

"Is Tom Bohlander a good car dealer?"

"I have no opinion on that."

"You and Mr. Bohlander became friends, didn't you?"

"I don't understand the question."

"You and Mr. Bohlander's families ever get together?"

"I don't remember."

"Do you have any knowledge of how Mr. Bohlander came to be awarded the Nashua site?"

"I don't remember."

"Mr. Bohlander ever loan you any money?"

"Not that I can remember."

"Did he assist one of your children with their college tuition?"

"Not that I'm aware of."

Two hours into the deposition, McNamara had heard enough. "Is English your first language?" he asked Pedersen. Lyon & Lyon attorney David Ritchie objected to McNamara "badgering" Pedersen.

"Well, you're lobotomizing the witness," McNamara protested.

It was clear to McNamara that Lyon & Lyon had coached Pedersen to lie. "If I try this case, I can't wait to show this to a jury," said McNamara, "(Pedersen) answered 'no' or 'I don't remember' to virtually every question, in addition to denying ever receiving any gratuities."

McCarthy claimed that, because McNamara asked about Bohlander paying Tim Pedersen's college tuition, that McNamara knew about incidents of gift giving at Honda and was withholding the information. In other words, the same thing McNamara was accusing McCarthy of doing.

On the plane home from Atlanta, McNamara drafted a motion for default judgment. Between Lyon & Lyon not complying with the rules of discovery and Pedersen's evasive testimony, McNamara felt he could convince the court to throw out the case and rule in Nault's favor. McNamara's motion was denied.

McNamara offered Honda a chance to settle the case for $9.1 million, a considerable savings over the $40 million that McNamara claimed he would seek in court. McCarthy declined.

On September 24, McCarthy and Budnick met in Boston to prepare for Budnick's testimony in a case in which a Boston Acura dealer had filed suit over Acura's placement of a new point. This was Budnick's chance for revenge on Pedersen.

Budnick claims he informed McCarthy about Pedersen receiving the $100,000 Holtham gift. And by the way, said Budnick, Pedersen received an Acura Integra from Nashua dealer Thomas Bohlander and Tim Pedersen's college tuition was paid by Bohlander. McCarthy later claimed that Budnick did not mention either incident during their meeting.

Judge Stahl decreed that December 13 was to be the last day of discovery. On December 12, Budnick was to give his second deposition. The night before, he again told Lyon & Lyon attorneys about the Pedersen gifts from dealers Bohlander and Holtham.

Budnick testified that he had picked up a thick manila envelope from Holtham and delivered it to Pedersen. He claimed that he later learned from Holtham that the envelope contained $100,000. He said the only dealer gifts he had ever received were candy, turkeys, and liquor.

I first talked to McCarthy about the $100,000 Holtham/Pedersen gift back in April, said Budnick, and I told him about the Bohlander deals in September. When I told McCarthy about Bohlander, he looked away and then changed the subject.

McNamara flew into an apoplectic fit. His suspicion about Honda hiding evidence about payoffs was confirmed — McCarthy had known details about the Holtham gift and had not disclosed them in Interrogatory #22. The information appearing on the final day of discovery smelled of cover-up between McCarthy and Budnick, since Budnick had been acting as a paid consultant to Lyon & Lyon.

In January 1992 McNamara filed a second motion for default. He charged that Lyon & Lyon had covered up its knowledge of the Holtham-to-Pedersen-and-Budnick bribe in Interrogatory #22. "The only reasonable conclusion," read the motion, "is that the information was available to American Honda's attorneys on May 2, 1991, but was intentionally and contemptuously withheld. . . . Defendant's attorneys have intentionally perpetuated a fraud on (the) court." The motion also stated that Lyon & Lyon "may well have allowed David Pedersen to perjure himself at deposition." McNamara's charges were among the most serious that one attorney can bring against another.

Lyon & Lyon vehemently denied the charges in its response to the motion. The Bohlander and Holtham gifts were merely "unsupported assertions" said the response, and McNamara knew about the Bohlander bribes before we did. Lyon & Lyon asked the court to consider sanctions against McNamara for filing "scandalous matter." Lyon & Lyon now had to clear its own name before the attorneys could clear American Honda's.

In January 1992 Lyon & Lyon faxed Budnick an affidavit for him to sign. It stated that the first time Budnick had informed McCarthy about the Pedersen gifts was on December 11. "I'm not signing this piece of shit," said Budnick to a Lyon & Lyon attorney. "It's not true." Budnick decided to switch camps and become a consultant for McNamara.

During a March 1992 hearing, Judge Stahl tried to cut to the heart of the case. "Gentlemen," began the judge, "I guess I'd have to say that I'm blessed and amused by all the filings that have been made by everybody in this case. I've spent a lot of time wading through page after page of accusation on both sides as to what this case is about. I now have before me a mini-trial which involves the date when Mr. McCarthy first learned about the alleged bribery of American Honda officials."

The judge threatened to unseal the protective order on the proceedings. He placed a several-hundred-dollars-per-page fine on any more filings by either side. He asked McCarthy point-blank whether he had knowledge of any bribery at Honda at the time of Interrogatory #22. McCarthy said no.

Nault Acura's motion for default was denied.

McNamara's frustration was compounded by something else — someone was watching him. His wife observed a man snapping photographs of their house and children. McNamara is convinced the man was one of

Honda's investigators, looking for a way to discredit him. Around the same time, Budnick faxed Judge Stahl a note concerning a man he had observed sneaking around his home and taking photos.

In February 1992 Frank Holtham admitted to McCarthy that he had given a briefcase stuffed with $100,000 to Budnick in early 1990, in exchange for Acura granting him permission to dual his pending Acura franchise with Mercedes-Benz. He said that he thought Budnick was going to give the money to Pedersen.

In April 1992, under threat of a lawsuit, Tom Bohlander agreed to cooperate with McNamara. He confessed to providing Pedersen with the Acura Integra automobile and tuition payments.

Lyon & Lyon turned over the information about the Bohlander-to-Pedersen gifts to Honda's human resources department. Honda had just begun its internal investigation, forced as much by the Nault case as by the Peck checks. In June, David Pedersen became the third executive forced to resign in Honda's housecleaning, after Jim Cardiges and Dennis Josleyn. Lyon & Lyon attorneys assured Honda's Japanese executives that they were "winning" the Nault proceedings.

The Nault case spun round and round. In late 1992 Judge Stahl was promoted to the First Circuit Court of Appeals. He was replaced by Judge Steven McAuliffe, the widower of Christa McAuliffe, the schoolteacher who died in the tragic 1986 explosion of the space shuttle *Challenger*.

Judge McAuliffe would display little patience with the goings-on in the Nault case.

Concurrent with the Nault hearings were those of other lawsuits that had suddenly emerged in 1992 alleging corruption at Honda. Lyon & Lyon's tactics were similar to those they were using in New Hampshire.

West New York, New Jersey, Honda dealer John Lindsay was surrounded by dirty Honda retailers. When Honda announced plans in 1991 to establish a new franchise in nearby Jersey City, Lindsay and another dealer protested the action before the New Jersey Division of Motor Vehicles. The new point was granted to a player named Bob Ciasulli Jr., a member of a multi-car-dealer family whose gift giving to Honda executives dated back to a Rolex watch that Ciasulli's father gave to Jack Billmyer in 1979. Ciasulli Jr. had promised $100,000 to Cardiges for the Jersey City deal and was also slipping a few thousand dollars every Christmas to New York zone sales manager Roger Novelly.

The other dealer in the proceedings was given a letter of intent for a

Honda point in Budd Lake, New Jersey, in exchange for his dropping the matter. Lindsay pressed on alone. He charged that the Jersey City point was awarded in exchange for "extortion payments" from Ciasulli. Lindsay had no evidence of the bribery, basing his allegations only on rumors swirling in the Jersey car community about Honda executives' relationship with local dealers.

In June 1992, with a Lyon & Lyon attorney at his side, Honda vice president Takeo Okusa was deposed. He was asked if he knew of any Honda executive receiving money in exchange for granting a new dealership. "I don't know," said Okusa. He knew about the moneys split by Cardiges and Temple in the Peck deal, but technically that was from the sale of the dealership, not the granting of the franchise. Okusa could have responded by answering "no," but either way he walked a fine line between truth and perjury.

With a Lyon & Lyon attorney representing him, Roger Novelly denied receiving kickbacks from any Honda dealer.

Honda backed off. The company offered John Lindsay a settlement, and he withdrew his protest. Bob Ciasulli Honda was established in Jersey City. Lyon and Lyon had deflected another bullet aimed at Honda.

A few months later, Don McCarthy was deep in another legal war. Ford dealer Rick Hunt and former Honda dealer Edward Mixon were partners in a deal to build a Honda dealership in Warrenton, Virginia. Mixon held the letter of intent and was selling it to Hunt for $900,000 plus a share of the dealership's profits. Hunt encountered problems obtaining the capital to construct the facility and backed out of the arrangement. In 1991 Mixon filed suit against Hunt, citing breach of contract.

It was alleged during proceedings, but never proven, that then–Washington, D.C., zone sales manager Dennis Josleyn was to receive $90,000 from Mixon for having issued the letter of intent for the Warrenton point.

Under deposition, Mixon stated that he had made the $90,000 offer because "(Josleyn) was basically a nice guy."

Though Honda had forced Josleyn to resign six months earlier, the company provided him with legal counsel in the case. With McCarthy as his attorney, Josleyn testified that he had never received money from Mixon or any other dealer. He stated that his exit from Honda was unrelated to any unethical activities and that he had never seen Honda's conflict of interest policy. He deemed the charge about the $90,000 mere "cocktail conversation."

Also with McCarthy at his side, current Washington, D.C., zone sales manager Hugh Cooper gave his deposition. Cooper was a few days away from being confronted by Honda about kickbacks he had received. A nervous Cooper testified under oath that he was never involved in, nor knew of any, bribery at Honda. He said that he did not know why Cardiges left Honda.

A bolt of lightning did not strike down Josleyn or Cooper, just as McCarthy had always promised.

Hunt decided to drop the lawsuit and settle with Mixon, in part because Lyon & Lyon hinted that if he would settle, the firm would help him obtain the Warrenton point. Cooper had canceled Mixon's letter and reissued it to another applicant, so Hunt's attorney asked Honda for information on the new dealer. Lyon & Lyon forwarded a copy of his application in late 1992.

The new dealer was to be Paul Stephens, the Illinois farmer set up to be the straw dealer by the Ed Temple enterprises.

Hunt and his attorney were unaware of who Stephens really was or that he was a only a sham dealer until Temple could sell the letter of intent. But something about Stephens's application smelled funny, so they did a little investigating. They discovered that the address in Warrenton for the proposed dealership did not exist. Stephens's home address was fake. He had never worked at the companies listed on the application. His dealership corporation did not exist. Hunt's attorney contacted Honda executive vice president Tom Elliott, questioning the veracity of Stephens.

McCarthy responded in a letter on behalf of Elliott, defending Stephens as a qualified dealer applicant.

McCarthy may not have known about Stephens, because there were dozens of letters of intent orphaned when Cardiges left Honda. Or he may have been hiding his knowledge of Stephens being a phony dealer from Hunt, just as he was concealing information in the Nault case in New Hampshire.

Honda woke up and rescinded Stephens's letter of intent in March 1993. Hunt discovered shortly thereafter of Stephens's real occupation. It confirmed what he could not prove in his case — that Honda executives had sold the rights to dealerships. Hunt is also convinced that McCarthy coached Josleyn and Cooper to lie under oath.

The owner of a West Virginia dealer also filed suit against American Honda in 1992. He claims he was denied an Acura franchise because he refused to pay off David Pedersen.

In early 1993 the *Nault vs. Acura* case finally shifted out of first gear.

Pretrial proceedings still revolved around the issue of when Don McCarthy of Lyon & Lyon first learned of the Holtham and Bohlander gifts. McCarthy and Nault's lawyer, Richard McNamara, were still accusing each other of misconduct. Almost forgotten was the core charge that Nault's Acura franchise had been wrongfully terminated by American Honda.

McCarthy asked the judge to strike McNamara's "scandalous" pleadings about Lyon & Lyon committing a fraud upon the court and that McNamara be forced to pay Honda's legal fees as punishment. McNamara again asked the judge to have Lyon & Lyon removed from the case.

Judge McAuliffe, tired of the tirades, levied fines on both attorneys. He sanctioned McNamara for making unsupported allegations about Lyon & Lyon and McCarthy for not adhering to the rules of discovery. He ordered the lawyers to write letters of apology to each other. In a stinging reprimand of Lyon & Lyon, the judge wrote:

> The record before the Court reflects a disturbingly polished skill on the part of Lyon and Lyon for hair-splitting interpretations of discovery requirements . . . for strained employment of the common speech . . . when answering interrogatories and defending depositions, for unsettlingly facile explanations when caught in what ought to be exceedingly embarrassing failures to comply with straightforward production obligations, and for a curiously dull unfamiliarity with most incriminating facts about Honda and its employees despite an impressively detailed grasp of all other facts. It is a provocative and suspicious history without doubt.

On February 22, 1993, the judge presided over the beginning of three days of evidentiary hearings. Over the protest of Honda's attorneys, he granted a motion by McNamara that the case's protective order be lifted.

"We are not going to have secret proceedings," said McAuliffe, "and we are not going to seal anything else from here on out. The public is supposed to know what's going on in the business community, especially where you're bringing an action against a public statute." McAuliffe's decree was bad news for Honda. From that moment forward, anything said in court was public information.

The battling lawyers became witnesses. McCarthy took the stand, again claiming that he knew nothing about the Bohlander-to-Pedersen bribes until told by Budnick on December 11, 1991, and thus his answer to Interrogatory #22 was the truth. McNamara took the stand and stood by his charge that Lyon & Lyon had withheld evidence of bribes.

Tom Bohlander testified that he gave the Acura automobile to Pedersen and paid the college tuition for Pedersen's son. He said he did it because Pedersen was his friend.

Damien Budnick took the stand. Warren Nighswander, an attorney for a New Hampshire firm retained by Lyon & Lyon, grilled Budnick about the Holtham and Bohlander gifts. Yes, said Budnick, I picked up a package from Holtham in March 1990 and gave it to Pedersen. No, I did not know what was in it. McCarthy told me on April 11, 1991, about the $100,000 Holtham gratuity rumored to be given to me. I told McCarthy on September 24, 1991, about the Bohlander gifts to Pedersen.

Budnick was still hiding his involvement in the Holtham deal and still firm in his recollection of the dates when he relayed information to Lyon & Lyon. He was asked by McNamara's partner, Gregory Holmes, about a phrase in the Acura world that Budnick had mentioned in a previous deposition.

"Mr. Budnick, can you tell us what 'passing the football' means?"

"That's a term that was used by the reps when a dealer paid for or had done something over and above to acquire a point, a dealership."

"Had a dealer paid someone for a dealership?"

"Yes."

"Was there a certain amount that would follow that decision?"

"Usually, it was a hundred thousand plus."

"And to your knowledge, who would that football be passed to?"

"Top management at Honda."

Budnick testified that the wide receivers were Jack Billmyer, Jim Cardiges, and former New York zone sales manager John Conway. He named two Connecticut dealers as having paid off Honda executives. Budnick's testimony hit the national news wires.

The Big Secret at American Honda was now out, but things were about to get much worse.

At the close of the hearings on February 24, Judge McAuliffe had another item to cover. Hearing the testimony about possible violations of a federal crime in open court compelled him to uphold an obligation of his position.

McAuliffe asked Honda's local counsel Nighswander, "What's been done about referring these apparent violations to the proper authorities; anything? Your company done anything?"

"No, your honor," replied Nighswander, caught somewhat off guard. "It's been considered . . . and found not to be a specific obligation of (Honda) to report specific allegations of misconduct."

"My inclination," said Judge McAuliffe, "is to refer Mr. Pedersen for prosecution, Mr. Bohlander for prosecution, Mr. Holtham for prosecution, (and) investigation of American Honda. I don't know that any felony has been committed. I just know that there has been sufficient evidence produced in this courtroom the last three days to suggest that one has been committed." He added that he might refer information on the antics of Lyon & Lyon attorneys to the California Bar Association for disciplinary action.

The judge gave another plea for the two sides to negotiate a settlement, adding that he doubted it would happen due to the "poisoned" relationship between McCarthy and McNamara.

The following day, Judge McAuliffe took the suspicious information from the Nault case upstairs to the New Hampshire offices of the Federal Bureau of Investigation and the U.S. Attorney. No decision had to be made to investigate the participants and American Honda; the feds were obligated to pursue the allegations.

Media reports trumpeted the impending FBI investigation of the corporation. The start of Honda's darkest days was at hand.

In June, Lyon & Lyon admitted in court that Honda had conducted an internal investigation of its executives. The corporation was in danger of details of the inquiry being introduced at trial, which was on the horizon after four years of legal wrangles. Equally damaging, McNamara introduced evidence showing that Lyon & Lyon had utilized its unethical methods in other court cases, on behalf of both Honda and other clients. Honda promptly settled with Richard Nault for a rumored $5 million. If Lyon & Lyon had directed Honda to settle with Nault before the February 1993 proceedings had begun, as the judges begged them to for two years, Honda would not have faced a federal inquiry.

The misdeeds by the Acura executives and Lyon & Lyon attorneys placed American Honda under the heat lamps of the Department of Justice. Honda's problems in New Hampshire were only beginning.

CHAPTER 15

The Race to the Courthouse

The most valuable commodity I know of is information.

—Michael Douglas, from the film *Wall Street*

AMERICAN HONDA was in deep trouble. An FBI investigation of the corporation and its executives might lead to widely publicized confirmation that the Honda world had been rife with corruption for years and that top company officials had ignored it. Honda retailers might initiate civil lawsuits, claiming they were victims of the favoritism shown dirty dealers. Worst of all, the government might find evidence of crimes that could lead to an indictment of the corporation or Honda's Japanese executives.

Auto industry observers recognized the connection between the Richard Nault case revelations about Honda's internal investigation and the fact that Jim Cardiges and several of his cronies had unexpectedly departed Honda in 1992. Information from the Rick Hunt case about Dennis Josleyn possibly receiving $90,000 for an open point also hit the news.

The media was all over Honda. *Automotive News* reporter Lindsay Chappell reached Jack Billmyer at his North Carolina home. Chappell asked about Damien Budnick's allegation that Billmyer had received upwards of $100,000 for handing out Honda franchises.

"I've never heard of anything so absurd," Billmyer insisted. Honda insiders laughed when reading the comment. "Jack's telling the truth," said one. "He wouldn't touch a deal for only a hundred grand."

Anonymous Honda employees and dealers slipped *Automotive News* information about the combo platter of crimes that had occurred. The trade journal reported rumors about the advertising, sales training, and used car scams, the first public mention of possible embezzlement by Honda executives.

Honda struggled to keep the lid on. A small number of employees left the company last year, said Honda, and we will not comment further.

On May 2, 1993, the *New York Times* published a feature story about the rumblings of corruption at Honda. Penned by noted automotive writer Doron P. Levin, the piece was titled "Honda's Ugly Little Secret." Levin quoted former Ohio dealer Tom Roulette, who detailed his payoffs to Honda executives. Levin noted a recent development in the William Shepherd case, the Concord, California, dealer who was suing Honda over its policy of forcing dealers to falsify sales reports. Shepherd charged that former Honda vice president Cliff Schmillen held a 10 percent interest in a neighboring Honda dealer and that the store's allocations were manipulated to gain advantage over Shepherd Honda. Levin talked to dozens of Honda executives and dealers who anonymously admitted that the Honda car distribution system had been wrought with fraud since the 1970s.

The Honda file floated around the New Hampshire U.S. Attorney's office for several months. Federal lawyers assigned to the case were not motivated to look much beyond David Pedersen and Damien Budnick. The FBI followed up on Judge Steven McAuliffe's referral and interrogated the two former Acura managers.

Budnick got the $100,000 from Frank Holtham, said Pedersen.

Pedersen got the $100,000 from Frank Holtham, said Budnick.

The FBI spoke with Connecticut dealer John Orsini, whom Budnick had fingered in the Nault proceedings as having paid Billmyer for a dealership. Despite his payoffs to Billmyer and Pedersen, Orsini denied having given anything to Honda executives. "I did not want to get involved in this matter," said Orsini later.

In July the case was assigned to Assistant U.S. Attorney Michael J. Connolly. The articulate, quietly ambitious 34-year-old New Jersey native had resigned from a position as a Manhattan corporate attorney two years earlier for the government job and the idyllic life of New Hampshire. He quickly established a successful record of prosecuting complex white-collar crime cases. Connolly had a hunch there was more to the Honda case than gifts accepted by Budnick and Pedersen. His first clue that the activities might be widespread came from the *New York Times* story. "The article made me believe that this could go right to the top of the company," says Connolly.

If he could break the case, Connolly figured he would send a message to the business world that commercial bribery would be dealt with as severely as is government bribery. "This type of insidious corruption has a pernicious effect on our economy and on the atmosphere in which business is conducted," says Connolly, "and for those reasons I thought it was an important case." He appointed FBI Special Agent John Mulvaney to be his lead investigator, and the pair went to work.

They first had to determine what laws had been broken by the executives. "I thought it was an easy case to convict Pedersen, because the perjury was so obvious," recalls Connolly. "I thought there was probably a fraud case here, too, although that was not immediately apparent, because you're dealing with intangible property and the law has changed on this."

Federal fraud statutes allow for convictions predicated on "theft of honest services." In other words, if someone is paid a salary for his or her loyal services, any breach of that loyalty is assumed to carry with it some loss to the employer, even though no money or property has been stolen. Thus, by Honda executives violating the company's conflict of interest policy by accepting gifts over $50, they had committed a crime by defrauding Honda of its rights to the executives' honest services. The company was not getting what it paid for. A 1987 U.S Supreme Court decision eliminated the "theft of honest services" provision of the fraud law. In 1990 Congress overruled that decision but disallowed the prosecution of any acts occurring before 1987, thus preventing Connolly from pursuing gift giving that had occurred during the Honda heyday. Regardless of the status of the vague provision, common sense held that fraud by officials who had received gifts from dealers would be tough to prove in court. Chasing Honda executives who were showered with random gratuities would not be worth Connolly's time — there was quid, but where was the quo?

Fortunately for Connolly, most of the Honda officials were multitalented. He concluded that the legal rights embodied in a letter of intent for a new dealership belonged to Honda, because it held the exclusive authority to decide who would receive those rights. By selling the letters of intent, or arranging to grant them and then splitting the proceeds from the sale of the dealership, Connolly deduced that the executives were stealing Honda property. He knew the most airtight charges involved crimes that were still only whispers in the media — the misappropriation of the advertising and sales training funds. Discovering executives who had siphoned off Honda cash would make for a slam-dunk conviction for defrauding the corporation. The new dealership arrangements and the ad and sales training swindles were what Connolly wanted to unearth.

More than just fraud charges were at Connolly's disposal. Executives who were working on common schemes could be charged with conspiracy. The more productive of the gang could be nailed for engaging in a pattern of racketeering, a charge that allows for the seizure of the guilty party's property. Anyone who lied to the feds could be indicted for perjury or obstruction of justice. Those who did not pay taxes on their ill-gotten gains could be referred to the Internal Revenue Service.

Connolly's next move was to contact American Honda. His early attempts to persuade the company to cooperate with his investigation failed. Honda did not want the Department of Justice exposing the scope of the scandal to the world. The corporation also realized it stood on shaky legal and ethical grounds by never having reported the crimes to the authorities or their own shareholders. Neither side will say much about the tense meetings between Connolly and Honda attorneys, the latter group led by Honda's associate general counsel Mark Brooks, but some things are clear: Honda provided information about the firings of Pedersen and Budnick, but little else. It said there had been isolated incidents of executives receiving gifts from dealers and that the company had handled the matters swiftly. Honda refused to reveal specifics about its internal investigation, claiming client-attorney privilege. The company's practice of hiding its sales executives' activities in the Lyon & Lyon safe had just paid off.

Go away, said Honda to Connolly, this is none of your business.

Connolly left his first encounters with Honda armed with another clue that something was amiss: the company had engaged an army of attorneys to fight his advances. Lawyers representing Honda hailed from Concord, Boston, and Los Angeles. "Three layers of law firms are not necessary to deal with a local problem," notes Connolly. It reinforced to him that the rumors might be true, that the corruption at Honda went way beyond New England.

Others dodged the approaches of Connolly and Agent Mulvaney. "We reached out to a lot of dealers early on who were alleged to have been involved in corrupt payments or to have knowledge of corrupt payments," says Connolly. "They uniformly resisted our overtures or out-and-out lied to us. It became clear that nobody involved in this thing wanted to divulge what they knew had been going on for the past decade. So we were meeting resistance everywhere we turned and it was frustrating. . . . Everyone seemed to know about it, but nobody wanted to talk about it."

Connolly made another run at Budnick. Under threat of being charged with a potpourri of crimes, Budnick rolled over. He detailed gifts he had received from Acura dealers. His latest spin on the Holtham deal was that he took $6,000 and the remaining $94,000 went to Pedersen. Budnick told Connolly that Jack Billmyer had a driver or mechanic from his NASCAR race team on dealer John Orsini's payroll.

Mulvaney dispatched a North Carolina FBI agent to visit Billmyer. The Patriarch of Payola knew nothing. He stated that he had never received money from Honda dealers. He had never heard of anyone in the corporation taking bribes. "I've never had a driver or mechanic on a Honda dealer's payroll," said Billmyer, speaking truthfully — the person on Orsini's books had been his race team's crew chief.

Two FBI agents knocked on Cardiges's door. He told them that he had never received gifts or cash from dealers, nor had hidden ownership in any Honda dealership. He claimed that he had left Honda under a voluntary retirement program. At the conclusion of the interview, the agents informed Cardiges of Title 18, Section 1001, of the United States Code, which defines the act of making false statements to federal law enforcement officials as a crime. They asked if he would like to change any statement he had made. Cardiges said no.

"It scared the hell out of me," says Cardiges of the interview. Both Cardiges and Billmyer would refuse all subsequent overtures by the Department of Justice.

By early fall, the government's investigation was stagnating. The resistance by the parties involved kept the feds at bay. Connolly had only a few dealer gifts, a possible no-show employee on a dealer's payroll, and a ton of rumors — hardly enough evidence to substantiate that a significant corruption and embezzlement scandal had occurred. He lacked the power of information to pry open the mouths in the Honda world.

And then Connolly's phone started ringing.

Members of the broken boys' club were not concerned about the government's probe, despite the possibility of a trip to Club Fed to any caught. Masters of denial, most of the departed Honda crew figured the FBI was only chasing Budnick and Pedersen. Only one man understood the bigger picture.

His name was Ed Temple. The Master. Omnipresent Ed. Friend to millionaire car dealers, shy Japanese executives, and the soybean farmers of America. Smarter than the average briber.

Temple the freelance broker kept wheeling until early 1993, when an open point deal turned sour. A letter of intent was issued to a non-car-dealer friend of Temple's for a new Honda store in tiny Waycross, Georgia. Cardiges had approved the deal before his departure from Honda, and interim corporate sales management did not recognize the applicant as being phony. Temple had supplied the capital for the straw candidate's application and found a dealer willing to pay $275,000 for the letter of intent. The new dealer had a tentative arrangement to assume a lease on a Chrysler-Plymouth facility. The day the dealer license was issued in February 1993, everything started to unwind. As the first shipment of Honda automobiles, parts, and computer equipment were en route to the store, the dealership's landlord filed for bankruptcy and canceled the new lease. Chrysler Corporation seized and padlocked the facility in order to protect its property. Honda was now shipping to a dealership that did not exist. Atlanta zone sales manager Bob Mazzitelli scrambled to have the Hondas moved from the store to a K-Mart parking lot. The next day he was fired by Honda for his involvement in the corruption, and Temple lost the only man who could have revived the deal. Honda quickly terminated the franchise, and the dealer refused to pay Temple his $275,000 fee.

The pattern of Honda executives selling rights to dealerships had started in Georgia in 1975, when Jack Billmyer first tried to shake down a retailer for a Honda franchise, and ended in the same state with this rare shutout for Temple in 1993.

Soon after Judge McAuliffe turned the allegations from the Nault hearings over to the Department of Justice in February 1993, Temple began consulting with his attorneys. Throughout the year, his nationwide contacts kept him apprised of who was being interviewed by the FBI. One of Temple's lawyers was a former New Hampshire Assistant U.S. Attorney, with his ear to the ground in Concord. Temple realized where he stood in the scandal, that he ranked with Billmyer and Cardiges in terms of moneys gained. He knew those two had been contacted by the feds and that he might be next. He heard that Connolly was not going to go away. Temple figured that he who talks first, walks first.

In September, Temple made the toughest decision of his life—he told his lead attorney, Washington, D.C., criminal defense lawyer Jim Sharp, to contact the Department of Justice. Get me immunity, said Temple, and I will tell them everything—and I know more than anybody. It was just another business deal to Temple, this time with the government instead of some panting car dealer, and he wanted to win. Temple was also deathly afraid of landing in prison. Sharp called Connolly and offered to produce his client. I have the man who can break the case for you, Sharp bragged.

It was the first time Michael Connolly had ever heard the name Ed Temple.

Sharp indicated he wanted to negotiate an immunity agreement in exchange for Temple's complete cooperation. He forwarded Connolly some easily verifiable tidbits of information about the corruption to gain his confidence in the quality of information Temple possessed.

As Connolly considered the deal to immunize Temple, he received another call: Christiaan Walker's attorney was on the phone offering up the Peck checks. Walker was still employed as Honda's Oregon district sales manager at the time. His five years of babbling about the money passed from Arkansas dealer Cliff Peck to Honda officials had not made him a hero but a goat. Walker was scrambling to prevent Honda from firing him, and his contacting Connolly was among his final acts. He would be pressured into resigning two months later.

The paranoid Walker was somehow convinced that Honda was going to press Connolly to indict him for extortion and forgery, so he decided to strike first. Walker's attorney sent Connolly copies of the Peck checks made out to Temple, Cardiges, and Fred Meis, the latter originally made out to a Peck dealership investor and altered to show Meis as the recipient. Honda has been covering this up for five years, Walker's lawyer told Connolly.

Walker had unwittingly used the Peck checks to sucker-punch Temple once again. Knowing he could now convict him on the Peck deal, Connolly refused to offer Temple complete immunity. If Temple had beaten Walker to the courthouse, he would have escaped all charges.

Armed with the information provided by Walker and Temple, Connolly was able to have his first productive meeting with Honda in early October. The company turned over a portion of its investigative files, including the copy of the forged Peck check. Connolly agreed with Honda's conclusion that Walker had altered the check in an effort to frame Meis. "It is extremely unlikely that Mr. Peck himself would have fabricated a phony name on one of his checks," says Connolly. "Walker was the only one who could have done it." (The FBI later interviewed Peck and his office manager, Michelle Bregard, who both confirmed that there had been no check to Meis.)

Connolly's investigation was finally rolling. "There was a constellation of events happening at the same time," recalls Connolly. "We had Honda coming to us, we had Christiaan Walker coming to us through his attorney, and we had Ed Temple reaching out to us at the same time. There was a synergistic effect from all this, because we could talk to Honda, knowing things they didn't think we knew. We could talk to Temple, knowing things he didn't think we knew. We could talk to Walker, knowing things he didn't think we knew. We could leverage the knowledge we were getting to provide a credible front and motivate these people to provide information to us in a candid fashion."

During the last week of October, Temple told everyone at Costa Mesa Honda that he was going home to Georgia for a week. Instead, he and

Sharp flew to New Hampshire. In exchange for Temple's cooperation, the government agreed to prosecute him only for his receiving $162,500 from Cliff Peck. Temple agreed to plead guilty to one count of mail fraud, which carried a maximum five-year prison term—a good deal for one of the most prolific fraudsters of the Honda crew. Knowing that Temple was probably involved in other deals, Connolly stipulated that he agree to pay the maximum fine of $250,000. In return, Connolly pledged that he would try to get Temple a suspended sentence.

For the next five days, Temple led Connolly and Mulvaney on a guided tour through the Honda underworld. Temple provided a stupendous amount of information to the government. Between his near-photographic memory, an extensive collection of checks, and the notes he had taken over the years, it seemed like Temple had long been preparing for this moment.

Temple started with Cardiges. He told Connolly that Cardiges had visited him the week before and was visibly nervous about the FBI investigation. Temple handed Connolly a list of 33 Honda dealers who had compensated Cardiges. He itemized Cardiges's automobiles and other personal property, naming which dealers had provided them. He proffered a copy of a $183,000 check made out to Cardiges from a California dealer as his split for granting an open point. He provided the names and addresses of Cardiges's accountant, lawyer, real estate broker, and insurance agent. He recalled Cardiges instructing Honda employees to take the money they received from dealers and invest it into real estate. Temple told of visiting one of Cardiges's unrented condominiums, where the sales chief had stashed a paper bag stuffed with $100,000 in cash. He reviewed Cardiges's odd family history, noting that the Cardiges offspring were "not worth shooting." The Master had just crossed The Mentor.

Temple named Jack Billmyer, Dennis Josleyn, Bob Rivers, Fred Meis, Hugh Cooper, Tom Caulfield, Roger Novelly, and two of his employees at Costa Mesa Honda, ex–Honda executives Bob Mazzitelli and Mark Benson, as having been major players. With remarkable detail and accuracy, he itemized each official's underhanded dealings and which ones owned front companies, the classic hallmark of a fraud scheme.

Temple talked about the Hong Kong shopping sprees hosted by Dah Chong Hong and other dealers. He told of industry consultant J. D. Power bringing the corruption to the attention of Honda's Japanese officials. He told them which Honda dealerships were secretly owned by Rick Hendrick. He disclosed which East Coast Honda dealers were rumored to have ties to organized crime, noting that he was putting himself in peril by doing so.

And then Temple detailed what Connolly wanted to hear: that some of the executives had stolen from Honda. Even though the embezzlement occurred after his tenure, Temple told how Josleyn and his brother had organized the sales training and advertising schemes and how Caulfield was the point man. Temple correctly identified the managers who received kickbacks from the Josleyn companies. He gave Connolly a copy of a $50,000 check that Rivers had received from Sales Training Technologies. He mentioned that Cooper had told him the week before that he had taken in $100,000 from the ad scam.

Temple cheerfully came clean on his own involvement in the chicanery. Over the coming months, he would admit to Connolly that he had received about $1.6 million in cash and gifts from dealers, the majority of which came from the open point deals he had arranged after leaving Honda. Among his confessions was that he had profited $100,000 on the Santa Paula Honda deal. He admitted to the payoffs he had made while a dealer, including giving $1,000 per car to Josleyn for some used company vehicles.

The Japanese executives knew about the corruption, said Temple. American Honda president Koichi Amemiya was scared to fire Cardiges after the Peck checks surfaced, because it might expose the problems. The corporation's inquiry did not look into the matter of "burning" the sales cards, Temple informed Connolly, because the Japanese were involved in it. Temple clued Connolly in on the Mercedes-Benz convertible given to Amemiya by California dealer Ted Stevens.

Temple's meticulously organized presentation enthralled and entertained Connolly and Mulvaney. That did not know it yet, but no other witness would step forward with as much legitimate and useful information as Temple had offered. Past and present dirty Honda executives paid the price for their confiding in Temple over the years as he handed the FBI the backbone of the case against them. All the feds had to do was gather the evidence.

The case suddenly appeared bigger than Connolly had ever imagined. Not lost on him was the impact a successful investigation and prosecution might have on his career. "It was a rare opportunity for a small-time prosecutor from a back-water state like New Hampshire," says Connolly. "One of my biggest concerns early on was that the Department of Justice in Washington would not have the confidence in our office to handle this matter. I realized this case was national in scope, that there would be a tremendous amount of money involved, and that it would entail sending FBI agents out on leads across the country. No case had ever been done like this in New Hampshire or small states like it."

"The term I used was to 'drop anchor,' in New Hampshire before

Washington found out about the case. I wanted to drop the biggest, heaviest anchor that we could put together in New Hampshire so that there wouldn't be any suggestion that the case be prosecuted out of some other district." The Honda case was to be Connolly's baby.

Temple's mention that he was Cardiges's closest confidant gave Connolly an opportunity to check under Cardiges's hood before word of Temple's confessions hit the streets. Temple agreed to wear a body wire and tape-record a meeting with Cardiges as soon as he returned to Los Angeles. Find out what his plans are, Connolly instructed Temple.

The timing was perfect — Cardiges and his cronies were rattled. John Mulvaney had ordered FBI agents to pay visits to some of the new suspects while Temple was still in Concord. Connolly mailed "target letters" to the gang — the notification that they were under investigation and the official invitation to See New Hampshire. American Honda, aware of how serious the Department of Justice had become, reopened its internal investigation and called in surviving executives to grill them about the corruption. Cardiges and Josleyn were scheduled to give depositions in the *Shepherd Honda vs. American Honda* case in two weeks. The lawsuit filed by the California dealer accused ex–Honda vice president Cliff Schmillen of holding secret ownership in a neighboring dealership. Honda notified Cardiges and Josleyn that it would no longer pay their attorneys' fees for the Shepherd case: in effect, Honda was going to allow them to hang themselves. At the same time, Honda unsuccessfully tried to convince the fired employees to come back in and confess to everything. This flurry of activity had the phone lines buzzing as the former executives asked each other: what the hell is going on?

On November 2, Cardiges drove Effie's red Civic wagon into the service department of Costa Mesa Honda. He strolled into Temple's office. Mark Benson poked his head in the door, and the three men joked about Cardiges's perfectly groomed ponytail. The room was briefly filled with the hearty, macho laughter of the old days. Cardiges had missed that.

Cardiges and Temple walked next door to an empty office in Temple's Infiniti dealership. The wired Temple was not the best sleuth. He began the conversation by nearly blowing his cover — he tried too hard to maneuver Cardiges into a chair close to his desk, prompting Cardiges to wonder aloud why he had to sit there. When telling how three managers had stolen $9,000 from the dealership's F and I (finance and insurance) department, Temple referred to it as the "FBI department." Cardiges would not pick up any clues that something was amiss during the meeting but thought it odd that the normally calm Temple appeared agitated.

"I know that it's getting ready to blow," said Temple. "I smell it. I feel it."

"I think it's gonna blow," Cardiges agreed.

"Did you ever think it would get to this?" asked Temple

"Jack always told me about the possibilities," replied Cardiges. "Jack always thought it could happen."

Temple said that former Atlanta zone sales manager Bob Mazzitelli "went in his pants" when the FBI visited him the day before. "He's gone berserk," moaned Temple. "He wants to go to Honda and cleanse his soul. He's just one of ten or twenty guys who could go off like that."

"Well, that's the risk in life we all face," Cardiges responded.

"Why are you taking it so well?"

"Because I know that when the dam breaks, we're all gonna have to pay the price. I've already reconciled that in my mind the past two years." The intuitive Cardiges said he was resigned to the fact that he was in trouble. He figured he would get hit for the advertising scheme and Temple for the Cliff Peck deal. He urged Temple to stick to their story about the Peck payments being a loan, should Temple be contacted by Honda.

"What the hell am I going to tell the FBI when they knock on my door?" asked Temple. "Kiss my ass?"

"The same thing I did," said Cardiges. "Nothing."

"Jim, goddamn, I have been up all night, this is the worst I've been since day one on this thing."

"Just calm down. You and I are going to jail. You gotta put it in your mind that you'll go to jail for a while."

"Who do you think they're gonna nail?" asked Temple.

"It'll probably be Josleyn, you, me and Meis," said Cardiges. "Mazz will probably go. Pedersen will go. I don't know about Rivers, because he's been out of the loop the past five years. We've got four or five different things that we're fighting at one time. STT, Cliff Peck, advertising. They're all interrelated."

Cardiges had faith that Temple would never throw him under the bus. "I've never worried about you," said Cardiges. "I've worried about a lot of other dealers. Ted Stevens will get up there and cry like a baby. The other dealers back East who we were close to will disenfranchise themselves from us."

Cardiges was mystified that Honda was apparently going to allow the Shepherd case to become what Nault was to Acura: a public pronouncement of the corruption. "I feel the potential for it exploding as a result of testimony from the Shepherd case is very good," said Cardiges. "Not from me, but I'm worried about Josleyn. It's not in Honda's best interest to have all this shit break nationwide. It is possible that Honda will try to settle this thing between now and the court date." Cardiges was unaware that Honda was under Connolly's scrutiny and thus was playing it straight in the case — no Lyon & Lyon coaching of executives or courtroom mischief. If the Shepherd proceedings revealed more of the corporation's dirty laundry, so be it.

Cardiges tried to soothe Temple's faked fears by repeating what his lawyer had told him. Attorney Phillip Israels had already earned about $60,000 from Cardiges in exchange for some questionable legal advice. He told Cardiges not to worry about an FBI probe. He said local FBI offices would not be able to coordinate investigative efforts with the New Hampshire bureau and that state law enforcement agencies would have to be involved. It's way too complicated for them to crack, said Israels.

More amazing was Israels's counsel about Cardiges coming forward. "My lawyer said, 'you didn't do anything wrong,'" Cardiges remarked. "'But besides that, whether you've done anything wrong or not, our legal system can not feel for somebody who comes up front and says I'm guilty, I did this. They throw a longer sentence at you and punish you harder than if you fight.'" Temple was living proof that the opposite was true.

Cardiges confided that he had considered the idea of fleeing the United States. "If you go international and you establish a home, then you can avoid this," explained Cardiges. "But you're not going to be able to come back for ten or fifteen years." It was Cardiges's responsibility as a father and husband that kept him from running. He asked Temple to enlist a certain dirty dealer's help in taking care of Effie and his children if he had to go to jail. "I've got Effie up to a level where she knows that I run the risk of being in trouble," said Cardiges. "So that when things do break it won't be like the biggest surprise."

Cardiges vowed to fight the government but was certain he was going to lose. He told Temple how he planned to present the right image when arrested.

"I know how I'm gonna look when they take my mug shot," said Cardiges. "I'm gonna have my chin up and I'm gonna have a stern, far reaching look in my eyes."

It was time for Cardiges to head home. "Don't call anybody and don't talk to other people," he advised Temple. "Don't worry about the Shepherd case. Save yourself, Ed. And I still love you."

"I appreciate that, Jim," said Temple. "I feel the same way. I hate that it all has come to this. I think I finally realize that this is just the beginning of the end."

Cardiges picked up his wife's car and joked to Temple about the dealership's service department. "I wish you guys would take better care of me," said Cardiges as he drove off. Temple turned off the tape recorder and walked back inside to call Agent Mulvaney.

Temple and Cardiges would never see each other again.

Connolly learned from the tape recording that Cardiges was not a flight risk. He seemed like a reasonable fellow who knew he had done wrong.

One of Cardiges's statements was of huge significance for Connolly's strategy development. "This thing goes back fifteen or twenty years," Cardiges had said. "It's not a thing that happened just three years ago with the advertising thing." Statute of limitations for conspiracy cases is five years. However, if the crime involves one continuous conspiracy, the statute of limitations is five years from the date of the last act, in this case 1992. With the exception of certain "theft of honest services" charges, Connolly could prosecute any act of the scandal dating back to the 1970s based on Cardiges's statement and supporting evidence.

Connolly made more determinations about the scope of the probe. He realized he could charge scores of executives and dealers with fraud charges, that the investigation would be limited only by whatever guidelines he set forth. Connolly decided to concentrate on pursuing the Honda executives because they were the ones who had abused their positions. Indicting Honda dealer principals, who could claim they were victims of extortion, would not be easy. The dealers were also going to be the best source of hard evidence. And like with most corruption cases, the party receiving the money gets charged with the crime. It was also difficult to measure the value of what dealers had gained by their involvement, but it was easy to count the money in the executives' pockets.

Connolly's unofficial parameter was to investigate Honda executives who had held the rank of zone sales manager and above, those with the authority to determine who would receive new dealerships. They also had participated in appropriating the advertising and sales training funds. Connolly knew of two executives who would be exceptions to that rule—former association advertising manager Tom Caulfield and former assistant zone sales manager Mark Benson—because they were involved in fraud charge–worthy schemes. At the bottom of the chain was Damien

Budnick, only a district sales manager but a man who was not initially forthcoming with the FBI. "Lying will get you indicted no matter what your rank," Connolly explains. The sea of dirty Honda district sales managers and assistant zone sales managers had just been handed clemency by Connolly.

Connolly concluded that American Honda was the victim of the actions of its executives, that the company had been defrauded. The attorney utilized the standard definition of a corporation — that the entity is composed of and owned by the shareholders, not the employees. The shareholders did not participate in, nor were they aware of, the corruption, so the company could therefore not be held criminally culpable.

Connolly walked a thin line by choosing not to pursue an indictment of the company — Jack Billmyer had sat on the corporation's board of directors, as had Lyon & Lyon attorney Bud Smoot and president Koichi Amemiya, three officers who knew the score and who had the closest ties to the shareholders. To Connolly, they were high-ranking employees and not owners. The obvious lack of action by top executives to stop the corruption did not matter to him, either. He was simply after a gang of criminals who had cost their employer money.

Honda was lucky. Corporations can be held liable for the actions of their employees, particularly when there is no enforcement of a conflict of interest policy, as was the case at Honda. Companies indicted on federal fraud charges also face fines that can be multiplied as much as 80-fold if the company failed to take measures to stop employee misconduct.

Indictments of corporations can also occur when individuals are harmed by the company's negligence. If Connolly or a consumer group had found proof that Honda officials' practice of forcing dealers to falsify sales cards had shortened the warranties of Honda automobiles, or that car prices had been adversely affected by the corruption, Connolly might have gone after the corporation. As it was, Honda was fortunate that Connolly's criminal investigation was to focus only on its executives.

"We're a victim! We're a victim!" cheered a relieved Honda in-house attorney Mark Brooks to another executive in the headquarters parking lot, upon learning about Connolly's determination.

As the fall foliage dwindled in November in New Hampshire, the tourists went home, only to be replaced by a brood of former Honda executives rushing to Concord. Temple told Benson, his longtime partner in crime and current employee of Costa Mesa Honda, what he had done. If you go now, said Temple, you might only get probation. Benson jumped on a plane for Concord, accompanied by an attorney from the same law firm that represented Temple.

Connolly and Mulvaney conferred with Temple before each suspect came to New Hampshire, reviewing the rascally resume for each. They played good cop/bad cop with Benson and the rest of the Honda boys. Cooperate with us, they said, and we will charge you with only one count. Mess with us, and we will nail you with every dirty dime that flowed through your old territory. Benson agreed to plead guilty to a tidbit supplied by Temple: that he had made $250,000 for granting a dealership in New York during the frenetic 1991. Benson detailed how Josleyn had received over $400,000 from Norm Reeves Honda for selling the retailer used Honda company cars. He provided information about regional manager Larry Finley's secret ownership in a Florida dealership. Like others, Benson "forgot" to mention a few gifts in his meeting with the government—a BMW convertible completely slipped his mind. But Connolly would later discover it.

After Benson rolled over, Temple told the panicked Bob Mazzitelli that he had heard that the feds were on to them all. "His 'connections' is how Temple said he knew about what was going on," says Mazzitelli. Having already received a target letter from Connolly, Mazzitelli and his attorney headed for New Hampshire. Mazzitelli agreed to plead guilty to one count of conspiracy, for splitting $375,000 with Temple in a Florida deal. He admitted to making $103,000 on the advertising scheme, saying that Josleyn and Cardiges had masterminded the plan. He supplied a list of 30 dealers who had given him gifts.

"Connolly didn't really ask much about Temple, which surprised me," said Mazzitelli later.

Former Washington, D.C., zone sales manager Hugh Cooper burst through Connolly's door a week behind Mazzitelli. He pleaded guilt to one count of conspiracy for his role in the advertising scam. Cooper revealed his mentor Josleyn's deal with minority dealer Joe Pope. He told of Roger Novelly's secret ownership in a Honda store in Detroit. He revealed Cardiges's hidden ownership in two Maryland dealerships. He told of Cardiges preaching to the sales executives about "getting on the program." Cooper confessed to receiving $203,000 for a Temple-arranged open point deal in South Carolina, $150,000 from the advertising scam, and $100,000 from selling used cars through a rigged system.

Cooper tipped off Connolly to one of Bob Rivers's deals in Virginia, and Connolly invited the dealer to Concord. The dealer called Rivers, saying he felt he had no choice but to tell the government about the payoffs. Rivers immediately flew to New Hampshire and pleaded guilty to one count of racketeering. He admitted to making over $1 million on the side while at Honda.

Fred Meis and Roger Novelly received invites to Concord. They came forward to add ballast to Connolly's anchor in exchange for the government charging them with only one count apiece. Meis admitted to receiving over $500,000 over the years, primarily on open point deals. I never solicited any of the cash or gifts, said Meis, and I always had a reputation as a guy who does not come around with his hand out. Novelly also insisted that he had never asked for a single gratuity, that $200,000 worth of dealer gifts just came out of the blue.

The Honda managers were falling fast and squealing like stuck pigs. Each guilty plea came packaged with scores of new leads. Connolly rented an office away from the cramped U.S. Attorney's bureau to store the piles of paperwork and to interview suspects. "John (Mulvaney) and I were so overwhelmed," says Connolly, "that we would just sit back and look at each other and shake our heads because there was so much information coming, we could not process it fast enough. We could not get the (FBI) leads out fast enough. We realized that we were dealing with one of the biggest commercial bribery cases of all time."

"Every day that a former Honda executive would fly in with his attorneys and enter a guilty plea, we would go back to the office and pinch ourselves. We were astonished that it was happening out of this sleepy little hamlet in northern New England."

Most of the Honda dealers received immunity agreements from the government in exchange for their agreeing to tell all. You are either a participant or a victim, Connolly would tell them, it's your choice. Faced with irrefutable evidence of their involvement, the majority of the dealers contacted by the government rolled over. Connolly or an FBI agent would walk into a dealer's office with one piece of evidence and walk out with a dozen more.

More than 50 dealers gladly supplied documentation on money and gifts they had given to the Honda managers. Officials of Dah Chong Hong admitted to forwarding over $300,000 in cash and prizes to Honda executives. Cliff Peck, Rod Ryan, and Joe Pope confirmed their payments to the officials for new dealerships. Dave Conant of Norm Reeves Honda told of paying Josleyn for the used cars and outlined his payments to Cardiges and other officials. The FBI confronted a Virginia dealer about a Rolex watch he had supposedly given to Cardiges. The dealer trotted out a computer printout of 48 other gifts he had bestowed on Honda managers, from a $1,000 gift certificate to Billmyer to a $29 box of almond toffee to Cardiges. Dave Trainer, the dealer who sold Cardiges the Buckskin Lane house, produced receipts for a dozen payoffs made to his good friend.

"This mass of information was growing under us," recalls Connolly. "I felt like our building was rising off its foundation. Every time we pursued a lead from one of the reliable sources, it would be corroborated. It was like a checklist. We'd go out and confront the dealer, and bingo, it would be a hit."

To a man, the dealers swore they had never paid off officials from other automakers. Some insisted they had been victims of extortion, that they were innocent victims afraid of losing their franchises. Others stated they bestowed cash on the Honda men because they were their friends. Did you give other friends large sums of money, the feds queried. Well, ah, no, the squirming retailers replied.

The FBI interviewed accountants, lawyers, contractors who remodeled executives' house, ex-wives, and friends of the crew. Connolly even interviewed a recalcitrant Frank Sinatra about the loaning of the singer's jet to Honda executives. The feds subpoenaed bank accounts and dealerships' records. The Internal Revenue Service confirmed the income of the executives and their front companies, including the fact that Cardiges had been pulling down over $1 million dollars a year on the side—not counting gifts in cash. Cardiges's accountant validated the sources of the outside income as being from Honda dealers and the Josleyn companies.

Connolly was stymied by the lack of hard evidence he found on Billmyer. The trail was too cold and Billmyer had been too discreet. Says Connolly, "Billmyer was perhaps the shrewdest person involved in this conspiracy in terms of making sure that there was no paper trail." An informant slipped Connolly a photograph circulated at Honda headquarters during the early 1980s, which the attorney pinned on his office wall for inspiration. The shot showed a grinning Billmyer sitting in a bar, a girl on each arm, giving the finger to the camera. Every morning, Connolly entered his office to the sight of being flipped off by Billmyer. Try and catch me, Billmyer seemed to be saying. Connolly also tacked up a picture of a group of eight smiling Honda executives gathered for Effie Cardiges's 50th birthday party. Connolly would eventually convict seven of them.

Connolly aggressively pursued the advertising and sales training swindles. He subpoenaed Tom Caulfield's bank records and discovered that over $800,000 had flowed through the account during 1991, the former Honda ad man never having set up a front company to hide his stash. Connolly sent Caulfield a target letter. Caulfield found a lawyer in the Orange County yellow pages and the next day called Connolly and pleaded guilty over the phone. Caulfield flew to Concord and provided details on the advertising kickbacks. He claimed he had tried to convince Cardiges to stop the embezzlement but to no avail.

Caulfield's confessions broke the advertising scheme wide open. Connolly subpoenaed the records of the Bergmann and Garey vendors and found over $2.5 million paid out to Honda executives in the advertising scheme. He discovered the kickbacks to Cardiges, Josleyn, and Rivers for the sales training seminars. Connolly had just scored big.

Connolly had never seen a case where so many suspects laid down so easily. "Everyone of us was petrified," explains Mazzitelli. "None of us had ever been in trouble before. The only people we have to blame for this is ourselves, by making it so easy for the government. We made the case for them."

Connolly threw a few undersized fish back to Honda. He found evidence on $20,000 worth of gifts received by zone sales manager Frank O'Neill, declining to prosecute him due to the small amount of money involved. Connolly gave the information to Honda, which handed O'Neill his walking papers. O'Neill should have been fired for stupidity: he continued to shake down dealers after Cardiges and Josleyn were forced to resign in 1992. Soon after replacing Josleyn as California zone sales manager, O'Neill visited Ed Temple at Costa Mesa Honda. Saying he wanted to find a "few select friends he could trust," O'Neill asked Temple for $6,200 to pay his children's private school tuition, noting he was unable to make ends meet in California on his salary. Temple paid the school directly so he would have a record of the transaction.

By December, 90 days after Ed Temple had come forward, Connolly and Mulvaney had unearthed over $10 million in embezzlement and bribe payments over a ten-year period. "Anytime you uncover that much, you know you're not getting all of it," says Connolly. Tens of millions of dollars procured by the executives in the early 1980s would never be found, but it did not matter — Connolly only needed one piece of evidence per suspect to throw the book at them. He had bagged eight criminals and was chasing at least ten more.

Connolly correctly concluded that Billmyer was the originator of the corruption, that Cardiges "ratcheted up" the program and likely benefited the most, and that Josleyn was the key man in setting up the advertising and sales training scams. Connolly was not concerned that the trio was refusing to meet with him. "We had information gushing through the windows," said Connolly. "Once Temple and others opened the floodgates, we weren't begging the others to cooperate with us."

News on the investigation began leaking to the press. A government mole tipped off the *New York Times* about the impending indictments in mid-February. Knowing revelations about the secret plea agreements by the executives might compromise the continuing probe, Connolly and Mulvaney began working 100-hour weeks assembling the indictments of five men: Cardiges, Billmyer, Josleyn, Budnick, and Pedersen.

Back in Laguna Hills, the invisible noose tightened around Jim Cardiges's neck. Connolly informed Cardiges's lawyers of the morass of evidence he had gathered on their client. Though the FBI tried to put ziplocks on the mouths of those who had pleaded guilty, Cardiges knew that his compadres were ratting him out. He was also broke. He shut down Worldwide Dyve, having lost over $1 million during the company's short-lived tenure. His heavily leveraged real estate holdings had plunged in value over the previous three years due to the collapsing California economy. The few properties in which he had equity were signed over to his attorneys in lieu of fees. He threatened Temple with a lawsuit to recover $166,000 that he believed Temple owed him as his share from a 1991 open point deal. The split between Cardiges and Temple was now complete.

Everything that Cardiges held sacred was gone: his job, his best friend, and his real estate. He turned to the people he was certain would be there for him, the owners of Honda dealerships.

Cardiges wrote Shau-Wai Lam, the president of the Dah Chong Hong dealer group, pleading for help in paying his mounting legal fees. We'll pass, said Lam. Jim Cardiges was not Soichiro Honda.

Cardiges tried to reach Rick Hendrick, but Honda's biggest dealer refused to take Cardiges's phone calls. In January, Cardiges wrote Hendrick a note:

> It appears that I may be taking the fall. Please be sure that Effie and my family is taken care of while I'm away, and do everything possible to make sure that she doesn't have to move out of our home.

Jim who, Hendrick wondered. In February, Connolly informed Cardiges's lawyers of the charges he planned to file. Cardiges wrote Hendrick again:

> My attorneys and I have read the informational charges leveled against me, other Honda people, and Honda dealers and *we are not guilty.*
>
> Please help me with a legitimate fully disclosed loan to my legal

defense fund. Rick, please help me fight this for you, the dealers and my family.

Please help me!

Hendrick again did not respond. Cardiges still did not understand that Hendrick had only used him to get what he wanted and that he had never considered Cardiges his friend.

Connolly and Mulvaney planned a surprise attack on Cardiges. On March 7, Temple provided them with a detailed description of the layout of Cardiges's home. He told them where to find Cardiges's personal records and which furnishings were provided to him by dealers.

The knock on the door of Cardiges's Buckskin Lane house came at 4:55 P.M. on Friday, March 11. FBI agents raided the home and spent five hours combing the premises for incriminating evidence and seizing property. Cardiges was arrested and led away in handcuffs. He kept his chin up and had a stern, far-reaching look in his eyes when they snapped his mug shot.

The timing of Cardiges's apprehension was designed to ensure that he would spend a weekend in jail while he arranged bond. On Monday, Cardiges mortgaged the mansion to secure the $200,000 bond. He was charged with racketeering, conspiracy, and mail fraud and faced up to 30 years in prison if convicted. The grand jury indictment included a laundry list of moneys and gifts purloined by Cardiges: cash for 15 letters of intent for new dealerships, eight automobiles, $24,000 worth of furniture, three Rolex watches, ten $1,000 suits, $100,000 from the sales training seminars, and an undetermined split of $2.5 million from the advertising scam. Connolly was still gathering evidence on dozens more allegations about Cardiges, including his financial arrangements with Hendrick, planning to use them in a superseding indictment.

On March 14, Jack Billmyer surrendered at the Raleigh FBI office. He was charged with one count of mail fraud for having dealer John Orsini pay his NASCAR crew chief in exchange for an Acura letter of intent. He was released on an unsecured bond of $100,000. Dennis Josleyn self-surrendered and was charged with racketeering, conspiracy, and mail fraud. David Pedersen and Damien Budnick turned themselves in and were both charged with conspiracy to commit mail fraud and obstruction of justice.

The indictments and arrests of the five former Honda executives were announced by New Hampshire U.S. District Attorney Paul Gagnon at a press conference in Concord on March 14. He also revealed the one-count guilty pleas entered by Temple, Mazzitelli, Benson, Cooper, Rivers, Novelly, Meis, and Caulfield. Connolly reported to the press that the nationwide scandal had been going on since the 1970s and was likely the largest commercial corruption case in American history. He stated that the investigation was ongoing.

A man held a cellular phone up among the microphones gathered in front of Connolly. The phone was a feed to a satellite truck parked outside, which beamed the press conference live to Honda's Tokyo headquarters.

American Honda issued a statement saying it was "outraged and saddened" by the revelations about the activities of its former managers. The company vowed to take legal action against the officials and was quick to point out that the U.S. Attorney's office had portrayed the corporation as the victim of the corruption. Honda began a strategy to characterize the executives as a "small number" of rebel former employees. To anyone outside the car business, this would make sense — no one would know that 13 high-ranking executives at the lean Honda made up a sizable portion of the corporate hierarchy.

Honda's proclamation danced around the topic of its inactivity, stating, "The complexity of the schemes to defraud American Honda made it difficult for us to immediately detect and identify them."

The company also announced it had locked the barn after the horses escaped. In a brilliant public relations move, Honda trumpeted that an employee ethics program would be instituted. Included in the plan were financial disclosure requirements for senior officials, company-wide ethics seminars, and a toll-free number for employees to report any suspected wrongdoing. If Honda were serious about a strong ethics plan, it would have been instituted in 1992 as the company was showing the criminals the door, not two years later in a transparent attempt to counter the indictments. Honda's housecleaning and the government investigation were much more effective tools than the corporate ethics program to discourage any repeat occurrences of corruption or embezzlement.

Honda's worst day had arrived. National news media blared reports about the 15-year-long nationwide pattern of bribery and embezzlement. An *Automotive News* editorial blasted the company: "American Honda now has a rigorous ethics program. It comes too late. And it comes before the surviving company officials have explained how American Honda could have experienced so much criminal behavior for so long." Honda wisely refused to answer questions from the press, citing the government's ongoing investigation as an excuse.

The rumor-riddled auto industry questioned why none of Honda's

Japanese executives had been charged. The Department of Justice must have had an agreement with Honda, said the whispers. Scuttlebutt had it that the White House was asked by Japanese government officials not to prosecute any Japanese nationals at Honda and that U.S. Attorney General Janet Reno had ordered Connolly to comply with the request. "That's a joke," says Connolly. "There was never any limits put on who we would or would not indict. That is absolutely fabricated out of whole cloth. The FBI wanted to hear everything." Connolly did not speak with Reno about the investigation until three days before the indictments were handed down.

Connolly concluded that the fraud food chain was headed by Cardiges and Billmyer, not the Japanese. He pursued several leads about gifts received by the Japanese executives, one being a $50,000 painting supposedly given to president Amemiya by a Texas dealer, a rumor repeated by several of the executives. Connolly could find no proof of the transaction. The only significant gift Connolly uncovered was the old Mercedes-Benz convertible that Amemiya had received from California dealer Ted Stevens. Connolly deemed the gratuity trivial, since there was no indication that the dealer benefited in any way from the transaction. He did not perceive Amemiya as a criminal, though the gift did trigger an indictment of Stevens for obstruction of justice—he had made the mistake of lying to the FBI about the car.

In early 1994 Honda Motor Company was notified by American Honda about the government's discovery of Amemiya's Mercedes-Benz. Headquarters ordered Amemiya to pay for the vehicle, which he quickly did, forwarding a $10,000 check to Stevens. American officials receiving gifts of that magnitude were summarily fired, but the Japanese executives were allowed to play by different rules. The Americans were disposable, the Japanese untouchable.

Every Honda official told Connolly that the Japanese executives were aware of the problems, but none could offer proof, only recollections of remarks made by the Japanese that intimated they knew about the bribery. Meis recalled hearing Amemiya and Takeo Okusa talking about how dealers had gotten used to paying off Honda executives and how Billmyer and Cardiges had gotten rich while at Honda.

The only scheme that Honda's Japanese officials were clearly involved in was encouraging dealers to falsify warranty registration cards, but Connolly had yet to find evidence that consumers had been hurt by that practice.

There was more work to be done. The day after the indictments were announced, Connolly's phone started ringing again. Other Honda dealers and ex–Honda employees had more information for the government.

Within 30 days, attorneys for a half-dozen dealers announced they were preparing to file civil suits against Honda, claiming their clients were deprived of profits due to the partiality shown the dirty dealers and by Honda's lack of response to stop the corruption. In May, a California dealer filed a class-action suit against Honda. The lawsuits were a gift for Connolly: he could now show a jury exactly how Honda had been harmed by its ex-employees, since the company faced millions of dollars in legal fees and possible settlements by being engaged in litigation with the dealers.

In April, Damien Budnick changed his plea to guilty for one count of obstruction of justice. He provided more evidence implicating his nemesis David Pedersen, who quickly changed his plea to guilty for one count of racketeering. Only Cardiges, Billmyer, and Josleyn were left to stand trial. All three flew to Concord to enter not-guilty pleas.

Between Connolly forwarding evidence to Honda and the corporation's continuing internal investigation, the company forced ten more managers to depart in 1994. A Honda dealer, tired of being shaken down by a Honda rep who continued to solicit gifts after his peers had been terminated, called headquarters and turned over evidence on him and another Honda manager. Both were fired.

Connolly picked off more ex–Honda executives. Frank Pisano pleaded guilty for having hidden ownership in a New Jersey Honda dealership and for receiving about $100,000 in gratuities from owners of other Honda stores. Former zone sales manager John Conway, a partner with Rod Ryan in several New Jersey Honda stores, was one of the participants who both gave and received kickbacks. He pleaded guilty to one count of conspiracy. Another of Conway's partners was John Fincher, who, along with Honda's Eastern regional sales manager Larry Finley, conspired to lie to the FBI about Finley's secret ownership of a Honda outlet. After Fincher's accountant provided the FBI with the company's records, Fincher and Finley both pleaded guilty to obstruction of justice. Honda terminated Finley after Connolly informed the company of the impending indictment. The government would later dismiss the charge against Fincher.

In June, a civil lawsuit was filed in Pennsylvania against American Honda by two men denied a franchise because they had refused to pay off Honda executives. The suit also named Raymond Hovsepian, a Ferrari-driving attorney for the late Honda megadealer Marty Lustgarten. The East Coast retailer had been one of the top players in the Honda game before his death in 1989. Hovsepian had continued to arrange payoffs to the Honda gang for new dealerships after his boss's death, and his demanding $250,000 from the plaintiffs for himself and three Honda officials ignited the lawsuit.

Connolly sent Hovsepian a target letter. Although the only gratuity Connolly could document with the attorney's fingerprints on it was $5,000 given to Cardiges, Hovsepian was likely charged because he was affiliated with one of the most prolific dirty dealers. Hovsepian agreed to plead guilty to one count of conspiracy to commit mail fraud — the only person charged for giving gifts. He spilled his guts on the hundreds of thousands paid by Lustgarten to Honda executives over the years, including a significant amount to Billmyer.

Ed Temple put Connolly on the trail of former Beverly Hills and Palm Springs, California, dealer Peter Epsteen — after he admitted shaking down Epsteen for $60,000 to approve the sale of Beverly Hills Honda. The tip led the feds to two pieces of incriminating evidence on Billmyer: the swimming pool Epsteen had installed at Billmyer's Palm Springs home and a $200,000 "consulting" fee Epsteen had paid to the sales chief. Epsteen initially lied to Connolly about his dealings and was charged with obstruction of justice.

Connolly's concentration on the Honda executives meant many dirty Honda dealers were shown mercy. He only convicted four dealers — Hovsepian, Epsteen, Temple, and Conway — the latter two being ex–Honda executives who had worked both sides of the fence. (The indictments against Ted Stevens and one other dealer were later dropped.) Only Hovsepian was charged for making payments to Honda officials. It is important to note that the dealers Connolly chose to charge were all major players — Fincher and Conway were part of the Rod Ryan group that owned 13 Honda and Acura dealerships. Epsteen and Hovsepian's dealer groups were also among the biggest bribers. The convictions sent Connolly's message to the car dealers of America.

One dealer not offered an immunity agreement to speak with the Department of Justice was Rick Hendrick. Connolly had other plans for Honda's biggest dealer, another man "honored" with the posting of his photograph in Connolly's office. Hendrick annoyed Connolly with his public pronouncements that he had done nothing wrong. He told the *New York Times* that his payments to Honda executives were "arm's-length deals. I got nothing for it." The FBI confronted Hendrick's employees. One provided details on the BMW automobiles leased for Billmyer. Another proffered information on the airfreight packages stuffed with cash sent to Cardiges for his house payments. A Charlotte banker supplied documentation on the Hendrick-backed home loans for Billmyer and Cardiges. A Hendrick dealership manager remembered his boss bragging about how he could "get anything he wanted from Honda." Connolly had the goods he needed on Hendrick's dealings—about $825,000 worth of gifts forwarded to Honda executives.

Bonnie Sikora, the lowest-ranking Honda official and the only woman to be charged by the government, pleaded guilty to taking $120,000 in bribes from the Hendrick organization in exchange for extra cars. Sikora's crime was the only clear example of quid pro quo for extra automobiles of the entire case. The 51-year-old former car distributor pleaded guilty to one count of conspiracy to commit wire fraud. Honda terminated Sikora.

Honda's investigation also uncovered allegations about a manager at the Marysville, Ohio, assembly plant. As with the activities of sales execs, rumors had circulated for years about kickbacks between Ohio plant managers and vendors eager to do business with the high-volume factory. In April, Honda discovered evidence that the manager of the Marysville automobile distribution center, Terry Goodwin, had received money from a maintenance company. Goodwin was terminated.

Michael Connolly had indicted 21 people so far, 18 of them agreeing to plead guilty. The federal trial of Billmyer, Cardiges, and Josleyn was set for early 1995 in Concord.

In December 1994, Cardiges wrote Hendrick yet another letter asking for help. He was still in denial that Hendrick had long abandoned him.

> It has become quite apparent to both myself and others that when an individual finds himself under scrutiny by a U.S. Attorney's office, that many long time friends and former employees have a difficult time demonstrating their trust, loyalty, perception of the truth. . . . I still have an outstanding balance which will be owed to my defense team. . . . I need financial assistance as soon as possible. . . . Rick, if the circumstances were reversed, I would hope that you have the same confidence in me that I have in you; that I would be there to assist you and your family.

Hendrick turned the letter over to the FBI.

Honda resisted Connolly's attempts to talk to its Japanese executives.

Retired president Tetsuo Chino and current executive vice president Takeo Okusa both suddenly bolted back to Japan in late 1993. Rumors said their exit was designed to help them avoid the U.S. Attorney's advances, though Okusa did return in 1994 to be interviewed by the FBI.

In late 1994 American Honda agreed to produce president Koichi Amemiya and mid-1980s president Yoshihide Munekuni. The pair were among the last of more than 500 people interviewed by the Department of Justice, a number that included over 100 owners of Honda dealerships.

Connolly and Mulvaney flew to California to meet with Amemiya and Munekuni. Honda attorneys knew that the government was not planning to indict the corporation nor any of the Japanese executives. Maybe it was time to come clean.

Maybe not.

Munekuni said he had never heard allegations of Honda officials receiving gifts from dealers. He did not remember meeting with automotive consultant J. D. Power in 1983 to discuss complaints Power had received from dealers about the widespread corruption.

Amemiya contradicted what numerous Honda managers had told Connolly. I never encouraged anyone to have dealers falsify sales cards, said Amemiya. I never used the term "golden telephones." I don't know what "gray cars" are. I never saw a report detailing the discrepancies between true and false sales numbers. I don't know what "bad boys" means.

Until the Peck checks came along, said Amemiya, I never heard any allegations of Honda sales executives receiving payoffs. I told Sherry Cameron to start an investigation one month after I heard about the Peck deal in early 1991.

Connolly turns grim when asked whether the Japanese executives were telling the truth.

"The record speaks for itself," is Michael Connolly's only reply.

Adding to the public headache of the FBI investigation to American Honda were the corporation's massive efforts to bolster its products and services. The company's endeavors were similar to how it handled its internal investigation — all the right moves, but five years too late.

A four-year-long recession in Japan and another round of the sinking dollar battered the corporation's profits in the early 1990s. Honda's sales continued to drop, bottoming out at 608,255 units in 1993, down more than 100,000 vehicles from the record set in 1990. Accord sales fell 16 percent in 1993, despite Honda spending a record $200 million in dealer incentives to move inventory.

There was nothing wrong with Honda's automobiles — the company simply missed key consumer trends. Customers' sudden love affair with sport-utility vehicles (SUVs) in the 1990s caught Honda without any such products for its loyal customers. Having steadfastly refused to build pickup trucks over the years, claiming it might hurt the company's image, Honda did not have a truck chassis on which to build an SUV. Honda began development on an SUV but knew it could not bring it to market until 1997. The corporation resorted to the unthinkable to quickly jump into the booming SUV market — it reached out to another automaker to supply it with a vehicle. Isuzu Motor Company agreed to build 25,000 units annually of its Rodeo sport-utility vehicle for Honda. The Rodeo was a four-year-old vehicle with a General Motors engine and below-average ergonomics and quality. Honda's version was christened the Passport, an old Honda scooter name, and introduced in late 1993. Isuzu priced the Rodeo $750 less than the Honda Passport and offered a longer standard warranty, thus enabling it to sell two Rodeos for every Passport moved by Honda. The Passport was a stop-gap measure for Honda that threatened to tarnish its reputation for building superior vehicles, but it quieted dealers rightfully screaming for SUVs.

The introduction of the Passport was also aimed at luring more men into Honda showrooms, sport-utility vehicle buyers being predominately male. The number of men buying Hondas had been steadily shrinking over the previous five years. The corporation's products were perceived as being neither sporty nor rugged — Hondas offered great quality and value but nothing to stir the blood of young, active men. Focus groups showed the Passport was destined to become, in the words of a female Honda market researcher, a "chick truck," and buyer profiles bore that intuition out.

The company's discontinuation of the CRX sport coupe, wildly popular with young men, and replacing it with the oddball del Sol open-roofed car in 1992, had also thinned the ranks of male Honda owners. Honda was fighting a battle against its image of being a women's brand by expecting men to flock to the Passport or del Sol.

In late 1994, Honda finally introduced its first minivan, the Odyssey. Though highly innovative, featuring a third seat that disappeared into the floor when not needed, the four-cylinder Odyssey was deemed too small and underpowered for American tastes. Over 92 percent of the 1.3 million minivans sold in 1994 were by Detroit automakers, and their minivans offered the power and size demanded by consumers. Honda was keenly aware that the Odyssey could not compete with Detroit's offerings. It announced plans to sell 25,000 minivans a year in the United States, a projection in line with the vehicle's sales potential, but it left some industry observers wondering why Honda didn't step up and build a "real" minivan. Honda's practice of building vehicles that suit both Japan, with its narrow streets and tax laws that limit vehicle size, and America did not work with the Odyssey. The only saving grace for the vehicle was that it became a best-seller in Japan, perfectly sized for the cramped country.

As part of Honda's agreement with Isuzu on the Passport, Isuzu dealers in the United States were given their version of the Odyssey. Hondas were now being sold at Isuzu dealerships and Isuzus at Honda dealerships. Honda's tradition of product independence was officially over.

Honda announced plans to offer a V-6 engine in the 1995 Accord, a move the company had resisted for years because of its confidence in the superior technology of the four-cylinder motors. Despite Honda's four-cylinder engines being as quick and smooth as any competitor's V-6, not to mention getting better gas mileage, customers were abandoning the Accord for six-cylinder Toyota Camrys and Mazda 626s. Honda's move to a V-6 came only after years of dealers' pleadings, the retailers now teaching the factory about the realities of what customers wanted rather than the other way around.

New Honda sales chief Richard Colliver provided badly needed leadership for the sales division. A shoot-from-the-hip manager, Colliver was not shy in admitting Honda's faults, incurring the wrath of dealers by publicly calling the process of buying a Honda automobile "five hours of humiliation." He announced his intentions to add 100 new dealerships. Disbanding the antiquated dealer advertising association system, the one that fed the dirty executives and produced advertising not always consistent with Honda's brand image, he replaced it with a Honda-controlled regional marketing program. He persuaded the corporation to charter a Learjet for a group of executives to tour the country to announce the new program.

Colliver even managed to get approval from the Japanese to create a half-dozen new management positions.

Colliver's boldest marketing move stemmed from his impatience with Honda's captive finance arm, American Honda Finance. He was annoyed with its noncompetitive vehicle residual values, the key component in low consumer lease payments, and dealers' complaints about Honda Finance's slow service. Colliver engaged General Electric Capitol Auto Leasing (GECAL), one of the nation's largest lease companies, to offer leasing options to Honda customers. National Honda advertisements featured low Accord lease payments from GECAL rather than Honda Finance. An automaker turning its back on its own bank was unheard of, but Colliver needed to move cars and send a message to Honda Finance.

In 1994, Honda's sales rose to 676,093 units, the best sales year since 1990.

The year was not without failure. Honda's first-ever attempt at IndyCar racing was a bust, the Honda-powered open-wheeled race cars not having the speed or reliability of the competition. At season's end, Honda dealer and former IndyCar champion Bobby Rahal announced plans to abandon Honda engines for the 1995 season, another public embarrassment that shook Honda headquarters.

The worst was yet to come. The looming federal trial was not going to be simply about crimes committed by Jack Billmyer, Jim Cardiges, and Dennis Josleyn. American Honda and its Japanese executives would also come under attack.

CHAPTER 16

The Trial

> The simple fact that the company was represented by apparently corrupt and dishonest lawyers does not excuse stealing.
>
> —Michael Connolly

IT IS a little-known fact that when law students are trying to pass the bar exam, they are required to recite the Attorney Anthem: "I'm jest an ol' country lawyer." Even if they are from Park Avenue, attorneys have to repeat the phrase three times daily throughout their careers or face being disbarred.

Chichester, New Hampshire, attorney Paul Twomey, mud on his jeans and smelling of sheep-dip, has been granted exemption from that requirement. Twomey really is a country lawyer, shielding his intelligence under a veneer of country hick. Sitting in his sparse office overlooking a dark woods, the 45-year-old farmer/attorney reflects on why he chose to represent former Honda executive Dennis Josleyn in federal court.

"I thought it would be a hell of a lot of fun," said Twomey. "Getting to cross-examine dirty car dealers, you can't have more fun with your pants on. It's like the Yankees playing slow pitch softball. You'd have to be brain-dead to not score points against car dealers."

Twomey and partner Mark Sisti have handled the majority of New Hampshire murder cases over the previous decade. They are known as defenders of the underdogs, ready to fight for the working class. In 1991 Twomey unsuccessfully defended Pamela Smart, a high school teacher who directed her teenage lover and two of his friends to murder her husband, in a case that inspired two motion pictures and a book.

Twomey's courtroom dress and demeanor resembled disheveled 1980s TV character Lieutenant Columbo: hair unkempt, shirttail out, the bottom of his tie resting six inches above his belt, perpetually scratching his head. His New England accent and toothy grin endeared Concord jurors. Twomey was the only New Hampshire attorney with a prayer of successfully defending Josleyn in the face of the overwhelming evidence collected by the government.

Only three men were left standing after the FBI investigation: Josleyn, Jack Billmyer, and Jim Cardiges. All three tried to retain Twomey, although lawyers for Cardiges and Billmyer wanted Twomey to act as local counsel only. Twomey did not want to play second-fiddle to an out-of-state law firm: he was confident he could successfully defend the case himself, no matter which of the trio he chose. Twomey agreed to be the lead attorney for Josleyn.

"In my infinite wisdom, I had to pick the one that went bankrupt before the trial," laughs Twomey. Josleyn claimed to be penniless, having lost money on the sale of his Laguna Hills house and in several business ventures. In late 1994 Josleyn drove to New Hampshire to begin preparation for the trial. Twomey found him a cheap apartment, and the former Honda high-roller lived on bologna sandwiches, a mere three years after he had the world by the ass.

In early 1995, Michael Connolly picked off two more suspects in his 18-month-old investigation of the Honda case. Josleyn's brother, Gary, pleaded guilty to mail fraud for sending a $100,000 kickback check to Cardiges for the sales training seminars.

The 20th person to plead guilty was former Honda zone sales manager Jim Mortimer. The dollar amount of Mortimer's sins was relatively small—he received $85,000 from the advertising scam and $33,333 for his split in a New Mexico open point deal arranged by the ubiquitous Ed Temple. Connolly took pity on Mortimer, an articulate man with a masters degree in business administration who cooperated fully with the investigation. Mortimer agreed to plead guilty to one count of misprision—an obscure charge meaning to have knowledge of illegal activities by others and not report them—a count that would likely lead to probation only.

The total number of Honda executives fired by the corporation and/or indicted by the government for their participation in the corruption stood at 33, a number equal to one-fourth of the number of employees of Honda's sales division at any given time.

A grand jury handed down superseding indictments for the three defendants, piling on evidence gathered since the original complaints were issued. Cardiges and Josleyn were each charged with four counts: two counts of conspiracy to commit mail fraud, one for peddling letters of intent and one for organizing the advertising scheme; one count of mail fraud for profiting from the sales training scam; and one count of racketeering, the government gold medal award given to those involved in a multitude of crimes. The racketeering charge included 42 separate acts committed by Cardiges and Josleyn, ranging from the embezzlement schemes and 21 letter of intent deals to Josleyn's take from selling Honda company cars and Cardiges's dealer-provided Rolex watches and automobiles.

Billmyer was charged with one count of conspiracy to commit mail fraud for receiving cash and gifts in exchange for granting new franchises. Connolly could have charged Billmyer with the lesser charges of mail fraud or obstruction of justice, but he wanted to nail the patriarch with the most serious crime possible. This was a move of great confidence, as Connolly knew the conspiracy charge could be challenged in court on several fronts. The evidence against Billmyer was irrefutable—$800,000 in gratuities from a variety of dealers—but the question of his participation in one overarching conspiracy was not clear. Connolly held that the conspiracy had lasted 13 years, starting in 1979, the year of the oldest piece of evidence gathered, and ending when Cardiges and Josleyn were forced to resign in 1992. He theorized that Billmyer was a member because he shared in the goals of the conspiracy: to defraud American Honda of tangible and intangible property and to enrich the defendants who participated.

The issue of Billmyer as a member of one long conspiracy was tenuous at best. If the jury did not find that Billmyer was part of a single conspiracy, the case could be thrown out on venue issues, Connolly having tied Billmyer's participation in the conspiracy to New Hampshire because David Pedersen was part of the same conspiracy when he received gratuities from Nashua Acura dealer Tom Bohlander. (In the case of Cardiges and Josleyn, the question of venue was clear because a sales training seminar was held at the Nashua Marriott hotel in November 1990.)

Connolly also had to dodge a statute of limitations deadline that mandated that at least one overt act in furtherance of the conspiracy had to occur after March 11, 1989, five years before Billmyer's indictment date but one year after he retired from Honda. Dah Chong Hong's payment of $100,000 to Billmyer in mid-1989 meant the jury could consider all acts committed by Billmyer during the conspiracy.

If convicted, Billmyer was eligible for a maximum jail term of five years, while Cardiges and Josleyn could received up to 35 years' imprisonment on each charge.

Cardiges's lead attorney, Phillip Israels, and his crew postured to the media about their assorted strategies. We will prove that Cardiges is innocent because gift giving in the car industry is standard practice, was the lawyers' first story. "Some clients give me flowers," said Cardiges attorney Rikki Klieman. "In the car business, they might send autos, jewelry or a Rolex watch." Later the team pronounced they would prove that the case was a conspiracy by the U.S. government to pressure Japan to lift trade barriers on automobiles. Israels claimed that Washington was going to use information about Honda's Japanese executives' knowledge of the crimes as a bargaining tool during concurrent trade negotiations. Cardiges's attorneys were grandstanding — they had no proof for any of their theories.

Cardiges's attorneys finally settled on a core defense, the same one Twomey was planning for Josleyn: that Honda's Japanese executives knew about the corruption and they gave tacit approval for it to continue — in other words, Honda could not be a victim if it knew what was going on. Israels hired a consultant to analyze automakers' pay plans to try and prove that Honda's Japanese managers purposely undercompensated their executives and thus expected them to moonlight. This defensive strategy was a long shot, but it was the best they could muster under the circumstances.

Billmyer's attorneys, David Long of Raleigh and local counsel Kevin Sharkey, planned a different defense. As expected by Connolly, Billmyer's core defense was the issue of "multiple conspiracies." His lawyers contended that Billmyer's activities were separate from those of his peers and thus he could not be charged with being a participant in a conspiracy. They planned to show that Billmyer withdrew from any conspiracy when he retired from the corporation. They also questioned the issue of New Hampshire being the proper venue for the trial.

Both sets of defense attorneys hoped to convince the jury that if Honda and its dealers and executives got rich during the glory days, where was the harm? This "victimless crime" tactic had a chance to work for Billmyer and for some of Josleyn and Cardiges's activities, but the latter two's embezzlement was a violation that clearly victimized the corporation and its shareholders.

Dozens of pretrial motions flew back and forth between defense lawyers and Connolly. District Court Judge Joseph A. DiClerico Jr., the man who would preside over the trial, denied defense motions requesting a separate trial for each defendant. Trying all three men together was going to hurt Billmyer the most, because the evidence about the embezzlement by the other two might taint his character.

Connolly filed a pretrial motion to prohibit any mention of Honda's

Japanese executives during the proceedings. He did not want a race card played before what was likely to be an all-white jury. In November 1993, American Honda had lost a lawsuit in a Concord courtroom due in part to anti-Japanese remarks made by a plaintiff's attorney. The case involved a snowmobile rider who was injured when his vehicle collided with a Honda all-terrain vehicle on a frozen lake. He sued Honda, claiming the corporation should have provided warnings to riders on the hazards of operating the vehicle on ice. In final arguments, his lawyer mentioned a comment made by a Japanese government official about American workers being "lazy and stupid." The jury found for the plaintiff, awarding him $1.4 million. (In January 1997 the New Hampshire Supreme Court overturned the verdict because of the racist reference.) Connolly did not want a jury focusing on Honda's Japanese officials rather than the crimes themselves.

Judge DiClerico indicated he was going to grant Connolly's motion banning Cardiges and Josleyn's defense that the Japanese knew about the corruption. Though the judge later declined to approve the motion, his leanings devastated the pair's attorneys. Klieman resigned from Cardiges's team to become a television reporter covering the O. J. Simpson murder trial in Los Angeles, scheduled to begin one week before the Honda trial.

This turn of events gave Cardiges pause. His attorneys told him that without their key defense, he was sunk. He had dropped over $400,000 in legal fees over the previous 18 months, despite a nagging feeling that he would be found guilty. He faced the possibility of spending the rest of his life in prison and fines totaling $1 million. It was time for him to do the right thing.

One week before the trial was to begin, Cardiges told one of his attorneys, Boston barrister Steven Lyons, to call Connolly and tell him that he was going to change his plea to guilty and that he would tell federal prosecutors everything. Cardiges hoped that his cooperation with the government's case against the others might lead to a lenient sentence.

"I was tired of denying this thing for seventeen and a half years," Cardiges said. "I was tired and I was wrong."

Connolly cut Cardiges no slack. "We told Mr. Lyons," recalls Connolly, "that if Mr. Cardiges wanted to plead guilty, he would have to plead guilty to the indictment and take his chances as to whether or not he would receive any recognition for cooperation that he might provide. Mr. Cardiges, in a gesture that I think can only be regarded as courageous, decided to accept the government's offer which essentially was an offer of nothing."

On February 7, Cardiges opened his Concord motel room door to face one of the worst blizzards ever in the Northeast. Shivering under his light overcoat, Cardiges headed for the courthouse, where he pleaded guilty to all four counts. Although the response to the questions asked by the judge required only *yes* or *no* answers, Cardiges repeatedly stated that, although he did participate in the crimes, Billmyer and Josleyn had been the originators.

Cardiges's agreement to provide information and to testify was a gift to Connolly as significant as the day Temple came forward with the bribery road map. Nobody knew more about the two other defendants than did Cardiges. His polished public speaking expertise would make him a compelling and believable witness.

For five days, Cardiges spilled his guts to Connolly. Cardiges told how Billmyer had stressed the importance of secrecy. Jack taught me how to take care of favored dealers in return for kickbacks, said Cardiges, and Josleyn was the one who concocted the advertising and sales training scams. Connolly had already collected evidence of $2.2 million worth of dealer gifts and embezzlement proceeds gained by Cardiges — the former Honda senior vice president filled him in on an additional $3 million worth.

Cardiges said he suspected that Honda's Japanese executives knew what was going on but could offer no hard evidence that was the case. "I had nothing," said Cardiges later. "I had no proof and that's what the FBI kept hammering, 'Do you have some written proof? Do you have pictures?' Do you have this, do you have that, and I did not have any hard substantial proof."

Connolly had assumed that Cardiges was the victim of poor legal advice ever since he reviewed the 1993 taped conversation between Cardiges and Temple. His debriefing with Cardiges confirmed it. "We were astonished," says Connolly, "to learn the level of ignorance that (Cardiges) was operating under as to what the evidence was in this case, as to what the law was which would govern his case. Mr. Israels, despite being involved in the case for more than a year, had failed to show Mr. Cardiges even the most inflammatory documents which would surely have been used repeatedly by the government throughout the trial." Cardiges fired Israels a few days after his meetings with Connolly.

American Honda was shrewd enough not to engage Lyon & Lyon to monitor the proceedings — the law firm's antics in the Nault case were well-known to the New Hampshire court. The corporation instead retained Concord criminal defense lawyer Steven Gordon to prepare current Honda executives called to testify and to ensure that Honda's stance of being a victim of its officials' activities remained intact. A flamboyant and funny man, Gordon once defended clients charged in the largest drug bust in New Hampshire history and was a veteran of late-night poker games at Paul Twomey's farm.

It was Gordon's client who would really be on trial.

The trial was Michael Connolly's to lose. He had collected a mountain of irrefutable evidence and had dozens of bright, credible witnesses lined up to testify. He had garnered 20 guilty pleas since Ed Temple first appeared on his doorstep, but it all would be for naught if he could not convict the final two suspects. Connolly had history on his side—the Department of Justice had garnered convictions in 87 percent of the fraud and embezzlement cases it had brought to trial over the previous decade.

Connolly planned to present the jury a case that "sticks you in the gut" about what is right and wrong by boiling down the complex crimes to an easily understandable level.

Presiding judge Joseph DiClerico was nicknamed "Hanging Joe" by the local law community, a reference to his being the toughest sentencing federal judge in New England. DiClerico was a large, authoritative man in his mid-50s with an intimidating presence, yet he was also a low-key, gracious judge. He always looked out for the comfort of jurors but would not tolerate any nonsense in his courtroom.

Proceedings in the trial of *United States of America vs. John W. Billmyer and Dennis R. Josleyn* began on a snowy New Hampshire morning on February 27, 1995. Attorneys and members of the press filled the audience, awaiting what promised to be a boisterous case. Before an all-white jury in the windowless federal courtroom, a buttoned-down Connolly presented the government's opening statement.

"Ladies and gentlemen," Connolly began, "this case is about property theft. It's about the theft of property from the American Honda Motor Company. The evidence will prove that Mr. Billmyer and Mr. Josleyn took American Honda property, they stole it, they sold it, and they stuffed the money in their own pockets."

Connolly cited "Billmyer's Rules" on how to accept gifts discreetly and how some of Billmyer's followers broke those rules. He emphasized how Honda was the victim of the crimes and that the resultant dealer lawsuits were going to cost the company millions. "It was well known to Mr. Billmyer and Mr. Josleyn," Connolly told the court, "that if they took bribes and they allowed other people working for them to take bribes that the likely result was American Honda was going to incur exorbitant litigation expenses, and the evidence during this trial will show that that's exactly what happened."

Connolly detailed how Honda's sales had fallen in the early 1990s, leading to the embezzlement. He simplified how each scheme worked. "Mr. Josleyn approached Mr. Cardiges," said Connolly, "and he said: Jim, can we use my brother's advertising company to do these advertising programs for all these dealers? And he said: Jim, if we do it, there will be a lot of money available for you and for me. Well, that was all Mr. Cardiges needed to hear. He approved it. He let Mr. Josleyn use his brother's advertising company and that's what Mr. Josleyn did."

As is tradition during opening statements, Connolly finished by telling the jury that, by the end of the trial, he would have proven beyond a reasonable doubt that the defendants were guilty on all counts.

Sixty-five-year-old Jack Billmyer sat solemnly at the defense table, dressed in a gray suit and wisely devoid of gold jewelry or his beloved Rolex watch. His local lawyer, Kevin Sharkey, presented the opening statement. Sharkey attacked the government's position that New Hampshire was the proper venue for the trial, citing that Billmyer was not involved in the David Pedersen transactions that triggered the investigation. He argued that Billmyer was not part of a continuing conspiracy dating from 1979 to 1992, since Billmyer had retired from the corporation in 1988. Sharkey characterized Billmyer as a man so important to American Honda that the Japanese officials tried to talk him out of leaving.

Sharkey pretended to be flabbergasted when countering Connolly's contention that Honda was injured by his client's actions. "How did Honda become a victim in all of this?" asked Sharkey. "How does Honda become a victim when Jack Billmyer works hard to sell all of their cars? How does Honda become a victim of Jack Billmyer's doing when Honda goes from selling hardly any cars in the United States to the top of the import car sales list?"

Paul Twomey, looking like a man fresh from a tractor crash, mispronounced Josleyn's name the first time he spoke it during his opening statement. He quickly fired his first salvo at Honda.

"If a business wants to let its employees get kickbacks," said Twomey, "God bless them, they can go right ahead and do it. That's what went on here. American Honda set up a system and a structure that encouraged people to seek out kickbacks, encouraged the dealers to make the kickbacks, and encouraged the employees to take them."

Twomey rebutted Connolly's assertion that Billmyer and Josleyn's superiors had been duped by the pair's secrecy. "The government's going to want you to believe that these higher-ups of American Honda, the most astute businessmen in the world, are just plain old stupid and they are deaf, dumb, and blind," said Twomey. "Essentially they are going to want you to believe that American Honda itself as a corporation was like a giant ostrich with its head in the sand saying, I'm in the swimming pool, I'm in the swimming pool, I'm in the swimming pool!"

Twomey built his case about top Honda officials condoning the fraudulent activities. He told the jury how American Honda president Koichi Amemiya had initially ignored the Cliff Peck checks and how he had granted Temple a letter of intent for a dealership despite his knowledge of Temple's involvement in the Peck deal. Twomey accused Lyon & Lyon of being a coconspirator in covering up the corruption, claiming the firm's attorneys taught Honda officials how to lie under oath.

"You won't hear anything about the United States government indicting anyone from Lyon & Lyon for doing that," said Twomey. "That's what we call suborning perjury. That — unlike getting a kickback in a commercial setting — is a federal crime, but you don't hear anything about any indictment about that."

Twomey turned and pointed to Honda's lair of lawyers sitting in the gallery. "The foes we have are powerful and have unlimited resources," said Twomey. "You take a look out in that courtroom and look at all those folks out there with the fancy suits taking notes. This isn't a field trip from some high school around here. There is a lot of money involved in this case for American Honda and they are willing to spend it, and you are going to hear about it."

Round One had gone to Twomey, the defender of the little guy against the big bad bureaucracies.

Connolly wanted to build the case against Billmyer first, knowing he would be tougher to convict than Josleyn. He wanted the first transactions between dealer and executive that he presented to the jury to be easily understandable. Assistant U.S. Attorney Donald Feith handled the questioning of the government's first two witnesses. He called to the stand Mitchell Gontarek, owner of a California construction company. Gontarek testified that Beverly Hills Honda dealer Peter Epsteen paid him to install a pool, spa, and fence at Billmyer's Palm Springs home in 1982. In what would be the first of many character assassinations of the trial, Billmyer attorney David Long tried to discredit Gontarek, citing trivial discrepancies between Gontarek's testimony and what he had earlier told the grand jury.

Feith next examined Michael Lake, sales manager for Rick Hendrick's Corona, California, Honda dealership. Lake testified that his dealership prepared and delivered the BMW sedans that Hendrick provided for Billmyer's use. The paperwork for the cars, like all evidence in the trial, was displayed on high-tech television monitors stationed around the courtroom.

The Honda dealer principals on Connolly's witness list were not the most sympathetic bunch: all were very wealthy and very dirty dealers. In a brilliant move, the first retailer Connolly called to the stand was Los Angeles dealer Lathrop Hoffman, a gentle, grandfatherly man straight out of a Norman Rockwell portrait—and more importantly, a squeaky-clean dealer. Hoffman made a great witness. He detailed how Billmyer had attempted to shake him down for an Alabama dealership and how he had refused to play. He outlined Honda's structure and how its allocation system worked. The defense team's cross-examination was brief and friendly, the attorneys not wanting to appear to crucify Saint Lathrop.

Connolly next called executives of the Rod Ryan/Clarence Fincher/John Conway dealer group of New Jersey, owners of 13 Honda and Acura dealerships. For two days, they detailed $200,000 worth of payoffs to Billmyer and other Honda officials, including two who were still employed by the corporation.

Ryan told of his 1984 clandestine rendezvous with Billmyer at an out-of-the-way Los Angeles restaurant, where he had handed the Honda sales chief an envelope containing $25,000 in cash, hoping to get favorable treatment in return.

Connolly asked Ryan to summarize the meeting. "Hello and goodbye," said Ryan, "took five, ten minutes. How do you do, this and that. And I got up and left. He remained there."

"How did you present the money to him?" queried Connolly.

"I simply put it on the table and said: This is for you, and pushed it across the table and I left."

"What, if anything, did he ask you about the contents of the envelope?"

"I don't remember him asking me anything."

"Was he surprised?"

"Didn't seem surprised," Ryan replied. "Didn't seem anything."

Ryan testified that he received a letter of intent for a new Honda dealership a few weeks later. Despite Ryan's whining about how uncomfortable he was paying off Billmyer, his testimony was powerful. Connolly used Ryan and the supporting evidence to actually take the jurors inside one of the transactions between dealer and executive.

Under cross-examination by Long, Ryan admitted that Billmyer had never solicited him for any money or gifts and that there was no agreement between him and Billmyer as to what he would receive in return for his contributions.

Connolly turned his attention to Josleyn. He called to the stand Sales Training Technologies speaker Bob Davies. The motivational trainer told how he asked Josleyn how he was going to sell the $185 seminars to Honda dealers for $395 and that Josleyn responded by saying that dealers who did not participate would have their flow of new cars halted. Connolly showed the jury copies of the kickback checks to Josleyn, Cardiges, and Bob Rivers for their split of the profits from the seminars.

Next came the dealer advertising association scheme. Patti Bergmann, the bookkeeper for Josleyn's company Bergmann and Associates, identified the checks totaling $2.5 million she had written out to Josleyn, Cardiges, and the rest for their kickbacks of the profits from the advertising scam. A California retailer testified how Josleyn had attempted to strongarm his dealer advertising group into using Bergmann and Associates' direct mail program.

Former ad manager Tom Caulfield was the first ex–Honda executive to testify. Under questioning by Feith, Caulfield described how Cardiges and Josleyn had funneled the dealer ad funds through Josleyn's company. Feith proffered copies of checks totaling $816,000 that Caulfield had received for his share of the kickbacks. Feith used the records of Bergmann and Associates to establish the payola pattern: a check would arrive from an advertising group and was quickly followed by kickback checks sent out to Caulfield, Josleyn, and other executives.

Feith asked Caulfield why he had agreed to participate in the scheme. "Mr. Cardiges at the time was a senior vice president," said Caulfield, "someone that I looked up to in a mentor type way, and just thought that, you know, if I did, then I'd be promoted, and I guess that's the main reason."

Twomey tried to get Caulfield to admit that Honda's Japanese executives knew of the corruption and embezzlement. "My understanding," said Caulfield, "is that the management definitely did not know about the thing that I was involved in, and that was the advertising portion of it. However, I felt that—again it's just my feelings, that the upper management were probably aware of some of the other things that were happening at the company at the time."

Former Honda Western regional sales manager Bob Rivers testified about the money he received from Sales Training Technologies. He told about how he and others were careful to hide their activities from Honda's

Japanese executives. Under cross-examination by Twomey, Rivers indicated that he had no reason to believe the Japanese knew anything about the corruption.

Former Honda executive and dealer John Conway testified about Billmyer receiving gifts from dealers, adding that Billmyer had once told him that Honda wouldn't pay a million dollars but the executives could still live like millionaires.

Under cross-examination by Twomey, Conway said that he had heard a Lyon & Lyon attorney tell a group of Honda executives about the lightning bolt theory of testifying. Former Acura official David Pedersen testified that Lyon & Lyon lawyers had taught him how to be evasive in his depositions during the Nault Acura proceedings. Connolly objected to Twomey's insistence on grilling witnesses about Lyon & Lyon's dark methods. "It is relevant to whether or not Lyon & Lyon is dishonest, unethical and immoral," said Connolly to the judge, "but that has nothing to do with the issues in this case." The judge overruled the objection.

Conway and Pedersen's testimony about the Lyon & Lyon attorneys' coaching of the executives convinced Twomey that the law firm and Honda had conspired to hide information about the shady dealings. He filed a subpoena ordering Honda to produce its entire internal investigative files, not just the portions turned over during discovery. Twomey wanted to crack the Lyon & Lyon vault, the receptacle of information about deeds done by dirty Honda managers over the years.

On March 10, the proceedings recessed for 11 days to give the jury a rest. The government was clearly winning, having introduced a preponderance of evidence against Billmyer and Josleyn. Defense attorneys tried to impeach the convicted executives by suggesting that, since they were testifying to curry favor with the government in hopes of a reduced prison sentence, they might not be telling the truth. Connolly rebuked that assertion, saying the officials would be in violation of their plea agreement if they perjured themselves on the stand and would be subject to tougher sentences.

Whenever defense attorneys tried to lead the jurors on a side trip — the burning of sales cards or the coaching of Honda executives by Lyon & Lyon attorneys — Connolly objected and reminded the jury that those issues had nothing to do with the theft of Honda's property.

The courtroom atmosphere was relaxed. Jurors brought in home-baked cookies for Judge DiClerico and the lawyers. The judge allowed jurors to listen to radio headphones during the numerous breaks. He joked about the length of Long's shaggy gray hair.

Josleyn kept to himself during breaks, but Billmyer bantered with observers. Noticing a U.S. Marshal studying automobile brochures, Billmyer offered to help him get a new Honda.

"But, Jack," said the officer, "that's why you're in here in the first place."

"No," laughed Billmyer, "I mean legitimately!"

The majority of the first two weeks of the trial had been mind-numbingly boring: long reviews of Honda's policies, structure, hierarchy, and subsidiaries and prolonged questioning about the witnesses' meetings with Connolly during the FBI investigation. Sidebar conversations between the judge and lawyers seemed to happen hourly, as they gathered at the side of the bench to quietly argue over minutia. The judge tried to keep the proceedings moving along. "We don't want this turning into another Los Angeles," he said at one point, referring to the concurrent O. J. Simpson murder trial, an affair moving at Yugo pace.

Testimony resumed with Honda vice president of human resources Sherry Cameron taking the stand. Connolly, trying to deflect attention from Honda's Japanese executives, moved to disallow any reference in her testimony to the Mercedes-Benz given to Koichi Amemiya by a Honda dealer, saying it was irrelevant to the trial. The judge refused to grant the request.

Cameron made a believable and entertaining witness. Connolly had her outline Honda's corporate structure. She explained the conflict of interest policy. Connolly wisely did not ask her whether she enforced the requirement of employees signing the document.

Connolly knew he had to make the initial strike about the Japanese executives — if the defense first broached the subject, it would appear that Honda or the government was reluctant to mention it, lending credence to Twomey's core defense. Connolly asked Cameron about Amemiya's Mercedes-Benz. She claimed not to know any details about the arrangement, saying the matter had been handled by Honda of Japan.

Cameron testified that Amemiya told her in February 1992 to initiate an internal investigation of sales division officials. In remarkable detail she discussed her confrontations and firings of Cardiges and six other officials. Her recollection was so thorough, it seemed like the events had taken place only the day before.

Connolly asked about the termination of Josleyn. Cameron told of asking Josleyn about his interest in his brother's advertising companies.

"Then I asked him about Donald Gary Josleyn," said Cameron. "He responded it was his brother. And I asked if he was connected to Garey and Associates and he said no, not tied to Garey and Associates."

"Was the mood changing at this point, Ms. Cameron?" asked Connolly.

"Yes, it was."

"How was it changing?"

"He was getting very nervous."

"What did you talk about next?"

"He is not aware of any relationship that his brother has with Garey and Associates. Then I asked what is your response if I say to you that we have seen documents to say that your brother, Donald Gary Josleyn, was president and officer of the company. And Dennis Josleyn responded: Your information is not correct. You know more information than I do. And I put very nervous, sweating."

"Why did you write that?"

"Because he had sweat pouring down his face," Cameron responded, "and I've interviewed a lot of people on some very serious matters and many people have responded different ways, which you'll see in my notes. But he was very nervous and sweating and both Jim Quirk and I observed this to be very, you know, a difficult subject matter for him to speak about."

Cameron stressed that during her investigations she took "a rumor just as serious as if we had a copy of a check."

Cameron's second day of testimony was interrupted by a closed hearing about Twomey's subpoena demanding that Honda turn over its investigative files. Honda attorney Steven Gordon moved to quash the subpoena on the grounds that the material was subject to client-attorney privilege.

Portions of the investigative files had already been provided to the defense during discovery: Cameron's notes on her firings of the executives and selected items from the so-called Tony Piazza files from the mid-1980s, when the Honda security chief conducted an unauthorized investigation of the corruption, a probe that Honda higher-ups ignored. But Josleyn's team wanted the entire package, including the work of all law firms and private investigative agencies engaged in the probe.

Twomey suffered from a collapsed lung the day of the hearing, the first of several maladies that would plague him throughout the trial. He was taken from the courthouse in an ambulance. His partner, Mark Sisti, took over.

Sisti presented the defense's arguments to the judge as to why they needed the files. "The relevancy of whether or not Lyon and Lyon was engaged in a cover-up," said Sisti, "and the relevancy of whether or not American Honda and its executives were engaged in a cover-up is extremely important with regard to any criminal intent that can be imputed with regard to Mr. Josleyn in this particular situation. . . . it would be evidence essentially of misprision of a felony. That it was essentially the end product of a cover-up."

A Concord law firm representing Lyon & Lyon joined in Gordon's motion to quash the subpoena, claiming the documents were Lyon & Lyon's work product and thus protected under the work-product doctrine. Connolly also joined in Gordon's objection, reminding the court that the files had nothing to do with the guilt or innocence of Josleyn and Billmyer.

Gordon's move to prevent the documents from being presented in court had nothing to do with the trial—he was representing a client facing a billion dollars worth of lawsuits from 30 clean Honda dealers suing the automaker because of the favoritism shown dirty Honda dealers. If the files were introduced into evidence, they became public property and thus more fodder for plaintiff dealers' attorneys.

Judge DiClerico ruled that Twomey's subpoena was overbroad. He issued an order limiting the documents to be produced to a one-inch-thick "legal file," Cameron's notes taken during her meetings with Honda's attorneys. He ordered Honda to turn over the Cameron legal file. Gordon requested that the judge seal the documents and indicated he was going to appeal the judge's ruling on the release of the files to the U.S. Court of Appeals for the First Circuit in Boston. Judge DiClerico said he would not review the file until the appeals court had issued a ruling. At that time, he would examine the file and determine which documents the defense would be denied access to based on client-attorney and work-product privileges. Gordon reluctantly produced the file.

Immediately contacting the appeals court, Gordon was informed by a court officer that they could not hear the case for at least two weeks. He said the court could only consider the matter immediately if certain extraordinary circumstances were involved. Like what? Gordon asked. Like if you were incarcerated for contempt of court over the matter of the file, the court official replied.

Gordon was willing to go to that length to protect Honda. The next day, he proposed a plan to Judge DiClerico: that they start all over, that the judge return the Cameron legal file to him and order him to produce the file again. Gordon said that he would then refuse to comply, and the judge would have to hold him in contempt and throw him in jail, and the appeals court would take up the matter immediately.

Judge DiClerico called Gordon's plan a "charade" and refused to play along. The judge told Gordon that he would hold him in contempt on other issues if he continued to delay the trial. He made it clear that he planned to review the file and turn it over to the defense unless the appeals court told him otherwise.

Sisti told the judge that he could not cross-examine Cameron until he had the opportunity to review the file. Cameron's testimony was suspended while the appeals court ruled on the matter, and she returned to California.

The trial resumed with dealer John Orsini testifying that Billmyer had asked him to put NASCAR crew chief Doug Richert on his payroll in exchange for an Acura franchise. Richert took the stand and attested that he thought it strange that his paycheck was issued by a Connecticut Honda dealership.

Acura market representation manager Dan Crowe, the man who had terminated Nault Acura and was thus blamed by some Honda executives for the FBI investigation and this trial, took the stand. He stated that Billmyer had ignored company policy when he unilaterally granted Acura franchises to Hendrick and Marty Lustgarten just prior to his retirement. This account refuted the defense's latest argument: that Billmyer alone did not have the power to hand out dealerships.

It was time for the government's star witness. Stanley James Cardiges strode confidently to the witness stand, neatly dressed in a dark blue suit and *sans* ponytail for his final public performance.

Most of Cardiges's testimony on his first day consisted of a review of the American automobile industry during the 1970s and 1980s and Honda's meteoric rise to prominence. Connolly would ask a simple question, and Cardiges would answer with a monologue. Cardiges spoke of oil embargoes, Corvairs and Valiants, Civics and Accords, and how the 1981 Voluntary Restraint Agreement had led to dealers charging $2,000 over list price for Hondas. Cardiges played to the jury like they were a group of Honda dealers from the old days, the volume and tempo of his speech rising and falling. The jurors were enthralled.

Connolly asked Cardiges to review Honda's conflict of interest policy and the standard method by which Honda awarded dealerships. Cardiges itemized the gifts he had received from dealers, listing 50 retailers and every gratuity each had provided: from cash, cars, and dealership ownership interests to a ski jacket from a Colorado dealer and a helicopter ride from a Hawaii dealer. He estimated that he had received a total of $5 million in cash and prizes over the years.

"Mr. Cardiges," Connolly questioned the former Honda national sales manager, "who was the first person to introduce you to any kickback scheme that existed at American Honda Motor Company?"

"I saw kickbacks being received by Mr. Billmyer when I first came with the company in the late 1970s."

"And during the term of your employment with American Honda were you aware of other individuals employed by the company who became involved in the kickback scheme?"

"Many."

"Now, when American Honda had cars that were in strong demand among consumers, were dealers willing to pay money to get letters of intent?"

"They were willing to pay money, swimming pools, gift certificates, houses, cars, you name it. The dealers treated us like kings," said Cardiges.

Connolly asked Cardiges about gifts that Billmyer had received from Honda dealers. Cardiges happily buried the man who had promoted him all the way to national sales manager. He told of delivering checks and Rolex watches from dealers to Billmyer. He detailed how Rick Hendrick provided BMWs and home financing for Billmyer. Cardiges mentioned how Billmyer and he granted Hendrick franchises through the use of straw dealers to prevent the Japanese from detecting the extent of Hendrick's holdings. He said he broke Billmyer's edict about never taking checks from dealers and that Billmyer had chastised him for his overt house-rental arrangement with Hendrick. Cardiges avoided Billmyer's stare throughout his testimony.

Connolly turned the questioning to Josleyn's activities. Copies of checks from dealers Joe Pope and Bill Frink to Josleyn were produced, and Cardiges outlined how each deal went down, fingering Josleyn as the instigator. He testified that Josleyn had initiated the advertising and sales training scams.

Connolly asked Cardiges how Honda had been harmed by the corruption. "This undermined the loyalty and the confidence in Honda by the dealers who were honest, the dealers who didn't give gifts," Cardiges responded. "It also undermined the loyalty of the employees of Honda. You didn't know whether you were going to be loyal to the people who were giving you the money, the gifts, or whether you should be loyal to Honda. When one dealer was able to get a franchise as a result of giving myself or (others) money, then Honda probably missed the opportunity to perhaps get maybe a better dealer."

Cardiges was adamant that he had no solid substantiation that Honda's Japanese executives had known what was going on.

Connolly asked Cardiges about Lyon & Lyon, another preemptive strike to assure that the jurors recognized that the government was not hiding controversial issues. Cardiges stated that Lyon & Lyon attorneys Bud Smoot and Don McCarthy had communicated their lightning bolt theory of testimony to him numerous times, but they never directly told him not to tell the truth on the stand.

Connolly made his last move with Cardiges: "Mr. Cardiges, why did you plead guilty to those four felony charges in the indictment that was pending against you?"

"Because I've been denying that I've been doing this thing for 18 years now, and I'm tired of doing that."

"Nothing further, your Honor," Connolly finished.

Twomey, fresh from the hospital, leaped up from the defense table and walked swiftly across the courtroom to cross-examine Cardiges. He skipped the formality of introducing himself to the witness — he wanted a smooth segue from Cardiges's last words.

"You are not tired of lying though; are you, Mr. Cardiges?" demanded Twomey. "Mr. Cardiges, you told this jury that you made a commitment to the government to tell the truth. Do you recall saying that?"

"Excuse me?"

"Do you recall telling this jury about three or four, five minutes ago that you made a commitment to the government to tell the truth when you testified here?"

"I did."

"That's not the first time you've made a commitment to tell the truth; is it?"

"I don't know what you mean."

Twomey tried to trap Cardiges by showing discrepancies between his testimony and what he had told the FBI in February, but Cardiges stood his ground.

"Why didn't you tell Mr. Connolly that you did suspect that Lyons & Lyons knew what was going on?" Twomey asked.

"I didn't lie to Mr. Connolly," Cardiges responded calmly, "and if you read the question from Mr. Connolly and see what my answer is, I think it will be apparent to you that I didn't."

"Sir, the question from Mr. Connolly as near as I could get it down —

was do you have any reason to believe that Lyon & Lyon knew about kickbacks, and you said no."

"No, I don't."

"But you did suspect they knew about it; right?"

"That's correct," said Cardiges.

For four hours, Twomey asked Cardiges to recall every gift he had received from dealers, state by state, looking for any discrepancy between his testimony and what he told the FBI in February. Twomey wrote each gratuity on a giant easel.

Cardiges's memory was faltering, unable to answer the demands of Twomey's hammering.

"Let's go to Oklahoma," said Twomey. "Don Carlton?"

"Yes, he gave me $100,000," replied a weary Cardiges.

"Why did he give you that?"

"I don't know if it was as a result of the sale of a dealership that he had or whether he wanted a letter of intent. I don't recall the exact reason."

"Is the reason you don't recall what you received it for because you received so much from so many different people it's hard to remember what any $100,000 payment was for?"

"That's very true," said Cardiges, "because this is eighteen years now that you're going through and I'm having a difficult time remembering what I ate in the last eighteen days. And I apologize for being so vague about it but, you know, I had a lot of responsibilities at the time."

Cardiges's stories were compelling under direct examination, but their rehash was getting stale. Twomey did not catch Cardiges in any lies, but it was obvious that Cardiges was being very guarded under cross-examination.

Mercifully, Twomey changed gears. He zeroed in on the Japanese. He brought up each item gathered by the government that might imply knowledge of the crimes by Honda's Japanese officials, the majority of which were rumor and hearsay.

The most intriguing tidbit was a letter that Ed Temple had written to Koichi Amemiya in February 1992, a few months after he became Honda's Costa Mesa, California, dealer. If any document ever proved that Temple had been planning his Emergency Roll-Over for years, this was the one:

> It was certainly good to talk with you today. . . . When we last met in June of '91, you asked me to keep an eye open for a good Mercedes SL model. Well, I found one. This car is a 1986 Mercedes

> 560 SL model, red in color. Has only 19,000 miles. Please see attached pictures. The interior is medium gray in color.

Amemiya never took delivery of the car. Temple did not write that he was going to provide the automobile for free, but he had created an incriminating paper trail in case the transaction occurred. Cardiges said that it did not prove that Amemiya had solicited gifts from dealers.

Twomey pressed on. You knew Amemiya got a Mercedes-Benz from dealer Ted Stevens, right?

"No, I didn't say that I knew it," said Cardiges. "I said that's what I had heard."

Why did Amemiya grant Temple a Honda dealership despite knowing about the Peck checks?

"I'm the one that signed the letter of intent. I don't know if Mr. Amemiya okayed it."

Why did your attorney tell the press that Honda management knew about what was going on?

"Well, it's probably the defense that he was going to put on. I did not authorize him to say this."

You knew Amemiya got a $50,000 painting from a dealer, didn't you?

"I had no information. I don't know who told me that."

Doesn't Amemiya saying "you don't need this" when he handed you a bonus check prove that he knew about the corruption?

"I didn't have any proof whatsoever of Mr. Amemiya or Japanese management knowing about it," Cardiges responded.

Twomey ended the cross-examination by questioning Cardiges about the dollar value of a Honda franchise and about how the Japanese officials knew the company could have charged a fee for the rights to a dealership.

"Well," asked Twomey, "do you agree with me a system in which American Honda chooses to allow people like you to give away franchises that are worth millions, literally millions, is a system that invites kickbacks?"

"If the individuals took the same attitude that I took, that's correct."

"Well, it's not just you. It's you and just about everybody who worked in that sales force for Honda, isn't it?"

"I did by example and my people did by example, that's correct."

"Doesn't the structure which Amemiya/Munekuni put in place and chose to keep in place, wasn't that a structure that was designed to result in exactly what happened?"

"I can't answer that."

"No further questions," said Twomey, disgusted.

Twomey had failed. In two days of scatter-shot cross-examination of Cardiges, Twomey could not prove that the Japanese executives knew anything about the corruption. The government, the witnesses, Cardiges, Honda — they're all in cahoots, thought Twomey.

Cardiges's testimony was interrupted on its fourth day by more fighting over the Cameron legal file. The U.S. Court of Appeals declined to consider Gordon's motion to compel the court to return the file to him. In a closed hearing, Judge DiClerico stated that he had decided not to honor Gordon's local motion to return the file. Gordon had been under the impression that the judge would return the documents, no matter what the appeals court ruled. Over Gordon's loud protests, the judge said that he was going to review the documents and then turn them over to defense attorneys.

"You tried to appeal that order," the judge explained to Gordon, "they said it wasn't right, they returned it, and now we're going to move on."

"And I asked this Court to return those documents to me in the event that this took place," screamed Gordon. "I feel that I've been sandbagged by this Court by you not willing to hold me in contempt for failing to return it, and I would ask the Court to return it to me. And I just don't think it's fair or appropriate. Judge, c'mon. Look at me and tell me that that's not wrong. Look at me and tell me that that's not the truth."

Courtroom observers were stunned by Gordon's bravado — lawyers never talk to federal judges that way. DiClerico again indicated that the matter was closed and waved Gordon away from the bench. If the exchange had occurred in front of the jury, Gordon likely would have been slapped with a contempt of court charge for his behavior. (The jurors never knew who Gordon was. All they saw of him was when he demanded to be heard during sidebar conversations, after which they usually noticed an exasperated Judge DiClerico.)

The Court of Appeals indicated that it would consider the matter if a thorough record of the case was submitted. Honda and Lyon & Lyon immediately filed the appropriate appeal to have the higher court consider prohibiting the judge from turning over the file. After further wrangling, Judge DiClerico decided he would hold off giving the file to the defense until the appeals court ruled.

David Long cross-examined Cardiges for two days. He tried to separate Billmyer's activities from those of Cardiges and the others to bolster his "multiple conspiracies" theory. He had Cardiges again recite all his dealings and admit that Billmyer had nothing to do with the majority of them. Long also got Cardiges to concede that Hendrick was an outstanding automobile dealer, the implication being that Billmyer had done good for Honda by granting so many franchises to Hendrick. Long jumped on Twomey's bandwagon and attempted to force Cardiges to say that the Japanese executives had received gifts from dealers. Cardiges held his ground.

Under redirect examination, Connolly had Cardiges reiterate that he had no evidence about the Japanese executives' knowledge of the corruption.

"Please tell the jury," said Connolly, "what the first thing you told the FBI was about your personal knowledge of Japanese management knowing what was happening at American Honda."

"I said that I didn't have any specific knowledge of Japanese management at American Honda being involved in or having knowledge of the corruption that existed at the company," Cardiges replied.

"Mr. Cardiges, please tell the jury about all the documents that the Government has that show the Japanese condoned these kickback practices."

"I saw no documents that either indicated or shown that the Japanese knew anything about kickbacks or gifts or anything like that."

Nothing incurred Connolly's wrath more than references to his employer having a hidden agenda in the case. He was annoyed that the defense had grilled Cardiges about his former attorney telling the press that the government was prosecuting Honda officials to pressure Japan to ease trade barriers.

Connolly asked Cardiges: "Does Mr. Israels have pictures of me and Mr. Feith meeting with the Japanese prime minister and Mr. Clinton—ironing out the terms of the trade agreement with Japan?"

"No, sir," Cardiges answered quickly.

"Is that what this case is about?"

"No, absolutely not."

"You know about any other stupid comments Mr. Israels made to the press?" Connolly asked in a rare display of anger.

On his final recross-examination of Cardiges, Twomey tried to discredit Cardiges's previous testimony. He wrote the words *yes* and *no* on the easel and asked Cardiges to read the words out loud.

"There, you can do it," coaxed Twomey. "Now, when you talked to Mr. Connolly — in fact when you talked to the government's lawyer you can say the words 'yes' and 'no' very easily; right?"

"I can say the words 'yes' and 'no' very easily to any question that requires an answer yes or no," an annoyed Cardiges responded.

"Why is it that you can answer the government's questions with yes and nos, but every time you give an answer to David Long or myself you qualify the answer in some way?"

"I don't recall that I've done that."

The words *Billmyer* and *Josleyn* were rarely uttered by any of the attorneys during Cardiges's final five days on the witness stand.

Following the prolonged side trip of Cardiges's cross-examination, Connolly spent two weeks marching more Honda dealers to the stand. All detailed their payoffs to the Honda officials as Connolly displayed the corresponding evidence for the jury.

David Conant of Norm Reeves Honda told of paying Josleyn over $400,000 for used Honda company cars. Conant claimed he had paid because he was intimidated by Josleyn.

Shau-Wai Lam, the president of the American subsidiary of Dah Chong Hong Trading Corporation, owners of nine U.S. Honda and Acura dealerships, took the stand. Lam was a key government witness because he had paid Billmyer $100,000 in mid-1989, establishing an act of the conspiracy by Billmyer within the five-year statute of limitations time frame. He presented a bizarre excuse for his payoffs to the Honda officials, saying he was "trying to protect my position in the company," a corporation owned by his family and headed by Lam himself.

Minority dealer candidate Joe Pope admitted to paying Josleyn $150,000 for a letter of intent for a California dealership. Employees of Rick Hendrick's organization testified about the loans made to Billmyer and the cash-filled packages sent to Cardiges. An NCNB banker talked about Hendrick guaranteeing home loans for Billmyer and Cardiges. Defense attorneys continued to attack the credibility of the dealers, claiming they were stretching the truth to assure that their immunity agreements with the government remained intact.

Connolly called to the stand American Honda executive vice president Tom Elliott, the highest-ranking American at the corporation. Elliott reviewed the company's history and the tremendous amount of freedom given to the corporation's executives. He claimed to have never heard any allegations of Honda executives being compensated by dealers in exchange for new franchises prior to the internal probe. Elliott told of the damage done to the corporation by the corruption: millions of dollars in litigation costs, sinking employee morale, and a damaged relationship with Honda's dealer network.

Long attacked Elliott's handling of the Christiaan Walker incident, noting that he had contacted only Lyon & Lyon and not Honda's human resources department or Amemiya.

"Bottom line is," said Long, "you didn't tell anybody anything about that (Walker) telephone conversation, other than you picked up the phone and you called Bud Smoot; isn't that right?"

"That is correct," Elliott replied. "We were talking about serious allegations against a high executive of the company by a person that I suspected was perhaps not the most honest person in the world." Long got Elliott to admit that there was no written policy about turning over information to Lyon & Lyon about sales department officials' wrongdoing.

Sisti cross-examined Elliott with the intent of exposing Honda's inconsistency in dealing with employees who violated the conflict of interest policy. He forced Elliott to admit that former Honda sales chief Cliff Schmillen was never punished for his secret ownership in two Honda dealerships. Elliott also testified that he did not terminate advertising manager Eric Conn for receiving gifts from Honda's ad agency. Sisti reminded Elliott how Amemiya had been given special treatment by Honda regarding the Mercedes-Benz automobile he had received from a dealer.

Then Sisti moved in for the kill.

"Did you ever hear the expression about when a wild animal gets caught in a leg trap?" questioned Sisti.

"Yes, I've heard of that expression," said Elliott.

"Well, I mean there are instances and there have been stories written about savage Bengal tigers trapped in a leg trap, and the way they save themselves is they gnaw off their own limb. Did you ever hear of that?"

"I've heard of that."

"Well, the fact of the matter is," screamed Sisti, "the two limbs that American Honda are gnawing off and have been gnawing off for the last two months in this courtroom are sitting right here, Dennis Josleyn and Mr. Billmyer; right?"

"They aren't the only two."

"Well, they haven't gone for the head yet, have they?"

"I believe they have."

"What this is all about really is a situation where American Honda in its discretion sanctions certain behavior and doesn't sanction other behavior; right?"

"I don't believe that, no."

"In fact, it's been going on for years and some of the examples you testified to yesterday. Did you fire Mr. Conn?"

"No, he was not fired," Elliott answered quietly.

Throughout Elliott's testimony, the milk of amnesia flowed from his lips. He did not remember hearing anything about Honda executives receiving gifts from dealers until the internal investigation began. He did not remember hearing about the 1983 meeting between Honda officials and J. D. Power, an item even the lowliest sales division employees knew about. Elliott, who frequently interacted with dealers and sales division managers, would have had to have been totally oblivious to not know anything. The corporation's mandate of protecting the company during the trial was being well served by Elliott.

Steven Gordon once strutted back and forth in a New Hampshire courtroom in front of a witness who suffered from convenient memory lapses. Gordon mocked the witness by doing an impersonation of "Hogan's Heroes" television character Sergeant Schultz, a prison guard who saw a lot but remembered little. "I know noooothiiing," taunted Gordon. "Noooothiiing." If Gordon had been a defense attorney in this trial, he might have performed the same act in front of Elliott.

The battle over the Cameron legal file continued during Elliott's testimony. Judge DiClerico expressed his concerned about what might happen if the file were returned to Gordon, culled from his by-now deep understanding of how Honda litigated. "You might get those records back and Honda might order them destroyed," he told Gordon. "I have no idea what might happen to those records. . . . This trial must move forward. This matter has taken a tremendous amount of time and resources as it is. And it has been intrusive."

On April 19, the Court of Appeals notified Judge DiClerico that it would hear the case about the Cameron file. By law, the judge had no choice but to suspend the trial pending the other court's ruling.

After hearing oral arguments by Gordon, Twomey, and attorneys for Lyon & Lyon, the Court of Appeals ruled on May 4 that the Cameron file had been properly turned over and that it should be provided to defense attorneys. The court concluded that Honda had already waived its client-attorney and work-product privileges when it had previously submitted portions of the files to the government.

Judge DiClerico forwarded the disputed materials to the defense teams. He had conducted a painstaking page-by-page review of the files, blacking out portions of the documents he felt were subject to Honda's assertions of confidentiality.

Twomey only found a few usable nuggets in the 60-odd pages of the Cameron file. Whatever material Judge DiClerico redacted from the documents, and what notes Honda may have previously removed from the files, remains one of the big mysteries of the Honda scandal.

The trial resumed on May 9. Connolly, aware that Josleyn would not be taking the stand, found a backhanded way to get Josleyn's words in front of the jury. He asked the court if he could read excerpts from Josleyn's deposition in the 1992 *Hunt vs. Mixon* case, where Josleyn was accused of agreeing to accept $90,000 in exchange for a letter of intent. Over Twomey's loud objections, the judge granted Connolly's request. In a monotone voice, Connolly read the Q and A in which Josleyn denied ever receiving money from dealers and denied that his departure from Honda had anything to do with any misconduct.

Connolly returned to his seat without comment; none was needed.

Testimony resumed with the cross-examination of Cameron that had been interrupted six weeks earlier by the wrangling over her legal file. Armed with documents from that file, Mark Sisti was ready to discredit Honda for hiding information about the corruption.

"Were you open and honest," began Sisti, "when you spoke with the Government about what you knew about American Honda and the corruption and people involved taking money?"

"Yes, I was," Cameron replied.

"The fact of the matter is that you knew and American Honda knew for about ten years that people were taking money for dealerships and there were all kinds of side deals going on; isn't that true?"

"No."

"You never heard of anything like that before?"

"No, I haven't," responded Cameron.

Sisti displayed a blown-up copy of a page from her file for the jury. Cameron glanced at Gordon in the audience to see whether she could answer questions about this piece of evidence. Gordon subtly signaled "no." Despite the Court of Appeals ruling, he would not give up.

"Your Honor," Cameron stated, "I understand that this is a communication between our company attorneys and myself that was privileged. Am I required to answer this question?"

"The Court directs you to answer," said Judge DiClerico.

The document contained notes from her initial meeting with Lyon & Lyon attorney Bud Smoot about the internal investigation, the day the law firm opened the vault. Included was a memo from Smoot to Cameron, the majority of it blanked out by Judge DiClerico. What remained was intriguing:

> It has long been rumored that to get a Honda dealership Honda people had to be paid off. The rumor has been so widespread that J. D Power raised the matter with at least one Honda Vice President almost ten years ago. You are aware of some of theses charges. Tony Piazza raised questions regarding Jack Billmyer and Cliff Schmillen years ago.

Sisti pointed at the note. "What's the subject matter of that information?" he asked.

"Rumors regarding people taking money," said Cameron.

"And it has to do with the very subject matter that you and Bud Smoot were investigating; correct?"

"This was rumors. I was investigating facts."

"Well, you know, sometimes your investigations begin because of rumors, correct, Ms. Cameron?"

"You can't really do an investigation with a rumor."

Sisti missed a golden opportunity to catch Cameron in an inconsistency. Honda attorneys apparently were concerned about the information from the testimony that implied that the corporation did nothing to stop the problems. Their solution was to instruct Cameron to testify that she only investigated hard facts and not rumors. In her March testimony, she was adamant that the company pursued every rumor about corruption. Now she claimed that the company did not follow up on rumors. Sisti and Twomey missed the discrepancy, thus blowing a chance to lend credence to their contention that Honda had done nothing to stop the payola.

Sisti asked her why she did not contact Power. Because it was only a rumor, said Cameron.

Sisti asked Cameron if she could talk about the missing portions of the document, igniting an imbroglio among the attorneys and forcing Judge

DiClerico to call a sidebar meeting to discuss the matter. Gordon jumped up from the gallery's wooden pews and walked toward the bench.

"Your Honor, may I attend?" asked Gordon.

"No, you may not," said Judge DiClerico, annoyed. "You can step back. If there's a need, I'll call you up." Gordon slinked back to his seat.

The judge decided that the jury needed an explanation of the dispute over the Cameron file. He reviewed the situation and allowed Sisti to continue. The attorney asked Cameron why Smoot wrote that she was aware of the allegations.

"When he was reading from this document," replied Cameron, "I was writing down that I was not aware of these things. So that I am telling the truth. I have not heard this before. This was the first time."

"This is even more troubling," Sisti remarked. "You mean to tell me that the attorney that you were sitting with wrote down you are aware of some of those charges and in fact you were writing a note at the same time that says you are not aware of it?"

"Yes, that's correct."

"So the two of you had like a misunderstanding as to what your knowledge was?"

"Yes."

"Bud Smoot thought that you knew?"

"That's correct."

"But you're saying that you didn't?"

"I did not know."

"The fact of the matter is Smoot knew; right?"

"He wrote this note," Cameron shot back. "You'd have to ask him."

At the defense table, Twomey was throwing a fit. He loudly gasped and rolled his eyes after each of Cameron's answers. He was 100 percent certain she was lying. Connolly asked the judge to have Twomey stop his theatrics.

Sisti attacked Cameron about the company's handling of Amemiya's Mercedes-Benz.

"Well, did he have to give the Mercedes-Benz back, ma'am?"

"I don't have the details of it," said Cameron.

"Was he at all punished?"

"Again, I don't have the details."

"Are you at all interested in that?"

"I figured I didn't need to get involved," said Cameron. "It was taken care of and I had confidence that it was taken care of appropriately."

Sisti was getting nowhere — Cameron had been too well coached. He took one final shot at establishing that Honda had covered things up.

"The fact of the matter is," said Sisti, his voice rising, "you selectively picked and chose what information went out to the government."

"Objection, your Honor," Connolly interrupted. "That's just argumentative and harassing." The judge directed Cameron to answer.

"The answer is absolutely not," said Cameron.

The government rested its case following Cameron's testimony, after which the judge and attorneys met to discuss the order of the defense witnesses. Throughout the trial, Twomey dropped hints that Koichi Amemiya was ducking the proceedings, despite the fact that it was Twomey who arguably had the obligation to call Amemiya. It became a game of guts between Connolly and Twomey. Twice during the trial, Connolly literally dared Twomey to call Amemiya. If Connolly had summoned Amemiya, he would have appeared unsure of his case and it might have lent credence to Twomey's defense. Twomey was convinced that Elliott and Cameron had lied on the stand and believed Amemiya would do the same. However, Twomey had built an image of Amemiya as being someone larger than life, the evil man from Japan who roared around in his Mercedes-Benz and winked at Cardiges's indiscretions, and the soft-spoken Amemiya would have quickly dispelled that perception for the jury. Ultimately Twomey decided that the defense had the most to lose by calling Amemiya.

Twomey told the judge that he was not going to call Amemiya to testify. The judge later inexplicably ruled that the government had the obligation to call Amemiya, thus setting up a "missing witness" instruction to the jury prior to deliberation, a minor victory for Josleyn's lawyers.

Billmyer's lawyers declined to call any witnesses for the defense. Twomey's three scheduled witnesses were his final hope to prove his case.

A former Honda sales division manager named Walt Heyer took the stand. He claimed that Elliott had bragged about lying under oath in a dealer lawsuit regarding Honda's auto distribution system and that Elliott and other executives often joked about their Graft and Corruption Accounts.

Heyer was cross-examined by Feith. He forced Heyer to admit that he had undergone a sex-change operation and had informed Honda he wanted to be known as Laura Jenson. Heyer next confessed to having been treated for a multiple-personality disorder.

"Isn't one of the side effects of that disease a frequent and often complete gap in memory?" asked Feith.

"Yes," Heyer replied.

Twomey's first witness had not been very credible.

Next scheduled to testify in Josleyn's defense was former Honda vice president of purchasing Cecil Proulx. The 55-year-old Proulx was the man who claimed he had tried to alert Honda's Japanese managers about the corruption several times during the mid-1980s. Connolly fought Proulx's appearance, claiming he was not competent to testify. He told Judge DiClerico that Proulx's information was "quadruple hearsay" and that Proulx had contacted television news show "60 Minutes," which did not believe his claims. The judge denied Connolly's request.

Proulx took the stand and told of his and other executives' conversations with the Japanese about the corruption. His most intriguing claim was that he had been told in 1987 by Japanese vice president of administration Michiaki Shinkai that he "looked the other way" at the sales executives' thievery because the company could not afford to pay them on par with Detroit automakers. Proulx testified that he had heard that former American Honda president Tetsuo Chino refused to initiate an internal investigation. Proulx named Honda vice president Chet Hale, Acura sales chief Ed Taylor, audit division chief Doug Divall, and head of security Tony Piazza as people who had confided in Proulx about the problems.

Throughout his testimony, one thing was clear: Proulx knew much hearsay but none in the form of admissible evidence.

Connolly tore Proulx apart under cross-examination. Proulx testified he knew nothing about the sales training or advertising scams. The night before Proulx's testimony, Honda attorneys had faxed Connolly three maniacal letters Proulx had written to top Honda officials. In one of the letters, Proulx (who is white) complained of being "treated like an inferior plantation worker." Using the letters and Proulx's own words, Connolly exposed him as a bitter complainer and a man who possessed only water cooler talk.

Being a tattletale comes with a price. Of the three whistle-blowers who surfaced in the Honda scandal, one was accused as being a forger and a blackmailer (Walker), one was exposed as having personality disorders (Heyer), and one was discredited as a whiner and a rumor monger (Proulx). All three were forced to resign from the corporation.

Neither of Twomey's first two witnesses had helped Josleyn's case. On May 16, he called the final witness for the defense, J. David Power, the auto-market researcher who held the most convincing evidence that Honda executives had been aware of the corruption for years.

Power told of the complaints he had received from Honda dealers about the need to pay off Honda executives for additional cars and franchises. Power read to the jury his 1983 letter written to American Honda executive vice president Yoshihide Munekuni, warning him of a widespread scandal if the corporation did not take action to stop the veniality. He detailed his meeting with Munekuni and Cliff Schmillen.

"Did you have any further contacts with Honda about the same subject?" asked Twomey.

"I was contacted by the outside counsel. I believe his name was Bud Smoot of Lyon and Lyon."

"That name is probably familiar to everybody in this courtroom. Now, what did Mr. Smoot come to talk to you about?"

"He was informed by Mr. Munekuni of the situation and he wanted to find out if I could come up with any hard evidence that this was going on."

Power testified that none of the dealers would provide details of their allegations, all fearing the wrath of Honda. Power claimed he had told Elliott about the problems, contradicting Elliott's testimony that he did not remember speaking with Power about the matter. For Twomey, this inconsistency finally confirmed his feeling that current Honda executives were either lying or conveniently forgetting things while on the witness stand. It came too late.

Power's testimony that he had warned Honda in 1983 about the corruption was splashed all over the national news. It was the most embarrassing of any statements made during the very public trial for American Honda.

The testimony was over. Thirty-five witnesses had taken the stand during the three-month-long trial. More than 80 Honda dealers were exposed as being participants in the chicanery. Hundreds of pieces of evidence bolstered the government's case. Neither of the defendants had testified.

Connolly had built a powerful case. He clearly showed that the defendants had intentionally engaged in the fraudulent activities, had broken the law, and had concealed their operations from their superiors and the shareholders of American Honda. Billmyer's claim that New Hampshire was not the proper venue for the trial was rarely broached in court. It was a matter for the jury to decide based on the applicable laws. Billmyer's team also never convincingly separated Billmyer's graft from that of the other conspirators.

Twomey and Sisti did a great job of exposing Honda as a sloppy organization but did not prove that the Japanese executives condoned or covered up the corruption. Even if they had, there was no guarantee it would lead to an acquittal for Josleyn. None of the defense attorneys could tell where the case stood in the minds of the attentive, poker-faced jurors. They knew that the jury would most likely remember what was said during final arguments.

On May 19, Connolly began the government's final arguments by reminding jurors that the case was about a very simple concept: it is wrong to steal.

"This is a very basic principle that parents teach their children from the time they are young," said Connolly. "It's something that grandparents and teachers reinforce in children in helping to build good character. By the time you are an adult, like Mr. Billmyer and Mr. Josleyn, you don't need to be told don't take property and sell it when it belongs to your employer."

Connolly spent 90 minutes of his two-hour-long presentation detailing why Billmyer should be found guilty. He outlined the four elements of a conspiracy needed to convict Billmyer: two or more people engaging in conduct that is prohibited by the law, knowledge of the purpose of the conspiracy at the time they joined it, the committing of an overt act, and the committing of that act in the furtherance of goals of the conspiracy. Connolly reviewed the evidence and testimony that proved Billmyer's actions satisfied the requirements.

Connolly neatly tied two key pieces of evidence together. He read Billmyer's response to a letter from spurned dealer J. H. Thomas, who complained that he was denied a franchise because another dealer had paid off Honda officials. Billmyer wrote Thomas that "there is no fee involved in securing a Honda franchise."

"Ladies and gentlemen," Connolly stated, "that constitutes evidence of saying one thing and doing something completely different. This letter is dated July 31, 1984. Ten days later, Mr. Billmyer was sitting at a restaurant taking $25,000 from a man with a pending application for a new Honda dealership."

Connolly told the jury that deciding on the issue of New Hampshire being the proper venue for Billmyer's trial was a "no-brainer," reminding them that David Pedersen's gifts from Tom Bohlander in exchange for a Nashua Acura franchise were clearly part of the same conspiracy as Billmyer's.

Connolly rolled through a review of the evidence against Josleyn. He rebuked the defense's assertion that the Japanese knew what was going on, outlining how the defendants artfully hid their activities from their superiors.

"Now, I submit to you, ladies and gentlemen," said Connolly, "if Mr. Josleyn's so-called defense in this case had any merit whatsoever, why would all of these illustrations of deceit, of cover-up, of hiding been so consistently pursued during the course of this conspiracy? That consistent, irrefutable evidence I suggest to you shows Mr. Josleyn's defense for what it is: absolutely made up out of whole cloth for the benefit of you people in the hopes that he might get acquitted."

Connolly called for the jury to return guilty verdicts on all charges, then walked back to the prosecution's table to listen to David Long present Billmyer's final argument.

Long questioned the integrity of the current Honda executives and the government. "How about this tortured theory that's been advanced here by our government that American Honda's a victim?" asked Long. "They've had an ironclad resolve from day one to portray American Honda and the Japanese management as victims when the evidence is to the contrary. This is a cover-up. It's very troubling when witnesses employed by the alleged victim come into this courtroom, or any courtroom in this country, and evade answering questions."

"Elliott. Tom Elliott. Gee whiz. He stayed on that stand for two days and lied for two days. Mr. Power testified he told Tom Elliott about all this in 1983. They're playing games with you. They don't want you to know the truth."

Long argued that Billmyer was not part of a single conspiracy. "For the most part," Long explained, "these conspiracies which were alleged by the government, which there was testimony about, there isn't any interdependence among these deals. One doesn't contribute to the success of the other in any way. Or that each knew of the other. There isn't any shared benefit in these deals. What we have here at best is multiple conspiracies."

"I can say to this jury," said Long, "that under the evidence in this case that the government has failed to carry its burden of proof and that Mr. Billmyer is entitled to a verdict of not guilty."

Paul Twomey's final argument on behalf of Josleyn began with more attacks on the credibility of those who were called by Connolly. "Virtually all of the government's witnesses at one point in time worked for American Honda," said Twomey. "You know, those people were all schooled in lying. They got their Bachelor's degree in lying from Lyon & Lyon's little seminars that Bud Smoot and Mr. McCarthy put on telling people that it just doesn't matter if you lie. The only thing that matters is if you get away with it and protect the company."

Twomey summed up his core defense: "You cannot attempt to defraud somebody if you know they know what you're doing and they know that you know it, and they know of it and they condone it and everybody's aware of what's going on."

Twomey argued that the government had concealed evidence that Honda officials were aware of the corruption. He accused Connolly of ignoring Cecil Proulx's pleas to be heard because it would be "inconvenient" to the government's case.

Twomey reminded the jurors that the government had failed to call Amemiya to testify. He walked over to the empty witness box, pretending to be Connolly questioning Amemiya.

"Mr. Amemiya," Twomey asked, "did you know exactly what was going on throughout all these years at American Honda in regards to gifts and kickbacks to your dealers? Simple question. What's the answer?"

"Mr. Amemiya, were you aware that Dennis Josleyn's brother was associated with the ad agency with whom your company did business? Simple question. What's the answer?"

"Who's got the burden of proof here? Does it make a difference what the answers to those kind of questions would be? Can you be satisfied that you know the truth in this case when that's kept from you?"

Twomey the showman ended with one final assault on American Honda: "They thought they were going to hide Sherry Cameron's file," said Twomey. "They're hoping to use a verdict for the government in their favor in that other litigation. If you were to do the wrong thing, if you were to forget about our Constitution, our Bill of Rights, the fact that government has to prove a case beyond a reasonable doubt, if you were to rip those things up and forget about them and enter a conviction here, there would be a lot of laughter. The board room at Lyon & Lyon, the champagne would be flowing. They'd be right. It doesn't matter if you lie in the courtroom. If you get what you want in the end, you might as well do it."

"They'll just be yucking it up tonight. Torrance, California, American Honda, old Mr. Elliott, he'll be having one heck of a good party."

Saying the government's case had been built on a "foundation of sewage," Twomey asked the jury to return a verdict of not guilty for Josleyn.

Judge DiClerico spent the better part of May 19 giving the jury their instructions for deliberation. He reminded the jurors that, even though Amemiya was never called to testify, they could consider Twomey's contention that Connolly had been in the best position to call Amemiya. They were allowed, but not required, to decide whether Amemiya's testimony might have been damaging to the government's case or merely a repeat of others' testimony.

The jurors retired and developed a game plan: they would review the evidence and testimony and then decide on Josleyn's guilt or innocence first, all realizing that determining a verdict on Billmyer was going to be more difficult. They considered and quickly rejected Twomey's core defense about Honda's Japanese executives condoning the corruption. They did not consider the "missing witness" instruction about Amemiya, but most were disappointed he did not testify. They agreed that the preponderance of evidence against Josleyn weighed against the applicable laws made for a black-and-white decision. It took them only a day and a half to decide to pronounce Josleyn guilty on all four counts.

Most of the jurors were sympathetic toward the elderly Billmyer, helped by Long's plea that Billmyer should be allowed to go home to North Carolina and enjoy his grandchildren. "Nobody wanted to send him to jail," said one juror. Though both defendants had shown the strain of having fingers pointed at them by witnesses during the long trial, some jurors had detected remorse in Billmyer's face throughout, while Josleyn had sat emotionless. Three of the jurors took leadership roles, reminding the others that the decision was not a personal issue, that they had to dispassionately consider the evidence. After three days of deliberation, they agreed that Billmyer was part of one conspiracy and that New Hampshire was the proper venue. After that, the checks from the dealers and Michael Connolly's simple words about the issue of what's right and what's wrong were all that was needed to convince them. The jury decided that Billmyer had willingly done wrong.

On June 1, the jury foreman read the verdicts: John W. Billmyer and Dennis R. Josleyn were guilty on all counts. Billmyer's legs nearly buckled when the verdict was read. Josleyn did not flinch. The only sounds in the courtroom came from the weeping wives of the two defendants.

"We feel that this jury was a victim of a cover-up and we think it will come undone sooner or later," Twomey told reporters outside the courtroom. "Certain people with American Honda were able to cover up their involvement with this."

The American justice system has traditionally been soft on punishing white-collar criminals. In 1996 New York automobile dealer John McNamara was sentenced to five years in jail for defrauding General Motors

Acceptance Corporation (GMAC) out of a whopping $436 million in a scheme in which he tricked the bank into loaning him money on nonexistent vehicles. Savings and loan magnate Charles Keating was convicted of defrauding thousands of elderly investors out of $285 million during the 1980s and was sentenced to 12 years in federal prison.

Those two scoundrels would have received the death penalty from Judge "Hanging Joe" DiClerico.

Federal sentencing guidelines are intricate and confusing, based primarily on the dollar amount of gains grabbed by the defendants. Sentences can be reduced by a variety of factors: if the defendants accept responsibility for their crimes, cooperate with prosecutors, or are deemed to be "minimal" participants in a conspiracy. Sentences can be enhanced if the criminals refuse to confess their guilt, perjure themselves, or are deemed instigators of a conspiracy. The entire Honda gang would benefit from being first-time offenders.

The punishment phase for the convicted Honda conspirators began in August. Connolly assured most of the cooperating defendants that they would likely receive probation, based on his knowledge of other first-time white-collar criminals who stole $500,000, the average take for the majority of the crew. It looked like Cardiges would be the only cooperating defendant destined for prison.

Tom Caulfield was the first former Honda official on Judge DiClerico's scaffold. Connolly gave a plea for leniency for Caulfield, saying he had cooperated fully and had provided key information about the advertising scam. DiClerico was not impressed. He noted that Caulfield's $816,000 take from the advertising scheme was more than anyone else's, including Cardiges and Josleyn. The judge sentenced Caulfield to 24 months in prison and ordered him to pay a $67,000 fine. Caulfield was assigned to a federal minimum-security prison in Boron, California, ironically located only a few miles from American Honda's Mojave Desert test track.

Connolly was stunned by the severity of Caulfield's punishment. He and Mulvaney cornered the next man scheduled for sentencing, Bob Mazzitelli, in the hallway outside the courtroom.

"Bob, this is going to be a tough one," Connolly warned. "Where do you want to go?"

"I want to go home," Mazzitelli replied.

"No, I mean where do you want to serve your sentence?"

"Atlanta. What's going on?"

"Bob, you made the right decision by coming up here in '93," Mulvaney encouraged him. "You'll get through this."

Mazzitelli was sentenced to 20 months in prison and levied a $10,000 fine. Mazzitelli and others felt they had been set up, that Connolly's pledge to assist them was a sham. "Connolly came across as a nice guy, like he was going to help me and all that stuff," said an angry Mazzitelli later. "In the meantime, he was nailing me to the cross."

The sentencing hearings were interspersed with DiClerico's complaints about the "sweetheart deals" cut by Connolly with the defendants. The heart of the gang — Caulfield, Mazzitelli, Mark Benson, John Conway, Hugh Cooper, Larry Finley, Roger Novelly, David Pedersen, Frank Pisano, Bob Rivers, and Bonnie Sikora — the 11 ex-Honda middle managers, whose documented ill-gotten gains ranged from Finley's $50,000 to Caulfield's $816,000, received sentences ranging from 10 to 24 months in jail. They were fined an average of $50,000 apiece. Each was required to be on supervised release, a monitoring program where they are allowed to travel only to and from work, church, or a doctor's office, for a period of two to three years after their prison terms.

Damien Budnick received seven days in prison for perjury. Jim Mortimer was granted probation on his misprision charge. Peter Epsteen, the dealer principal convicted of lying to the FBI, was sentenced to six months in jail and a $256,000 fine. Advertising agency owner Gary Josleyn was sentenced to 12 months for mail fraud.

Lawyer–turned–Honda dealer broker Raymond Hovsepian received six months' imprisonment for his tipping Cardiges $5,000. He was the only person convicted solely for giving gifts.

Judge DiClerico had denied motions by those who wanted a change of venue for their sentencing. Fred Meis's attorney exploited a technical error made by Connolly into having the court agree to allow Meis to be sentenced in his home town of Dallas. Meis was facing a probable 16-month sentence from Judge DiClerico. A Texas federal judge sentenced Meis to probation, much to the outrage of the other defendants.

The convicted crew all expressed remorse to Judge DiClerico for their actions, likely borne more out of their regret over being prosecuted than for having done the crimes. Several asked for alternative venues to serve their sentences. Former Eagle Scout Benson said the Boy Scouts organization was willing to let him work for them in lieu of prison. Judge DiClerico denied all such requests.

Rivers's attorney, Randall Hite, summed up the band of people parading before the court: "This is one of the strangest groups of criminals I've ever seen, because the victims, the supposed guys who paid the money, are probably some of the sharpest automobile dealers in the world and were so successful, they had that kind of cash laying around to pay, and meanwhile the guys that they are paying it to are some of the best, most college-educated, all-American, cream-of-the-crop young executives you'd ever want to find."

Judge DiClerico used time at the sentencing hearings to ask the question that had nagged him during the trial. "There's a pattern that runs throughout all of these cases," he said to Hugh Cooper. "You all were raised with strong values and yet when you saw something was wrong, I haven't seen anyone yet who had the courage to stand up and do anything about it. Why isn't it that nobody had the strength to really say this is wrong and we've got to speak up and let's do something about it?"

"Who was it basically, your Honor," asked Cooper, "that we could go to with this information? Everybody was involved, and in often cases, your Honor, these cases were sanctioned by the highest executives of the company." Cooper told the judge about Amemiya saying that, at American Honda, "we have no priests." Roger Novelly also told the judge about a conversation with Amemiya that implied the president knew what was going on.

"I guess I've learned," said Judge DiClerico, "during (this) series of sentencings, I've learned a little bit more about Mr. Amemiya all the time. I can't help but wonder why he hasn't been standing in this courtroom."

On October 2, the two defendants in the trial appeared for their sentencing hearings. Connolly asked the judge to throw the book at Billmyer. Long objected that the length of Billmyer's sentence might be enhanced based on the government's premise that Billmyer had been an organizer of the conspiracy. The judge denied Long's objection.

Billmyer declined to address the court. Judge DiClerico sentenced Billmyer to 60 months in prison and assessed him a $125,000 fine. Billmyer was the only participant to be sentenced to the maximum prison sentence the law allows for the particular charge. Long indicated that he was going to appeal Billmyer's conviction on venue and single- versus multiple-conspiracy grounds. Judge DiClerico ruled that Billmyer's appeal had merit. Billmyer was not required to report to jail, pending an appeals court's ruling.

Paul Twomey transformed Dennis Josleyn's sentencing hearing into a three-hour microcosm of the trial. Connolly asked the judge to pronounce the maximum sentence allowed by law, calculated to be 87 months in prison on each count, based on sentencing provisions that allow for consideration that Josleyn never accepted responsibility for his actions and was an organizer of the scams.

Twomey claimed that Josleyn should not be penalized for being an originator of the corruption, that he was only a "foot soldier" following Cardiges's orders. As he did during the trial, Connolly reviewed evidence that clearly showed Josleyn as the organizer of the two embezzlement schemes. The judge rejected Twomey's argument.

Twomey had Josleyn give his apology to the court, to help argue Connolly's claim that Josleyn had never accepted responsibility for his actions. "Your Honor," said Josleyn, "I would just like to apologize to this Court, to my family and friends, for the wrongful actions that I participated in. The legal issues, whether they were legal or illegal, is still unknown to me and way above my head. I do acknowledge that they were wrong, and I would like to apologize for those actions." Connolly referenced a sentencing guideline that said a defendant who is found guilty and then admits guilt and remorse is not necessarily eligible for a reduced sentence based on acceptance of responsibility. The judge ruled for the government.

Twomey gave one last shot at arguing that what went on was part of Honda's corporate policy. Judge DiClerico interrupted him: "There was no company policy. At best you come away from the case with a reasonable inference, and that is that this company was negligently managed. The red flags were up. J. D. Power was pointing out to this company back in the mid-eighties that there was trouble, and they ignored it." Twomey had just lost his final argument.

Judge DiClerico came down harder on Josleyn than on all the defendants, sentencing him to 78 months in prison on Count I and 60 months each on Counts II, III, and IV, all to be served concurrently. Josleyn was not assessed a fine because the court determined that he was destitute, despite Connolly's assertion that Josleyn had money hidden away. Twomey asked that Josleyn be allowed to self-report to jail, giving him time to return a rental car and thus avoid being charged with automobile theft. Judge DiClerico granted the request. It was Paul Twomey's only victory in the case — but he'd had a hell of a lot of fun.

It was time for Ed Temple's sentencing hearing. Connolly passionately argued for leniency for the man who broke the case for the government. "His cooperation was singularly more productive and successful than any other person who participated in this case," Connolly told the judge. "If Mr. Temple had not become involved, I think we would still be heavily involved in the investigation today." Connolly credited Temple's information in leading to the indictments of Cardiges, Josleyn, Billmyer, and ten others. John Mulvaney and another FBI agent also spoke before the judge, praising Temple's assistance in the probe.

Temple stood and addressed the judge: "I'd just like to say I am truly sorry for the hardship and pain I've caused anyone over this ordeal. I used poor judgment in my decision making. I have tried my very best to right the wrong I have done. I thank my family and friends for their support and will now pledge to all to be a better person."

Temple was shaking when Judge DiClerico read the sentence: six months in prison and the previously agreed-to fine of $250,000. The judge declined Temple's attorney's request that Temple serve his time working for the Veterans Administration but allowed Temple three weeks before incarceration because of his need for surgery — anal-retentive Temple had come down with a case of hemorrhoids.

Jim Cardiges was sentenced the same day as Temple. Citing Cardiges's "extraordinary" cooperation, Connolly argued for a light sentence for the man he had spent 18 months building a case against. Judge DiClerico countered by pointing out that Cardiges was in the center of each scheme and personally had grossed a total of over $5 million.

Attorney Steven Lyons gave an impassioned plea for his client. "Mr. Cardiges's career is in a shambles," said Lyons. "By his plea of guilty he is a disgrace to the community, and I don't say that lightly. He has lost or will lose all of his assets. He will be forever a convicted felon. In short, Mr. Cardiges as he approaches his fiftieth birthday a few days from now has nothing to show for his life except for the humiliation caused by his criminal conviction and his mistakes." Lyons presented letters from Cardiges's friends and his priest, all praising Cardiges as a good family man who gave to his community.

Cardiges then stood and gave his final speech.

> In these times when many individuals appear to be shifting and deflecting blame on others, I would like this Court and quite frankly the rest of the nation to know that I accept full responsibility for my misdeeds, for my personal transgressions, and for my illegal activities during my tenure within the automobile industry. I apologize and I ask forgiveness from this Court, from my United States federal government, from the people of New Hampshire, the innocent people at Honda, in the automobile industry, my friends, and each and every member of my family. I understand that my sentencing will be a deterrent to others, and I would like to say that for the last three years I have lost not only material things and my family's assets and will lose all those, I've lost self-esteem, I've lost respect, and I've lost a career. However, I've gained something and that is a profound healthy appreciation for the difference between what is right, what is wrong, what is moral, what is immoral, what is ethi-

> cal, and what is unethical. When given the opportunity, your Honor, I intend to assist my United States federal government and any person or any corporation to help prevent any of this type of abuse from occurring in the future. Prior to the beginning of this year I was part of the problem. After the beginning of this year I have strived to be and will continue to be part of the solution so that this won't occur again. Your Honor, I'm deeply sorry, and I'm deeply remorseful for my actions.

"I have had a nagging question throughout this case," said Judge DiClerico, "and it's a very simple question. Why didn't you know the difference between right and wrong for years and years and years? Just a very simple notion of what is right and what is wrong. Why?"

"I fell into a pattern early on in my career," Cardiges explained, "and I followed at the time in Ford Motor Company the crowd and I didn't have the fortitude to stand up and say when I was 26-years-old that what was happening is wrong. My sense of wrong and right, as I mentioned in the trial, went right out the window in the first year of my career in the automobile industry."

The judge pronounced the sentence: "Stanley James Cardiges is hereby committed to the custody of the Bureau of Prisons to be imprisoned for a term of 60 months on Count I and terms of 60 months on each of Counts II through IV, all to be served concurrently." Cardiges was also assessed a fine of $364,000. He was assigned to the federal minimum-security prison in Lompoc, California, the former home of renowned Wall Street embezzler Ivan Boesky, as well as that of H. R. Halderman and John Dean, aides to former president Richard Nixon convicted for their roles in the 1974 Watergate scandal.

Lyons pleaded that Cardiges be allowed to self-report to the slammer to avoid a three-month-long prison bus ride to California, a trip where convicts are relayed from jail to jail as transportation becomes available. Court officials refer to the junket as the "federal express." The judge denied the request.

Cardiges was handcuffed and led from the courtroom. He turned and stole one last look at a sobbing Effie, who was being comforted by one of the jurors who had convicted Billmyer and Josleyn.

Stanley James Cardiges was taken to the county jail in Manchester, the first stop on his long journey to Lompoc.

CHAPTER 17

Ethics/Epilogue

"There can be no offense where none is taken."

—Japanese proverb

THE HONDA scandal was preventable. Whether key American Honda executives were recklessly indifferent to the corruption, or gave tacit approval to it, will be debated ad nauseam. The company was clearly more concerned about the corrupt activities' impact on litigation than about what is right and wrong.

Honda's corporate culture, combined with the mistakes made by officials over the years, resulted in a primer for what not to do to prevent the initiation and spread of corruption within an organization:

- Unchecked authority to too few managers.
- No system of internal controls relating to proper vendor and dealer selection.
- No prescreening of applicants by officials outside the sales division.
- No consistent enforcement of employees signing the conflict of interest policy.
- No consistent notification to employees and dealers that corrupt practices would not be tolerated.
- Employee compensation plans below industry average.
- Consistently ignoring dozens of warning signals (e.g., J. D. Power, Peck checks, company cars sold at below market prices, and executives' lifestyles).
- Unwritten corporate policy of keeping information on violations from the human resources department.

- Slowness in taking action to terminate offenders.
- Failure to notify law enforcement authorities of the criminal activities.

Honda has instituted a corporate ethics program, with the hopes that it will prevent a recurrence. Managers have been dragged through boring ethics seminars. A confidential toll-free number to report violations is available to employees. And everyone signs the conflict of interest policy. In 1996, Honda fired a 34th employee involved in the corruption, when the man confessed to a few minor, decade-old indiscretions during preparation for his deposition in the civil suits filed against Honda. He claims that Honda attorneys hinted that he would get a deal similar to Koichi Amemiya's, an opportunity to make restitution for the gifts, if he told the truth. He was wrong. Once too slow to pull the trigger, Honda is now taking no chances.

Whether Honda's ethics plan was driven by the embarrassment of the federal indictments or by a genuine desire to clean itself up remains unclear. Although it is impossible to stop all employee abuses of trust, particularly when a field sales staff by its very nature operates fairly independently, Honda is at least making an effort.

When news of the Honda scandal became public, industry observers felt that some consumer group would file suit against Honda or its dealers, claiming that customers were forced to pay more for Honda automobiles as a result of the kickbacks among dealers and Honda officials. The wisdom held that, since some dealers paid extra for Honda automobiles and franchises, they would have to pass the costs onto the consumer. No such lawsuit has yet been filed because of the difficulty of proving such a contention.

Ironically, the opposite of that theory may be true. Many of the dirty dealers sold Honda automobiles for lower prices than the clean operators. An analysis of financial statements of various dealers supports this claim. The reason for this dichotomy is twofold: (1) Most of the dealer principals predisposed to bribing Honda officials were those who sought a shortcut to profitability, the same way they operated their dealerships. They did not invest in proper training or screening of their salespeople or in customer satisfaction programs to nurture the consumer, both of which can lead to higher gross profits on new vehicle sales. The best cars in the world were parked on their showroom floor, but all their crew could do was sell price rather than product. Their underqualified sales staffs simply waited for customers to pile in the door and then undercut another dealer's price to make a deal. (2) The dealerships that became high-volume operations due to an abundance of product had to sell Hondas for less to keep the units moving and to continue to receive large allocations of automobiles from the factory.

Naturally, there are exceptions to this rule. A few of the major bribers were above-average dealers, such as Rick Hendrick, and offered value-added services and reputation that drove customers to pay a little more money for a Honda than they might at another dealer. Some of Honda's operators were double clueless: they neither paid off Honda officials nor took care of their customers, resulting in poor sales and low profits per unit.

The difference in sale prices among all dealers was insignificant—about $200 to $300 per car, or less than 2 percent of Honda's average mid-1980s manufacturer's suggested retail price. No consistent pattern could be identified that proved consumers had paid more or less for their Hondas when purchasing from clean or dirty dealers. Ultimately, the market determined the sales price of the vehicles. Even dealers who were forced to pay $500 to $1,000 over invoice to buy Hondas from other dealers or brokers could not pass the costs onto the consumer. They simply had to swallow the difference to remain competitive.

The dealers who paid Honda executives up to $750,000 for a franchise that others received for free also could not raise prices on automobiles to cover their added debt—the market could not bear the price. This point will also serve to refute one of car dealers' favorite advertising campaigns: "Our low overhead means low prices for you!"—the battle cry of small-town dealers outside metropolitan areas bragging about their tiny facilities. Dealer overhead has little impact on the ultimate transaction price of a vehicle.

The primary reason consumers paid sticker price and above for Honda automobiles during the 1980s was the Voluntary Restraint Agreement, limiting the number of Japanese cars that could be exported to America. The resultant rise in prices of Japanese autos, along with Detroit's ill-advised price hikes, cost American car buyers an estimated $50 billion dollars.

Consumers were more hurt by Honda's lack of control over its dealer body and its tightwad policies than by any of the payoffs. Customers endured some Honda dealerships with shabby facilities and 1950s sales pressure tactics, two items that innovative franchises such as General Motors' Saturn dealerships are required to avoid. Had the key American executives concentrated solely on their business and the Japanese executives gotten off their wallets, Honda might have assisted, or forced, the dealers to adhere to customer sales satisfaction and dealership standards. The Japanese executives' hatred of the American legal system prevented the corporation from ever attempting to cancel any Honda dealers' franchise — no matter how poorly the dealer treated customers. Instead, cloaked in the rationale that "we have too much respect for our dealers to tell them what to do," Honda missed an opportunity to become a superpower in the United States. A customer-friendly corporate philosophy of Saturn combined with the Honda product would be an unbeatable combination. Despite Saturn automobiles not possessing the drivability or quality of a Honda Civic or Accord, Saturn has overtaken Honda in all measurements of customer satisfaction, thanks almost entirely to a dealer body given marching orders from the factory on how to behave.

According to a J. D. Power survey, Honda continues to rank in the bottom 20 percent of automakers in America in terms of how the customer is treated during the buying process. The days when a customer unhappy with a Honda dealer automatically sought out another Honda dealer are over — there are too many other quality automobiles on the market. Periodically, Honda announces to the dealers an upcoming program designed to increase customer satisfaction during the sales process, but the plans are never implemented. The executives' workload, combined with a lack of funding from the Japanese, is usually the excuse for the programs dying.

A customer proving that he or she paid more money for a Honda automobile because of the corruption is unlikely. In the end, the American consumer was apathetic to the scandal. As long as the automobiles were still good, they were unconcerned.

"If the public likes the car, it won't remember the scandal," industry analyst Ron Glantz told *Automotive News.* "They'll say, 'Gee, the franchise was hot, the car was hot and there was some bribery. So what?'"

The Honda scandal was not without its victims. Michael Connolly decided that the corporation had been victimized, and Honda happily agreed. Given the evidence of the corporation's lack of effort to stop the problems, the company as a victim is another issue that can be disputed. Honda's image was tarnished within the automobile industry, but key clean officials had ample opportunity to stop the bribery years before they ultimately took action.

Many promising careers of clean Honda executives were cut short due to guilt by association. Honda hired outsiders rather than promoting many qualified managers, resulting in a mass of resignations. Those who sought employment with other automakers found dead ends. A personnel manager at another import automobile company said resumes received from ex-Honda managers "go straight into the trash."

Some of the dealers miss the departed executives. "Baptize 'em and bring 'em back," says a Texas Honda dealer principal. "At least you could negotiate with the old guys."

Jim Cardiges earns a salary of $50 per month at the Lompoc federal prison. He teaches fellow inmates how to read. Twice a week, he holds seminars on public speaking and marketing. His priest visits him regularly, as do an army of attorneys involved in the civil suits. Effie Cardiges lives in a modest Orange County condominium. She teaches school for $8 an hour.

An official of the California Tax Board read about the Honda scandal. The state subsequently demanded $650,000 in back taxes from Cardiges, based on the value of his graft and embezzlement proceeds.

Ed Temple worked in the dental lab of the Atlanta federal prison during his six-month term. He now lives in seclusion in Florida.

Dennis Josleyn remains in federal prison in Colorado.

Michael Connolly was honored by U.S. Attorney General Janet Reno for his excellence in litigation in the Josleyn/Billmyer trial. He received the John Marshall Award, singling him out from among 7,500 assistant U.S. district attorneys.

In October 1996, a federal appeals court upheld the convictions of Josleyn and Jack Billmyer. In February 1997, the U.S. Supreme Court denied Billmyer's appeal of his conviction. He was ordered to report to prison.

In April 1997, attorneys for Josleyn and Billmyer filed a motion for a new federal trial, claiming the government had hid evidence that Honda's Japanese executives knew about the corruption. In a stinging response to Billmyer's motion, Michael Connolly wrote:

> Billmyer has watched his marquee defenses—multiple conspiracies and venue—fizzle our before the jury, the First Circuit and, most recently, the Supreme Court. In this motion, Billmyer descends to the desperate, government-bashing tactics favored by his co-defendant throughout the trial. Billmyer now argues that he took kickbacks from dealers in return for American Honda Motor Company Letters of Intent in the "good faith" belief that it was an ac-

> ceptable business practice, and that "new" evidence, some of which allegedly was suppressed by the government, proves that point. Under well-settled principals of law, Billmyer's motion falls far shy of the requirements for a new trial.

Both Billmyer and Josleyn cited a mysterious gift, given by American Honda president Koichi Amemiya to a woman in Ohio, as proof the government withheld evidence. In late 1990, Amemiya notified New York zone sales manager Roger Novelly that he wanted a Steubenville, Ohio, Honda dealer to supply a used car to a woman, the sister of a friend of Amemiya, for free. The dealer complied, giving her a 1984 Buick Skylark worth $1,600. Intriguingly, the chosen dealer principal had previously given Novelly co-ownership of a Detroit Honda dealership. Defense attorneys claimed that Amemiya had chosen that dealership because he was privy to Novelly's relationship with the dealer and thus knew of the corruption. In truth, it was simply a coincidence that the woman happened to live near Steubenville.

Connolly noted that the FBI had investigated the incident before the trial and found it to be insignificant.

It was not too bright of Amemiya to prevail upon a dealer to give the car away, but the incident took place in 1990, before all the problems came to light. A Honda spokesperson deemed Amemiya's action an act of charity by the president to help a woman down on her luck.

Billmyer and Josleyn's motions for a new trial contained several other trivial illustrations of their points, the last desperate gasps by their attorneys to save them.

On July 17, 1997, Judge Joseph DiClerico denied Billmyer and Josleyn's motions for a new trial. Paul Twomey called Connolly and indicated that he was going to file yet another motion for a new trial—he claimed to have unearthed new evidence that top Honda officials knew about the corruption.

"You won Round Three," Twomey taunted, "but the bell is about to ring for Round Four."

The majority of the members of the gang were released from prison in 1996 and 1997. Most have gone to work in the retail car business.

The convicted men are angry and bitter, claiming that Tom Elliott and Sherry Cameron lied on the stand. They think the government had an agreement with Honda not to prosecute the corporation or the Japanese.

None of the crew are happy with Temple. "They call those types 'rats' in the prison system," wrote Bob Rivers from his Las Vegas jail cell, ironically the city home to Angelo Falconi's Honda dealership, the one that Rivers co-owned and went to prison over. "Temple really hurt me bad," says Bob Mazzitelli. "I considered him a friend."

Christiaan Walker became a district sales manager for Isuzu of America. His lawsuit against Honda never went to court; Honda was able to successfully block the suit on technicalities unrelated to Walker's core claims of harassment and wrongful discharge. In October 1996, shortly after Walker's final request for a trial was denied by a federal court, he was asked to resign from his position at Isuzu because of substandard job performance. Walker continues to insist that he did not alter the $100,000 Cliff Peck Honda check to reflect Honda executive Fred Meis as the recipient.

Dave Conant of Norm Reeves Honda is still a member of the Honda National Dealer Council, despite his history of paying off Honda officials. In 1996 Honda also approved him to become majority owner of the dealership. Norm Reeves Honda remained the number-one-volume Honda dealer in America in 1996, just ahead of Rick Hendrick's Gwinnett Place Honda in Atlanta. Dah Chong Hong's Gardena Honda is number five.

Steve Shuken of the former Santa Paula Honda has filed suit against Dah Chong Hong, claiming the group violated racketeering statutes when it blocked his dealership's move to Ventura in 1989. American Honda has approved Shuken's relocation and is fighting the DCH-owned Honda of Oxnard's protest of the move before the California motor vehicle board. DCH officials are now claiming there was never a financial arrangement between their firm and Soichiro Honda during the 1960s, despite its employees previously bragging about the connection.

Sherry Cameron resigned from American Honda to join the Disney Corporation. The law firm of Lyon & Lyon no longer represents American Honda in disputes with dealers.

Koichi Amemiya remains the president of American Honda Motor Company. He has sold his Mercedes-Benz.

The litigation that Honda's Japanese executives feared so much arrived in spades. If Honda had stopped its executives' corrupt activities in the early 1980s, it might have cost the corporation a few million dollars in claims from a few Honda dealers who would have sued because neighboring dealers were enjoying the fruits of favoritism. Instead, the current pile of attorneys' fees and possible settlements may cost Honda billions.

Over 70 Honda dealers have filed suit against American Honda. Included as defendants in the suits, along with the corporation and Honda Motor Company of Japan, are the convicted former executives, Honda's top current and past Japanese officers, dozens of the dirty dealers, and Lyon & Lyon. The dealers are planning to seek an estimated $4 billion in damages, claiming their dealerships' profitability suffered because of the corrupt activities and favoritism shown the dirty dealers and that Honda looked the other way when informed of the problems. They charge Honda and the conspirators with violating the Racketeer Influenced and Corrupt Organization (RICO) and a myriad of state statutory laws. Conviction of RICO calls for mandatory triple damages. One of the dealers is asking that his suit be certified as a class-action, representing all 1,250 Honda and Acura dealers in America. Attorneys representing the majority of the dealers have banded together and invested several million dollars in a war chest to battle Honda. The plaintiffs' cases benefit from the overwhelming amount of evidence already gathered during the FBI's investigation. The cases should go to trial in 1999.

Incredibly, among the dealer principals suing are several who aggressively paid off Honda officials themselves. Apparently they now feel they did not get their money's worth from their bribes. Equally mysterious are the motives of some dealers, not located anywhere near a dirty dealer, suing Honda.

Many of those filing suit rank at the bottom of the dealer chain, those who could not have sold more Hondas even if they had been allocated them. Most of the 16 Los Angeles–area retailers suing Honda constitute a veritable Who's Who of Lousy Car Dealers, a mixed bag of operators with ramshackle buildings, shoddy customer handling, and ownership by dealer principals who rarely set foot in their stores. Their engaging in litigation against Honda represents another short-term approach to making money, the same way they operate their dealerships. Unhappy Los Angeles dealers need only look at some of their neighbors, clean Honda retailers who thrived during the good times without engaging in any of the malfeasance, to see the outrageousness of their claims.

Some of the dealers have legitimate beefs. Those who lost money because of a needless Honda dealership being put in their backyard. Those whose allocations were subtly lowered so Honda officials could force the dealer to sell his store to one of the favored few. A dealer granted an open point, only to see it yanked and given to a dirty dealer. A dealer in a metropolitan area surrounded by dealers who were paying off Honda officials. The dealer peeved over Acura officials conspiring with another dealer to steal his NSX customers. Those who were denied allocations of Hondas because of their refusal to falsify warranty cards, if there are any dealers in that category.

One of the dealers simply wants his money back from Ed Temple, the man who sold him his letter of intent. A North Carolina dealer is not only suing Honda but has also petitioned the state to revoke Rick Hendrick's dealer license.

New Hampshire dealer Richard Nault is among those suing Honda. When Honda settled with him over the Concord Acura debacle, the company failed to have him sign a release that prevented him from suing on behalf of his Manchester Honda dealership. Concord is still without an Acura dealership, as it has been since Nault's store was terminated in 1989. Neither Lexus nor Infiniti has established a dealership in Concord.

Rick Hunt, the Virginia dealer who stumbled upon farmer Paul Stephens receiving a Honda franchise, is also suing.

Honda has vowed to fight the suits to the end. The company has asked to have the cases dismissed on the grounds that the dealers cannot prove they lost money because of the scandal. Indeed, for dealers suing solely over allocation issues, it will be very difficult to identify their losses. They will have to prove that, because a another dealer earned more money, they earned less. Honda's lack of dealer development programs over the years may help the company here, since it will be able to point to the deficiencies in the plaintiff dealers' operations as the reason they did not sell, and thus earn, more Hondas through the allocation system. For every dealer who claims he has been injured because a favored dealer received increased car allocations for paying off Honda officials, Honda will be able to trot out nearby clean dealers who did fine.

Most of the convicted Honda executives have agreed to cooperate with the plaintiffs' attorneys, in exchange for being dropped as defendants in the suits. One of the few exceptions is Temple, who is not talking to anybody.

Throughout the litigation, Honda will continue to plead the company line: We were just a stupid victim of the corrupt officials' actions. We did not do anything wrong. We knew nothing about the corruption until 1991, and we took action in 1992 to terminate the executives involved. It is a claim that will be challenged.

The pretrial motions for the suits were all consolidated to be heard before a federal judge in Baltimore. Over Honda's protests, the court ordered the company to produce three executives from Japan for depositions, including Yoshihide Munekuni, the former American Honda president who had declined to initiate an internal investigation into the corruption during the early 1980s. The issue of the Japanese executives' knowledge and participation in the corruption was merely a sideshow in the Josleyn/Billmyer trial, but it will take center stage in the civil suits. Depositions in the suits have already turned up new information about gifts received by some of Honda's current executives, information that might cripple Honda's defense and lead to another FBI probe, similar to what happened in the Nault case.

A statement about the civil actions by the company read, "American Honda has complete faith that at the conclusion of this unfortunate litigation the company will again, as in New Hampshire, be found to have been victimized and defrauded by this group of unscrupulous former employees and Honda dealers."

Rick Hendrick found himself tangled in a different legal web in late 1996, at the end of another glorious year for his enterprises. He remained the largest automobile dealer in America, with 67 dealerships selling over 105,000 vehicles annually. (Honda has refused to grant him further franchises, freezing his number of Honda and Acura stores at 26, still far more than any other dealer.) His Hendrick Motorsports' NASCAR stock car racing team won its first Winston Cup championship in 1995, with Jeff Gordon at the wheel of a Chevrolet Monte Carlo. Hendrick teammate Terry LaBonte edged Gordon for the 1996 crown.

Also during the 1996 season, Hendrick Motorsports entered a car in the NASCAR Late Model stock car racing series. The car's owner was listed as being Jack Billmyer.

On December 4, 1996, three weeks after his team won the 1996 Winston Cup championship, and the day before he was to fly to New York City for the gala NASCAR awards banquet in New York City, Hendrick was indicted by the Asheville, North Carolina, office of the U.S. Department of Justice. He was charged with 13 counts of money laundering, 1 count of mail fraud, and 1 count of conspiracy, for his role in paying off Honda executives. Most of the counts involve the packages containing the $15,000 to $20,000 in cash that Hendrick sent to Cardiges as payment on the mortgage on Cardiges's Laguna Hills home. Another is for the house payments and leased BMWs that Hendrick provided Billmyer. Hendrick's brother and minority partner, John, was indicted on one count of conspiracy for paying off Honda traffic assistant Bonnie Sikora. The conspiracy and mail fraud counts each carry a maximum penalty of five years in prison and a

$250,000 fine. Each money laundering count carries a maximum of between 10 and 20 years in prison and fines of $250,000 to $500,000.

Hendrick clearly had been the target of the feds since their investigation of Honda began in 1993. A few months before the Hendricks' indictments were handed down, the government put Cardiges on the "federal express" bus for a three-week ride to North Carolina to testify before a grand jury against his former friend. Hendrick's indictment was designed to send one final message to U.S. car dealers about the potential downside of bribing automakers' officials.

One of the charges against Rick Hendrick was not previously unveiled by the New Hampshire investigation. The indictment alleged that between 1991 and 1993, Hendrick paid a Lexus zone sales manager $34,000 in cash in exchange for additional shipments of Lexus company cars to his Charlotte dealership. If proven, this charge may confirm the rumors that circulated in the Torrance car community during the start-up of Lexus in 1989: that Lexus executives were Honda-like in their raking in cash from dealers in exchange for granting franchises and additional cars. An official of Toyota Motor Sales, U.S.A., the parent company of Lexus, called the government's charge "groundless."

Brothers Hendrick pleaded innocent. According to one of his attorneys, "Mr. Hendrick's position is that he was a victim of extortion in this case, and we are dismayed that the government would seek to prosecute him under these circumstances."

Included in the Hendrick indictment were two potential bombshells for American Honda. Noting that part of the conspiracy between Hendrick and Honda officials was the practice of falsifying warranty registration cards, the government noted that owners of Honda automobiles were among the victims of the scheme because some did not receive full warranties on their cars. The Department of Justice decreeing that Honda customers were hurt by the conspiracy could lead to consumer groups filing suit against Honda.

Worse, the Hendrick indictment stated that another group of victims of the scandal were dealers who did not participate in the bribery "and were defrauded of profits on the sales of Honda automobiles each would have received under a fair and uncorrupted distribution of Honda automobiles." In other words, exactly what the plaintiff dealers in the civil suits against Honda are claiming. The statement was a huge blow to Honda's defense of the suits.

Three weeks later, Honda fought back. It followed through with its hollow promise of three years earlier by filing civil lawsuits against both the convicted former officials and the owners of some Honda dealerships involved in the scandal. Supposedly, the suits were filed to recover the fortunes gained by the parties due to their defrauding Honda, but the move was more designed to strengthen Honda's position in the civil suits by reinforcing the company's position as victim of the crimes, particularly in light of the government's proclamation.

The 22 dealer principals Honda chose to sue own approximately 60 Honda franchises that account for about 10 percent of Honda's U.S. sales. The common denominator among them is that they paid Honda executives for a letter of intent, thus obtaining a Honda or Acura franchise through fraudulent means. Included is the Dah Chong Hong dealer group, the company partially responsible for funding Soichiro Honda's automobile development program in the early 1960s. Hendrick is also among the owners being sued, as are Bill Schuiling, Angelo Falconi, Peter Epsteen, Dave Trainer, the Ryan/Fincher/Vince group, and the widow of Marty Lustgarten. Dealer principals who only gave gifts to the executives in return for additional automobiles were not sued, since it would bring up the issue of quid pro quo in relation to cars, damaging to Honda's defense of the civil suits.

By this legal action, Honda has placed itself in an odd factory/dealer relationship position, one almost certain to cost the company sales. We want you to sell our cars, says Honda to its dealers, but we are also going to make life miserable for you. Dealer principals will have to scramble to keep company morale alive, as employees will likely abandon ship, fearing additional retribution from Honda.

If Honda were serious about its outrage over the dealers' actions, it would have moved to terminate their franchises a long time ago. Honda has canceled only two dealerships involved in the scandal, and both were open-and-shut cases. In 1994 the company terminated Ed Temple's Costa Mesa Honda because of franchise agreements and state laws forbidding ownership of an automobile dealership by a convicted felon. (Temple is now suing Honda for wrongful termination of his franchise.) In the case of Atlanta dealer Barry Alexander, one of the few who had outlined in writing his gratuities to Honda executives, Honda proved to the state of Georgia that Alexander had "secured his franchise agreement through commercial bribery." The state revoked his license in 1994. Honda is attempting to cancel the franchises of Las Vegas dealer Angelo Falconi and California dealer Hank Torian, claiming both obtained their franchises fraudulently.

In response to the suit, the Hendrick Automotive Group filed a cross-claim against Honda. It accuses the corporation of failing to supervise its executives and permitting the corrupt environment to flourish.

In January 1997 Rick Hendrick filed a petition to have his federal trial moved from Asheville, North Carolina, to his hometown of Charlotte. He announced that had he learned in November that he had chronic myelogenous leukemia, a rare form of bone-marrow cancer, and that he needed to undergo six months of treatment in Charlotte. An overwhelming outpouring of sympathy came from the NASCAR world and the public. An Asheville federal judge denied Hendrick's motion for a change of venue for his trial.

On August 14, 1997, Rick Hendrick gave up his fight. In a plea agreement, he agreed to plead guilty to one count of mail fraud, for the cash he sent to Cardiges for payments on the Buckskin Lane home. He was expected to be sentenced to between 10 and 16 months in prison and pay a $250,000 fine. Federal prosecutors agreed to let Hendrick serve his jail time at home due to his illness. Hendrick's brother John agreed to make restitution for the money he had mailed Bonnie Sikora, and charges against him were dropped.

Though Hendrick's plea agreement stipulates that he will cooperate with the "ongoing" federal investigation of Honda, it is likely that the probe is over. After Hendrick's plea made him the 22nd person convicted by the government, Michael Connolly deemed the Honda investigation and prosecution a "complete, unmitigated success."

The week of Hendrick's plea, Connolly announced that he was going to return to private practice, for a law firm in Boston. Recruiters for legal firms had beaten his door down after the federal trial. He admits he may never have another case as interesting and challenging as the Honda investigation.

The paper mill of lawsuits flying in and around Honda add up to the largest legal quagmire in automobile industry history. The only certain outcome is that a lot of attorneys are going to make a lot of money.

The nonlitigious events of 1996 and 1997 at Honda reflected a remarkable microcosm of the company's history.

In its 38th year of continuous manufacture, the tiny Super Cub motorcycle, the machine that helped build Honda's brand image in Japan and America, is revolutionizing transportation in emerging nations. Honda set up production facilities to build the motorbike in China, Vietnam, and Thailand, the latter being expanded in 1997 to become the first factory ever to produce over 1 million vehicles annually. Sales have been through the roof in those nations, as well as in India and Indonesia. The current Super Cub looks almost identical to the original, though it has undergone substantial mechanical refinements over the years. Over 32 million Super Cubs have been sold worldwide since 1958, making it the best-selling motor vehicle in history, far ahead of the runner-up Ford F-150 pickup's total of 26 million. Nations whose streets are now buzzing with Super Cubs will no doubt eventually see larger Honda motorcycles and then Honda automobiles as their economies strengthen, the same product strategy that has worked for Honda for years.

Worldwide, Honda sold over 2 million automobiles in one year for the first time in 1996, but it was the Super Cub–led motorcycle division that made Honda Motor Company's profits soar. Though automobile sales accounted for six times the revenue of motorcycle sales, operating profits for the motorcycle division were actually higher than for those of the automobile division for the first time in years. Somewhere, *Kaminari-san* is smiling.

In America, Honda won its first IndyCar racing manufacturer's championship, the first Japanese automaker to win the prestigious open-wheeled racing crown. Honda-powered cars won 11 of 16 races, with Honda driver Jimmy Vassar winning the individual championship. Honda's competitors' race cars featured motors ostensibly from Mercedes-Benz and Ford, though they were actually built by specialized racing engine corporations. True to form, Honda developed and manufactured its racing motors entirely itself.

After being in the doldrums product-wise since 1991, Honda automobiles came roaring back in 1996. The car that had started it all in America, the Civic, shone the brightest. Completely redesigned for the fifth time in its 24-year history, the 1996 Civic was nearly the size of the 1989 Accord and filled with technological advancements unavailable in other automobiles. The Civic coupe offered the option of a continuously variable transmission, a technology that other automakers had tried and failed to perfect for years.

As they had in the 1970s after the enactment of the federal Clean Air Act, domestic automakers deemed new year-2000 California clean-air standards impossible to achieve, saying the target could not be reached with an internal combustion engine. And as with the introduction of the 1975 Civic CVCC hatchback that easily met the new standards without a power-robbing catalytic converter, Detroit engineers were once again embarrassed by the introduction of the 1996 Civic hatchback, which met the tough emissions goal. Additionally, Honda announced plans to offer an Accord in 1998 that also meets the 2000 California standards. The company revealed plans to market a natural-gas–powered Civic in 1998, a car that Honda says will produce almost no exhaust emissions and will be the cleanest vehicle with an internal combustion engine ever made. Honda was racing away from the competition once again.

Automobile magazine named the 1996 Civic its Automobile of the Year. Throughout the year, American dealers screamed for more Civics. Honda had been supplying U.S. dealers entirely with North American–built Civics, but it began to import Civics from Japan to catch up to demand in 1996.

More people were still buying Honda Accords than any other car. The Accord was the best-selling retail car in America for the eighth straight year and the Civic was number three. The Ford Taurus was the overall number-one-selling car for the fifth straight year but ranked only tenth when sales to rental car companies and fleet accounts were excluded.

Early in 1997 Honda introduced its first sport-utility vehicle (other than the Isuzu-built Passport), the CR-V, a vehicle that had been a sales sensation in Japan since its 1994 introduction. Based on the Civic chassis, the CR-V is a mini sport-utility vehicle, smaller than the majority of the vehicles in the category. Cute as a bug, the roomy four-wheel-drive vehicle features a unique foldout card table stored in the rear and seats that can be transformed into a pair of single beds. With the booming full-size sport-utility vehicle market being close to maturation, and prices of those vehicles hovering around $30,000, Honda's entering into the largely untapped mini segment of that market is a clever move. American Honda officials predicted that all 50,000 CR-Vs to be imported in 1997 would sell quickly. With prices starting at $19,300, the CR-V will attract young buyers into the Honda fold. Much to the delight of Honda dealers, customers began leaving deposits on CR-Vs four months before its introduction.

In 1996 the Honda division sold 735,920 vehicles in the United States, an all-time record that bettered the 1990 mark of 716,495 units. Sales at the Acura division, buoyed by the introduction of four new models, increased to 108,008 units, up from 1995's record-low 97,151 cars. If the momentum of both brands continues, American Honda may be able to achieve total U.S. sales of 1 million vehicles annually by 2000, the corporate goal first set for 1990.

Honda dealers' profits were among their highest in history in 1996, spurred by solid profits on Civic sales, a strengthened dollar that helped Honda hold the line on prices, and a steady flow of dealer incentives.

Honda was hot again.

And the rumors of kickbacks from Honda dealers to American Honda executives, the type of rumors that were ignored for so long, those rumors that for 15 years turned out to be true and brought shame to the corporation, the same rumors returned to the world of American Honda Motor Company.

Acknowledgments

American Honda Motor Company did not cooperate with the writing of this book. The entire sordid mess that is the subject of this tome has been a major embarrassment to the corporation, and I understand their reluctance to speak with me. Fortunately, many other people did not hesitate to help.

The people I ache to thank the most are those who have requested anonymity: the dozens of current and past Honda employees and dealers who shared their insights with me, but feared retaliation from Honda if their names were mentioned here. Assorted lawyers who lent advice also requested their names not be published. You all know who you are and what your help meant to me.

My editor, Susan M. Brehm, somehow turned my lump of a manuscript into a book. Her expertise in all areas of book production was also invaluable.

Several friends knew of this project before anyone else and offered much advice and encouragement: Steve Doubet, Alice Christian, and John Fitzgerald. The latter also provided an insightful critique of the manuscript, as did Craig Webb, John Morzenti, Deana Faucett, Gene Reilly, and Judy and Errol Dauenhauer.

The staff of *Automotive News* took a risk by publishing excerpts of this book long before it was finished and endured the wrath of American Honda for doing so. It was the vision of Keith Crain, Pete Brown, Dave Versical, and Lindsay Chappell that first brought this material to light and I will always be grateful. Chappell also provided important observations on his own investigation and on the Josleyn/Billmyer trial.

The kindness shown me by the New Hampshire trial participants was extraordinary. Assistant U.S. Attorney Michael Connolly was more than generous with his time and insights. His return to private law practice is the government's loss. I met with attorney Paul Twomey as he sweated out a jury's verdict in a double-murder case. Judy Prindiville, Jan Caron, and Diane Wildfeuer of Connolly's office showed much patience with my requests for documents. U.S. Marshal Edward Hubbard and juror Nancy Berardi also provided key help in this project.

Finally, Honda dealer turned country music songwriter Bill McDavid ("Me and the Drummer") kept me motivated during this long journey.

Steve Lynch
Dallas, Texas

Notes

With the exception of those noted below, the quotes in this book came from the testimony and evidence from various court cases, from my conversations with the people quoted, and from my recollections and notes from my years at Honda.

Chapter 1

Lee Iacocca: "Almost everywhere . . . ," Lee Iacocca with William Novak, *Iacocca, An Autobiography* (New York: Bantam Books, 1984), p. 35.

Ohio dealer: "These guys were so cocky . . . ," *New York Times,* May 2, 1993.

Jack Billmyer: "I can teach . . . ," Robert Shook, *Honda: An American Success Story* (Englewood Cliffs, N.J.: Prentice Hall, 1988), p. 64.

Chapter 3

Soichiro Honda: "I was literally intoxicated . . . ," Sol Sanders, *Honda: The Man and His Machines* (New York: Little, Brown and Company, 1975), p. 19.

Honda: "I learned about the feelings . . . ," Sanders, p. 38.

Honda: "No matter how good . . . ," Sanders, p. 43.

Honda: "I probably . . . ," Shook, p. 20.

Honda: "First, each individual . . . ," Shook, p. 13.

Honda: "I don't want to walk . . . ," *Inc.,* November 1986.

Honda: "We knew that . . . ," Sanders, p. 83.

Honda: "If you want to control us . . . ," Shook, p. 19.

Honda: "A front-wheel drive . . . ," Tetsuo Sakiya, *Honda Motor: The Men, the Management, the Machines* (Tokyo: Kodansha International, 1987), p. 157.

Henry Ford II: "No Jap engine . . . ," David Halberstam, *The Reckoning* (New York: Avon Books, 1986), p. 544.

Cliff Schmillen: "From the outside . . . ," *Automotive News,* May 24, 1976.
Honda: "I found doing business . . . ," *Time,* October 23, 1989.
Billmyer: "Nobody really . . . ," *Automotive News,* October 9, 1995.

Chapter 4

Billmyer: "You don't know a . . . ," *Automotive News,* October 9, 1995.

Chapter 5

Jim Cardiges's friend: "He was very status . . . ," *Los Angeles Times,* March 23, 1994.

Detroit executive: "After Honda announced . . . ," Maryann Keller, *Rude Awakening: The Rise, Fall, and Struggle for Recovery of General Motors* (New York: William Morrow and Company, 1989), p. 23.

Chevrolet dealer: "Let me put it this way . . . ," Brock Yates, *The Decline and Fall of the American Automobile Industry* (New York: Empire Books, 1983), p. 68.

William Van Dalsem, "I just wondered . . . ," *New York Times,* July 10, 1994.
Rick Hendrick: "We won't . . . ," *Carolina Business,* September, 1987.

Chapter 6

Cardiges: "Ron, I hope . . . ," *Washington Post,* August 7, 1994.

Chapter 9

Tom Elliott: "We felt that Honda . . . ," Shook, p. 69.

Chapter 16

Rikki Klieman: "Clients give me . . . ," *Automotive News,* April 11, 1994.
Paul Twomey: "We feel that this jury . . . ," *Wall Street Journal,* June 2, 1995.

Chapter 17

Hendrick's attorney: "I promise you . . . ," *Charlotte Observer,* December 5, 1996.

Author

Steve Lynch grew up in the shadow of the Studebaker automobile factory in South Bend, Indiana, and attended Indiana University. Lynch spent 13 years in the world of Honda, rising from a Honda dealership showroom floor to the executive offices of American Honda Motor Company, where he was in charge of regional marketing. Lynch also worked for Honda's advertising agency. He lives in Dallas, Texas.